the rock concert industry in the nineties

Design: David Houghton
Printed by: MPG Books

Published by: Sanctuary Publishing Limited, 82 Bishops Bridge Road, London W2 6BB

Copyright: Mark Cunningham, 1999

Photographs: courtesy Mark Cunningham, except where indicated

Cover photographs: courtesy Diana Scrimgeour and Nik Milner

ISBN: 1-86074-217-3

the rock concert industry in the nineties

Live
& KICKING

mark cunningham

For Mum

acknowledgments

It all began in September 1993 when I was failing miserably at dividing my time fairly between my young family, a full-time position as the manager of a large company's Media Division, and a newly-established sideline as a freelance writer for a number of musicians' magazines.

Interviews with Paul McCartney and his band during tour rehearsals soon led to an invitation to see several of the New World Tour shows. During informal conversations with Macca's crew – specifically John Roden – it dawned on me that the production aspects of this particular tour might be worthy of coverage. Having played in bands professionally since my teens, I had always maintained a keen interest in this area of gigging, but as a writer I had yet to explore this potential. Neither did I know of any specialist magazine in this field. What next?

After writing up the Macca tour story and scouring a media directory for the name of a suitable publication, I came across *Live!* – it sounded about right, so I picked up the phone. Five minutes later, I had sold my first production article to *Live!*'s then Editor, Jerry Gilbert, and in less than a year my increasing level of work within this niche area of publishing encouraged me to turn full-time as a writer in August 1994. Thanks, Jerry, it was all your fault! Hopefully, this tale of desperate improvisation will serve as an inspiration to others who may be contemplating a career in journalism.

Two other individuals who have loomed large in my career and who also deserve credit are Ian Gilby and David Lockwood for their support in developing *SPL* magazine, without whose sudden closure I may never have formed my own publishing company and launched *Total Production*. Every cloud has a silver lining, as they say.

Thanks to all the manufacturers, PRs, rental companies and production personnel involved in the tours covered in this book, and those who have arranged for me to be in the thick of the action. I have met so many gifted and wonderful people on the road and in rehearsal, and I appreciate them taking time out to discuss their work. There are too many to name here, but read on and you'll find out!

I must thank Diana Scrimgeour for helping me to create a consistently excellent visual vibe in *Total Production* (and *SPL*) with her outstanding photography and assistance on countless tour projects. Also, to *Total Production*'s co-founder Andy Lenthall, PH, JO, Julie Hilder and our friends at Compugraphics in Eastbourne for keeping my feet on the ground and making the magazine happen, Mo and Kay Foster, Michael Bettell and Gordon Giltrap for preserving my sanity, and Jeff, Eddy and Penny at Sanctuary for giving life to this project.

Finally, and as always, I thank my mother Joan for her endless support, and send my everlasting love to my wife and best friend, Paula, and my four lovely children (Rosie, William, Jordan and Lucy) who endure my long working hours, regular trips away from home, and creative torments and tantrums. They are ultimately the reason I do all this.

about the author

Born in East London in the early 1960s, Mark Cunningham was engaged throughout the late 1970s and 1980s as a professional bass guitarist, singer/songwriter and record producer at all levels of the music industry.

By the early 1990s, he had turned his attention towards professional audio and concert production journalism, and quickly earned a favourable reputation through his work for specialist magazines including *Pro Sound News*, *Lighting + Sound International*, *Live!*, *Professional Sound*, *Billboard* and *Audio Media*, as well as a variety of musical instrument (MI) monthlies and mainstream titles such as *Mojo* and *Q*.

After turning full-time in this field in 1994, his first book for Sanctuary Music Library, *Good Vibrations: A History Of Record Production* was published in May 1996, and was quickly followed by his work as Editor on session bassist/composer Mo Foster's Sanctuary book *Seventeen Watts?*.

In the spring of 1997, Mark quit freelance writing to develop a new live industry magazine with SOS Publications, entitled *SPL*. This short-lived but highly-respected monthly was re-invented the following February when Mark and business partner Andy Lenthall formed Pulse Publications Co Ltd to launch *Total Production*, the definitive international live production magazine, of which Mark is Publishing Editor and principal writer.

Mark Cunningham is an associate member of Re-Pro (The Guild of Recording Producers, Directors & Engineers) and BASCA (The British Academy of Songwriters, Composers & Authors). He lives in Essex with his wife Paula, twin sons William and Jordan, and daughters Rosalie and Lucinda.

contents

From The Humble Microphone To A Multi-Media World

Thirty years on from the psychedelic era which brought about a new set of technological demands, the 1990s will be remembered as the decade which more than any other defined concert production and the way it will continue for decades to come. The live concert production industry as we know it today hardly existed thirty years ago, although its enabling technology can be traced back to a vital nineteenth century invention.

The word "microphone" first appeared in 1827 in Weatstone's description of an acoustic device. It was later used by Berliner in 1877 and Hughes in 1888 for their "loose contact transducers", later called carbon microphones. The credit for the first workable microphone is given to Bell, when developing in 1876 his "harmonic telegraph", although the first credited use of a microphone for music reproduction came almost fifty years later.

Interestingly, the business of live performance technology shares a similar line of development to that of the recording industry which I researched for my book *Good Vibrations*. Until the 1940s, musicians, whether in music hall orchestra pits or in featured jazz bands, would mostly play without any form of amplification, relying on the natural sound pressure levels of their instruments to create a balance. The advent of the guitar amplifier made it possible for jazz guitarists' solos to be heard above horn sections, while small and very basic "public address" systems, together with the classic chrome-grilled ribbon mic, served the same purpose for vocalists.

A similar line in technical minimalism was maintained throughout the rock 'n' roll era of the Fifties and the beat boom of the early Sixties, at a time when, in the UK at least, promoters caught on to the commercial potential of "variety" tours. These tours, which continued beyond the late Sixties, often visiting a nationwide chain of cinemas, featured an odd mix of the latest teen idols and groups, interspersed with comedians and magicians, with a popular radio or TV personality as the compere. Eventually, and for good artistic reasons, the bills of concert tours began to be reduced to one main band and a support, or in the case of Deep Purple who revolutionised the tour package circa 1972, just a single act.

Arguably, there were two events in the mid Sixties which more than any other influenced a revolution in live performance production, the ripple effects of which still resonate today. Owing to the legendary hysteria which greeted The Beatles' live shows, by August 1965 it was almost expected not to be able to decipher which song they were singing on stage. It was then that the band played the biggest pop concert ever at the time, a sell-out at the 55,600-seat Shea Stadium in New York. Flown in by helicopter, the four uniformed Fabs took to a small riser in the middle of the baseball park and played their hearts out to a crowd who, if they really concentrated, might just about have guessed that the opening number was 'Twist And Shout'.

Afterwards, $160,000 better off, The Beatles drove away from the show in their armoured car, frustrated that their music could not be heard, and imagined what concerts might be like if this was not a problem. It seems a preposterous thought now but they were amplified only by the timid house Tannoy system – the same used to announce baseball scores to the Shea's regular sporting patrons. Much was learned from the Shea experience. PA systems got bigger.

Over on the west coast of the United States, meanwhile, the peace movement was beginning to tighten its grip on youth consciousness. Amidst a heady atmosphere of recreational narcotics and an overtly liberal attitude to sex, bands such as The Grateful Dead kick-started the "Love-Ins" or "happenings" – haphazardly organised, word-of-mouth-promoted free festivals of music and art, originally focused on the San Francisco area before the idea spread across the country. The psychedelic flavour of the music was enhanced further by "liquid light shows" – weird and wonderful coloured oil slides, manually mixed and projected on to the stage to create a distorted, floating, mysterious visual setting.

This treatment soon found its way across the Atlantic and into the clubs of London, where bands such as The Pink Floyd (together with lighting experts Mike Leonard and Peter Wynne-Willson) experimented with their own projection formulae. They, among others in the mid Sixties, also introduced the moving image to performance, with off-beat film projections providing yet another dimension to work alongside the musical improvisations. The influence of these Sixties visual innovations is evident today in scanner and gobo projection technology, and the now widespread use of video at large events, such as Jean Michel Jarre's 1997 *Oxygene* tour featured in this book... more of which later.

The American free festivals of 1965 and 1966 which helped to define the hippie culture inspired the well-organised Monterey Pop event in the summer of 1967, which boasted Jimi Hendrix, The Who, Janis Joplin and the Mamas And The Papas, among many other new generation artists. This, along with 1969's mammoth Woodstock festival, was all the encouragement British promoters needed to stage their own UK alternatives, and since the end of the Sixties, even in the face of the most inclement weather, summer festivals – from the Isle of Wight events of 1969 and 1970, the Weeley Festival, Dylan at Blackbushe Aerodrome in 1978, Reading, Glastonbury, Phoenix and "V" in the UK, to Lollapalooza, Lilith Fair, HORDE and Furthur in the USA, and Pink Pop, Torhout/Werchter, Roskilde and Doctor Music in Europe – have played a major part in modern culture, as well as boosting sales of Wellington boots!

Although The Beatles had pioneered the concept of staging shows in sports stadiums, it was not until the early Seventies, with the huge audience pulling power of festivals showing such potential, that this began to be commonplace. To a large extent, The Who were responsible in Britain for the move towards open-air stadium venues when they headlined a Bangladesh benefit concert at the Oval cricket ground in September 1971 on a bill which also included The Faces, Atomic Rooster, Mott The Hoople and Lindisfarne. Three years later, in May 1974, The Who played their first of two concerts at Charlton

Athletic as the giants of the pop world began to make the transition into stadiums, signifying a major turnaround both in terms of profit and scale of production.

Such events marked the end of a long and healthy reign for Charlie Watkins' enduring WEM PA column systems (complete with the massive "Reading Horn"), as developments from the likes of Dave Martin, Bill Kelsey and Tony Andrews (such as the two bin and horn systems that are still the template for many loudspeaker manufacturers) began to influence high output sound system design.

It was in the early Seventies that the arrival of genuine rock theatre venues sprang up in the UK, inspired by the success American promoter Bill Graham enjoyed with his Fillmore East/West endeavours. Indeed, the Fillmore production team, including Joshua's Lights, were invited to the UK to help John Conlan achieve his aim of establishing Sundown Theatres in London, in Mile End, Edmonton, Brixton and Charing Cross Road. These venues, together with the Rainbow (previously the Finsbury Park Astoria), became the heart and soul of rock culture in London throughout the Seventies, serving as a brilliant development ground for many rock and pop legends.

At the other end of the scale, large arenas were gaining popularity, with promoters, if not the fans. Because of their ability to accommodate more than 15,000 people at a time, vast indoor spaces such as Earl's Court were finding favour with big draws like The Osmonds, Pink Floyd and The Rolling Stones. While most bands were content to concentrate on delivering powerful live performances based solely on their music, there was a small, elite club of artists who, given the budget and the appropriate size of venue, began to integrate a theatrical element into their shows, just as the Stones did in 1976 with their enormous, sprawling "petal" stage. Only rock 'n' roll? Not anymore, mate!

While Cat Stevens created a magic sequence with Doug Henning for one of his shows, Donny Osmond flew down a wire from the back of the auditorium to the stage amidst much hysteria (I remember it well!), and Supertramp's Crime Of The Century tour broke new visual ground in the mid Seventies, the art of concert production was propelled in leaps and bounds by Pink Floyd, whose live presentations of *The Wall* at Earl's Court in 1980 and 1981 are still regarded as some of the greatest ever seen.

Who would have thought that the wild idea of building a polystyrene wall between the audience and the band, gradually during the first half of the concert, would go down well with ticket buyers? And yet this was high drama, complemented by an army of lifelike Gerald Scarfe puppets, the trademark inflatable pig, an exploding Stuka bomber, and Cinemascopic film projections across the entire width of the "wall", which, at the end of the show, was ceremoniously "blown up".

How to follow that posed an enormous problem for Floyd's contemporaries as The Wall paved the way for the "super shows" of the late 1980s and 1990s. Whilst the theme of the show originated from the seemingly tortured mind of Roger Waters, the fabrication of his nightmarish visions owed everything to the skills of designers Jonathan Park and Mark Fisher (several of whose productions are covered here, including the Stones' Bridges To Babylon, U2's PopMart and the Carlsberg-sponsored Songs & Visions event).

Lighting, and especially its control, remained a relatively basic technology throughout the Sixties and Seventies, with only a handful of designers successfully delivering shows which could be labelled "visually astounding". With financial backing from The Who, lasers began to appear as the ultimate in-concert special effect. If you had lasers in the Seventies, you'd really made the grade as a live act!

The real progress in lighting was made in late 1980 when a team from the Dallas-based sound and lighting company Showco developed the world's first moving light, the Vari*Lite prototype. After a brief demonstration, Genesis, one of Showco's long-time "accounts", ordered fifty lamps, gave the product its name and became shareholders in the company. When Genesis debuted the VL1 production model on the first date of their Abacab tour in September 1981, the death sentence on wholly generic light shows was passed. Since then, other companies such as Light & Sound Design, Martin Professional, High End Systems and Clay Paky have contrived their own moving light products, all of them successful, but still the name Vari*Lite continues to be as synonymous with moving lights as Hoover is to vacuum cleaners. A great name for a revolutionary idea.

At the time of the introduction of this technology, moving light systems required their own dedicated control consoles. Now we see a combination of generics (ie Par cans, Molefays (or audience blinders) and ACLs or aircraft lights) and "disco lights" working harmoniously with each other and run off integrated boards, such as the Wholehog, Celco and Avolites brands.

Set designs, such as those commissioned by the U2s and Stones of this world, are ever more thrilling and sophisticated. The key to this increased trend towards "mega-production" ultimately lies with the audiences who have grown up with the concept of MTV. When MTV burst on to the music scene in the early 1980s, not only did it provide an ideal vehicle for the talents of a whole new generation of imaginative promotional video directors, it also increased the public's expectations of live concerts. By the time the promo phenomenon reached its peak in the mid to late Eighties, with the complexity of many videos rivalling Spielberg blockbusters, the image of performers had taken on an almost super-human glow. Projecting that image on stage was the next step and bands reacted by extending their production budgets in an attempt to match the sophistication of their video personae.

No longer was it acceptable for these bands to saunter on stage with a few pretty lights and expect to wow the crowd. And with CD quality accessible to every record buyer, only the best live sound reinforcement would suffice in the concert arena. Audio, of course, is a very subjective area and generally speaking the fidelity of stadium sound is rather limited by the unfriendly acoustic environment. However, while loudspeaker technology has improved greatly since the days of Shea Stadium's overworked Tannoy system, the most recent advances have been made in the area of digital processing, enabling cleaner signals, and the science of loudspeaker array design, to channel the sound to the audience more accurately.

Mixing control, too, has improved tremendously with the introduction of fully automated consoles which can memorise and instantly recall various parameters of mix settings, and thus minimise the threat of a poorly balanced performance. The sections here on Rod Stewart's and Phil Collins' tours clearly explain the virtues of automated mixing, while the sophistication of on-stage monitoring (again, largely pioneered in the "good old days" by The Who) does not get any more clever than the system adopted by Tori Amos on her 1998 Plugged tour. In-ear monitoring, gradually established as a standard during the 1990s, has brought with it numerous sonic and aesthetic benefits, all of which are explored in various chapters here.

Creative video reinforcement for rock concert touring has come a long way since the early Nineties, when the pioneering work of Anton Corbijn and Presentation Services Ltd on Depeche Mode's Devotional tour and the use of tracking Sony JumboTrons on Genesis, Michael Jackson and the Hyde Park Masters Of Music all-star concert opened our eyes to the medium's future potential.

As the technology has become more sophisticated and the screens have grown in size, the arrival of U2's PopMart with its record-breaking screen from Belgian company Lorrymage, opened up the debate as to whether the new LED format, which this tour largely pioneered, was superior to the conventional Cathode Ray Tube (CRT) technology embodied in the Sony JumboTron and Mitsubishi Diamond Vision. The flames were fuelled further when less than a year later XL Video produced a higher resolution and comparatively lighter weight, modular LED screen, as used on The Spice Girls' SpiceWorld tour.

However, the choice of which video screen format to use on a show will normally fall to the set designer, who will have a clear idea of what the audience should see and how it should manifest itself on a stage. Clearly, the venue, whether indoors or outdoors, will impact upon the ultimate choice and there is a variety to choose from, including front or rear projection on to soft screens (as seen on Jean Michel Jarre, Supertramp and Oasis's Be Here Now), or video cube walls – a format favoured for motor shows and exhibitions, although after U2 took out 190 cubes (with two crew) for the Zooropa tour in 1993 it started to become popular for concerts and was used to good effect on Blur's 1998 tour.

In the future it is likely that we will see greater interaction between video and lighting, and it is only a matter of time before the ever-changing "virtual set" – enabled by still or moving image projections – points the way forward to a new standard in concert presentation.

Hopefully, the touring "case studies" in this book go some way towards exploring how a cross section of productions from 1993 to 1998 have taken on board various technologies and applied them to their specific needs, in order to make the shows look and sound the way they should. Music fans without direct involvement in the industry may well be intrigued by this "backstage" view of touring, while professionals should regard *Live & Kicking* as a handy reference book wherein they can see how their contemporaries "did it".

Covering these tours has been very rewarding and the good experiences certainly outweigh the bad. Yes, there have been moments when last-minute refusals of backstage access have made my job impossible, or when over-sensitive PRs have clearly not understood why I've been more interested in "the knobs and faders" than the latest love trauma of their client...and yet I still do not possess an anorak!

Nevertheless, some crews with whom I've mingled, especially those working for U2, the Stones, Oasis, McCartney, Tori Amos, The Spice Girls and The Who, for example, have been so welcoming and accommodating that it is has been a joy to spend "quality time" in rehearsals and on site, and therefore document the evolution of their productions in deserving tones.

How standards in production technology and techniques develop past that magic 2000 date is anyone's guess. The interaction of mixed media will certainly be at the forefront of show designers' minds, and the Millennium is being regarded by many as a turning point. Whatever the future holds, concerts will still have to sound good, look stunning and leave the audience fulfilled – the rest is just the icing on the cake. I hope to be there.

Mark Cunningham

CHAPTER ONE

Paul McCartney

The New World Tour – 1993

Unlike fellow top shelf artists such as Pink Floyd and The Rolling Stones who had made sure to include Earl's Court as their key London venue on world tours, as far back as 1973 and 1976 respectively, it took until 1993 for Paul McCartney to join the club, inevitably with some prodding from promoter Barrie Marshall. It was at that giant exhibition complex that Macca's second global trek in four years, the New World Tour, came to rest that September – with a 140-minute show studded with no fewer than sixteen Beatles numbers.

Brilliant though they were, however, the Earl's Court concerts were something of a logistical compromise. Overseas fans who had seen the colossal outdoor shows in Australia, New Zealand and the United States earlier in the year must surely have felt sorry for the British folk who were witnessing a vastly scaled-down production. But the sheer presence of the world's greatest living songwriter was more than enough to satisfy.

Singing with youthful tones, McCartney bounced around the stage with chummy "thumbs aloft" vitality while he, his omnipresent wife Linda, and his crack band – guitarists Robbie McIntosh and Hamish Stuart, drummer Blair Cunningham, keyboard player and one-man orchestra Paul "Wix" Wickens – displayed a high level of versatility, exchanging instrumental roles with matter-of-fact ease. Sadly, after accompanying her husband on every live engagement since The Beatles, this was to be Linda's last tour before the discovery of the cancer which so tragically took her life in 1998.

As with the 1989-90 Flowers In The Dirt tour, Floyd and Springsteen LD Marc Brickman designed the lighting, relying heavily on a Vari*Lite rig. To bring out the best in his design, cracked oil was used. When indoors, four or five machines could fill an arena the size of Earl's Court with a fine mist to thicken the air and show off the follow spots and Vari*Lites to maximum effect. Brickman commented: "I may be using a similar Vari*Lite system to the one on Pink Floyd's last tour [Delicate Sound Of Thunder], but the main difference is that the lighting and effects were the real personality of their show. With Paul, however, we just need to enhance his presence.

"Everyone's got their own interpretation of what they see in their mind's eye when they hear Beatles songs, and you don't want to confuse them. So when it comes to 'Can't Buy Me Love' or 'All My Loving' we use a lot of white light for a neutral stadium feel. If there's one thing I've learned, it's that lighting should make the performer appear larger than life and focus the audience's attention. It should illuminate and enhance, but not distract."

The first visual highlight of this nostalgically-flavoured experience was the opening eleven-minute video documentary which traced the ex-Beatle's thirty years as an international star. Projected in tryptych on to a huge single rectangular screen across the back of the stage, using three separate Xenon projectors, this intro video came at a time in the early Nineties when the incorporation of moving images into a live production was poised to take off, initially among major acts. The video was assembled from archive material by Dick Lester, the director of the seminal Beatles movies *A Hard Day's Night* and *Help!*.

Lester explained the reasoning behind this intro sequence: "The film that precedes Paul's entrance to the stage on the tour is a means of placing him in the context of his work as a performer from the early Sixties to the present – the songs he's written, what he looked like when he did them, the mood of the times and the spirit of the age that The Beatles captured and sometimes initiated – and place that in an historical documentary context."

Halfway through a live insert of 'Bluebird' from the Wings Over

America tour of 1976, the film metamorphosed into a grisly visual protest against animal cruelty, with stomach-churning scenes of monkey experiments and whales executed in seas of blood. A thought-provoking introduction, the like of which John Lennon would have been mighty proud.

Kicking off the live set with 'Drive My Car', other visual stimuli included a huge Brian Clarke backdrop design which appeared intermittently throughout the show. Clarke first met McCartney in 1977 through his then art dealer, Robert Fraser. A close friend of McCartney's since the mid Sixties, Fraser was among The Beatles' social clique and behind some of John and Yoko's more eccentric "happenings". At his Park Royal studio, Clarke said: "Robert introduced me to Paul and we quickly started working on some things. I initially worked for Linda. We both share a passion for photography, she obviously being more at the sharp end. Then she and Paul commissioned me to do some stained glass windows for their home in East Sussex, and by this time they had already collected a number of my paintings. Later, Paul asked me to design one of his album covers – *Tug Of War* became our first public collaboration."

Seven years later, Clarke's help was enlisted for the visuals accompanying the *Flowers In The Dirt* album, and McCartney's 1989-90 tour, his first for ten years – anxieties following John Lennon's murder in December 1980 being largely responsible for the delay. The "matrix" theme present in much of Clarke's paintings and stained glass design, since his 1978 painting 'Attack, Decay, Sustain, Release', was the main focus of his work on the tour, with his huge set backdrops painted in Los Angeles by theatrical stage painter Ron Strang.

When the partnership with McCartney was re-activated in preparation for the New World Tour, Clarke's role was extended to incorporate not only the paintings, but a wider range of visual elements. "With the experience of one major tour behind me, I approached this in a different, more informed way," he said. "To accompany Paul's modern-day peace anthem, 'C'Mon People', I had the idea to use a large selection of Linda's portrait photography to form this giant wall of stark projections. One has to remember that this projection wall is 300 feet wide – the biggest that there has ever been. [Four years later, U2's PopMart screen, at half this width, would become the largest touring LED screen.]

"At Anaheim Stadium, the full stage was lit up with the stained glass image collage I'd put together for 'Let It Be'. It was a 'history of stained glass' theme, using images dating from the eleventh century, up to my own latest works which evoked the same feelings as the song. I heard 70,000 people gasp and that's a hell of a sound! It was overwhelming and incredibly rewarding for me. I'm very close friends of Paul and Linda, and because of that I have a good understanding of their sensitivity and sensibilities involved in the rhythms of their work."

To Clarke, working in the abstract is not enough – he needs to live and breathe the subject matter, be it music, architecture, or a combination of both. "Norman Foster described my paintings for Paul's 1989-90 tour as 'transient, nomadic architecture', and it's a phrase which has stuck," he said. "I didn't want to design it and just let the people in LA make it big for me. I really wanted it to work with the music. There are physical constraints in that the paintings have to fit inside a jumbo jet. But the real architecture is the music and, if you like, my architect is Paul, the music's author. I thought I would treat this as if working in a building. I'm going to get intimately acquainted with this running list of songs and the show's rhythm, especially as it is very different to the last tour."

How did he set about "getting a feel" for the 1993 production? "I asked Paul if he would mind me attending the rehearsals down at his studio for a month. He was fine and I made myself a little makeshift studio up in the loft, and had a perfect view of the band. While they were playing, I was making drawings and having ideas. It meant that the initial stages of the design were all a direct visual result of a musical experience. I had the time of my life!"

It was patently clear from Clarke's infectious enthusiasm that the collaborations with his ex-Beatle ally gave him lasting joy and satisfaction. "You have a large audience standing in front of these paintings and visuals for over two hours," he admitted, "and they develop a very intimate relationship with them, whether they realise it or not. By the time they leave, they've got to know them very well and that's great! The stage design continues my life-long wish to make art for public display, and you couldn't be more public than Paul's stage set."

The middle section of the show partly reflected McCartney's recent *Unplugged* performance (and subsequent album) for MTV. A stunning Chet Atkins-style guitar cameo from Robbie McIntosh allowed the crew to set-up for a "busk-along" acoustic set, with Wix assuming the role of a wandering minstrel as he gently pumped his accordion on 'Michelle', against a backdrop of still black and white images of Parisian cafe life. Many agreed that Hamish Stuart's version of the soulful 'Ain't No Sunshine', on which Macca played drums and Wix thumbed bass, was a real highpoint of this set, and indeed rivalled Bill Withers' original for supremacy.

The pinnacle of the show was arguably the sound and light crescendo of 'Live And Let Die' – as good as it ever was back in '76, '79 and on the previous world outing. "This one was covered recently by another group," introduced McCartney, referring to the Guns N' Roses hit. And it's amazing how effective a touch of pyro can be. "The pyro system was specially built for the 'Live And Let Die' explosions in the middle and at the end of the song," said an enlightening crew member. "It consists of four lighting stands of adjustable heights with four flash pods on each, laid out on a metal sheet. The flash pots include 4ft diameter pods filled with powder from M&P Associates for each explosion. It's connected with a battery-operated console and the operator, Mick McGuire, can sit anywhere to remotely set off the blast."

Paul "Pablo" Boothroyd was operating a Midas XL3 mixing desk and running the Showco Prism PA system from front-of-house, while John Roden looked after the monitor system, mixing the wedges with a thirty-two-channel Harrison SM-5 console and two twenty-channel extenders. Roden found the boards easy to see at a glance, allowing quick reach of controls. The system was also able to create audio scenes, with monitor mixes "following" the performers through a number of locations on stage.

Roden's professional career began in the mid Seventies, after which he engineered for Entec and Tasco before turning freelance in 1984. The first band of note with whom he worked was Squeeze, on their 1979 Argy Bargy tour. During Macca's tour rehearsals at the star's rural studio in East Sussex, Roden said: "I've been pestering Showco to build me a new smaller wedge which, although only at prototype stage, is being used on the tour and is near completion. Everyone in the band is very pleasant to work for and they're all happy with a straightforward mix. Paul has four wedges on three mixes – a left and right mix and a central mix when in his down stage position. Everyone else has two wedges – Blair and Wix each have a stereo pair, Linda, Hamish and Robbie have a pair in mono, as does Paul for the piano. For the side fills, I use three Prism blue cabinets per side with a downstage left and right mix, and mono for upstage which includes vocals, drums and keyboards. These are controlled by a Showco crossover control system.

"Everything changes for the acoustic and piano sets and again when Paul plays drums on 'Ain't No Sunshine'. But the thirty-two-channels allow me to cope with the contingencies involved with all the shows changes. I use a Yamaha DMP for playback at rehearsals, and it's also used for the soundtrack of the opening film."

At the first of four shows at Earl's Court, nerves were understandably a little frayed. "The Saturday was really hectic," said Roden. "It had been decided it would be a good idea to transmit our soundcheck live on Radio One. So we were all pretty tense, but that's typical of Paul to set us these challenges."

Of course, things do not always go to plan even under the tightest control. At the beginning of 'Paperback Writer', six giant size drapes masquerading as book pages were unfurled on rollers. Very effective on the Saturday and Tuesday gigs. But on the last night only two appeared stage left, provoking some confused looks on the bands' faces. That wasn't the only problem experienced on the tour, according to Roden. "In the early stages we got Wix's keyboards patched the wrong way around. That wasn't really noticeable until 'Magical Mystery Tour', when the bus got confused and went from left to right. I don't think the audience realised, but to us it sounded like the bus was returning instead of going! It's little things like that which are hilarious at the time...but you really had to be there!"

Mesa/Boogie amplification was used exclusively on the 1989-90 tour by McCartney and his fellow axemen, and although his colleagues continued to use some of the gear, Robbie McIntosh reverted to his favoured Marshall amps and 4 x 12" cabinets. He commented: "I couldn't get a warm distortion out of the Mesa/Boogies. I'd either get a really over-the-top, boxy, flat distortion like a Rockman, or it would be too hard. I'm now using Marshall 9000 Series amps which have been modified by Pete Cornish."

In keeping with the nostalgic flavour of the tour, Macca, when playing guitar, returned to Vox amps with a vengeance, as John Hammel, his personal assistant since The Beatles split, explained: "On the last Wings tour in 1979, Paul was playing the occasional number on his Epiphone Casino guitar through Vox AC30s, and he's back to using them again with two Vox 4 x 12" cabs. For bass, though, both he and Hamish use Boogie 400 amps and Boogie 1516 and 2 x 15" bass cabs."

Guitar Technician Keith Smith helped advise McCartney on new technology: "When I first joined the team in 1989 after working with Pink Floyd and The Who, Paul's equipment was getting a bit old, even though it was good gear. He hadn't toured for ten years so there was a lot of catching up to do. We first agreed on the Mesa/Boogies, then I set about building him a new effects rack system which would cope with modern touring demands. We eventually settled on a custom-built Pete Cornish system not only for Paul, but Robbie and Hamish as well."

Keyboard maestro Wix's introduction to the Macca camp came through partnering Robbie McIntosh and Blair Cunningham on The Pretenders' *Get Close* album in 1987. It was McIntosh who recommended Wix during the *Flowers In The Dirt* album sessions and a new touring band was born.

Wix's keyboard set-up, along with his musical virtuosity, helped to re-create some of the most memorable orchestral lines in the vast catalogue of Beatles and solo McCartney material, including the piccolo trumpet of 'Penny Lane', string quartet of 'Eleanor Rigby' and 'Yesterday', brass of 'Got To Get You Into My Life' and symphonic frenzy of 'Live And Let Die' — all of which sounded incredibly accurate. "It all keeps me on my toes," said Wix. "I'm playing classic lines and riffs, and to the audience, they automatically suggest the original sounds anyway."

One of the greatest testimonials to Wix's dedication to authenticity came from (Sir) George Martin himself. "He was very kind," Wix continued. "When he came down to watch us, I felt like he was looking over my shoulder, especially on the Beatles songs where we stick to his arrangements. He was quite impressed by how I got those sounds and didn't realise it could be done like that. You can't really mess around with those arrangements."

For Wix, whose long list of session credits also includes work with Tasmin Archer, Texas, George Michael, The The, Barry Manilow and Alison Moyet, the moment of the set which gave him the most satisfaction was the brilliant re-creation of the 'Golden Slumbers'/'Carry That Weight'/'The End' medley from *Abbey Road*. "It was fantastic to do," he admitted, "especially as *Abbey Road* was the first album I ever bought, and it was my idea to include it on the tour. When I was a kid I used to sit at home with the headphones on, imagining I was on stage playing it. So doing that medley at the end of every show gave me a real sense of achievement. It was a phenomenal buzz!"

Fifteenth of November, 1993 saw the release of *Paul Is Live*, a double live album recorded during the American and Australian legs of the New World Tour. It was a faithful representation of the kind of tour which doesn't come around that often, and with the sad loss of wife Linda it marked the end of an era for the man who would soon become Sir Paul McCartney.

CHAPTER TWO

Eric Clapton

100 Not Out! – 1994

For ten years between 1986 and 1996, February in the music business meant one thing: Eric Clapton's annual timeshare at London's Royal Albert Hall. This musical and ultimately corporate phenomenon had become a tradition by 1994, the year of Clapton's eighth consecutive Albert Hall run which also included his 100th show at the celebrated venue.

As usual, everyone wanted a ticket and the escalating celeb guest list was causing Production Manager Mick "Doc" Double severe grief. "Townshend fancies dropping by... Jeff Beck wants to come... can you accommodate Curtis Stigers?" Naturally, the Duchess of York had little problem getting her VIP laminate for the "centenary" show. Although lacking the pomp and circumstance one would have expected from such a milestone, the RAH management did see fit to take the entire entourage to dinner afterwards at San Lorenzo's!

A cropped-haired, bespectacled Clapton stepped out under the Vari*Lites sporting a baggy T-shirt and faded jeans – no Armani suit! Seated solo, and embracing his National steel guitar, he began in country blues tradition with renderings of Robert Johnson songs. With Andy Fairweather-Low accompanying on 'Malted Milk', the band, including bassist Dave 'Less Is More' Bronze, gradually filled the stage for a whistle-stop tour of the blues and R&B that had inspired the young Clapton. Cream classics and a searing cover of Hendrix's 'Stone Free' followed before 'Tearing Us Apart' and other solo greats bought the audience screaming into the Nineties.

Clapton's re-creation of some of the more emotional moments from his best-selling *Unplugged* album – 'Circus Left Town' and 'Tears In Heaven' – justifiably provoked weeping in Kensington Gore, and backing vocalist Katie Kissoon brought a new freshness to that lovers' chestnut, 'Wonderful Tonight'. 'Layla' was as superb as ever, with that seven-note opening riff still reigning supreme.

EC's Production Manager for the last ten years, Mick Double was one of only three crew members to have been present at every one of Clapton's Albert Hall residencies, the others being guitar tech, Lee Dickson and security officer Alfie O'Leary. Double "fell into" the production side of the biz via his long-term role as Keith Moon's drum roadie, from 1970 until The Loon's death in 1978. He explained Clapton's remarkable allegiance to the Albert Hall. "Eric likes the building and the atmosphere. I don't know if he did when he played here with Cream [the band's 1968 farewell show] but he's certainly taken more than a shine to the place in recent years. He feeds off the crowd, and at the Albert Hall he enjoys the fact that they're so close to the stage."

Clapton's personal guitar technician since 1979, Lee Dickson's stage left cockpit resembled a well-stocked guitar shop. He discussed his role while restringing the master's instruments: "This type of show governs the choice of instruments, and Eric will get through around eight, from Dobros and National Steels to jazz guitars, Gibson Les Pauls and Fender Strats." As well as his regular Soldano amps, EC was using Lee's own small National amp, with a Fender Champ combo as back-up for some of the jazzier blues material. "It was the sound he was looking for, and it suited his choice of large-bodied jazz guitar, like the L1."

In his fifth year as Clapton's lighting designer, Irishman Tom Kenny was keen to point out that his design would never detract from the music. "You've got this brilliant musician on stage who does not need a light show, but obviously I need to bring out the best in his performance." How did he keep each year fresh? "I've learnt that simplicity is best and fortunately with Eric we all get a lot of rehearsal time. Last year [1993] we had a very different sort of lighting rig, all scrimmed off and very pretty. As it's Eric's 100th show I've decided to go big, and that means more trussing. I wipe the slate clean every year and take a completely new approach. We tend to spend the budget on other things."

The lighting company was Light & Sound Design – "great people to do business with," according to Kenny. "We're using sixty Vari*Lites [forty VL3s and twenty VL2Cs] which I'm very happy with, 300 Par cans, thirty Dataflash, twenty LSD colour changers, twelve Molefays, four truss spots, four front-of-house Xenons...and a lot of goodwill. I'm driving all this with a Celco desk. I always used Avolites until I worked with someone who used Celco, and now I won't use anything else."

Concert Sound's front-of-house engineer Robert Collins first worked with EC at the 1985 Prince's Trust Concert and later engineered the epoch-making twenty-four nights at the Albert Hall in 1991, which resulted in a superb live album. His control desk for "Show 100" was a 40/16/2 Midas XL3 with eight VCAs, plus another sixteen-channel stretch. Reinforcement was provided by a EAW KF850 system (twenty-four boxes per side). "This really is a difficult venue from a sound balance perspective," Collins said, mirroring the view of virtually every sound engineer that has worked at the Albert Hall. "The sound just goes round and round, and there are no corners in which to hide. Anything that is played on stage just comes flying out, so level is a problem. You really have to battle to keep things under control. But this is a dream compared to the pressures we were under during the twenty-four nights. We were going from a small band one night to orchestra, and all points in between, again with a Midas board and an EAW system.

Fellow Welshman and Concert Sound engineer Kerry Lewis took care of the on-stage sound. His desk was a one-off custom-made 4/20 Concert Sound console. "I personally think it's the best around," he said. "You can set it up and mix very easily and there's an excellent VCA section which I use for all my cues. It's ideal where you've got musicians seated on some numbers, standing on others, lots of guitar changes and the horn section on some numbers. Our wedges are all Concert Sound-designed. They are quite unique monitors with a configuration you will find nowhere else in the world. This whole system goes everywhere with Eric."

Support artists all gained from Lewis's expertise and he upheld a philosophy that all engineers should subscribe to. "Working for a sound company, you have to take the view that today's support acts could be tomorrow's stars. That's why Nine Below Zero [the R&B support act for Clapton's 1994 shows] get exactly the same treatment from me that I give Eric."

In 1997, Clapton broke with tradition and was noticeably absent from the Albert Hall calendar, with the exception of his appearance at the all-star Music For Montserrat concert. The next year, the guitarist released *Pilgrim*, his first all-original studio album since 1989's *Journeyman* and returned to the UK live scene with shows in the decidedly less intimate confines of Earl's Court.

CHAPTER THREE

Take That

...To The Max! – 1994

The screams and whines of hundreds of teenage nubiles at the backstage gate provided a clue as to what could be expected that evening when Take That came on stage at Wembley Arena in September 1994. The shrill crescendo of the young audience which greeted the five wonderboys as they rose from the centre stage trap door, was like Beatlemania all over again, but ten times louder. And despite the vastly increased power of PA systems since the Sixties, Take That's first number, 'Satisfied'/'I Can't Get No Satisfaction', was barely audible above the din of ecstasy.

With costume changes a-plenty and a set that seemed to metamorphosise every fifteen minutes, the show was a non-stop exercise in arena excess. The nearest Take That ever got to an "Unplugged" performance occurred midway through the set when two Yamaha pianos rose through the stage and Jason Orange strummed his guitar for 'Why Can't I Wake Up With You' and 'A Million Love Songs'. Then it was time for the highlight of the show. Out of nowhere it seemed, a steel catwalk, half the length of the arena, was lowered on to the stage. The five blue mohair-suited lads darted along it to a circular B stage in the middle of the audience, 100 feet away from the main stage and ten feet above the mixing platform. This is where the screaming reached its peak. Ironically, they performed a medley of Beatles classics – 'I Want To Hold Your Hand', 'A Hard Day's Night', 'She Loves You', 'I Feel Fine' and 'Get Back' – culminating in the timeless 'Hey Jude' "na-na-na-na-na-na" mantra. The place was cooking!

An on-screen interactive video sequence animated 'Babe' and as four of the boys appeared to get closer, the real life ones walked on to the stage through splits in said screen. Very effective! Encoring with 'Pray', Gary Barlow, Robbie Williams, Howard Donald, Jason and Mark Owen decked themselves out in their most risqué outfits and completed their extravaganza with the much talked-about 'Relight My Fire' sequence, featuring Lulu as a vampire. This was one of the last opportunities to catch the five-piece Take That before Robbie Williams took indefinite leave, and the band's eventual split – a memorable show for the kids and adults alike.

For the technically-minded it was just as memorable for the presence of personal in-ear monitoring, a discipline which had won the hearts of a number of performers and engineers since the turn of the Nineties, and whose popularity was now on the brink of becoming truly widespread. Along with Peter Gabriel's Secret World Tour and U2's Zoo TV, the Take That shows of 1994 became a benchmark by which the Garwood Radio Station wireless in-ear monitoring system was to be judged for some time.

An idea devised by engineer and Garwood founder Chrys Lindop after working with Stevie Wonder in the late Eighties, and then subsequently built by Garwood's Martin Noar, the Radio Station system was designed to dramatically reduce stage volume, eliminate feedback and, in conjunction with the now widely-used radio microphone, give artists complete freedom to wander around a stage whilst experiencing a consistent, high quality monitor mix, regardless of the environment. With a mix fed directly to an ear-piece set via a UHF radio link, artists not only focus complete concentration on their performance, but with a volume control-equipped belt pack can also determine their own comfortable listening level.

"Although our monitoring is predominantly in-ear, we are using some speakers," said Take That monitor engineer Ian Newton. "Most of the time I am monitoring on a set of headphones out of the desk. On the Midas XL3 that's okay because I can listen in stereo. I used to have the cue output wired to a spare transmitter and plug my headphones into there, but now we are getting into so many frequencies, I am working on the theory that the less frequencies broadcasted the better, so I don't do that anymore. It keeps the airwaves a little bit clearer of RF. I also have a cue wedge if I need it.

The original plan was to build monitor grilles into the stage for hot spots in case of radio system breakdown or RF crises. But, said Newton: "They got rid of that idea and instead I just have a wedge tucked in behind the side fill. It's only really drums in the side fills, just to add a bit more energy and vibe on-stage, especially for the dancing. The bass player and guitarist are on radio systems, but they also need some kick and snare thump in a wedge otherwise it all feels too sterile for them. If there's a problem with the boys, such as if their ear-pieces fall out or get broken, I just send the vocals through the side fills while we're fixing the radio problem. They can break them just because of the sheer physical nature of the show. They are breakdancing and doing back somersaults and headstands, so it's easy for them to pull the wires out of their ear pieces or pull the antennae or jack sockets out of their belt packs. But the boys are pretty good in difficult situations like that and they don't panic. They let me know if there's something wrong. There are a lot of costume changes throughout the show and if something does go down, we give them some vocal in the side fill and once we get around the back, we have spare parts for the radio systems.

"It is a much more complex show this time from the wireless aspect, because all the musicians are now on the radio system as well as the boys and everyone gets their own separate mix. There's a lot of wandering around and the only way we could give everyone a personal mix was to put them on the radio system. On the last tour, the boys were very mobile but the musicians were very static and for this tour it was decided that the band would be free to move around. The percussionist and keyboard player are both wearing ear-pieces, but being the only ones to remain static they are hard-wired rather than on the radio system.

"When you start getting into lots of different frequencies, a good thing to have is a mobile scanner, so that if you are experiencing problems at least you can work out whether it's down to an RF thing where someone is breaking in or if it's a problem with the unit. Most of the time it will be due to someone else operating near your frequency. But, of course, we never ever use it to listen to the mobile phone network!"

Performing the ten-minute Beatles medley on the centre B stage posed a technical problem for Newton and his pals from Garwood. "We've used two Yagi long throw antennae to give an extra transmitter throw to the boys on the centre stage and so far we've had no RF problems. The problem with the delay is not them hearing the speaker system, it's the microphones hearing the speakers. They pick up the delay which then goes into the in-ear monitors. So when they go out there, there's a lot of changing around, soundwise. The boys listen to each other quite a lot, but out there because of the spill with the PA going into the mics, I have to dial everybody out of everyone else's mix and push the snare drum right up, almost as loud as the vocal, as a reference for timing. I don't know how they manage it to be honest because the level of the screaming is ridiculous when they're out there!"

Garwood's Martin Noar said: "Take That used six systems on their last tour but have been using twelve systems this time, ten of which are on the Channel 69 frequencies with the other two doubled up on frequencies and acting as back-ups. Technically, the difficulty with doing that was remaining within the law. If there were no constraints with the amount of frequencies we could use, then obviously we could have fifty units working simultaneously. But we have to operate within a very small band and we put a lot of work into calculating intermodulation which is a phenomenon that happens when you have more than one radio system of any description running. You have to calculate carefully to ensure you don't get interference from unwanted signals on your system.

Noar added: "If you can bring a band out into the heart of the arena, right into the audience, you will give a whole new depth to a production and I think that must excite lighting and set designers terrifically. I'm sure that their understanding of this technology will become reflected in future stage designs. They can progress to another plane now because of the equipment. Even console designers are now taking in-ear monitoring into account when designing new products, so that's a good third-party endorsement of the concept and a positive sign that the idea is now in people's minds as they look ahead."

Ian Newton controlled his sixty input channels of sound on two Midas XL3 desks, employing an extra twenty-four-channel stretch from a Soundcraft 8000. Newton said: "I need two desks for the number of mixes I am doing and I can't get enough sends out of one desk once we start getting into stereo mixes. My number one console has been fitted with buffer outputs and number two gets the inputs from number one's post gain, post EQ and post insert pots, which keeps me happy because I don't have to have inserts on number two desk. Because there aren't enough channels on a forty-channel desk, I mix down a little sub group of toms and percussion on the Soundcraft board and bring them in on a couple of channels on number one.

"Outboard-wise, I am using graphics across the radio mixes, mainly for some high-end boost, even though the belt packs have a high-end boost on them. Although they sound bright enough to me, the musicians still ask for a little more high end. So we just give a little nudge here but that's about the only EQ that gets put on them. I have a compressor across the radio groups, but I've found that I have just about wound them all the way off now because there is plenty of compression in the transmitter unit. I have them in for safety, when people drop microphones."

Tragedy struck the Take That crew during production rehearsals at London Arena when FOH Engineer Tim Warhurst of Capital Sound sustained a fractured skull and broken neck after falling from a PA tower. Colleague Dave Pringle was seconded as a replacement but as he said: "It was a hell of a way to get a job." Pringle responded to the challenge which he modestly described as being straightforward, apart from the large amount of wireless technology involved in the in-ear monitoring, guitar transmitters and twelve Shure and Sennheiser radio mics. It was the audience noise which gave Pringle his biggest headaches, in more ways than one.

"When Take That are on the circular stage above me, they are obviously in front of the PA system," he explained, "so I'm not going to get a whole lot of level out of them and the mics do drop out occasionally. There's also a lot of radio mic muting going on when the lighting rig comes down at different points, otherwise there would be a lot of interference. But that's always between numbers so it doesn't compromise the performance. The costume changes are very quick and you'll find that the guy who leaves the stage thirty seconds before the end of a number will come on and introduce the next one while the others are getting changed."

Pringle used a Capital Sound-supplied Yamaha PM4000 console with a total of sixty inputs to control the standard Martin F2 PA configuration. "The good thing about the PM4000 is that you can put lots of stereo modules in it to increase your input capacity," he said. "There are a couple of reverbs in the outboard racks, two Yamaha SPX 1000s and an Eventide H3000, but it's not really a show that relies too much on outboard effects. I have to compress the vocals quite a bit because with such a loud audience, the dynamic range is reduced somewhat. It gets very manic out here and I've never experienced anything like it. When the screaming reaches its peaks, I have to go on headphones because it's the only way I can make any sense of what's going on with the sound."

A comprehensive discussion with the band's chirpy Antipodean stage manager, Paul Bradman – known to Gary Barlow as The Fat Controller, but to everyone else as Skippy – revealed all about the impressive stage construction. "We've got a Serious Structures stage with infills built by Brilliant Stages," he explained. "Towards the downstage edge we've got our front trap where the boys rise from at the start of the show and come down at the end. Underneath stage right there is a makeshift dressing room which allows very quick costume changes between songs and the guitar amplification is kept down there away from the audience's view as we don't really want to have any unnecessary visual distractions. We also have special braces that prevent the stage from wobbling too much when the boys are really active on-stage.

"There's a set of steps allowing the boys to walk all the way up to the back wall. That wall goes up to a height of 28' and as it rises to its full height, some flaps are lowered to reveal all the rear scenery at the start of the show. The two keyboard players also double on sax and trumpet, and they are on stock 8' x 4' rolling risers. We have two 9' 6" x 9' 6" rolling risers for the drums and percussion which start off on the hydraulics lowered as far as they will go. The idea was that the show would start off with almost nothing on stage, so it looks like there's nothing there. Then suddenly the drums and percussion start coming out of the holes, and in next to no time this whole set just appears out of thin air."

On entering the empty arena before the show, the first thing one noticed was the giant spaceship-like lighting rig. "It's a beast," laughed lighting crew chief, Mike Humeniuk of Samuelsons as he surveyed his team's work. "Logistically, to build it here at Wembley within the time allowed was quite hard because it's a real monster. Fortunately, I have an A Team crew that can cope very well in these situations. There's no space in this bloody venue and the stage should be another eight feet wider either side because our mother grid is 96' wide.

"There are nine pods which are all independently controlled from stage right and in total there are about 1,500 individual lighting elements plus the Vari*Lites. We are using VL6s and I believe we were the first tour in Europe to go out with them. There is a separate dimmer system for the catwalk/circular stage sequence. There are four moves during the show and there is a separate computer control adjacent to the FOH sound mixing platform which runs the catwalk/circular stage sequence, so in effect I have two lighting crews to look after. We are using two Celco Gold consoles and a Celco thirty-way console, all linked together to give us 210 channels.

"It's the mother grid that flies all the pods which are TTR folding truss and Minibeam. There are two 96' runs of TTR on-stage and two 16' off-stage, plus seventeen lengths of Minibeam across the lot to pick up all thirty-six points on the pods, thirty-two of which are computer-controlled."

Humeniuk summed up the feelings of the crew when he added: "From a lighting perspective, the show is a real challenge, but it's well worth it because at the end of the day it's bloody spectacular and the biggest thing in arenas in 1994."

CHAPTER FOUR

Del Amitri

Twisted World – 1995

For rock audiences and bands alike, London's Labatt's Apollo (formerly the Hammersmith Odeon) is sacred ground, a venue associated more with heart-stirring atmospheres than acoustic clarity. But in the claustrophobic heat of July 1995, on their Twisted World tour, Del Amitri proved they could generate both.

With a set drawn largely from their most recent albums, *Change Everything* and *Twisted*, the Glaswegian Dels delivered a fine slab of no-nonsense rock, rather like The Faces with a kilt! The folky acoustic moments which were more in evidence on earlier albums played second fiddle to gritty blues tones, largely provided by the Les Paul-wielding Iain Harvie. Bass player and bushy sideburns campaigner Justin Currie, meanwhile, justified himself not only as a magnetic frontperson but also a rare singer whose live voice transcended even its best recorded moments.

Unlike many shows witnessed at Hammersmith since the Seventies, the sound approached an almost studio-like quality. At the rear of the stalls, next to the FOH mixing platform, Currie's bass was extremely present without the normal inherent muddiness, David Cummings' and Harvie's guitars cut through loud and clear, though not offensively, and every vocal uttering was clearly defined.

Much of this aural success was the product of FOH engineer Andy Dockerty's use of the much-applauded BSS Audio FDS 388 Omnidrive loudspeaker management system and FCS 926 Varicurve dual equaliser analyser. Used in conjunction with each other, these two systems provided a full, real-time, graphical indication of the performance of the PA rig and allowed the adjustment of a wide range of parameters. The Omnidrive itself incorporates two full-function four-way crossovers, parametric EQ, delays and limiters, with all functions accessible through the unit's front panel.

Dockerty, whose Liverpool-based PA company AdLib Audio provided the sound system for the Dels, was using the Omnidrive system for the first time on this tour and said it had made a huge difference as an aid to streamlining his tasks. "The Omnidrive is an amazing piece of kit. I'm not really into technology. I class myself as a straight ahead rock 'n' roll engineer who puts the faders up and sees what happens. I'm not naturally MIDI minded and in the past I've tended to pooh-pooh new developments, but the Omnidrive is so easy to get your head around once you've been through it once or twice. It made me wonder why I never got into MIDI earlier because this is the Nineties and the new technology in live sound is here, so I say let's grab it! There are now less things for me to worry about. I just hit one button and all the audio events and scenes change.

"The system has a set of parameters that I would call the basic control system, such as crossover points, EQ shapes and delays. I then use the Varicurve to fine tune the EQ from show to show. We spent a fair amount of time working all this out for the first couple of shows and we tend to leave the Omnidrive settings as they are for each date. Depending on the venue, I may play around with some of the EQ settings. On the first two or three shows, because of the facilities available, I made the mistake of playing around with it too much. I was like a kid in a toy shop, asking myself, 'What happens if I do this or do that?' But I went back several steps and since then everything has been fine."

Dockerty said that one of the major benefits of the Omnidrive was that its use was not limited to one speaker system as most control systems had been in the past. "We can now look at the future and plan to go out on the road with four Omnidrives and four control racks with different speaker systems, whether they be AdLib's own DF1 system or DF2 which has slightly different components higher up. If a system has a different shape to the next, you can just programme the Omnidrive to align them. It opens up a whole new way of thinking for PA companies. With most pieces of kit, you are always finding little characteristics that you think can be improved upon, but I haven't found anything about the Omnidrive that I'd want to change or add to. I can say the same about the Varicurve, although it would be nice to have some more notching facilities sometimes. But if you need that, you can just throw a graphic in line for fine tuning. I basically use it as an FOH system EQ device and there are probably another 101 things on it that I'd never use it for. It's incredibly comprehensive."

The AdLib Audio-designed ground stack PA had twelve DF1 full range cabinets and twelve DF1 subs. The 2 x 18" subs were loaded with JBL 2241s, while the high pack had a JBL 2226 15" speaker, an RCF 750 10" and a JBL 2446 horn. AdLib's flying system, flown by Mann frames and steels, and Columbus McKinnon Lodestar motors, consisted of twelve DF2 full range cabinets and four DF2 bass bins. Amplification was provided by Crown VZ 5000 amps (subs/bass), C Audio RA 4001s (mids) and RA 3001s (highs). Dockerty said: "We were using Crown 1201s on the mids and highs until recently, but the C Audio amps provide a much cleaner sound.

"On the cabinet side, we recently did some experiments with different bullets but we've waived them since the advent of the Omnidrive because I can put a little curve in to counteract the need. I find it's a far more consistent way of going about things. The biggest cut in there is about 4.5dB at 6kW which is just top end tuning. There's a dip of about 3dB at 500Hz and another small dip at 125Hz at 2dB. That's on the main cue that I have on the system.

"Apart from the compression drivers, the most expensive cost with our high pack was the development of our own classic horn flare for the 15" and 10" speakers. It's all one unit which just slides into the cabinet. We discovered that using a plastic as opposed to a wooden horn flare gave us a cleaner sound that was about 0.5dB louder. It is quite an expensive way of doing it, but when you compare the costs of building our cabinets against some of the more established manufacturers, ours are still less expensive."

At the front-of-house position, Dockerty manned a 40-16-2 Midas XL3 mixing console, on which he used thirty-one input channels with the remaining channels reserved for effects returns. In his outboard rack, he had a Lexicon PCM70 multi-effects unit, two Yamaha SPX 900 multi-effects units, a Yamaha REV 5 and delays via a Roland SDE 3000A and a Yamaha D1500. All his effects were MIDI-controlled via the Varicurve FPC 900 remote equaliser analyser controller. On drummer Ashley Soan's kit, the kick was inserted into a Klark Teknik Quad DN504 compressor and a Drawmer DS201 gate before being returned to the XL3. His hi-hats and overhead mics were sent via two aux channels on the XL3 to a stereo BSS DPR 402 compressor/limiter. The snare's top and bottom mics were gated and compressed at the aux channels, then routed to the mix. Justin Currie's vocals were compressed by both the DPR 402 and (secondly) the newer BSS DPR 901 Mark II, then returned to the desk.

Debuting on the latter part of this tour as Del Amitri's monitor engineer was the youthful Dave Kay of AdLib, who originally joined as a PA rigger. Although Kay had gained much experience as a monitor engineer in the past at a variety of events, this tour marked the first time he had worked for a major band in this capacity.

The Soundcraft SM24 console he used was on loan to AdLib from the Hertfordshire manufacturer for this tour, and Kay was clearly in his element. He said: "A lot of thought has obviously gone into designing the SM24 with the engineer in mind and both Minnie, my predecessor, and I fell in love with it. It has all the features you could ever want from a desk; everything's big and in the right place."

Kay used thirty-six input channels on the SM24, many of which were dedicated to Justin Currie's Garwood in-ear mix. Kay said: "Justin's the only one using the in-ear system but he also uses wedges to add a bit of warmth to the sound he hears on stage. His wedge mix is predominantly drums, with hi-hat, kick and snare upfront, which is important for his timing as a bass player. Although the system is great for monitoring most instruments, it isn't fully capable of delivering a meaty drum sound, so he needs the wedges to 'feel' the sound better. The in-ear system tends to make the user feel isolated, so we place an ambient microphone on top of each of the side fills to pick up a bit of the on-stage and audience sound to make him feel more at home. I have my own pair of ear moulds which I plug directly into the Radio Station so I can hear exactly what Justin is listening to. But you have to be careful not to listen at too high a volume level, otherwise the top end of your hearing just disappears. I tend to just monitor his in-ear mix for the first three songs to make sure he's getting the right mix, and then I will listen only occasionally throughout the rest of the set."

AdLib's own-designed monitor wedges and fills were used extensively with BSS crossovers and powered by Crown amps. There were three separate mixes along the front, two mixes at the rear and a rear pair of monitor fills to project the guitars into the middle of the stage for solos. Kay said: "We're actually using Black Box side fills which we just had lying around and put to good use. The bass bins have two JBL 2226 15" drivers while the mid highs have two JBL 12" speakers and two JBL E140 2" horns. The drum fill has two JBL 15" drivers, plus a 2" horn. Accompanying the Crown amps in the monitor control rack are two Drawmer DS201 dual gates, two Behringer MDX 2000 dynamics processors, four BSS FCS 960 dual mode graphic equalisers and four BSS FCS 360 frequency dividing/limiter system units."

An ingenious AdLib invention in use with Del Amitri was a pressure pad system for muting backing vocal microphones when they were not being used. Dave Kay explained: "There is a pad situated behind each backing vocal mic stand which the singer has to stand on to gain access to the mic. When he stands on it, the mic is open, but it closes as soon as he steps back. It's a very useful tool for controlling sound bleed from drums and backline amps through the monitors, especially in smaller venues, and it obviously also helps the FOH mix."

Production manager and lighting designer Derek McVay had worked with Del Amitri since 1989, exactly one year before the band scored its first major chart successes with the hits 'Nothing Ever Happens' and 'Kiss This Thing Goodbye', from the *Waking Hours* album. McVay was using a Celco 60 series II Special Edition console to control what he described as a traditional rock 'n' roll lighting rig, designed to enable heavy saturation of colour when much white light is being used.

"The rig has been designed not for me, the manager or the band, but for the punters," he explained, "and I've seen some great local reviews while we've been on the road that confirm that we're capturing the audiences in the right way. I'm not into aesthetic lighting design; it bores me. I like to use lots of ACLs and big fans, and although some of the things I do might seem corny, if the audience leaves having had a good night, then I've done my job."

The truss was 44' wide, trimmed at 25', with two 10' legs descending like goalposts. There was a white cyc at the back with four Rosco ground rows on it, while on the floor there were three 1.2kW CCT Turbo Sils with gobo rotators, four bars of ACLs, three floor cans and four Megastar strobes. The front truss was exceedingly minimal with only six Strand Lekos and three Thomas four-lite Molefays. Aside from colour washes, there were four bars of four to each side with number five bulb-loaded Par 64s with simple colours. The back truss had eight mixed bars with six different 650 watt CCT Profiles on each and Par 64s with number one and number two bulbs. Each top and bottom lamp on the bar had a colour changer on it and was hung on the truss vertically, then angled diagonally across the truss to form a "V" shape. Here, there were six bars of ACLs and six of 1kW Strand Lekos.

"Everything is open white apart from the Rainbow colour changers which I've used for years and are so easy to work with," said McVay. "The vast amount of white in the rig is a deliberate move. After being in America for about two months and having to suffer inferior rigs, Justin Currie and I got into using lots of white, although I've always been a fan of it. All the band members, especially Justin and Iain, are very aware of lighting and they like to give me some feedback. There is no set look for each song. I might use some memories where I've built something up for a song, but there isn't a script as such because we like to keep things spontaneous. So the look of each show will be slightly different. Most of the time, I will get an idea and just go for it on the night. It's the same way of thinking as the band's, because they are likely to change the set at short notice. They certainly never keep the same set for more than two shows."

Part of the reason for the rig's simplicity was budget constraint. Wearing both the production manager's and LD's hats meant that McVay was constantly fighting with himself where creative and economical factors were concerned. "I go to the band's management and ask them how much they want to spend on lighting," he said. "It's then left to me and the lighting companies to bring the show in within that budget. The tour manager looks after the hotels while I look after the production, and we've worked happily like that with Del Amitri and Deacon Blue for about six years now. We've had the same lighting guys for about three years now and lots of other guys in the crew have been with us for a long time, which I think that is a reflection of the happy family atmosphere. I'm very concerned that I should work with nice, youngish people around me who are prepared to learn and be sympathetic to crew guys in every department of the production."

CHAPTER FIVE

Rod Stewart
A Spanner In The Works...
And In The Round – 1995

Not even torrential rain could dampen the high spirits of the 85,000 strong crowd gathered at Wembley Stadium in June 1995 to see Rod Stewart's dazzling display of pop artistry. An impressive in-the-round stage design situated in the centre of the venue's hallowed turf provided an innovative platform upon which "The Mod", his fourteen-piece band and twenty-two-piece orchestra presented songs from his latest album, *A Spanner In The Works*, while a generous and faithfully executed back catalogue of over twenty-five years had the fans joining in on every line.

Showing no sign that he turned fifty that January, Stewart's voice was back in fine form after some years of difficulty and he left the audience breathless at the sight of his athleticism as he jumped, ran and kicked footballs by the dozen into the crowd, and generally twisted the night away. By complete contrast, the weather was hot and sunny during the previous day's load-in and set-up when various members of the production crew waxed lyrical about many technical developments being introduced on this tour.

One such development was the much talked about forty-eight-channel Midas XL4 audio mixing console, of which three were put to good use for the first time on this Stewart tour which began in Aberdeen. With the exception of pre/post switching on aux sends, virtually every switch on the XL4s was automated, courtesy of Out Board Electronics who were commissioned by Midas to design a bespoke, upgraded version of its SS2 snap shot automation software package for the new console.

On the eve of the Wembley show, Out Board's Robin Whittaker commented: "There is a phenomenal amount of automation on the console which I think really sets it aside from just about any other analogue non-assignable board. There are around sixty switching functions per channel automated as well as faders. There are some really nice touches, such as when you power the console down, irrespective of what happens to it before it's powered up again, everything will reset automatically. In terms of specifying the automation, I canvassed the opinions of Lars Brogaard (production manager/FOH engineer) to a reasonable extent. He had the experience of working with the automated XL3 package which was really just moving faders, and collaborated with Midas on the overall console specification.

"We try to adopt a Volvo approach to product development, so rather than redesigning something from scratch to give birth to a new product, we issue enhanced and improved versions of our old products. So what Lars is working with has a much larger memory capacity and a larger addressing capacity in terms of how many switches and faders it conforms to. It has an upgraded user interface and we now have an alpha-numeric display which was absent from the previous SS2 system. We've also taken on board MIDI event management into the new processor rather than have it on an external software product basis. The SS2 solution was to use proShow, a remote programming and MIDI events management system, but that's now incorporated into the new processor.

"Within each scene or cue in the automation, you can programme a series of MIDI events that are executed when you hit the Go key. It still has event listing on the computer screen and we have a version of proShow on the XL4 which is an overall scene, cue and prompt listing package, as well as displaying VCA status in terms of being able to name VCA groups. Although there is virtually total automation, the engineer can intervene at any point. It's still essentially a snap shot-based system, so the automation is not ruling the show; it's still the sound engineer who is deciding on the moves. The automation serves as a scratch pad memory facility for him. It's only when the switch and fader movements are being recalled that the automation is active."

Lars Brogaard began his audio career in 1977 and toured extensively with ABBA, Lionel Richie, Traffic and Cher, among many others, before joining Rod Stewart's clan in 1984 as both FOH engineer and production manager. Why both jobs? "When I started, production managers didn't pay too much attention to the sound because most came from a lighting background," he explained. "So to get things done the way I wanted them, I had to be in that job too."

Brogaard's involvement in the automation design for the XL4 resulted in a console that was almost personalised to his own discerning requirements. How did he view the latest Midas creation? "One of the big changes is that there are sub-groups on this board which there wasn't on the XL3. The EQ is fully four-way parametric and there is both high pass and low pass on the mic and line inputs. They are just a few of the extra useful features. The metering is much better and the great sound coming out of the board means that I don't need to do much EQing, although if you pick the right microphone you shouldn't need to do much anyway."

For the first few dates on the tour, Brogaard worked with an incomplete automation package on his console. The VCA sub-groups and mutes were already automated, and within a few weeks the board's input channels were assigned to moving faders.

The in-the-round production meant that Brogaard and his crew had to approach elements of PA rigging and EQ differently. "We have two sets of PA system mirrored, so that we have two lefts and two rights," he explained. "There is a lot more EQing and phasing that needs to be sorted out, but having done it a few times, I can say that it gets easier. You certainly don't need such a long throw."

A moving Plexiglass dome in the centre of the stage provided an isolated "home" for the twenty-two-piece orchestra. "It works very well because you get a tremendous amount of level in there. There's no spill from the band, although there wouldn't be much anyway as everyone is on in-ear monitors. But the drum kit is still banging away in their direction. On the last tour, we had them sitting behind the band with a Plexiglass baffle in front of them. But we can get a much better sound now."

With the exception of some Shures and Neumanns on the drum kit, the microphones were exclusively AKG. "We have AKG C401 pick-ups on all the string instruments, C409s on the woodwinds, C451s overhead on the flute and there are some C414s picking up the ambience inside the shell. On drums we have a D112 on the kick, a Shure SM57 on the top and bottom of the snare, a C451 and a Neumann on the hi-hat, small AKG C408 bugs on the three toms (also on the horns), a C451 on the percussion and a couple of Neumanns overhead. The guitar cabs underneath the stage are miked with Shure SM57s. The vocals are all AKG TriPower C5900 and keyboard position mic is the only one which isn't wireless – everything else is a radio mic and we have twelve channels' worth of them!

"I was always trying to keep as many mics as possible on wires because I generally think they sound better than wireless. But the technology is improving all the time and we tried out the AKG stuff which I thought was so good that I couldn't distinguish between their radio mics and hard-wired products."

Adjacent to Brogaard's XL4 was a Midas XL200, functioning exclusively as the orchestra mixing console. The instruments were broken down into sub-groups, assigned effects for warmth, then sent in stereo to the XL4. The crew had to wait until until showday before the orchestra arrived. "It's rather expensive to have an orchestra on site for two days," Brogaard explained. "They will come in on showday at 8am and rehearse, then I will soundcheck them at 11am. It's not something that makes me nervous because once you've successfully mixed an orchestra live, it's more or less the same thing over again. We have just been using local orchestras for the first few dates, but after Wembley we will be travelling with our own orchestra for the rest of the European tour which will make things a lot easier."

The Electrotec Lab Q PA rig was controlled by three BSS Omnidrive loudspeaker management system units. Another interesting BSS product used on the Rod Stewart tour was the DPR 901 dynamic equaliser for all of the vocals.

Stewart's PA system consisted of a bass bin with one 18" driver and a horn loaded cabinet which had two 12" drivers, a 2451 horn and 2075s. These were powered by Crown 5000 amplifiers on the lows and mids, and Crown Reference amps on the highs, contributing to a combined amplification power of around 250,000 watts. There was a line speaker cabinet arrangement on top, with the remaining cabinets staggered in checkerboard fashion at the bottom. Some of the cabinets were turned upside down to provide a more forceful sound. The sub-bass cabinets all contained Aura 18" 1kW speakers and were positioned around the bottom of the stage, leaving one to fear for the health of the audience members seated in the front rows!

Brogaard assured: "Having the sub-bass cabinets so close to the front of the audience hasn't been a problem and certainly no one has complained. The way we run the sub-basses isn't like you might for a heavy metal or rock band where it can be offensive. We use them as part of the music, the entire mix picture. I had planned to position the subs in the middle of each of the four sides, but in that position they were shaking the orchestra to pieces and I couldn't leave it like that. So I had to move them out even though I was a bit nervous about phasing. I don't know if it's the best situation but it does work."

The entire FOH EQing was performed with BSS Varicurve units, while general outboard effects at Brogaard's console were largely care of vintage AMSs. "I'm not very keen on Japanese technology," he admitted. "It's not warm enough for me whereas I really like the warmth and natural qualities of this old stuff. I find that Yamaha equipment is much harder sounding on the reverbs. But I have heard guys doing some fantastic work with Yamahas, so I'm not saying there's anything wrong with them, just that it's not for me."

Rod Stewart and his band enjoyed the luxury of two monitor engineers. Mike McNeil's primary responsibility was to look after Stewart's personal mix, while David Bryson on the opposite side of the stage took care of the band, each being equipped with forty-eight-channel automated Midas XL4 consoles – one of two major world firsts for this monitor crew!

McNeil enthused: "I have been running with automation from the very first day and it's working great. It has MIDI in/out, so I've MIDI'd it to all the effects and everything changes with the press of the next button, because there are assignable MIDI channels on the board. The first time we used this system on the road was in Aberdeen and it's the first time anywhere in the world that an automated monitor mix has been attempted, but I've got it all going out pretty good and there are no problems whatsoever."

To add further fuel to the technological feats displayed on the tour,

McNeil was happy to point out that there were no conventional monitor wedges to be seen on the stage, as the performers were all using Garwood Radio Station in-ear monitoring (IEM) systems. In the spirit of this boundary-defying tour, there were fourteen Radio Stations running simultaneously to provide fourteen stereo mixes – a world record at the time!

"As far as I'm concerned, it's the future standard of live monitoring," said McNeil. "We have one Radio Station module and an Aphex Dominator per man. The Dominator is a peak ceiling limiter which is a protection unit aside from the internal protection within the Radio Station itself. It provides dynamic limiting which holds down the over modulation of the unit. If you over modulate you risk crashing one frequency into another.

"I don't hard compress anything in the in-ear mix like some other engineers tend to do. We're much more comfortable with open dynamics, but I do have the ceiling set so that anything really major happens it'll hold it down and not damage the listener's ears."

Stewart, McNeil affirmed, preferred to hear a full show mix, the quality of which was virtually hi-fi. "I have a full complement of effects here and I create a lot of ambience with a variety of effects. If you send a very dry mix into the performer's in-ear mix, it's really just too confining and too closed in, and not a nice experience. But we open it out with reverb systems that are dedicated to individual voices and instruments. That creates different types of ambiences which makes the overall sound appear much more natural."

The only wedges in sight on the lower stage level were situated below both McNeil and Bryson's consoles. "I use my wedge occasionally to check my cues, so that I don't have to wear my ear pieces all day," said McNeil. "We also hooked up a live hands-free selectable audiocom that we invented ourselves to enable a three-way conversation between myself and the other console engineers; we can designate it to any of the performers on stage, or all of them at the same time. The conductor is on an isolated in-ear mix and the orchestra players are listening only to themselves. The Plexiglass shell that they're in is acoustically resonant inside because of its symmetry, and it gets really loud in there so they can hear themselves just fine and they're isolated from all the extraneous noise."

McNeil eagerly took on the responsibility of introducing Stewart and his band members to the idea of IEM. Most were enthusiastic, although it was to his credit that he persevered with the doubting Thomases to ensure that everyone was "on ears". "I took each member one at a time and we demoed the ear pieces with a full stereo mix. The keyboard players were the last two holdouts and were on straight wedges last year, but on this tour they've gone over to the ear mix. Everybody is really happy with it. Because of the stereo imaging and the detail that you can put into a mix, it is a comfortable listening experience."

Colleague Bryson commented: "Drummers can also be difficult to win over because of the lack of power they experience without drum fill monitors. Dave Palmer has two of what I call butt-woofers or shakers. They are Aura solenoid drivers, mounted on the bottom of his drum stool. Each one is basically a coil and I reinforce the stereo signal through an amplifier to give the sound a lot more beef. It goes through a parametric EQ and I give it forty cycles as the signal goes to the stool. They constantly blast his spine with the physical sensation normally experienced with loud side fills. He has a hard-wired, stereo ear mix, although he wears closed-can headphones instead of ear pieces, so he hears a really fat sound."

A combination of radio mics, guitar transmitters and Radio Stations contributed to the use of a staggering thirty-two separate radio frequencies. Said Bryson: "We organised it very thoroughly with Hand Held Audio, ran some programmes and worked out all the frequencies for all the venues well in advance of the tour. As a result of the isolation on stage, there is a much better FOH sound."

The BSS Varicurve system with remote control was used extensively. McNeil said: "I have Varicurve inserted on Rod's main mix output, the three backing singers and orchestra conductor. There's a stereo insert on each one of the mix outputs and I use the remote control for all of this. It also has MIDI in and through, so that if I do want to brighten up for one of the softer ballads, and put some extended highs on it as I change the reverb programmes, all the EQ programmes change as well, via the XL4 which, I've got to say, is the most happening mixer I've had my hands on in eighteen years.

"David and I both use a Midas XL88 to sub-mix the orchestra. The sub-mixes come to me in four groups from Lars at FOH and I send them in stereo to Rod. That cuts down the channel usage somewhat. We've got a real versatile thing going here. We can change our set-up around and in any emergency situation I could theoretically pick up one of David's players and he could pick up one of mine. They are two matched monitor systems, and although mine is dedicated to Rod and David's, to the band, we have enough on-board flexibility to troubleshoot and save the show, in the event of the worst possible scenario."

The tour witnessed the first use in the live entertainment sphere of fibre optic cabling, used exclusively here for audio. Originally manufactured for missiles in operation Desert Storm during the Gulf War, the cable impressed Electrotec with its strength and durability, far surpassing that of traditional copper. Having withstood tanks rolling over it in the desert, Electrotec was confident that the cable could take the pressures involved in a Rod Stewart tour and hired engineer Greg Horn to look after all aspects of the cabling.

Horn said: "I've been involved with Electrotec for over six years and they wanted a crew member dedicated to this stuff. Lars wanted to bring this out on this rig provided there was someone around who knew how to terminate fibre and troubleshoot it. To date we haven't had anything to troubleshoot. We're running about seventy-six channels' worth of band and orchestra mic and line level to the FOH and about twenty-six channels of returns which include talkback.

"We have cables the size of a microphone line holding 128 channels of audio, and they'll run for three miles without any loss. In a regular situation, we would string the 'snake' up from the ceiling, put two ropes over the top and pull it up, then just drop it at the end of the show. The reason that Lars wanted to bring it was that we're doing a bunch of festivals where we're taking all our FOH gear and monitor rigs, and we'll want to pull out our snake before the show's over. We can do that in ten minutes! There's about a mile of this stuff and it weighs only 180lbs as opposed to 300' weighing 250lbs. On top of that there's no mechanical protection so we haven't spent five seconds running ground loops at all."

The lighting rig was designed by Lars Brogaard, together with LSD's Kevin Forbes and Jeff Grainger, and the brief to the lighting design team was keep it simple but bright. Responsible for making it all happen every night on tour were LD Martin McLoughlin and Icon operator, Mark Payne. Stewart's Wembley set kicked off at 8.15pm when there was still plenty of daylight and ended with the moving finale of 'Sailing', accompanied by Jeff Gilreath's spectacular pyro display and the cliched waving of ciggie lighters in the evening sky.

For the first nine or ten numbers, the lights remained an effective white. But, as McLoughlin explained, "We have a meeting before the show to decide at which point we go to colour. That is dictated to some degree by how dark the sky has become, but even in daylight, the white Icons give the stage a real edge. So adding colour for the first time is an impressive effect in itself.

"We were left alone to get the show together really. I believe in giving clients exactly what they want and if it's a big, simple show they are after, then that's what they get. In the past we've had more theatrical looks, but Rod likes to be the centre of attention with the lights around him. There are, of course, some moody ballads like 'Have I Told You Lately That I Love You' and 'Tom Traubert's Blues' in the 'Unplugged' part of the set where we keep the stage all blue with a white spot on Rod, but for the most part it has to be bright."

The Plexiglass stage was a completely new design by Ian Knight and Rikki Farr, built especially for this tour. The central part of the stage was an under-lit moving Plexiglass dome in which the orchestra sat. Payne said: "The core in the middle ejects Rod out for a rather slick entry. It makes for a slick departure as well! Rikki also had some involvement with the lighting and having been with Rod for many years, he is able to interpret Rod's wishes very closely. Everything's been designed from scratch including the roof which was designed by Mikel Brogaard Staging [run by Lars's brother] and the stage will no doubt go on to be used by several other artists as it has been very successful.

"We've only done three shows and we've locked in to what is a very successful, bold and effective look. In a stadium situation, if you're going to go red, everything's going to have to go red, and if someone's got a hope in hell's chance of creating any kind of atmosphere on stage, it's got to be bright. We have twenty-one LSD Megamags over the stage in two circles which are literally focused on the stage.

Generally we use one colour per song and sometimes split the Megamags half and half. There are also twenty Molemags and ninety-six C-Mags, and there are eight 3kW Gladiator spots around the stage and four 1200W HMI spots on stage. Martin covers filter spots, we cover solos with the spots, but most of the time everything is focused on Rod. The band plays quite a low profile; it's an excellent band, but they are very much in the background."

McLoughlin added: "The total power of the lighting rig is around 650kW since we added all the runways to the stage. We have three seventy-two-way dimmers, two thirty-two-way C-Mag controllers and I operate a Celco Gold ninety-way console. It's a fabulous desk, although on this show, not a great deal is demanded of it. It's just pushing chases and big washes. Mark operates the Icon console which controls twenty-four Icon active heads and, again, he's not doing anything complicated."

Payne, who previously worked with Stewart as a Vari*Lite operator, insisted that while the lighting for Stewart is important, it remained a secondary aspect of the production. "I think we've done a good job of making the lighting very effective while not overshadowing what's going on. It's quite refreshing to see a show that is very straightforward and uncomplicated."

One of the most visible equipment suppliers to the Stewart tour was Screenco which was celebrating its tenth anniversary as the leading rental company of giant CRT (Cathode Ray Tube) video screens to major outdoor rock concerts and festivals, as well as top sporting events. Its success was largely a result of its massive investment in Sony JumboTron video screens, each complete system costing in excess of £2 million. That, however, represented only one-third of Screenco's overall commitment to system inventory. But, as managing director David Crump said, for concerts such as Rod Stewart's Wembley appearance which boasted four screens suspended around the stage rigging, this technology was absolutely vital to audience appreciation.

The JTS80V in use on the Rod Stewart show was Screenco's first JumboTron system and was a joint venture with Arsenal Football Club (an unintentional coincidence for the soccer mad singer). Crump said: "This particular system is owned by Arsenal FC but we operate it for them, hiring it out between matches and out of season. It works very well for both parties because they use it for their matches and we generate income for them at other times. The system is actually being used for two weeks at Lord's Cricket Ground during a break in Rod's tour. The key to making it that versatile was in coming up with the right design and packaging of the equipment so that assembly and dismantling was quick and simple, and it could be used in all situations."

Physically, the JTS80V was identical to the screen used on Genesis' We Can't Dance tour in 1992 and its main advantages lay in its high resolution and lightweight, modular construction. The screen came direct from Sony in units of 352 x 352mm "building blocks". Each contained 256 pixels and Screenco mounted the standard Sony units four wide by three high to form a 1.408m x 1.025m, 220 kilo module – essentially an aluminium frame holding twelve units.

In the configuration used for Rod Stewart's show, Screenco constructed the screens three modules wide by three modules high (3 x 3) to give a total screen measurement of approximately 4.5m x 3m. "To do what we did with Rod Stewart would have been unheard of two years ago, because video screens were huge twenty ton lumps of equipment that had to be lifted in by a crane," commented Crump. "The configuration we've used on this tour is probably the smallest we would ever expect to go with a JumboTron system."

"The smaller you make the screen or the fewer modules you use, the fewer pixels there are and effectively the lower the resolution. If we had made the screen any smaller for Rod, I am sure that the picture quality would have been unacceptable, but most people's opinion was that the resolution at the concert was very good.

"I think we struck a good medium on the size because a bigger screen wouldn't have worked. Firstly, there was the cost factor; secondly, a bigger screen would have added too much weight to the rigging. Each of those four screens had 192 pixels horizontally and 144 vertically, giving a total of 27,648 pixels which is an awful lot lower than a conventional TV picture. When we designed the modules we specified TV aspect ratio, four units wide by three high, so that if we wanted a TV shaped screen we would simply configure the modules in a 3 x 3, 4 x 4, 5 x 5 arrangement, and so on. But there is no reason why you cannot make screens with a different aspect ratio, in a narrow or extended wide shape, although they are conventional aspect ratio for Rod Stewart."

Each module was fed with horizontal and vertical data cables, with one cable for each column of units, and they were addressed on a matrix basis to enable calculation of which item of visual information each unit should be showing. The modules were each fitted with one sixteen amp power connector and the main image control was performed by a separate rack at floor level. It received a normal composite video feed, converted it from analogue to digital [A-D] and sent it out to the screens as a multiplex datastream.

Crump said: "As we are running four screens for Rod Stewart, we purchased from Sony a £20,000 splitter system which was originally designed for basketball arenas, and we are the only rental company in the world to have purchased one. It takes the output of one image controller and splits it equally four ways, so that the image on each screen is identical. We couldn't really put different pictures on each screen. This kind of technology is ridiculously expensive in comparison to the cost of other equipment which goes out on the road."

On the mixing platform it was easy to pay more attention to the on-screen video images than the real-life action on the stage. That in itself spoke volumes for the quality of the JumboTrons. Crump agreed: "Everybody I've spoken to said that it was difficult to keep their eyes off the screen. But at the end of the day, the artist and staging is absolutely essential to the show, otherwise there would be no audience. People go to a stadium show for the atmosphere and excitement of the spectacle. But video screens are becoming an integral part of the set-up; it's visual amplification and I no longer believe it's fair for an artist to perform to a crowd of 85,000 people without screens.

"The concept of doing that show in the round was that it brought Rod much closer to his audience. The way the cameras were positioned, it meant that at all times Rod was facing a camera and could be seen clearly on a screen, no matter where he was on the stage or where you were positioned in the audience."

Creative Technology, which is owned by Screenco's holding company Avesco plc, provided all the video production equipment for the Stewart tour on sub-hire to John Basile of Videopac Systems who was one of several crew members beavering away in the claustrophobic under-stage confines. In charge of the raw video material being sent to Basile was video director Mick Anger who was clearly in awe of the technology at his fingertips. "Getting these JumboTrons is not something I could complain about!" he said. "I've worked with Screenco quite a bit over the last ten years and we did Genesis's Invisible Touch tour together in 1987. Starvision was the state of the art medium then but JumboTrons are in another league entirely."

Although the images shown on screen were predominantly close-ups of the live performance, some numbers included videotape inserts. Examples included a *Top Of The Pops* clip from 1971 with Stewart and The Faces performing 'Stay With Me', portions from the cartoon promo for 'The Motown Song' and "home movie" shots of Stewart's wife, Rachel Hunter, and children shown during 'Have I Told You Lately That I Love You'.

Anger said: "We shoot the show as close as we can to make the best use of the screens. If you were to put a wide shot up there it would make everything look a lot smaller, so we stay as close as we can comfortably work."

The essential tools for this job were Sony 70IS cameras, two Elmo "lipstick" remote cameras and a Grass Valley 110 switcher in the processing equipment. "We're using two 30:1, one 35:1 and two 14:1 lenses on the cameras near the stage," said Anger. "Five of the cameras are manned and two of them fixed – one on the drums, the other on Chuck Kentis, the keyboard player. The main duty of three of the cameras is to follow Rod and, obviously, since we are in the round I need several to capture his movements at any given moment.

"I'm really happy with the outdoor set, it's beautiful. When you consider that's all the steel required for the whole PA and everything, it's a marvellous feat. It takes ten guys six hours to put it all away. For a show like this you would normally be talking about three days to get rid of all the scaffolding."

By the time of this tour, Anger had been working in the video domain for seven years, and one recurrent problem he had faced was lighting directors' lack of sensitivity to the role of video. He said: "The best you can do with lighting people is to just go with them. Your best break is to have a good engineer and a band member who says that he can't be seen by the audience. Most LDs won't even enter into a conversation with me. I don't want them to change their show, but they have to realise that the human eye is different to the television camera. You just have to do the best you can and Rod's show, for me, is the best of both worlds. It's Europe in the summer, so we have daylight and I don't have to worry about the lighting guys, plus I have the luxury of JumboTrons. I think I'm doing okay!"

Employing Lars Brogaard to head the production again, and hiring virtually the same key crew members, Rod Stewart embarked on his next world tour in July 1998, following the enviable international sales of his album *When We Were The New Boys*.

CHAPTER SIX

The Greatest Music Party In The World — 1995

After massive achievements with the Nelson Mandela Seventieth Birthday Tribute Concert in 1988, Guitar Legends in Seville and Roger Waters' all-star The Wall: Live From Berlin, producer Tony Hollingsworth and his company, Tribute Management, had a lot to live up to when billing a week-long string of live concerts as The Greatest Music Party In The World – otherwise known as The Big Twix Mix, a big deferential nod towards sponsor Mars. But those who braved the bitter weather to venture out to Birmingham's NEC Hall 5 in December 1995 were in for a multi-sensory treat with a line-up of diverse stellar acts including headliners David Bowie, Rod Stewart, East 17, Eternal and Diana Ross, supported by some of the latest innovations in stage design.

Hollingsworth, who also created the Songs & Visions spectacular featured later in this book, is one of a small number of live event entrepreneurs who has seen, and acted upon, the growing interest of large corporations in rock 'n' roll. Another is Andrew Zweck who left Harvey Goldsmith Entertainments to form Sensible Events, a company devoted to binding the money of commerce to the coat tails of rock 'n' roll. "There was no doubt the audience spend and touring were shrinking," he said of the mid Nineties industry.

"Wembley Arena used to do seventy-eighty shows a year, but they've dropped at least 30% since 1994. What I realised when sponsorship first appeared in the touring market was that here were big companies with big, big money. When a corporation spends on a TV ad, one in 100 viewers might be their target audience if they're lucky. When they tie themselves to a festival or special music event, if young people are their target, then they're hitting 100% of the right people, as well as aligning themselves with a fashionable entertainment form. It makes their product look cool."

The five-night Big Twix Mix was recorded by The Manor Mobile and filmed by BBC Television for broadcast over the Christmas period both in the UK and abroad to an estimated 400 million viewers. Yet despite the apparent enormity of the exercise, plans for the production did not get underway until less than six weeks before the first night, as project manager, Chris Hey of PA suppliers Britannia Row Productions explained.

"We first learned about the shows about six weeks ago so we haven't had much time to plan it, although that hasn't really caused us a problem," he said shortly before the excellent Echobelly kicked off the proceedings. "Most shows have a much better lead time but the only real complications have involved the sound recording and filming. There have been no production rehearsals as such but there have been very well organised soundchecks for the artists, which is something you wouldn't have in a festival situation, and Bill Martin has done a superb job of stage managing the whole thing. But there's only a maximum of six acts per night and everything would have been fully checked out before doors open which means we are unlikely to get any nasty surprises."

Much of the talk backstage and among the audience concerned the elaborate Mark Fisher stage design, as built and fabricated by Star Hire. Central to the concept was Screenco's 5 x 4 Sony JumboTron JTS-35 vision screen which dominated the rear of the stage as a dazzling backdrop to all the artists. To form an extended landscape image, an additional four single columns of four screen units were placed 1' away from the main screen. The Screenco team had the unusual task of loading in the screens ahead of other riggers, four days prior to the first show, due to the staging being built around and underneath the screens.

Although Screenco, together with its sister company, Creative Technology, had provided camera teams and full vision mixing services at a number of previous high profile concert events, it was the BBC which, on this occasion, handled all the camera and mixing work. "We are literally taking a feed from the BBC," said Richard Ellis, who coordinated the three-man Screenco team and load in/out crew for the events.

Freelance director for the BBC, Gavin Taylor, whose previous credits included Channel Four's *The Tube*, added: "The screens are being fed from the BBC truck and they carry either images of the lead performers or video inserts which will be generic when the bands are playing, so it isn't specific footage. In between the bands, during changeovers, there will be a variety of promo videos on screen. So there is something running on the screens at all times."

To ensure a comprehensive mixture of wide stage images, the Beeb crew constructed a sixty-metre suspended camera track, running from the centre of the screen down to the far end of the auditorium. Remote operation of the camera on this track allowed tilt of focus and control of the camera's speed of movement. Taylor said: "We are using the new Ikegami chip cameras. The BBC has provided us with the very best equipment, I have to say. The cameras are feeding into the large BBC video mobile unit outside the building and I have all the cameras on separate monitors. We are deploying ten cameras through the vision mixer, plus we have small CCD chip 'lipstick' Panasonic cameras placed in some interesting positions on the stage. We also have a Steadicam which roams around the audience and which records on its own unit, as well as three cameras pointing at the stage from the pit. On top of that there is a camera backstage to do the presentations. So there is quite a lot of hardware here. Exactly how it is going to be packaged for transmission is something for the BBC to worry about. I am only involved in the hot edit of the songs that they want to use, and that is all done on the morning following each concert."

Richard Ellis explained that the original plan was to show video graphics on the outside single columns, with the artist close-ups sandwiched on the main screen. These graphics were assembled by producer Hollingsworth from backdrops used behind bands on an Asian music TV programme. "When the production team saw the way the graphics looked on *all* the screens, they decided that it would be good at certain points during the shows to have those images taking over completely from the artist close-ups," Ellis said. "In one respect, by having the graphics appear for long periods, it gives the lighting guys a rest from having to put on an all-singing, all-dancing light show throughout the entire performance."

Gavin Taylor in particular is a major fan of JumboTrons: "The output from them is tremendous, some of the brightest I've ever seen. I've worked with vision screens quite a lot in the past on a number of rock concerts and many of them carry these large JumboTron screens. They are generally either side of the stage, purely so that the audience can gain a good close-up view of the artists from afar, but on these shows, the screen is an integral part of the set and has to battle with the light, but it cuts through incredibly well."

Joining BBC's Taylor in praise of the dominant vision screens was the omnipresent LD, Patrick Woodroffe, fresh from his work on the design for Simply Red's Life tour. He said: "Screens have actually been designed into some of the last few shows I've worked on. The Rolling Stones had one at the back of the stage and AC/DC are using one for a production which goes out in January. They are increasingly part of the repertoire as video becomes more integral to shows. However, everyone's getting a little bored with having the screens either side of the stage because it means you are constantly forced to take your focus away from the real action. The idea of having something so powerful and strong right in the centre of the stage really appeals. You can't use front or rear projection anymore because it's not nearly as bright as JumboTron. So this was always a key part of the design."

Woodroffe was also keen to point out the importance of lighting the show with a bias towards the cameras and the screen. "To provide lighting that is friendly to the camera is essential whenever video or television crews are part of the equation. They are as much a part of the jigsaw puzzle as the front-of-house sound engineer, and all the really successful shows have come as a result of putting that jigsaw puzzle together thoughtfully to create something which is seamless. The shows that don't work are the ones where you have too many elements fighting against each other. So if you have video, of course you must light the stage in a way which enhances rather than overshadows the video effect. But at the same time you must not allow the video element to overpower the show. Because this is really a television show, we are constantly referring to video monitors so that we can see the effect the lighting is having on the camera work."

With a total of twenty-five rock, pop, dance and soul acts performing, a challenge was laid down for co-lighting designers Woodroffe and Dave Hill to come up with a scheme which helped cultivate an individual look for as many artists as possible, within the boundaries of a common stage

Paul McCartney with trademark Hofner violin bass at Earl's Court, September 1993

Brian Clarke's dynamic set drapes brought McCartney's New World Tour production to life

Wix, Linda McCartney and Blair Cunningham during an acoustic set

The Macca troupe salute the audience from an ascending platform

Macca's monitor engineer,
John Roden

Earl's Court welcomes the ex-
Beatle

Brian Clarke in his Park Royal studio

Lee Dickson, Slowhand's faithful guitar tech

Engineer Robert Collins

Clapton sings the blues at the Royal Albert Hall

Take That – the fivesome who kickstarted Nineties boy band fever

Mike Humeniuk, lighting
crew chief

Front-of-house engineer
Dave Pringle

The Take That boys
traversed this bridge to
reach a central B stage

TT at Wembley Arena

Garwood's in-ear pioneer Chrys
Lindop

Ian Newton, Take That's monitor
engineer

Del Amitri at the Labatt's Apollo, Hammersmith

The BSS Omnidrive system made one of its first touring appearances on the Del Amitri shows

A monitor engineer's view of the Dels' stage and Soundcraft console

The Dels' frontman, Justin Currie

Rod Stewart's Wembley Stadium appearances broke the venue's concert attendance records

The Mod still wears it well

Dave Palmer's drum monitoring – assisted by an Aura "butt woofer"

Above and below: Rod Stewart in the round at Wembley Stadium

Lars Brogaard – production manager and front-of-house engineer

Rod's lighting principals: Mark Payne and Martin McLoughlin

The Lightning Seeds (above) and Echobelly (below right) were among those on Screenco's Sony JumboTron at The Greatest Music Party In The World

Lighting visionaries Patrick Woodroffe and Dave Hill

Gavin Taylor in the OB truck

Mick Hucknall 1995

Mark Fisher designed a "snake" lighting truss for Simply Red's Life tour

Soundcheck mode for Simply Red at Wembley Arena

Simply Red: Fritz McIntyre

Simply Red: Velroy Bailey

set. One of the most significant features of the lighting design was a Tony Hollingsworth brainwave, turned into reality by Mark Fisher. This involved what appeared to be four giant, new age umbrellas, but were actually futuristic "technopods", each 15' tall x 20' wide, and weighing over two tons, which each carried a cluster of seven Vari*Lites and video monitors.

Woodroffe told me: "The only disadvantage to having these technopods, which has actually turned out to be a blessing in disguise, is that they remove the need for a big lighting system. To place enormous trusses, grids, boxes and blocks of lights around them would be completely self-defeating. What is so beautiful about them is that they float in front of a big empty space. The rest of the system is designed around them in that the low lighting position under the screen is really useful, especially when you're filming and the side lights give us some real depth to make the whole thing look very big and wide.

"In lighting any act, you are always dictated by the music and the performance. But there's no way you are going to make the stage look different twenty-five times. So we have concentrated more on the mood and the tempo, and how to light the principal artists. With Bowie, we light him in an arty, backlit manner. The poppier groups like East 17 will be much brighter with a lot more front light. That's where you strike the balance."

Some of the headline artists, such as Bowie who appeared as part of his Outside tour, brought in their own specialised sound and special effects lighting equipment as supplementary items. Apart from the 110 Samuelsons-supplied VL5 and VL6 Vari*Lites, a relatively modest (though none the less effective) lighting system was brought in by Concert Productions Limited for the five star-studded nights. CPL's principal lighting technician, Mike Humeniuk explained the extent of the rig: "It's essentially a Vari*Lite show. Generically, however, we have six bars of aircraft light on stage and a further twenty bars on five 80' long trusses over the audience. The audience trusses also have two six-lamp bars for a steel blue audience wash and a pair of truss warmers with Rainbow Colour Changers on the front. The generic lighting on stage is simply provided by two sets of ACs and there are two 1200W Panis per side. Also on stage there are ten Molefays with Molemags on the front to uplight the cargo net backdrop.

"At the front-of-house we have six 2kW Xenon Super Troupers. To brighten the tops of the technopods, we have six 60W and 80W bulk heads in the top, six 500W floods to uplight the underside of the canopy, six Par cans and a string of small strobes. We also have Par 36 up and down lights in a Toblerone shape sitting in the centre of it all. All the Vari*Lites are operated from an Artisan console and the generic lighting is run from a Celco sixty-way console. We also have a Zero 88 XL for operating the Rainbows and a standard Colourmag board for the Molemags."

Britannia Row's PA system at the NEC was standard issue for the company: a combination of thirty-six Flashlight narrow loudspeaker cabinets, eight Floodlights, fourteen underhungs and forty-eight bass enclosures. Jointly responsible for the two sixty-four-channel Yamaha PM4000 consoles and a massive wall of outboard equipment at the front-of-house were engineers Leon "Big Ears" Phillips and Dave Braviner, names then otherwise associated with the incestuous and eclectic Jethro Tull/Fairport Convention brotherhood.

For the entire audio side of the shows, an A/B system was in operation on the stage set-up, multicores, front-of-house control, monitors and the sound recording truck. Phillips explained why: "The idea behind it all is that while one band is on stage, everything can be set up for the following band at the same time on another desk. So by the time you come to use the B desk, it's already set up to go. Ideally, this cuts down changeover time and if we do encounter a problem we can solve it in the time that would normally be used for something else."

Chris Hey explained that the stage boxes fed the signals out to the Manor mobile truck. "There is a conventional split and they take ninety-six lines from us across the A/B system. We take a split for the FOH and a split for the monitors, and the other split goes to the mobile."

In addition to the two PM4000s, the headlining act on each night brought its own desk and engineer. "Bowie is also using two PM4000s," Phillips commented. "He is out on tour now anyway and it makes sense for him to bring in the desks that have already been set up, rather than compile new desk information. The only exception will be Diana Ross who is using one of our PM4000s when she headlines, so she won't be bringing a desk in from outside."

Surely an automated recall system would have been ideal in a situation where such a wide range of acts are performing. Braviner was surprisingly luke warm to the notion. "My own experiences of working with that kind of technology have not been good," he said. "The way we have approached it is rather like a better organised festival because we have soundchecked and rehearsed the acts in reverse order and people have had to mark up levels and settings."

The drive rack split the PA into the main flown system, left and right, with further amps to drive the underhung and side cabinets. Of the extensive array of outboard equipment, Braviner said: "It's all pretty standard band gear, with Drawmer compressors and gates, Lexicons and Yamaha effects. We're using the Turbosound LMS-780 Loudspeaker Management System, the predecessor to the Omnidrive, for graphics. The rack equipment has been specified by visiting engineers for different bands, and we are equipped for any eventuality which accounts for the rack's overall size."

Famous as the monitor maestro on Paul McCartney's 1989-90 and 1993 world tours, John Roden was operating two forty-channel Midas XL3 consoles, either side of a sixteen-channel XL3 stretch, to mix for a total of around forty wedges on stage. Roden, who shared monitor duties with fellow engineer Bob Lopez, explained the process of running the A/B system for monitoring: "We run out of the B board and into the sixteen-channel desk which just handles the effects in, returns from front-of-house and other sources such as DATs. The outputs from that stretch run into the A board which is regarded as the master because we go from there to the amp racks. So any band which comes in has up to forty channels and fourteen mixes to play with."

There was the obvious requirement to chart the consoles when running the A/B configuration, but the BSS Varicurve system helped to smooth the ride. "We have given every band a basic curve, but occasionally people want to expand on that in their own way," said Roden. "So the Varicurve gives them the facility to bounce into the mix, boost or remove a frequency, and save it for instant recall, and it's just for them. Whoever else comes on, without having to think about going back to your graphic, you can just knock in a programme on the Varicurve remote."

Along with the comprehensive wedges, Garwood Radio Station in-ear systems played a part in the overall monitoring scheme. On the first night of the Big Twix Mix, both Alanis Morissette and Bowie, along with his entire band, were "on ears", and it was expected that most of the other headliners and some support acts would be using this new standard in monitoring. "Bowie's in-ear transmitters are set up on the other side of the stage and we are just running lines back from there," Roden commented.

A Radio Station was also used for the sound crew's communications system which enabled interchanges between the stage, monitor, front-of-house and recording mobile engineers during line checks. "The guys listen via the Radio Station and talk through head-worn lip mics," said Roden. "Because this show is really run from the stage, communication is really vital otherwise we would come a cropper!"

The Big Twix Mix showed how a major concert production could successfully bring attention to the sponsor's product, and in doing so find a loop hole through the BBC's strict advertising ban, although industry veteran Mick Kluczynski (the production manager of the annual Brit Awards) emphasised that it was not a new phenomenon. "Corporate rock 'n' roll started creeping in when the top level of rock bands started on the second tours of stadiums. This is an industry that was really born in 1961 but blossomed in 1968 and continued to grow."

Corporate sponsorship, in Kluczynski's view, serves to keep the audience's attention by pouring otherwise difficult to raise finance into a production. Referring to his days with Pink Floyd in the Seventies, Kluczynski recalled: "Once we'd reached a point of saturation where we could do Milwaukee Stadium for three nights and outsell the Stones, financially things were stagnant and we were repeating ourselves. All you could hope for would be for the ticket price to rise each year by a certain percentage. You were already delivering a high-quality show, so where could you go from there?

"We've got into the cycle of bigger, better, bigger, better. Corporate sponsorship became necessary when productions became so top-heavy that additional funding was required to make it all work. We are now in an industry that is something like the third-biggest export business in the UK, but it's still one of the best-kept money-spinning secrets in the world."

CHAPTER SEVEN

Simply Red

Life – 1995

From both a visual and sonic point of view, the Simply Red concert production unveiled to UK audiences in December 1995 was a masterpiece. Governing most of the set were songs from the band's then new album *Life*, which may not have immediately boasted the same conviction as its best-selling predecessor *Stars*, however, there was no doubting Mick Hucknall's ability to command a stage and convey intimacy with an audience, even in a large venue like Wembley Arena.

Key to this was the configuration and relationship between the stage and lighting design, and the comprehensive Turbosound PA rig supplied by Britannia Row. Mark Fisher's stage set and Patrick Woodroffe's lighting theme evolved after analysis of Simply Red's 1991/92 Stars production which featured the band performing on a central stage for half of the show, after which they moved to an end-on stage for the remainder.

The idea for Life was to develop on the theme of two performance areas, while keeping the whole show inside the centre of the arena. The two stages – one larger than the other – were linked by a bridge which rose during the second half of the show (and, strangely, reminded one of a certain Monty Python scene). At the beginning of the set, the band performed from the smaller stage while Hucknall wandered freely over the bridge and jaunted to and from both stages. At around the halfway point in the programme, the Reds were reduced to the core duo of Hucknall and mainstay keyboard player, Fritz McIntyre for 'Wonderland', after which the band returned to perform the rest of the set from the larger stage.

Lighting designer Woodroffe believed that if anyone could handle a crowd in that environment, it would be Mick Hucknall who was celebrating his band's tenth anniversary at Wembley ("I've been called fat and ugly, but I'm still here!"). Woodroffe said: "As a result of the stage design, Mick is much closer to more people for more of the time than on any other of their shows, even though he plays on three separate areas. No one is very far from him, which could not be said in the case of end-on arena shows. This idea of two stages was developed with a bridge to link them, and the lighting system above them reflects the shape and it ends up as a very beautiful, sinuous snake, as we call it. I think it's indicative of the way a lot of design is going. The idea of just using trusses in different shapes or places and then filling them up with lights is slowly becoming outmoded. You are seeing more shows these days where people are building custom-built structures on which to put the lights. They become floating scenery as well as a lighting source."

Conventional lighting along with Vari*Lites and LSD Icons all ran from one Icon desk, manned by Mark Payne whose other responsibilities in 1995 had included the Rod Stewart Spanner In The Works tour, interestingly another in-the-round production. The entire stage area was lit from above by the large snake-like truss which carried VL5s, Icons and various architectural lighting elements inside the snake itself, such as Molefay lights hidden behind custom-designed bulbous panels. Payne commented: "In essence, we have produced something of visual interest, rather than being purely a functional truss. Both the music and the lighting begin in a fairly laid back fashion, and the lighting gradually rolls along from being neutral and soft, to extremely exciting and dynamic as the faster numbers are introduced. It all goes pretty mental on the last couple of songs and the Vari*Lites and Icons really earn their keep!"

Pyro and flames were on standby at the three pre-Christmas Wembley shows but were not used until the band's return to home shores in January 1996. Other effects such as a giant, moving metallic sun suspended over the smaller of the two stages were greeted with gasps from the crowd. The sun, which had VL6s attached internally, an Icon in the centre and Par 20s in several other places to light up architectural pieces, remained static until 'Wonderland' when it tilted backwards and forwards. Another good effect saved until 'Thrill Me', three-quarters of the way through the set, involved four telescopic lighting pods which rose from the large stage, surrounding the motorised drum riser, to create an instant high tech look.

Audience lighting, particularly during the second half of the show, played a major role. "Mick wanted everybody in the audience lit because there is normally a lot of participation on certain numbers, like 'Holding Back The Years'," said Payne. "It just opens it all up and the audience becomes a kind of cyclorama; you are literally looking through the stage at a living backdrop."

The Turbosound PA system supplied by Britannia Row was a configuration of 124 flown Flashlight speakers, forty-six underhangs and twenty-four sub-basses, powered by BSS EPC-760 and 780 amplifiers. Front-of-house engineer Robbie McGrath said of the rig: "The Turbosound box itself is very powerful and sounds incredibly good, and it certainly suits Simply Red. It's very hard to lose the vocals in this box – it provides a great deal of clarity but you have to ensure that you get the angles of the hang right and use very little of them, then you'll maintain the clarity."

With the performance based wholly in the centre of the arena, the production team decided to split each venue into six tight stereo zones. The whole perimeter of the two stages, however, was treated as one source. "I wanted to take the rectangular space that the stages were in and feed the sound into six smaller areas of the auditorium, rather than have two separate systems. The throw on the speaker cabinets isn't as long as it would be if they were all at one end of the room, and the result is that it all sounds a bit more personal and comfortable. It makes these places sound and look a lot smaller and more intimate than they are."

In a situation where it was not possible to couple the bass bins at floor level, McGrath and his team resigned themselves to placing the bins around the stage, although this initially caused a few time alignment headaches. After considering TEF and Klark Teknik, McGrath chose the Turbosound LMS-700 version of the BSS Omnidrive to align the system, which he said has simplified the whole process. "We literally plug in the measurement information and tell it to knock the delays back by 20' or three metres or x amount of seconds. To calculate the delays between the speakers and the stage at central position, we used a tape measure, which is a very old fashioned way for such a high tech situation. All the front speakers are delayed by 10' back into the stage. You have to give the impression that when you're looking at the stage, the drums are coming from the drummer and the vocals are coming from the vocalists, rather than somewhere else in the room."

In common with 1995's other main in-the-round production FOH engineer, Lars Brogaard, McGrath was a great advocate of the Midas XL4 console, and claimed its level of automation is both sensible and practical. "It doesn't completely run the show at the touch of a button. I still have a lot of hands-on work to do here," he insisted. A totally automated desk would not readily suit a man who had experienced mixing in real time for nearly twenty-five years, but McGrath said the facility did help to set up ballpark audio scenes for introductions of songs – the efficacy of which was plainly noticeable at Wembley where Simply Red employed a wide variety of musical styles – from soul and jazz, to reggae, house and pure pop.

"With a computer you need to adopt some pre-planning which does pay off in the long run. To be in the ballpark as soon as the band kicks into each number would be very difficult without automation. You have to be able to perceive the song's feel. With this it is possible to automatically go from a reggae number like 'Hillside Avenue' into a slow soul ballad like 'Holding Back The Years'."

Much use of samples was noticeable at Wembley, in the form of scratched loops, various percussion and brass ensembles, all programmed by the man in the pit, Merv Pearson. Keep Music Live campaigners might be horrified at the very thought of it, but in this instance the samples were used tastefully without overshadowing the human efforts from the stage. One of two Yamaha ProMix 01 mixers was set aside for the control of these samples which amounted to as many as fourteen on the show's closing number, 'Fairground'. An additional ProMix was responsible for various processing from Eventide H3000 harmonisers, a Lexicon 480, PCM-70s for the saxophone and drums, an SPX-1000 for drums and electronic-driven vocal delays.

Mark Fisher's stage design dictated that Hucknall's normally-favoured Shure wired mics could not be used. Wireless was the only option and the AKG WMS-900, supplied by Hand Held Audio, came out tops against Sony and Sennheiser during extensive evaluations. Eight UHF channels were in use for Hucknall and his two female backing vocalists on WMS-900s, an AKG C409 clip-on Micromic for saxophonist Ian Kirkham and a Samson transmitter for guitarist Heitor Pereira.

RF problems proved troublesome during the soundcheck on the second of the three Wembley dates. This, McGrath explained, was attributed to the Wembley stewards arriving and switching on their walkie-talkies! The problem, however, was cured by showtime when frequencies were switched to a clear band. "Last night, though," McGrath said during their stay, "it was really cold in here and it led to quite a brittle sound."

Bringing Hucknall's soulful vocals out of the mix and into the laps of the audience was a specialist challenge which McGrath knew only too well. It was even more difficult than normal to handle at Wembley Arena. The road to perfection, he said, started by sending the mic signal through a Focusrite, after which the vocal signal was sent to a channel on the XL4. "Then I have a Behringer Combinator which compresses four different sets of frequencies," he said. "So if there is a little instance of 3k peak you can take it out quite easily. The vocal then passes through the Summit DCL-200 tube limiter...and by the time it's gone through all that and then into the Midas EQ, it sounds big and powerful."

Conventional miking techniques were applied to deliver crisp, punchy sounds from Velroy Bailey's Pearl drum kit, with AKG C414s as overheads and other AKGs on hi-hats. In addition, an M88 was used in the bass drum and Shure 98 mics on toms. McGrath then used a Behringer Ultrafex across the kit sub groups to expand the low and high ends. He said: "Some of the drum sounds need a very rough, obvious reverb, especially on the reggae numbers, whereas other numbers require a lushness. So I have both a Yamaha SPX-1000 to provide the roughness and a Lexicon PCM-70 for the latter. Overall, I use Behringer gates and compressors because I find them very clean when you run a signal path through them."

Monitor engineer Steve "Flaky" Flewin was, like McGrath, using a forty-channel Midas XL4 with generous outboard including Klark Teknik graphics and Behringer gates and compressors. The main difference between his and McGrath's consoles was that the on-board automation options were not exploited to the same degree for monitoring, not until midway through the tour, anyway.

Every member of the band received their own personalised mix and more besides. Flewin had responsibility for twenty separate mixes – sixteen monos and four stereos. He said: "Working like this eats up the channels in no time, so I am working flat out across the desk. With the XL3 you could get an additional sixteen-channel stretch to spill on to, but you can't get the same for the XL4...yet. That would be great because, let's face it, you can never have enough channels!"

Rod Stewart's 1995 production may have demanded in-ear

monitoring and a wedge-free stage, but it was not the case for Hucknall and co whose stage was littered with boxes. Despite the band's purchase of a Radio Station system prior to the tour, the decision was made to go "earless". Flewin said: "Mick and Fritz, who is static throughout the show, weren't going to go in-ear but the others in the band were originally. We just didn't have enough time to get used to it in production rehearsals and it is quite an alien world to begin with."

McGrath added: "They are the type of band that for years have been grooving off each other and I think the trouble they've found with the in-ears is that it all feels too isolating to them. They also like to hear the whole sound of the room, they really get off on that."

"So because we were still so unsure about the mode of monitoring, we never got around to actually design a monitor system as such," Flewin continued. "So I had to try out a variety of wedges before I settled on what we have here."

Three mixes were sent through six Turbosound 1 x 12" cabinets fixed to the truss, pointing at the stage, while on the bridge there were six 2 x 15"s, plus another 2 x 15" for Fritz McIntyre on each stage. Heitor Pereira had a stereo mix through two 1 x 15"s and drummer Velroy Bailey had a 1 x 18" Turbosound bass bin and two 1 x 15" wedges on a stereo mix on both stages. "You can punch different musicians into others' mixes and with twenty mixes going on simultaneously, there aren't any dead spots," Flewin commented. "The only problem is when one member moves into someone else's space. Heitor has his guitar rig set up on the big stage and anyone standing near there is obviously going to hear a lot more guitar. I personally monitor through a 2 x 15" Turbosound wedge which is the same cab as used on the bridge and drums, and I also have a Meyer Sound UM1 wedge with a switching device to listen between them."

For general front-of-stage perimeter monitoring, Flewin opted for sixteen UM1s. He said: "The UM1 works very well with vocals because it delivers a bright sound which this group needs. I had previously used the Turbosound 1 x 15" on stage which doesn't sound as sweet because you have to pull too much out of them. If you want it loud on stage, the Turbosound monitors are fine, but this group doesn't need volume – they prefer clarity."

A new line-up of Simply Red emerged in 1998 to play a string of seven nights at London's Lyceum Theatre, prior to a full 1999 tour.

CHAPTER EIGHT

Masters Of Music

Hyde Park – 1996

The summer of 1996 was inches away from being perfect. The weather threatened to be the finest for years, England had narrowly missed out on a place in the Euro '96 soccer final at Wembley, and after releasing two "reunion" singles the surviving Beatles were rumoured to be "getting back" for the finale of the MasterCard Masters Of Music Concert at London's Hyde Park on Saturday, 28 June in front of 150,000 thrilled fans.

Despite the cloud and wind, England's semi-final defeat and the non-appearance of the Fabs, everything else about Harvey Goldsmith's benefit concert for The Prince's Trust, the flagship event of the year's National Music Festival, was as big, grand and entertaining as rock shows get. With a stellar line-up featuring Eric Clapton, Bob Dylan, Alanis Morissette and the all-star live premiere of *Quadrophenia*, it was the largest rock concert ever staged in London – the first to be held in Hyde Park since Queen graced the boards at the last of sixteen free concerts, in September 1976. Capital Radio's Party In The Park, held in the same spot two summers later with a youth pop-orientated artist bill, attracted a similar size of audience.

At Masters Of Music the joy of watching some of the most significant rock history-makers came at the expense of just £8 (although a whopping £95 for a VIP seat). This was a sure-fire way of filling the venue for the benefit of the television cameras which were filming the event for broadcast to an estimated 120 million viewers in forty countries, and effectively earning a right royal packet for the Prince's Trust.

Harvey Goldsmith filled in the detail behind his idea to stage the event. "One of the Board members of MasterCard is also on the Board of The Prince's Trust, and I was coming around to the idea of staging an event for the National Music Festival in Hyde Park. It suddenly dawned on me that if I could get MasterCard to underwrite the event, the Prince's Trust to be the beneficiary, and National Music Day to have its flagship event there, it would be a great marriage. It transpired that MasterCard were in discussion with the Hard Rock Cafe about a show in Hyde Park but felt they would be overshadowed. So they pulled out and thought this was a better idea, and that's how it started.

"I originally wanted to have bands like Blur and Oasis, but the Park Authorities wouldn't let us. It also didn't fit in with MasterCard's profile and we needed to be guaranteed a large audience. There have been too many people who have done charitable events where the charity ends up with virtually nothing. So wearing my Prince's Trust hat, I insisted that the charity got a guarantee of £500,000 from the income and I think the eventual bill had enormous pulling power."

It was fitting that The Prince's Trust's Rock School Band earned their keep, so to speak, by opening the proceedings. Other young hopefuls Leighton Jones and Imogen Heap, and comperes Frank Bruno and Billy Connolly, kept the entertainment going at the front of the stage while the main acts changed over behind the curtain. The first of which was Jools Holland and his Rhythm & Blues Orchestra who launched into a typical boogie-woogie routine in between characteristic quips. Alanis Morissette offered proof that she had become a figurehead for Nineties pop feminism. Her numbers 'You Oughta Know' and 'Hand In My Pocket' took on an anthem-like status, and were greeted with some of the most enthusiastic applause of the afternoon. Then cometh The Man... Bob Dylan, who together with guest guitarist Ronnie Wood, ripped through a no-holds-barred set of classics – including the evergreen 'Don't Think Twice, It's Alright' and 'All Along The Watchtower' – which spanned more than three decades.

The highlight for many was the first live performance of Pete Townshend's Mod-opera, *Quadrophenia*. Originally released as an album by The Who in 1973 and recreated as the 1979 Franc Roddam movie, *Quadrophenia* traced the mental anguish and subsequent spiritual epiphany in Brighton of school leaver Jimmy, during the Mods and Rockers clashes of 1964. The transference to the stage of the intellectual aspects of Townshend's work was always going to be the greatest challenge, especially in front of such a large crowd. But it worked, and in no small part due to Jonathan Park's complimentary stage design and the integration of JumboTron-screened video inserts, directed by Aubrey "Po" Powell and produced by Steve Swartz. From a musical viewpoint, however, the reunion of Pete Townshend with former Who colleagues, Roger Daltrey and John Entwistle, was perhaps the greatest crowd-pleaser of all.

Goldsmith commented: "Pete Townshend and I presented the first ever Prince's Trust Rock Gala and he was always very sympathetic to the charity. During the previous summer he performed a show on Long Island as a fund-raiser for kids with Paul Simon and Annie Lennox. So I called Pete up and said, 'Why don't you repeat the show for Hyde Park?' But it was really Paul Simon's gig and I didn't realise that Pete was a minor part of it. He called Paul but he was writing a musical [*The Capeman*] and couldn't really do it, and Annie didn't want to work. But Pete was really keen to do something and we talked it through. He said, 'I've got this idea. *Tommy*'s doing well, what do you think about *Quadrophenia*?' When Bill Curbishley [Who manager] returned from a tour abroad, we all met up started to put the whole idea together. Pete then asked Roger Daltrey and John Entwistle to get involved. Having a premiere of sorts at Hyde Park adds a kind of poignancy to the whole show."

This story of an adolescent with four personalities, together with the charitable nature of the event, presented a perfect opportunity to assemble an all-star cast, consisting of Phil Daniels in a narrator's role, Gary Glitter, Pink Floyd's David Gilmour, Stephen Fry, Adrian Edmonson and Trevor MacDonald as a news correspondent from the riot-torn Brighton beach.

During a soundcheck on the previous rain-drenched afternoon, Glitter accidentally swiped Daltrey's head with his microphone stand. The Who's singer struggled for more than ten minutes to find his feet and the soundcheck was brought to an abrupt halt as many wondered whether he would be fit for the show. But a hastily contrived eye patch, aptly painted with a Mod target design, enabled Daltrey to face the crowd as if nothing had happened.

Quadrophenia began six sold-out shows at Madison Square Garden on 16 July and a tour followed, with two London dates at Earl's Court in December 1996. Hyde Park was possibly an ill-matched venue for its premiere, but it served as a reminder of the unique chemistry between the three Who members that continued to distinguish them from other Sixties survivors. Daltrey, fit and agile as ever, was still capable of delivering his gut-wrenching roar as he ruled the stage with characteristic menace. Although lacking in the hair department, Townshend retained a devilish look in his eye and despite restricting himself to an acoustic guitar for most of the set (while brother Simon and Geoff Whitehorn handled most of the lead duties), his unpredictable nature kept the audience on edge. Entwistle, meanwhile, the rock world's greatest bass player, looked as unfazed by it all as he did in the era of 'My Generation', while holding down the rhythm like an anchor and letting rip with the occasional breathtaking flourish. Adding a sense of urgency was thirty-one-year-old drummer Zak Starkey, son of Ringo Starr, whose style was the nearest that any of his predecessors had come to matching the once-in-a-lifetime flavour of the late Keith Moon. Put simply, it was the best Who line-up since 1978.

Finally, the show closed with a classic hits 'n' blues package from Eric Clapton and his ten-piece band which featured the Kick Horns. Though wonderful tonight Clapton may have been as the skies darkened, one was left a little cold by the expectation of an historic finale that never came. The audience was, however, treated to a moving rendition of 'Holy Mother', complete with the thirty-two-piece choir Clapton had performed with at Luciano Pavarotti's Modena show a week earlier.

For most of the audience it was the end of a memorable show, and the beginning of a long struggle to leave the park. But for those graced with a VIP wrist band, a great night was to be enjoyed in the hospitality marquee, courtesy of The Mike Flowers Pops and MasterCard.

Creating a venue for a concert within Hyde Park has never been a mean feat and Unusual Services was chosen by Harvey Goldsmith Entertainments to site manage and coordinate the 500 metre deep ground infrastructure. Before anything could happen, a licence had to be obtained for the event from Westminster City Council which represents the interests of the Royal Parks.

One of the main service companies sub-contracted by Unusual was the omnipresent ShowSec International whose security team rose in number from four, upon Unusual's arrival on site on 17 June, to 450 on show day, with several remaining in the park until 5 July when the site was finally cleared. Among the other rarely acknowledged suppliers hired to assist Unusual with the creation of the concert venue were Arena Seating (5,000 seat VIP tribune), Eve Trakway (3,000 metres of trackway), Star Hire (2,000 metres of Steelshield fencing for the perimeter fence), Beaver 84 (control barriers), Black & Edgington (four clearspan VIP marquees), Search (portacabins and dressing rooms), Bowood (1,500 toilets and shower facilities) and caterers Eat Your Hearts Out. Templine, meanwhile, was supplying enough power for a small town in the shape of 5.25 megawatts laid on for the PA systems, lighting, the outside broadcast truck, backstage village and food/merchandising stands.

Together with his colleague, Tony Wheeler, site manager Chuck Crampton designed the backstage village which, due to the artist bill increasing in size during the planning of the event, was subject to amendments several times. Crampton, who took charge of forty-five staff, said: "Dealing with nine acts within a seven-hour period has made life very hectic, but Tony and I have a very good rapport. He knows the best companies to use for ordering materials, so he's the practical side of our team while I am more political." Four hundred people were expected backstage on show day, but that was a piece of cake for Crampton who had dealt with 28,000 backstage passes at the VE Day anniversary event the previous year – possibly an all-time "ligger" record!

Twenty-six years after working with The Who at the now-legendary 1970 Isle Of Wight festival, Mick Double was once again enjoying a rare reunion with Townshend, Daltrey and Entwistle. But his duties as production manager also extended to his regular "account" (of eleven consecutive years and beyond), Eric Clapton, so it was no surprise to find him with his hands more than full at a Clapton rehearsal in Hayes, five days before the show.

How did Double get involved? "When we were doing the Albert Hall shows earlier this year with Eric, I was asked by Harvey Goldsmith if I wanted to work with Dennis Arnold on producing a show at Hyde Park. When I discovered that both Eric and the ex-members of The Who were doing it, it was a bit of a shock but luckily I was able to delegate most of the production duties to a pal of mine, Ian Day, and Dennis and I gradually pulled a team of people together."

Double described the Masters Of Music venue as one of the best outdoor sites he had ever seen, but whether it was the largest ever in the UK depended on how one measured it. Statistics aside, the sheer technology behind the event and quality of the bill alone justified the use of the word "mammoth". Double said: "I first worked with Eric in the 1970s doing monitors and when he played at Blackbushe in 1978 he probably had more people there. But this is the biggest one-off rock show I've done and certainly the biggest ever seen in London. It's not like being in a football stadium for four nights. Where this show is different is in the way the acts are spread across the programme. It's not like there's a revolving stage, they are on for ten minutes and then get thrown off quickly afterwards. People don't really get value for money that way. The decision was made that all the acts are going to basically do their regular show, although *Quadrophenia* isn't what you'd call a regular show. Not yet, anyway! They are doing what can only be described as an extravaganza."

Stage management was hired by Mick Double and Dennis Arnold in the form of Steve Jones from Stage Miracles. "Steve has a team of thirty people working for him, while Dennis and I ensure the bands are ready and on time for their performances, because we were given a very strict 9.30pm curfew [which actually overran]. We fought it long and hard, but there was no way around it if we were to do the show. With the Euro '96 final at Wembley the following day, it was expected that several thousands of football fans would be hanging around in the area, so for safety's sake, the authorities decided to close Park Lane off to traffic for an hour after the show, and that's a first."

It was a busy year for Spencer-Hey Associates, the audio system design team formed at the beginning of 1996 by Steve Spencer and Chris Hey after leaving their posts at Britannia Row Productions. With Spencer taking care of Simply Red's show at Manchester United's Old Trafford ground and the Hyde Park audio "buck" stopping with Hey as sound consultant, 29 June certainly was a big day for the enterprising pair. Hey's call to relieve Double of part of his production burden came in late February. Four months later, the workload was beginning to take its toll. On show day, he said: "It's been a fantastic month for us, what with today's shows, the recent dates with M People and the rehearsals for Lord Of The Dance in Dublin which I only returned from a few days ago. I fly back to Dublin tomorrow and when I return I'll hopefully go to bed for a long time!"

"Big" is a word that could safely describe the Clair Brothers PA system, specified and designed by Hey for the event. In the middle of such a busy period for large scale outdoor shows, availability was a prime concern and the lion's share of the eventual rig was shipped in from Audio Rent in Switzerland, Clair Bros in the USA and also from Japan, following Bon Jovi's Japanese tour. A 1,000,000 watt system valued at around £3 million and weighing over 100,000 kilos, it was one of the largest ever assembled for an outdoor presentation.

The 266 JBL-loaded speaker cabinets spread around the park included 140 Clair S4s on the main front-of-house system, sixteen P4s for the infill and 108 S4s distributed among nine satellite delay towers. Seven Edwin Shirley trucks transported the huge rig which was subsequently manoeuvred by fifty-eight one and two ton motors. There were two types of S4 cabinet – the S4P long-throw and S4F medium/short throw – with thirty of each per side of the main stacks. The S4 consists of 18" lows, 10" mids, 2" compression drivers and tweeters in four-way boxes; the R4 is a three-way box with 18", 12" and 2" speakers, and the P4 has two different types of 12" and 2" speakers in a three-way box.

Hey pointed out that the sound was drawing around 400 amps,

three-phase. He said: "Although the system mainly consists of standard Clair S4 boxes, I basically specified how I wanted it put up, and the layout of the delays." To assist with the set-up and calculation of the nine delays, Hey used the TC electronic TC-1380 delay unit. Of the towers, Hey commented: "There's about 100 metres distance in between them, and they are in tiers with each carrying an average of 12 S4 cabinets."

A total of thirty-two Clair 12 AM wedge monitors were positioned around the stage and for Dylan and Morissette, extra S4s were placed on 1 x 18" bass bins. Dylan also used a bank of Clair 115s which each comprised of 15" and 2" drivers and a tweeter. A number of R4 monitor fills were required for *Quadrophenia*, for playback sound effects such as the roar of motorbikes. These effects were generated both by samples, "played" by keyboard player, Jon Carin, and the soundtrack of the video which occupied four channels on one of Dave Kob's Yamaha PM4000Ms at front-of-house. Adding further weight to the monitoring was a front fill of four blocks of four P4s under the front of the stage. The PA was driven by sixteen racks of eight mono blocks and four stereo Clair-modified Carver 2.0 amplifiers, plus 10004 Crests on the mid/high P4s and 9001 Crests on the low end. Fitted with two amps, each Crest amp rack was a standard European configuration, powering four cabinets. The entire system ran with Clair Bros CTS (Coherent Transfer System) and Electro-Voice X-EQ3 three-way electronic crossovers.

Despite the growth of in-ear monitoring, only Alanis Morissette, Roger Daltrey and Gary Glitter (for *Quadrophenia*) used the Garwood Radio Station, with Daltrey wearing just one ear mould. While Morissette used her own system, the others were supplied by Hand Held Audio, which also provided the radio microphones. Mick Shepherd of Hand Held said: "Because there are quite a few actors with speaking parts in *Quadrophenia*, there has been a sizeable requirement for radio gear. For Pete Townshend and the actors we have four Samson UHF Synth headset mics, and there are two hand held Samson UHFs acting as MC mics for the Clair Bros crew. We've also supplied two additional Samson UHF mics and two Garwood Radio Stations for the crew's 'shout' [communications] system which is run by Rick Pope."

The microphone selection for *Quadrophenia* largely reflected The Who's long-term choice of Shure, with ten of Daltrey's favoured SM58s, twelve SM57s, two Beta 52s on Zak Starkey's kick drums, four SM81s around and above his kit, SM7s on brass, four ECL 24/Beta 58 radio systems and a WCM16 headset on an ECL 114 radio system for Stephen Fry.

With regulars such as engineer Robert Collins then occupied on the Mark Knopfler Golden Heart tour, Eric Clapton's crew for Hyde Park was almost completely new. Mick Double said: "There's an arrangement we have with Concert Sound whereby we use members of their team regularly and on this show there are five of their guys looking after the Eric Clapton side of the show, in conjunction with Clair Bros, just so we are nicely self-contained. The rest of the Clair Bros crew have been mostly concerned with *Quadrophenia* rehearsals at Bray. We've used both companies in the past but for this show we really needed to pull together a big sound system and it evolved that we would use Clair with Bob Weibel as crew chief, in charge of fifteen technicians."

As a result of each act demanding its own FOH and monitor consoles, the combined audio input channels required for the main PA totalled a staggering 600. Mick Double commented that although all of the artists gave their services without charge, the artists' discerning technical needs were all catered for and, hence, the mixing tower became known as console city as each act brought its own desk! Hey said: "Eric, *Quadrophenia* and Bob Dylan are bringing the consoles and control equipment that they have been using for the past couple of weeks in rehearsal. The other control equipment is already here because those bands are not touring or rehearsing directly before the show."

Jools Holland & his Rhythm 'n' Blues Orchestra had a Yamaha PM4000 at FOH with Ron Burrows engineering and a Midas XL3 monitor board; Alanis Morissette also used a Yamaha PM4000 FOH with a Ramsa S840 on stage; and Bob Dylan's FOH engineer, Ed Wynne had a Clair custom board FOH while monitor engineer Jules Aerts mixed with a Ramsa S840 on stage. Long-time Who associate Bobby Pridden was overall sound consultant for *Quadrophenia* which used two Yamaha PM4000Ms both at FOH with Dave Kob and on stage with Dave Skaff, as well as a stretch desk to deal with the actors' mics. Eric Clapton had a PM4000 at FOH with Concert Sound engineer Chris "Privet" Hedge and a Midas XL3 monitor board in the hands of CS colleague Steve May, plus a stretch desk for the choir which appeared on 'Holy Mother'. Meanwhile, all of the front of stage "support" acts were controlled by Harrison FOH and monitor desks.

Dave Kob explained the configuration of his two forty-channel PM4000s: "There are nineteen people on the stage for *Quadrophenia*, so I am sub-grouping the inputs into percussion, brass, drums, bass, guitars, Pete Townshend, Rabbit on piano, synths, lead vocal and chorus. The two hand-held mics and two headset mics that are used for the actors and dialogue readers are sub-mixed on the monitor stretch and then sent out to me, because Dave Skaff on monitors can actually see what is happening on stage and know when to bring up the channels."

With the whole show being recorded for broadcast and a possible long-form video release by Chrysalis (for Allied Vision), Home Box Office (for American broadcast on 14 July) and Manor Mobiles' two audio recording trucks, a complex A-B-C audio switching regime which interfaced with BSS splitters was devised by Chris Hey to smooth the changeovers between acts. He explained: "There is a stage box for each of the A and B systems, and there is only ever one console connected to them at any given time. We start the show with Jools Holland's desk connected to the A system and Alanis Morissette's to the B system. As soon as Jools has finished we not only change all the input side of it, we leapfrog over to Bob Dylan's own FOH and monitor console which has to be connected to the stage box."

On top of this there was a C system for the ancillary video inputs, comperes, emergency microphones and the front of the stage acts performing during main stage changeovers, although this control system did not interface with the splitters. Hey said: "After each main act, videos are played for ten minutes, which doesn't involve us other than pushing up the fader. During that time, we set up one of the support bands on the front of the stage and they play for fifteen minutes. That is followed by another ten-minute video slot while we set the stage for the next main act which would already have been line-checked on the unused system. Simple really! But I certainly wouldn't want to have less time to change over!"

The presence of JBL at the show extended far beyond the inclusion of its loudspeakers in the Clair cabinets. The privileged partygoers were treated to an outstanding performance by The Mike Flowers Pops afterwards, for which contractors Entec Sound & Light specified a JBL Concert Series PA rig. This consisted of eight JBL 4873 full range and six 4788 sub bass cabinets, powered by two Crown Macrotech amp racks, each containing two 1201s and four 2401s. Harman Audio supplied a Soundcraft forty-eight-channel K3 Theatre console for the band's engineer, Steve Ludlum to use at FOH, while Entec's Paul Keeble controlled the monitors via a Midas forty-channel XL3, after the intended Soundcraft SM12 was kept busy by Chris Evans' TV show *TFI Friday*. A total of sixteen Entec bi-amp floor monitors (10 x APW-212s and 6 x 115s) were powered by three Crest Quad bi-amp racks.

After its busiest-ever twelve months as vision screen supplier to tours by Rod Stewart, M People, Oasis, Tina Turner and countless other discerning artists, Screenco scored a significant achievement at the Masters Of Music concert as the coordinator of all the video display aspects of the show, including sister company Creative Technology's camera work.

With the 150,000 crowd stretching back as far as 500 metres from the stage, the value of JumboTron screen technology had rarely been greater and Screenco was required to supply four screens – two JTS 35s on-stage and two new generation JTS 17s out in the field as delay relays. The *Quadrophenia* set demanded a central screen located above the stage in a landscape aspect ratio to enable the showing of 1960s Who footage, scenes from the 1979 *Quadrophenia* movie and the new footage directed by Aubrey Powell that was shown in a Cinemascope-type format. Producer Steve Swartz approached Screenco's MD David Crump for further screens to be added, but was politely informed that due to the demands of other summer outdoor events, particularly those connected with sport, none were available. To add a further headache, Crump was informed that Eric Clapton insisted on performing with the screens at either side of the stage.

How did Crump rise to the challenge? "We came up with the idea of having a pair of 1:1 aspect ratio screens, which are not standard television aspect ratio, and devising a way of moving them. They are two 5 x 5 metre screens, made up of twenty-four modules, which for most of the show are located in a typical PA position and flown from the roof of the stage. But for the *Quadrophenia* set only, we track them together on a track suspended under the Edwin's roof."

After consultation with Jonathan Park and Edwin Shirley Staging, the JTS 35 screens were built into the set design drawings and, to Crump's relief, it was fortunate that the ESS stage roof was able to tolerate enormous weightloads. Just before load-out to Hyde Park, he said: "The screens will be on a cantilever downstage of the main support towers, and they have to track out past those towers. Those two screens weigh almost five tons each and they are suspended from above and have to move in an accurate, controlled fashion, completely in vision during the show."

Suspended from beam trolleys which were fixed to an 80' I-beam, the screens were able to move from side to side, powered by a computer-controlled winch motor system from Unusual Rigging which would normally be used for the movement of scenery. It was fascinating to watch the two on-stage screens come together for the first time shortly before a soundcheck of *Quadrophenia*. A few adjustments later and the screens appeared to lock together seamlessly. "Those motors can control the screens to within a millimetre," said Crump. "It's a similar system to the one we used on Genesis's We Can't Dance tour where we had three JumboTrons tracked together which also moved apart, but they were ground-supported on trolleys."

While the use of winch motors to unite and separate the two screens solved the problem of satisfying the two main artists' requirements, it meant that the control of the video images to them needed further thought. Crump explained: "The screens need to carry two separate images at one point, and one strange aspect ratio image at another. So we are using Creative Technology's new OB truck which is switchable between 16 x 9 aspect ratio and the more conventional TV format 3 x 4 aspect ratio, and that allows us to output in either standard. We are using a two-channel DVE (Digital Video Effects) system to enable us to squeeze and manipulate pictures to fit in the different aspect ratio screens. A similar technique was used by Dick Carruthers on Oasis, but it is more complicated on this because we have to simultaneously output to conventional shaped screens down the field. The stage screens will be driven as one screen and even when they are apart they will be showing one image and what we feed them will have two images side by side, but split down the middle with one side per screen. By sending two separate feeds to the effects unit, you can end up with different shots on each screen, such as a close-up face on one and a shot of a guitarist on the other."

In order to synchronise the video pictures with the sound heard around the venue, Screenco installed its two additional screens at 100 metres from the stage, either side of the arena, with the video picture delayed by approximately one-third of a second. The most common way of achieving this was by the use of a Pioneer hard-disk video recorder which was able to record on one part of the disk and read on another, and then output a delayed signal. Suspended from conventional ESS structures, the two screens used for the delay system were the new 3 x 3 JTS 17s and Masters Of Music was only the sixth time they had ever been seen in Europe, after shows with Tina Turner and M People.

Despite costing twice the price of the JTS 35, Crump predicted a great future for the new JTS 17. He said: "The JTS 17 is a much higher resolution system, designed ideally for smaller screens with shorter viewing distances. These daylight TV screens use thousands of miniature cathode ray tubes which are mounted together in a matrix. On the JTS 35, the distance between each red-green-blue cluster is 35mm, and that's reduced to 17mm on the JTS 17, which automatically gave the highest resolution available for a daylight display system. Effectively, by reducing that distance to 17mm horizontally and vertically, the resolution is quadrupled because there are four times as many pixels in any given area. Therefore, it's possible to have a screen one-quarter the surface area and achieve the same resolution. Or, with a screen the same size as the JTS 35, four times the resolution. So on larger screens, you are getting very close to standard television resolution which no one has ever come near to achieving before with daylight screens. It also means that you can reduce viewing distances and you can comfortably watch it from 10-12' away, whereas historically you had to be between 25-40' away from the screen to appreciate the images."

Traditionally, the display devices manufactured by Sony for JumboTrons were designed for permanent installation. Screenco's business, however, was based on purchasing these devices and repackaging them for mobile configurations. But the advent of the JTS 17 saw Sony building bespoke modules and providing Screenco with them as a turnkey package. "We have now set up a manufacturing division," said Crump. "Not only is the arrangement with Sony saving us money, we also wanted to have the additional control by working with sub-contractors that we know and trust."

Another new development from Screenco in its early stages at Hyde Park was the replacement of its conventional co-axial video cable with fibre optics. "Traditional cable is prone to interference and signal loss, and it was thought that being such a huge venue, this would be the ideal place in which to introduce this new cable system which will provide distinct advantages in such a huge venue. It is a very thin cable which has a box on each end to modulate the video signal on to a laser and it fires down the fibre optic to a decoder at the other end. It will result in a much cleaner feed to the screens than would be experienced with conventional transmission technology."

Screenco's crew loaded the screens and control equipment into Hyde Park from its Eastleigh, Hampshire base on Thursday, 27 June, followed the next day by Creative Technology's OB truck. On site, Crump said: "With so many input and output feeds, we need maximum sophistication and CT's truck has a Bosch BTS thirty-two-input three mix effects mixer with a linked Abekus DVE. It's unique because it's a serial digital truck which is very rare, and it's actually bigger than the Chrysalis truck which is handling the televised show. It's all pre-configured beforehand and it saves a lot of time. We've had to set everything up so that we can load out quickly. Masters Of Music was put into our summer schedule at a relatively late stage and we have commitments for the screens at Clapham Common and

Edinburgh immediately after the show."

For future broadcast purposes, Chrysalis installed cameras and crew on behalf of Allied Vision. In the CT truck, vision screens director Kevin Williams took isolated feeds from Chrysalis's close-up cameras to add to CT's own camerawork. "CT are also controlling the three manned Thompson cameras, two of which are in the pit and one on side stage. We also have three minicams which we can put on drums, keyboards, guitars or other appropriate locations, depending on the act. That gives us six of our own sources, and we will also take around six feeds from Chrysalis's main transmission output. The difficulty is that we cannot direct those cameras, so we'll have to take whatever comes our way and mix it in as required. They have two cameras at front-of-house on long lenses which we have been told will concentrate on the main artists in close-up or mid shots, so we'll definitely take those two feeds. Obviously, with a show like this Chrysalis really rule the shots, because they are earning the majority of the money through selling the show to TV companies."

Other responsibilities on Screenco's and CT's shoulders included playing in commercials between acts and relaying messages, such as public transport and emergency information, via a graphics display system. Williams also supplied images from the OB truck to monitors in the press centre and backstage hospitality marquee, as well as ISO recording *Quadrophenia* on eight Betacam machines. The pre-recorded footage shown during that part of the show was run from two Sony CRV laser disc players and controlled by a Macintosh computer to ensure tight cueing. Even *Quadrophenia*'s musicians and actors were assisted by the Screenco/CT alliance, as Crump explained: "Everyone will need vision as well as audio monitoring, and we've put some monitors on stage so that they can minutely time the music and dialogue to synchronise with the footage."

This being a charity show for the benefit of the Prince's Trust, Screenco was asked, like most suppliers, to keep the cost of its services as low as possible and Crump believed that, under the circumstances, he and Dennis Arnold at Harvey Goldsmith Entertainments struck a favourable deal. But the increase in large charity events since Live Aid presented problems within the rental industry. "It has been increasingly difficult for suppliers to keep on doing charity events," he observed. "More so with companies like Screenco than PA or lighting companies, because we have a very narrow window through which to earn our money. We normally have three months every year in which we work flat out, while the other nine months are comparatively quiet, so we have to maximise the opportunities to earn revenue in a short space of time. It's fair to say with something like Hyde Park that because of the amount of touring work we have this summer, if it had not been a charity show we may well have turned it down."

But three days after the show, Crump was glad he accepted the job and reflecting on a hectic run-up to the event and all that the show entailed, he said: "Like the VE Day event, it was a massive challenge and a bit of a nightmare for everyone involved behind the scenes, and everyone was so exhausted by the end of the day. Unusual's tracking system worked perfectly and, technically, it was the highlight for us of an extremely rewarding day."

Hyde Park had become so increasingly synonymous with designer Jonathan Park that the uninformed might have been forgiven for believing he was named after the place. Park had already added his touch of genius to Handel's Tercentenary, Pavarotti In The Park and the aforementioned VE Day celebration in 1995, so it was no surprise to learn that he was chosen to conjure further architectural magic for Masters Of Music on the same hallowed ground.

Unlike those other memorable events, where the theme and performers were pre-defined, Masters Of Music was but a loose idea with little direction when Park first became involved in the project in February 1996. At that time, Harvey Goldsmith's Allied Entertainments was planning an untitled show with an unconfirmed list of possible performers, none of which was to appear on the final bill. It was, therefore, a tribute to Park's razor-sharp imagination that he not only dreamed up one of his most potent designs ever for a rock 'n' roll show but, on the day, the impression was that the stage had been purpose-designed for each of the legends who agreed to perform.

In his King's Cross office during the frenzied run-up to the big day, Park said of the project's evolution: "I did some little doodles of my ideas for the concert and everybody seemed to like them, so I took on the design of this very large event that had no performers! Neil Young and Rod Stewart And The Faces were the names being thrown around when I was first involved, but plans quickly changed and a long time passed during which very little had happened because getting acts together for this was a tough job. The biggest coup was, of course, having the world premiere stage performance of Pete Townshend's *Quadrophenia*. Ordinarily, that very important highlight of the show would have had a major influence on my stage design, but by a fortuitous coincidence, the architecture of the stage that I had already developed fitted very nicely with the concept of *Quadrophenia*. It is quite a large project to do in such a short time, essentially less than twelve weeks, so it has been hectic with lead times running very close to the edge. Most of my time has been spent specifying what is going to be there and making sure it's all going to work."

Knowing that the lion's share of the show would take the form of a celebration of rock 'n' roll, past and present, Park approached his overall design with dynamism at the forefront of his thoughts. He was also keen to provide the most exciting visual backdrop possible for the army of television cameras covering the show for an international audience. "You can't design a set specifically for five acts, but we've aimed to give each act their own identity and have a good looking stage with three-dimensional attributes. So when the camera is looking at the stage from different angles, it looks different and there's something behind the performers as well as the lights that gives the setting some sort of feeling. But ultimately, what you're concentrating on is the energy of the performer, so anything we do is only an enhancement.

"I was trying to portray some sort of animation in the middle of the day that represented rock 'n' roll and could be seen by thousands a long way from the stage, as well as reading on television with some stage architecture. So I chose some large multi-purpose white spiky shapes as a backdrop, which would add some kind of dynamism and also take colour from the lighting or gobos. What I normally do in these large concerts is attempt to create a stage picture which has a strong architectural form and is memorable. When you see these things from a long way back, they look flat anyway but when you are close to them and looking at the stage through a television camera, what you want is a bit of texture, grain and edge to it all."

In this particular case, Jonathan Park's "hook line" used as its source a deconstructed circle at both sides of the stage, pierced through each centre by what could only be described as a futuristic 120' high spike or mast, topped with an aircraft warning light. Although a large stage (overall 200' wide), the budget was not infinite, and Park was forced to design something fresh and original using only a standard Edwin Shirley roof and stage kit. The result, whilst also resembling a distressed ghetto blaster, appeared to pay homage to MasterCard's famous dual spherical logo.

He said: "I couldn't do anything with the roof but by the means of these big circles and the spikes, at least the architectural feeling could be transformed. Rather than have a normal monolithic tower block of PA at either side, I decided to hang it off one tower so that it had a lighter feel and the audience would look right past it.

"The stage does have slight allusions to MasterCard's logo. You have to take some departure point which doesn't need to be presented literally, but the departure point I took was two circles which I deconstructed. I did try to explain that it was not a representation of the MasterCard logo, but a departure from it. You can't design a set specifically for five acts, but we've aimed to give each act their own identity. I always make models of these things because it makes things so much easier to explain, and also three-dimensional drawings in the computer so I can see how everything relates to each other in scale, but the real sweat is in turning it into reality."

For the performance of *Quadrophenia*, Lady Luck was clearly on Park's side. He managed to incorporate his deconstructed circles theme into the show by making the roundels part of the set, pulling up a red bullseye disc in each middle and highlighting a small tail. Hey presto, two instant "Q" logos!

Park said: "In this section of the show, the inner stage picture changes to one that is very specific to this Mod opera, and we needed to bring visual information in behind the band as well as having lots of explanatory footage and graphics on the video screens. The original idea was to make big painted backdrops which represented certain parts of the scenic setting, but my feeling about those was that they would be both extremely expensive and difficult to change between each part of the performance. You could do it in a theatre after twelve weeks of rehearsals, but not in a show like this. Also, the stage is so big that it would be wholly impractical to start using huge scenic cloths. So I suggested that we shrink the intended backdrops down to a series of large, 16' x 10' 'postcards' which depicted parts of the story and the idea was well supported. So at various times during the performance these postcards rise or drop into position and as the show progresses, the backdrop to the stage will gradually fill up with a collage of these postcards, which starts with the terraced house in which Jimmy was born and ends up with the pirate ship he imagines as he rows out into the bay, which is different to what happened in the Franc Roddam film, of course. On television, the postcards will appear as large coloured backdrops to the close-ups of the performers, while to the audience they will still make sense even from a long way away.

"The vast audience who are more than 100' from the stage have to see a big picture which they can make some sense of, because of the performance being very small. So they can generally see the performers big on the video screens, but we also want to see things change on the stage so that they feel that not only are they watching this little person magnified but they are also seeing something which they can read as being part of the same action, and the brain puts the two together."

In the final stages of Park's design, lighting designer Tom Kenny's input proved invaluable. Park said: "It was useful to have someone who knew both The Who and Eric Clapton. When Tom came in, he not unnaturally wanted to put in quite a lot of lights because he's going to need to pour light at it to bring it out. Tom also needed to have a high degree of redundancy so that he could light the different performances from a variety of positions.

"We realised how essential it was that the last part of the show with Eric Clapton looks quite different from *Quadrophenia*, so Tom suggested lowering the lighting at that point and the set will change to a regular set piece that Eric is used to which luckily can be brought in and erected very quickly. The inner stage picture will change markedly with an energetic stage look that accentuates Eric's rock and blues, and Tom is doing everything he possibly can to get colour on to the stage."

Built on-site by Edwin Shirley Staging one week prior to the show, the stage was positioned to the north of the park to enable greater access for load-in and out, which Park said was a major improvement over the logistics of VE Day and other past shows. "It was intended that the trucks would have the shortest distance to travel to the stage once they enter the park and it also leaves a tremendous amount of park space left open. It limits the incursion into the park for as long as possible and the park officials like that very much. When we did Pavarotti at the other end by the Serpentine that locked up a central area of the park and it was difficult to get vehicles in. Over the course of the last few big events, our stages have gradually migrated around the park and I think we now hold some kind of a world record for Hyde Park!"

Edwin Shirley's Tower system stage featured a 60' high roof – the same one used for VJ Day on Horse Guards Parade, but without the front balcony. For Masters Of Music, this became a peak with the columns moved out to the sides to achieve a large covered inner area of approximately 80' square. The depth may have been colossal but only the front half was used for the performance, while the back half became a setting-up and storage area for equipment when not in use. With literally several scores of musicians appearing in the headline and support bands, it was imperative that the huge amounts of drum and percussion kits, keyboard rigs and backline were kept out of sight, behind the black backdrop which lifted up to 10' from the stage to allow the necessary items of equipment to be accessed quickly. In between the main performances, the front curtain was drawn to allow all the movement on stage to be obscured from the audience, while the support bands played at the front of the bow-fronted stage, their backline raised into position by a hydraulic lift, again to enable quick changeovers.

Not only was there no thrust at the front of the stage, but Park also decided to keep the traditional "ego ramps" out of his design.

He said: "Apart from everything else, they are quite difficult to use and they need a lot of rehearsal, especially if the performer goes out in front of the PA, for feedback reasons. We really wanted to contain everything in the one area, within the stage aperture."

Park stressed how eager he was to see the fruits of his labour come into full being. "I've really enjoyed this project and on the day I hope that we have achieved the three main things I always strive towards. Most importantly, the bands should feel sufficiently comfortable to be able to play; the next thing is whether the audience can see them; and the third is whether or not the setting is interesting. It has been amusing to have had a concept at the beginning which was to do with architecture and memorability, and some sort of theme without any discussions with artists or directors, and to find that all the performances can work within it."

With a summer show planned to start in the early afternoon and end mid evening, there was little that Tom Kenny could do for most of the production apart from enhancing what was already in daylight with large colour washes. Although a sunny day was forecast, the weather was fairly dismal for the most part, but looking on the bright side, it did at least give Kenny the chance to "shine" a little more than expected. But the only point in the show when the lighting became truly obvious was during Eric Clapton's set which began at around 8.30pm.

In the week prior to curtain-up, Kenny said: "The show has been bought by every major TV company in the world as an event, so what I'm doing is mainly for the cameras on the day. I asked lighting cameraman Eugene O'Connor to look at the vision screens and keep an eye on everything, because the television end of things is such a big deal. The reason that it is such a big lighting system is to make it look like a huge rock show. There's a lot of detail for the stage because it's so big and we have every part lit. It's a very gleaming show even for the people at the back, and that's a long way! Obviously, whatever sun there is will be in the audience's faces so the stage needs to be enhanced from behind for television, and for that we have six 4kW HMI lights and eight 2.5kW HMIs with colour changers. A lot of people would take the view that lighting isn't really necessary for a show in daylight, but I've done them so many times in the last few years and I think it's important to the punter to see a lighting rig because it's part and parcel of a rock show. I've done stuff with Page and Plant in Sweden where it didn't get dark until 12.30am, but we put in sixty Par cans so that people at the back of the field can get the feel of the show."

After liaising with Tony Panico at Meteorlites, Kenny designed a rig which included twelve front and rear follow spots (eight 2kW super troupers and four on-stage Pani truss spots), a total of fifteen Pallas 4 x 1kW ground rows, fifty-two Par 36 Molefay units, seventy-eight six-lamp bars, eight Wybron eight-light scrollers and eight Pancommand XL Ranger nine-light scrollers. To fulfil Kenny's wish for Icons and Vari*Lites, Meteorlites also hired forty Icons, an Icon desk and twenty VL5s from LSD. Meteorlites' Andy Stacey looked after the dimmers, as controlled by one Avolites forty-eight-way and four seventy-two-way systems. Kenny said: "The Icons are being run from their own desk by Pete Barnes while I operate the conventional lighting from a Celco Gold Series 2 ninety-way board and the intelligent technology end of things, such as the colour changers, is being handled by an Avolites thirty-channel Rolacue desk. The VL5s are operated by Pete from the Icon desk via an interface unit."

Kenny, who saved his programming duties until forty-eight hours before the show, added: "Because of all the artist variations we have a different focus for each act, so there has been quite a lot to take on. But it has been very well organised and there's been lots of rehearsal time, thank God! *Quadrophenia* is very theatrical and a bit like a Floyd show because there is so much going on. We are basically making it look very bright and white, using the Icons as key lights rather than moving them because there is little point."

Arriving in London on 10 June to make final changes to the lighting design in connection with the JumboTrons, Kenny returned ten days later to oversee a number of the *Quadrophenia* and Eric Clapton rehearsals. Hyde Park marked the first occasion where Kenny had joined forces with Meteorlites, and he hoped it would be far from the last. "I'm obviously used to working with LSD with Eric Clapton and various other artists, but I have to say that Meteorlites have done a really good job and they have a fine crew. The hardest task has been finding people to work on the show because so many are out on tour already, but the main players are all there."

He was not the only person pleased with the interaction with Meteorlites, a company which at the time was enjoying one of its healthiest years in recent history, with its involvement in Euro '96, various television dramas, Lord Of The Dance and Paul Weller. Tony Panico commented: "The team I have put together for Hyde Park have been truly wonderful and they have my deepest thanks. Tom Kenny is someone I've wanted to work with for a long time. He knows exactly what he wants and it's an absolute pleasure to help him realise his plans. Going down to production meetings allowed me to grasp the whole sheer concept of the show from Jonathan Park and other key players. But once you get on site things do tend to change."

Things certainly began to change three days before the show when the lighting was rigged. Lighting crew chief Paul Hawkes was one of many to scratch his forehead. He said: "Because the infrastructure of the whole show has been quite vast, you don't really know for sure how all the engineering elements are going to fit together until you get on site. It's all very well seeing something on paper but things can change dramatically when you're there and faced with a huge stage. But the way in which everyone has pooled together has been fantastic and we've all mucked in to solve little problems that have arisen from time to time in fitting the amount of equipment we have in this one space. We had to juggle the rig around to provide a decent set of sight lines for the JumboTron screens, estimate the trim height (the screens did not arrive until the Thursday), take into account that the screens move and also the weight displacement of the roof."

With 150,000 ticket holders all leaving the site at once after the show, and taking well over an hour to do so, Harvey Goldsmith instructed Tom Kenny to design some lighting which would both entertain and act as practical illumination upon exit. "Harvey wanted to have some kind of interesting lighting for people to see as they left just to make it look very eventful, so we have lots of different Icons and architectural lighting to make the whole place light up like a circus. The event has been designed so that from the minute people enter the venue to the minute they leave, it would be a show never to be forgotten."

The plan worked. It was a show which, like Live Aid, would be remembered for a long, long time. And even if The Beatles were absent, a splendid time was still guaranteed for all.

CHAPTER NINE

Bryan Adams

18 Til I Die – 1996

Wembley Stadium's famous Twin Towers and Brakeyard Tunnel had become very familiar by the end of the summer of '96 – on 27 July it was time for Bryan Adams to wow the crowd as he completed the European leg of his 18 Til I Die tour, with support acts Ricky Ross (ex-Deacon Blue), Melissa Etheridge and the brilliant Del Amitri.

The Dels in particular were on fine form and even managed to slip in the old favourite 'Kiss This Thing Goodbye', a song absent on their previous tour. By 7.30pm, the crowd was hot for Adams as he entered the stage and launched into an uncompromising slew of hits, including 'Run To You', 'Somebody', 'Cuts Like A Knife', 'Have You Ever Loved A Woman?', a truly electrifying version of the duet 'It's Only Love', with Etheridge returning to take the part of Tina Turner, and the unmentionable, painfully familiar ballad which occupied the Number One slot for most of 1991. All of which was being recorded by Bob Clearmountain in the Manor Mobiles truck.

There were two parts of the show which were particularly entertaining: the first, when Adams invited a bare-chested male reveller on to the stage to sing 'Summer Of '69' (an instant star!); the second, after ninety minutes, came when Adams and his band rushed through the crowd and leapt on to a central B stage to perform a pure, in-the-round rock 'n' roll set with (wait for it) Air Artists' enormous inflatable dancing underwear popping up for good measure.

Back on the main stage, on which a rear catwalk provided a memorable vantage point for a crowd of specially invited fans, Adams climaxed with his soft rock anthem, 'Heaven'. It was fascinating to witness his appeal among the masses and across such a wide span of ages, and with a show which lasted at least three hours, the acclaim was richly deserved.

Staging for this latest Adams trek was co-designed by Willie Williams and Bruce Ramus, who dreamed up its concept, and Edwin Shirley who designed and built the tower system, while also handling the trucking. Video close-ups were directed by Paul Becher and displayed on two Panasonic modular screens, which were developed for and supplied by Astravision. Like most of the crew, lighting director Mark Cunniffe was a freelancer – he took over from Williams while he began working with Mark Fisher on U2's international touring monster that would be known as PopMart.

For an *alfresco* performance, this LSD-supplied lighting rig was more than substantial, as Cunniffe explained: "We have around 600 Par cans and 290 Uni-Pars, which is a relatively new product from the USA. It is a clear plastic can that will take the heat of a 1,000 watt Par, and you can have the plastic in any colour that's desired. There are ninety-six LSD Washlights and thirty LSD Icons, as well as a considerable amount of floor equipment. For the conventional rig we are using an Avolites Diamond console and the Icon desk is running everything else including strobes.

"The idea is to get away from the huge metal monstrosities that you get on a lot of rock 'n' roll shows these days, and concentrate on delivering a lot of colour. With the Uni-Pars and the Washlights combined, you do get a really good sense of colour which blends in well with the PA. We've been doing some outdoor shows in southern Europe where it has been getting dark earlier and it's so effective as an outdoor rig. The catwalk at the back of the stage was a result of Willie's idea to get the total involvement of the crowd over 360° without playing a conventional in-the-round show. That works because it forms a really good backdrop with lots of light-coloured summer clothing to pick up the lights."

Vancouver's greatest musical export, Bryan Adams signed with A&M Records in 1979 and providing the sound system and expertise on his first nightclub date in his hometown in 1980 was Jason Sound Industries (JSI), arguably Canada's most successful audio rental company. Also from Vancouver, JSI was founded in the mid 1970s and worked alongside Adams on all his headlining tours since 1983. The JSI rig on tour with Adams in 1996 was a JBL-component custom system by the company's head designer, Jeff Berryman.

JSI President, Jeff Lilly said of the system: "We have 120 of our J60 boxes which are our full size boxes, and it is a three-box system. Thirty-six of them are used as under-stage subs and eighty-four are flown. Then we have twenty-four of our J30 half size boxes that are used for side, near and front fills as a two-box system. We believe in horn-loaded technology and think that the proprietary nature is in the horn throats, and the component count and general layout of the box is not something we try to hide."

In February 1996, JSI was acquired by the concert and theatre lighting specialist organisation, Westsun International. One of the results of the merging of these two normally opposed entertainment disciplines was the rather garish-looking flown speaker arrays. Lilly explained: "Lighting and sound have never really got along too well in the concert situation, and there are some large sound companies which are downright hostile to lighting and set design. They hate anyone touching their boxes or even lighting them! So this purchase was quite radical and we thought that this integration of sound and lights may even give us a competitive edge.

"We actively solicited set designers and told them that if they had ever thought of ideas that were rejected by a sound company they should let us know because maybe we would be more receptive. One thing that we came up with was to offer designers the opportunity to use multicoloured grilles on the PA speakers to get rid of the traditional black cloud at each side of the stage. Little did we realise that this germ of an idea would lead to what Willie Williams designed for this tour, and some of the crew felt that it was a little cartoonish, but it's a move in the right direction."

The front-of-house mixing platform was unusually positioned at 45°, stage left, which meant that the engineers were effectively mixing off one stack. Adams' man, Jody Perpick engineered a forty-eight-channel Soundcraft Europa console (forty mono plus four stereo channels) while a Midas XL3 was shared by the three support bands' engineers, including Del Amitri's Andy Dockerty of Liverpool-based rental company, Ad Lib Audio. Mixing the Dels under festival-type conditions clearly had Dockerty working by the seat of his pants. He said: "By the time I get to the desk for the Dels, I am using whatever Melissa Etheridge's engineer has set up in the way of EQ as my starting point and from there on I am estimating our own EQ and gain structures. It's basically a case of winging it for the first couple of numbers. There have been no soundchecks for the supports, just a quick line check and then we're on! If you're in a situation where the support is touring for three or four weeks, you can chart up your desk so that you know where you are. But we're only doing two shows on this so there's been absolutely no point. The last time I worked on a Bryan Adams tour was with Texas and they insisted on carrying their own board and that gave me a little more of an advantage."

The XL3 ran via the Europa and at a previous date at the Alfred McAlpine Stadium in Huddersfield, Dockerty noticed a suspicious amount of compression in the system whenever he attempted to wind the volume up for his band. This, he believed, had more than a little to do with the decibel limits set for each venue. "There is a ridiculous dB limit set for Wembley. It's 100dB at the desk, but it can't be more than 65dB outside the stadium. For it to average at 100dB over the course of the day, the support bands have to run at 95dB to allow Bryan to play at 105dB for that extra presence. But it's very difficult to mix at 95dB in a stadium this large."

It was strange to notice a complete absence of delay towers in the field, but Adams' sound crew chief, JSI's Dean Roney commented that the singer harbours a built-in opposition to them. He said: "We don't normally use delays because we feel that our speaker configuration produces enough energy of its own. Bryan is very involved in not having any large structures in the way of audience sight lines, which is why there is no roof over the mixing platform. That's very considerate of him, although it might cause us a few problems later if it rains [which it didn't]." He was also showing signs of extreme frustration with the venue's management. "Wembley Stadium is probably the most anally-retentive venue we have ever played and Valdis Dausts, our Production Manager, spends all day long dealing with inspectors of different kinds. I certainly wouldn't want his job today!"

Dockerty, meanwhile, felt it appropriate to air his views on the whole concept of stadium shows. "I'm not a fan of stadium sound, although from a technical perspective it's probably improving. The sound quality in a stadium in comparison to an NEC kind of show is extremely inferior, and the people who really suffer at the end of the day are the punters. But I don't believe that they appreciate just how much they suffer, which is why so many promoters have got away with cramming audiences of 50,000 upwards into stadia for so long."

The Shure name permeated all conversations on the microphone theme. The entire vocal mic selection exclusively consisted of Beta 58As, of which Roney said: "It's Bryan's favourite and although it may not be the most hi-fi mic in the world, it's remains the most used." Other mics included Beta and regular 57s, 98s and 91s, plus a variety of Sennheisers, Neumanns and AKGs. "We try to use as many Shure mics as possible," commented Dockerty. "HW International [Shure's UK distributor] look after us very well but I've always been a great fan of the 98s and 91s anyway. Jason Sound have been brilliant and I've simply told them that I'd go with whatever was easiest for them. You can get too precious about these things because in our situation, by the time we're getting the sound just right it's time to come off!"

An additional six AKG 3000 mics were required to pick up the "vibe" from the audience and deliver it to Adams and his band through their Garwood Radio Station in-ear monitors. A total of seven wireless systems was in use, including a spare set for monitor engineer, Glen Collett, who was running two Soundcraft SM24 consoles. In a similar approach to that of Rod Stewart's David Palmer, Adams' drummer Mickey Curry added weight to his in-ear mix by having a "bass thumper" attached to the underside of his stool to simulate some low frequency. Although a great believer in the IEM cause, Collett found that, in the rock genre at least, he needed to reinforce the IEM sound in some way.

"If you're working with guys who are used to getting a feel for what they're doing from wedges, they definitely miss them if they're not there," he said. "The drummer will be used to feeling some air move around him, so we have to adopt some unusual methods. I'm only using side fills for some vibe, plus a pair of wedges for the keyboard player and they are at low level."

Collett preferred not to add too much EQ character to the IEM mixes but added that he needed to work hard on "enlarging" the sound. "The first comment people make when they begin to use IEM is normally that it sounds small, so my whole effort is about getting it to sound as big as possible without saturating the little Radio Station. It's a bit of a balancing act but the benefits are huge."

He also said that as a direct result of the IEM approach, his input count has risen "beyond belief" to sixty-eight which, for a six-piece band, did seem rather excessive. "They now all want cymbals, ambience and all kinds of things you'd never put through wedges. I also end up splitting inputs and having duplicates, because people want different EQs. Before, everyone would hear the guitarist coming from his big stack. But now that I'm supplying it to them, the bass player doesn't want it as bright as the guitarist, so I have to split the input for that. But that's just the beginning. The drums that come out of the side fills sound big and fat, but I can't replicate that on the in-ears otherwise it'll cover up the rest of the mix for something else. So I split the kick, snare and tom inputs for someone else...it goes on and on! I'm listening on in-ears as well and I have a spare IEM wireless system that I hook up to the cue buss, so that it's always running and I can listen to what they're hearing. If one guy's goes down, I can quickly swap his mix into that spare."

Theoretically, IEM does deliver an enormously improved, hi-fi quality sound to the artist. But, Collett said, the hardest-working IEM engineers would always be the ones in the rock music field because of the constant desire to push the boundaries of the system's dynamic range. "For artists who work at low levels, the benefits lie in the nice, big spacious sound. Our on-stage levels are a whole lot quieter than they ever were before, so the musicians don't get the ear fatigue that was commonplace. Rehearsals are always bad news because you're normally in a small room somewhere, and they went on for seven hours on that first day. They removed their in-ear monitors and Bryan said, 'I can't believe this, I've got no headache!' They never realised how bad it was before. So now when they come off stage they feel as fresh as they did when they went on."

IEM probably came along at just the right time to prevent Adams (aged thirty-seven in 1996) from doing irreparable damage to his vocal chords, as Roney observed: "It may be too early to tell but my belief is that IEM can prolong an artist's career because by having monitors in his ears, he doesn't have to exert himself as hard vocally, so his throat may last a few more years than with wedges where he is fighting against loud on-stage volumes."

Adams and his band were not the only artists at Wembley to use IEM. For years, Del Amitri lead singer and bassist, Justin Currie repeatedly asked for his vocals to be loud on-stage but this often led to impractical ambient stage levels. The problem was solved by him being the sole band member to use IEM. The Dels' monitor engineer and Ad Lib Audio man, Dave Kay said: "All he has in his mix is his vocal, plus the drum overheads which also pick up some of the surrounding backline. But he also gets some wedge back-up for the bass and drums, and a tiny bit of the guitars on larger stages where the band members are wider apart. As a gesture to the support acts, Jason Sound brought with them a bunch of 2 x 12" and 2" loaded wedges, although at the Huddersfield gig, the Dels were complaining bitterly about the lack of them."

Kay believed that the Soundcraft SM24 console provided such distinct benefits for IEM that it could easily have been designed for it – in fact, the SM20, introduced in 1998, *was* designed for it. "The SM24 has eight stereo outputs. The first eight outputs are mono for wedges and you can use the stereo buss for running side fills. You can easily configure sixteen mono outputs or eight stereo outputs, so in that respect it is ideal for sending eight channels of IEM."

Driving the whole JSI rig was a massive complement of lightweight QSC Powerlight amplification, with 109 1.8s and forty-two of the newer, larger-powered version, the 4.0. JSI's embracing of QSC began early in 1995 after the company had spent its previous ten years as an exclusive Carver amplification customer. Jeff Lilly takes up the story of this drastic turnaround: "We had made some pretty serious commitments to Carver's lightweight technology and although we often visited QSC at audio engineering exhibitions, we felt that all they could offer us was fairly conventional technology. But Carver began to lose its grip, mainly because it was being managed by hi-fi specialists who were running the pro division into the ground, and eventually it closed.

"Prior to this closure, we had engaged in many conversations with

Carver about its next generation of lightweight technology and what we wanted to see. Noticing how badly the company was coming apart at the seams, we started looking for alternatives while maintaining our interest in this technology."

It was at the October 1994 AES Convention in San Francisco that Lilly caught his first sight of QSC's Powerlight products and he was immediately impressed. The news that Gordon Irwin, Carver's primary engineering specialist, had joined QSC was a further incentive in Lilly's eyes. "Although the Powerlight technology is QSC's all the way, it could be argued that this was the next generation of lightweight technology that we had been looking for and there was some continuity in the engineering that we appreciated. QSC needed to make an impression in concert touring and so was looking at appropriate vehicles to assist in its endeavours. The first two vehicles which became available were Sound Image of San Diego and JSI, and both of us were ready to buy, interested in the technology and had enough profile to make it worth the manufacturer's while."

JSI finally made the unreserved switch to Powerlights at the beginning of 1995 and never looked back. "Carver had lots of problems with its quality control over the years, but I assume now that Phoenix Gold has taken over the company, all those problems will be solved. Compared to what we had previously been using we have been rewarded with considerably improved sound quality and reliability by taking on QSC. We have been using Powerlights exclusively for six months and have been taken aback by the quality control. It's quite amazing."

CHAPTER TEN

The Eagles

Hell Freezes Over – 1996

If the Nineties are to be remembered for anything, musically speaking, it is bound to be the trend for Jurassic rockers to bite their lips, forget their differences and reunite with their estranged megastar band members for one more run around the block before expiring. If The Beatles could do it for their *Anthology* project, then why not The Sex Pistols on tour for huge wads of Filthy Lucre? The Eagles had not seen the light of day as a unit since their acrimonious split in 1980, when they vowed that the day they played together again would be the day that hell froze over. Appropriately, their 1996 reunion tour was titled Hell Freezes Over.

Profits made by the regurgitated Pistols paled into insignificance compared to the cash earned on this one. Although wholly unanticipated by the band (drummer Don Henley, guitarists Joe Walsh, Glenn Frey, Don Felder and bass player Timothy B Schmit) and probably their accountants, Hell Freezes Over was at one time the biggest grossing tour ever, shattering records previously set by Pink Floyd's Division Bell tour and The Rolling Stones' Voodoo Lounge. The Eagles' retirement fund was suddenly bulging at the seams.

The tour began in the USA on 24 May, 1994 and ended just over twenty-six months later in Edinburgh. For the audiences, who comprised mostly of the thirty-plus brigade, the show was a journey back to a time when long hair and faded denims were at their coolest, a time when hedonism among the rock elite, especially The Eagles, was embraced to the full.

Kicking off their set with 'Hotel California', one might have been forgiven for thinking that The Eagles had unwisely played their ace card far too early. But the remainder of their set was nothing short of country-fused rock excellence, with classic band numbers ('New Kid In Town', 'Lyin' Eyes', 'One Of These Nights', 'Life In The Fast Lane', 'Desperado' and many more) diplomatically punctuated by the members' best-known solo works, including bottleneck hero Walsh's 'Life's Been Good' and 'Rocky Mountain Way', Henley's 'The Boys Of Summer' and Frey's 'The Heat Is On'.

Four supporting musicians – Al Garth on horns and violin, Scott Crago on drums and percussion, and two keyboard players, John Corey and Timothy Drury – fleshed out a precision sound which remained faithful to the recordings of the Seventies. But The Eagles themselves traded instruments with effortless ease and natural dexterity, like old hands should. A fifteen-minute intermission halfway through the set enabled the stage crew to change the set around for a four-song acoustic section, before the band returned for the nearest they would ever get to a rock thrash-out, climaxing with one of their earliest hits, 'Take It Easy', a thought which undoubtedly came to mind after more than two years on the road.

It was a big day for Chris Lamb when he was asked to step into the production manager role and look after a crew of sixty-two people for this reunion tour. There was a certain mistiness in his eyes when he recalled working for Fleetwood Mac in the mid 1970s, during those decadent days when *Rumours* and *Hotel California* battled it out for West Coast soft rock supremacy. When the call came to join his former arch rivals, he was surprised to discover that the years apart had not affected the band's tight musicianship. "It's amazing how good this band is," he exclaimed. "When I went to their first rehearsals in 1994, we set out five folding chairs and they all sat in a semi circle with guitars, playing 'Lyin' Eyes'. I was in my production office and could not believe the sound I was hearing, considering they hadn't seen each other for so long."

The tour reached Wembley Stadium in mid July 1996, by which time Lamb had already voted Hell Freezes Over as his most enjoyable tour to date. "The Eagles' show is about the music and the sound, lighting and video projections reflect that simple fact," he emphasised.

"It's not a band made by MTV – these guys made their name on their music, not by how they could dance, so there are no explosions or hydraulics. For an indoor show we use nine trucks, and eleven for an outdoor show, plus a generator truck and four tour buses."

Another aspect of the show Lamb was eager to point out was the excessive number of guitars carried on the tour for use by Don Felder, Joe Walsh, Glenn Frey and, in his non-drumming moments, Don Henley. "With this show we carry seventy-four guitars because there is a guitar change for every number. Each guitar is tuned differently for each song, but with everyone having his own guitar tech, we have the changeovers down to just a few seconds."

A simple but impressive stage set was designed by John McGraw and Don Henley, and built by Edwin Shirley Staging, whose sister company also handled the trucking in Europe. The set, an angular mish-mash of broken architecture, was intended to convey a post-holocaust scene, such as that in the 1968 movie, *Planet Of The Apes*. To enhance that imagery and also add a flavour of the desert, so vivid in The Eagles' music, a sandy mountain range painted on to acoustically transparent scrim was placed in front of each PA tower.

Positioned on the outside of each PA tower was a 30' x 20' video projection screen, supplied by Nocturne in the USA. As with many UK shows in the summer, the lighting and video crews faced the insurmountable problem of attempting to enhance a show which was mostly in daylight. "The screens don't come up until the sun goes down," Lamb commented. "They are purely for close-up documentation and we have a four-camera shoot going on, with a team headed by video director Carol Dodds. There is a house camera in the mixing tower, one on a boom in front of stage left, another on a trolley in front of the stage and a hand-held moving around the band on stage. We're a little stuck over here in Europe because it gets dark so late. Normally in the USA and the rest of the world where we're playing, we wouldn't go on until dark, but we're forced by curfew laws and public transportation to start The Eagles' part of the show at around 7.30pm and end early."

LD Richard Schoenfield, better known as "Nook", began working on Hell Freezes Over with long-time Sting associate Nick Sholem who originally designed the lighting regime in 1994. Nook said: "When this started out, I ran the console and he controlled the spotlights, but he had a commitment to Sting and had to leave, so I've just been doing it all over the last few months. From a lighting perspective, it's a pretty basic show because this isn't a band that likes flash and trash lighting. It's more about painting a pretty picture and letting it be. We have fifty-six LSD Icons, over 200 different colour changers all over the rig, about 100 1kW groundrows and stacks of Molefays. We've hired everything from LSD for the UK and everything's been working fine. We've used different lighting companies for most countries and it has been a very different experience in each! We're taking the colour faders with us everywhere we go and contact local suppliers for everything else we need."

Nick Sholem was the among the first – if not *the* first – LD to use a Wholehog lighting console for a major tour (Sting in 1993-4), and a Wholehog 1 was specified once again for The Eagles. "This is about the fifth or sixth tour on which I've used a Wholehog board," said Nook. "It has twenty faders for bumping along and bringing up different stuff, and it runs all desk channels, colour rams, colour faders and mole scroll dimmers. Every cue on this is on time phase and it's a brilliant board that I swear by. I programmed this show with a Wholehog II because Nick likes the latest technology. If I have to close spotlights and keep hitting Go cues, that's enough for me, because I don't want to keep looking around for verse/chorus/verse/guitar solo movements and after a few shows it's all automatic pilot.

"For each song I have a list of cues come up on my computer monitor and the comments page, where I have all my spotlight cues programmed in, is fantastic. I'm talking all the time to my ten operators and it helps to have a foolproof guide. There are five guys in the band and you have to have a light on each of them because of the video cameras. The Stones did it the same way and you could always see them clearly on the video screens, but on other shows like Page and Plant, they had the front spots in red which may have looked okay on the stage at times but it meant that the video guys were in hell! Having the guys in the band lit at all times does take away from the show, but you can't just light one or two of them."

If there was one Eagle who created a challenge for Nook, it was Joe Walsh. Nook laughed: "They're a pretty good unit but Joe is tough –

he won't allow a front spot. He's the result of thirty years of hard living, but now that he's been completely straight for a few years, he doesn't want a light in his eyes, even though that's hard for video. So I hit him with truss spots from every side, but then he complains about heat. I just tell him, 'Joe, you're wearing a flannel shirt and it's July!' He's a strange cat but we go to great pains to make sure that an Icon never hits him."

Outside of the UK, Nook used around thirty Wybron mole scrollers, but he was satisfied with LSD's alternative supply of Molemags. Of the rest of his equipment, Nook commented: "I have twenty Cyberlights, a bunch of Wybron Par 64s, lightning machines (for the show intro), Martin lights and a Cloud projector. I also have a 2.5kW Pani slide projector and a 2kW glass loop wheel projector that was bought from Phoebus in San Francisco, but we can't use that in Wembley because it's not dark enough!"

Operating sixty Icons from his Icon desk was Ken Delvo who began the tour as a technician but took over from Chris Barron when he went on to another project halfway through. Nook also periodically stepped out of the tour to work the lights for Lenny Kravitz, Sting and Megadeth, but said that Hell Freezes Over was one of those tours that seemed as if it would never go away!

Rarely does the issue of sound quality feature large in the reviews of the national press, but in the weeks leading up to the Wembley dates, column inches were devoted to praising the clarity of the Clair Brothers 120-cabinet S4 PA system, much of which had been shipped to Dublin for the start of The Eagles' European tour immediately after use on the Masters Of Music concert in Hyde Park.

The front-of-house engineer on the tour was JD Brill who landed his job after working on Frey and Walsh's solo outings, and proving himself to be an all-round good guy. Hell Freezes Over was, in fact, a combined audio effort between Clair Bros and Brill's own company, front-of-house control equipment supplier Schubert Systems of North Hollywood.

Brill was using two Gamble EX Series consoles, appropriately manufactured in California, which between them provided the possibility for 112 channels. He said: "I have two spare channels and a lot of effects returns. I try to set up my front-facing board as the one

I'm going to be using throughout the show and have all the main channels on my left hand board subbed across for ease of use. For instance, my eight channels of toms are grouped as two channels on my main board, because rarely will I need to bring up the level of one tom over another when I'm actually mixing the show. So I am basically working with eight different groups and it cuts my working area down. The width of the Gamble desk is very friendly and channel one to fifty-six is easily within arm's reach. I have a lot of trouble focusing on two areas but fortunately I only need to touch my sub board about ten times during the whole show. Don Henley plays drums for about 65-70% of the show and his feel is mellower than the more rock 'n' roll Scott Crago. Similarly Glenn Frey's approach to playing grand piano is totally different to the other guys'. They are really the only times I have to ride the individual faders and respond to those changes in attack."

A total of eleven live Shure Beta 87 vocal mics was on stage, although until the European tour, the favoured mic for vocals was the Beyer M700. Brill commented: "The Beta 87 is a closer proximity mic and because we have eleven mics, I'm looking for the highest rejection I can get and those mics do it for me. We're using the new Beta 56s on all the guitars and on the snare drum, and SM98s on the drums. In the kick drum we have two different mics. There's an SM91 for my front-of-house requirements and there's also a Beta 52 in there for Chris Lantz's monitors."

Antiquated technology in the form of a Helpinstill pick-up system was used to model an attractive grand piano sound, as Brill explained: "Many years ago there was an actual Helpinstill electric grand piano and the way it was amplified was by integrating single coil pick-ups, as found on a Fender Stratocaster although longer. They look like metal yardsticks and are secured to the soundboard of the piano, positioned over the strings. On the lower strings, you have to place one of the pick-ups under the strings to achieve the optimum sound. The idea is that every string is covered equally and it's actually a pretty good way of getting a loud sound from the piano, over a large PA system. It's not the most open sound, of course. The other way would be to place a pair of 414s or Neumann mics in there, but with a lot of speaker power close to the stage, they run the risk of feedback."

A large bank of effects processing was employed on the tour, including some items of equipment new to Brill. The seemingly endless spec list included a TC 2290 digital delay, three dual engine TC M5000 digital reverbs, two Lexicon PCM 70 multi-effects units and the new PCM 80. Brill was also using two new Yamaha Pro R3s and a Lexicon 480L. For vocal compression, he chose Summit TLA-100 compressor/limiters and additional control was provided by a BSS DPR-504 Quad gate and a BSS DPR-402 dual compressor/de-esser/limiter, for which he found an interesting application. "As well as using it on vocals, I use one channel to de-ess Al Garth's saxophone. When he's screaming really loudly on the horn, the BSS will cut the 2.5kHz out and leave everything else in, the result being an exciting but controlled sound. When he's playing quieter, the 2.5kHz that is then needed will return to give a more natural sound."

A liberal helping of Behringer equipment was also to be seen, including a Denoiser for the keyboard rigs and twelve channels of Intelligates. Brill commented: "In my opinion the clicking and the opening and closing of the Intelligate is far quieter than on the Drawmer gates, and it's pretty much comparable with an Aphex 612 or 622, so that's why I'm using them. There are three Behringer Composer stereo compressors here on my drum and percussion sub groups and the compression circuitry is actually superior to the dbx 160A. You get all the attack, speed, release and hold features that are on the 165A, a $1,000 compressor that I use on the kick and snare drums, but this costs only $350. The 160As I use on the drum and percussion overheads because there are an awful lot of soft parts in the show and I don't so much compress them as limit them. I put a lot of gain on those overhead mics. There's much use of shakers and all kinds of things that are very quiet but they need to be in the mix, so I drive those mics harder than I might on most other gigs. When Don and Scott slam on cymbals, the 160A cuts in and limits pretty hard."

Brill's Schubert Systems Group designed and manufactured a bank of six-band parametric EQs for use on the beautifully chiming acoustic guitars and Schmit's DI'd bass, while a Yamaha SPX 990 was used for guitar processing. To EQ the PA system generally, Clair Bros' standard issue of a TC 1128 EQ system with ten channels all controlled by a TC 6032 graphic EQ remote with flying faders was the set-up, as also used by the monitor engineer, Chris Lantz.

A rack of Clair CTS-2 crossovers was in situ for the giant Clair/Crest Audio hybrid amplifier-driven front-of-house PA, of which each stack was configured six cabinets wide by ten high. Brill said: "Although it appears that they are all identical boxes, there is in fact a right and a left box, with the horns mirror-imaged as you look at the stage. The stacks consist of both S4 short throws, and P4 long throw boxes, and each are JBL-loaded but they have a completely different sound. Our top six rows of PA are long throw because they have further to project, and our bottom four rows are short throw. To handle all that we have two sets of crossovers which strive to make the sound of the boxes as equal to each other as possible. I run my long throw boxes about 5dB louder than my short throws, so when you walk towards the PA during the show, it doesn't appear to sound any louder."

Unlike most shows at Wembley Stadium where the stage has traditionally been positioned at one end of the venue, with a long, narrow area to cover, sound-wise, The Eagles' became the first band to ever perform side on from the Royal Box position – few others have chosen to go this route, although Elton John did so in 1998 with a notable depreciation in sound intelligibility. This presented obvious new challenges for Brill and his team, which included his assistant and sound crew chief, Brian Ruggles. "After there were problems with the first Wembley show, Brian turned the on-stage columns down in volume so that more of the energy focused off stage," said Brill. "If I am producing a 95db level at the console and everything is equal in volume from left to right, obviously the off-stage boxes will have further to throw. So now, the on-stage boxes I am hearing will be quieter and although I won't know it, the off-stage boxes will be louder.

"We've been touring with four delay poles which are 40' high, each with eight horns, and they stand in the shadow of the mix position. Two face backwards and the others are at 45° angles, so we get an arched array of 2" drivers delivering the top end, where the percussion and vocals are critical. Here though, we are in a slightly bizarre situation because our throw is relatively short, except for shooting down the sides, so for these gigs we are counting on the stadium's own delay system which is time-corrected by computer."

Brill's goal for the Hell Freezes Over tour was to make each venue a hi-fi environment and deliver a controlled sound without resorting to excess volume. "One of my favourite tools is my little Radio Shack decibel meter. You will never see that go over 100dB. I think it has been up to 99dB, but that's the most it's ever been on this tour! We have moments during the show when you can almost hear a pin drop but at the other extreme, we do crank it up on some of Joe's songs, like 'Rocky Mountain Way'. I like working at a level where I can increase the band's dynamics, whereas a lot of engineers will compress and nail the volume down to one area, but I don't like that. People can do that with a CD at home but when they come to a show, they want to hear a sound that varies in emphasis with the music and their reaction to it."

In his monitor control cockpit, Chris Lantz was running seventy channels and twenty-two on-stage mixes from a Yamaha PM4000 console and a Harrison SM5. A total of twenty-six Clair 12 AM wedges and two drum fills consisting of two 12 AMs and two ML 18 cabinets covered the stage, while nine Garwood Radio Station in-ear monitoring systems (backed up with four spares) were also in use for all of the musicians except Joe Walsh.

Lantz said: "The Harrison is used purely to route to the wedges and I sub them into the main desk, the PM4000. The only effects I'm really using are delays and reverbs from three Yamaha SPX-1000s for vocals. On the acoustic set, when the five of them come down and sit on stools, we add a couple of wedges and move them out front a little further. At that point, the wedges are mainly concentrating on the vocal mix, whereas on the rock set they are carrying a full mix of everything.

"The band members use the ear monitors in one ear only, mainly to hear the vocals and vocal enhancements, but they are also listening to the wedges which fill out the sound. For EQ back-up I have sixteen TC Electronic TC 1128 twenty-eight-band graphics, but with the ear monitors I just rely on parametric EQ from the desk. I feel I need to add some reverb and sweeten up the EQ on the ear monitors and take some of the high end out of them. I find that the combination of the one ear and the wedge is excellent because when you use both ears you're stuck in the same world wherever you are on stage. For some performers, that might be good, but with one ear you can walk around the stage and feel the different pockets of sound and warmth of the speakers with your open ear as well as maintaining a balance with the ear monitor. At the beginning I thought that would be kind of a weird experience, but in reality it works well.

"I've worked with a lot of singers who don't like in-ear monitors and some of the people who do persevere will consistently back off the microphone because their voice sounds so strong in their heads, but it makes it hard for the front-of-house engineer to get a good signal. Personally, I'm a great believer in in-ear monitoring, but it takes some time to get used to." Unlike the desert-hued musical tones of The Eagles, that is, whose internal bickering remained the only obstacle in the way of further live reunions. Money isn't everything, but it's an attractive incentive to some.

CHAPTER ELEVEN

Shed Seven

A Maximum High – 1996

Just as it was in the 1960s, England in the mid Nineties was once again divided into musical regions with their leading bands jostling for pole position in the charts. While Oasis headed the national pack as Mancunian ambassadors, Ocean Colour Scene ruled the Midlands and Blur rated as top Essex lads, Yorkshire's great hopes were Shed Seven whose single 'Going For Gold', well-timed with the Atlanta Olympics, brought them instant acclaim.

November 1996 saw Shed Seven on a UK tour in support of their newest single 'Chasing Rainbows' and second album *A Maximum High* – a fine collection of infectious tunes, albeit over-influenced by the Stones, The Doors, Stone Roses and Oasis, but executed with the kind of commercial BritPop venom that had been dominating the airwaves in recent years.

Less convincing was their copycat live persona, not that this bothered the spirited fans at the Forum in London, but what the band lacked on stage was countered by a dazzling and thoughtful light show, designed and operated by erstwhile Sheds production manager and former Rory Gallagher and Wildhearts LD Pete Sarson, whose choice of Celco's then brand new Ventura 1000 console marked this product's live touring debut.

This Celco innovation followed in the footsteps of its Navigator, Aviator, Major and Gold boards, and was designed to compete favourably with its nearest rivals the Wholehog II, Avolites Sapphire and Compulite Animator. Featuring DMX 512 and Lightwave Research sixteen-bit high resolution output, the Ventura allows the control of 1,000 channels of up to 100 automated fixtures of mixed parameters, with 240 dimming channels over ten pages with 1024 DMX dimmer channels arranged on two lines, and eighteen playback and twenty-four preset faders arranged on two banks of twelve. Its memory stores 500 multi-parameter cues, each of which recall up to three sequences, and there are ninety-nine sequence patterns of up to ninety-nine steps and ninety-nine stack/lists, each with the capacity for 999 entries.

The development of the Ventura could be traced back to September 1995 when Celco originated the specification, although the physical work on the prototype did not begin in earnest until May 1996, leaving just enough time to have a finished model available for viewing at the annual PLASA entertainment technology exhibition in London that September.

Celco's business manager Keith Dale said that many of the ideas for the board were put in place in 1991 with the Navigator. "There was always this concept of having a professional extension wing for the Navigator, with most of the features that we have seen lately in the Wholehog and Wholehog II. Due to other commitments, however, it never got off the ground at the time.

"This has been an expensive R&D project because of the amount of software designers involved. They were just part of a large team dedicated to the Ventura who each worked on specific aspects, such as the screen displays, front panel hardware, the core CPU programme and DMX handlers, and it's all come together in a very short space of time. The experience of seeing it all through has really proved to me just how much the business has changed over the last ten to fifteen years. Back then, it didn't take too long to produce a piece of software but hardware was very time-consuming. Nowadays it's the reverse because of today's sophisticated demands of software, but with modern computer-automated techniques, hardware and circuit design is so quick and easy."

During his ten years in lighting, Sarson had regularly used Celco consoles, his choice often governed not only by the inherent quality but also their compact designs. "When I work abroad with bands, I like to be able to take my preferred board with me," he said. "Sapphires are too big to carry about really and there aren't that many of them around for hire in Europe and Japan. The Navigator was a really small board that came to me recently and its size allowed me to take it on an aeroplane without a problem. When I was in Thailand, I had some difficulty running the board with Intellabeams and I got in touch with Celco to help me solve everything by supplying some personality cards which I tested out for them. I started to develop a relationship with Keith and while I was out all over the world with the Navigator, in clubs and other venues, they began sending me software upgrades and I gave them my opinions on how they worked with specific types of lighting equipment. Eventually, Keith told me about this new board that was coming out and asked if I would contribute to its development, which I did happily."

Bizarrely, Celco's decision to debut the Ventura with Shed Seven, rather than a higher profile act, appeared to have been inspired by a visit to a barber shop. Said Dale: "We thought Pete would be an ideal candidate to take out the first Ventura. He told me he was working for Shed Seven and as a coincidence, I heard the band on the radio in my barber's and thought they were bloody good! We knew several months ago that Pete would get the first bite of the cherry and it's great because although he is a brilliant board operator, he's not so big in the industry that we might lose a degree of communication."

One week before the start of the Sheds' tour, which climaxed at the Barbican in their home city of York on 21 November, Sarson spent three days at Celco learning the ropes on the new desk. He commented: "The first time I saw the Ventura was on a schematic drawing; the second time was a photograph; the third was in the flesh but without software, but even the look of the board had me hooked. When I started learning how to use it, there was no question...it was going on the Shed Seven tour!"

Sarson began working for Shed Seven in 1993 when he and a roadie colleague traversed the country in a Renault van carrying just two Golden Scan 2s and backline equipment. With a truck full of lights for the late 1996 tour, courtesy of Prism Lighting, things had somewhat progressed and the LD reserved much praise for the new Celco product.

Scene Wizard is a facility on the Ventura which offers a selection of preset animated "looks", such as Jungle Greens, Ocean Waves and Moody Blues, from which the user may run an entire show and therefore reduce programming time. Meanwhile, the Auto Select function tracks the current output and permits the user to busk a show by quickly altering the current lighting state. Cue programming is significantly eased by auto tracking which defines three trigonometric positions for lamps to which all stage positions are then referenced.

Sarson commented: "For me, the Ventura offers enormous benefits, not least the fantastic speed of programming. You don't have to go through different menus in screens to find out how to programme a group and edit chases, for example, because it's all in front of you. There is a library of effects which helps you work quickly and you can programme in a colour sequence and get your Scans to circle in a matter of seconds without having to plot the stage. As soon as you programme in a Golden Scan HPE1 as Lamp 1, it does very similar things to the Sapphire only the Ventura's layout of the buttons and faders makes things a lot easier to grasp.

"On the colour palette, it automatically puts in ten colours and four rotating gobos into the beam palette for you. It also selects some preset focuses, so you immediately get ten positions at your disposal. Once you've done that, you really are ready for action. There are twenty colour buttons and to choose red you will, for example, hit button A. If I wanted twenty lamp groups to be in red, I would choose the last selected lamp – number twenty – and select Colour A (red), then enter that by holding down A and pressing Lamps. I would then press Save which effectively saves twenty Scans in red. If you were using a Sapphire or a Jands Hog for the first time, you would have to be shown how to do that. But with the Ventura, if you were shown how to input Lamp 1 as an HPE1 and then told that the colours and beams were already available by selecting these buttons, you would be able to operate the board in minutes...it's that foolproof!"

The addition of a monitor for use with the board is a necessity, not a luxury, said Sarson. "There are four rotaries which can do so many different things and the monitor gives you instant access to so much information about configuration changes, more than you would see on a regular board. You might need five channels for Skyroses and twelve for HPEs, and without the monitor you can't actually see what those rotaries are doing. And the monitor readout is absolutely brilliant.

"People who have told me that they can't understand the Sapphire without being guided around it for a whole day could go on to the Ventura and within an hour would be able to run a show. In that respect, it is the ideal board for festivals. Every reputable hire company used to own a Gold and a Major which were sixty- and ninety-way boards and all the festivals I used to do tended to have one or the other. To programme in cues you very simply pulled back a fader and pressed Enter, and the LDs who looked for that level of simplicity in other boards will, I'm sure, be very impressed with the Ventura."

The Forum was the only venue on the Shed Seven tour where any in-house equipment was used – a decision influenced no doubt by the high premium charged by the management for removing the in-house wares to allow space for touring rigs. (Yorkshire Audio and Prism Lighting serviced the remainder of the tour.) Sarson's own specified rig consisted of six Golden Scan HPEs, eight Martin Pro 400s, two Skyroses driven with DMX colour changers, profile spots with gobo rotators, Mega strobes and a new DMX smoke machine and a DF50 on the front and back truss. These were augmented by 150 of the Forum's own Par cans (gelled with Sarson's own colours) and fourteen Vari*Lite VL5s, controlled from the in-house Avolites board. Sarson limited his use of the VL5s to just five songs, and adopted his normal approach of using specific effects once only in order to give each song a different look.

"The first song, 'Dolphin', starts off with lots of strobing, then slows down and builds up again," he explained. "Their songs are subject to a lot of mood swings, so I react by having the stage looking quite dark and desolate one minute, and then introduce bright flashes of light everywhere. 'Out By My Side' is a very slow and moody number, for which I keep the stage reasonably dark and use just one wash. 'Going For Gold' features the Skyroses and a dot spread gobo in the Scans, as well as coloured sequencing moves and chasing Par cans. That song goes into 'Parallel Lines' at the end of the main set. I focus the Scans on to the mirror ball at the start of that number and then bring in the ACLs as the song warms up. The band had been talking about having a backdrop but I wasn't keen on the idea. I compromised by suggesting that when Rick sings the words 'a maximum high' in 'Parallel Lines', those words would appear on the rear screen. So I made some frames with special video screen paint and the backdrop was painted in the same colour, so it would take the Scan projections and all the different effects. I then painted the words 'a maximum high' in invisible UV paint so that it would only be seen when I introduced the UV guns on that number."

Features aside, cost was a consideration which swayed most customers towards the Ventura, especially as its price tag was around half of the cost of one of the desks it aimed to compete with: the Wholehog II. "In terms of price and performance, and the market slot we have targeted, I believe we have achieved our aims," Keith Dale commented. "When we put together our specifications we have a good history within [Celco's parent company] Electrosonic of knowing exactly how much materials, time and labour will cost. We ended up being only £15 over the Ventura's target cost which by anyone's standards is pretty amazing! We put a lot of quality features in our products and there are elements that we never want to remove, such as the quality of the buttons and faders or just the paint finish. We could get the costs even lower but it would be moving away from the Celco concept."

The interest in the Ventura grew to the extent that within a few months of the product's appearance in the market, Celco had accumulated a £500,000 order book – a phenomenon which the Dartford-based company has not experienced for a number of years. Celco also took on a number of sales and software development staff, including Pete Sarson who, for the moment at least, was happy to come off the road after the Shed Seven tour and pour all his efforts into building the success of the Ventura desk.

"There are so many rental companies that are coming to us whom we haven't heard from in ages and it's all down to this wonderful new desk," says Dale who formed Celco in 1978 as a designer with a rental company before moving into manufacturing.

"When we launched the Aviator desk in 1992, we began to focus more on theatre and television than rock 'n' roll, out of necessity rather than choice. The Ventura is a genuine all-purpose desk which has a place in theatres, but it certainly puts us back into rock 'n' roll and demonstrates our strength at being able to focus on different areas of the performance industry with ease. I feel at home working with road crews; I like that mentality and attitude. So it's great to be back."

CHAPTER TWELVE

East 17

Insomniax Tour – 1996

In terms of advances in concert production, 1996 is likely to be remembered for a major push in the creative use of video. Good camera skills will always find a home on the big screens, but there was a marked increase in the integration of special effects and purpose-shot video footage. British "boy band" East 17 was one such act to embrace the possibilities in this area, and their Insomniax tour of the UK in late 1996 – which culminated in a show at Wembley Arena on 23 December – indicated great potential for their contemporaries.

The visual production relied almost wholly on this blend of live camera shots and pre-recorded footage projected on to three video screens, courtesy of PSL (Presentation Services Limited). Pete Barnes' lighting design was also noteworthy. His LSD-supplied rig consisted of thirty Icons, twelve VL5s, twenty Colourmags, ten Molemags and thirty channels of generics, all controlled from a single Icon board. Few special lighting effects were needed, as most of the visual budget had been reserved for the giant Lorrymage digiwall above the boys.

At the start of the show, an intro video inspired by the Insomniax theme of East 17's latest album was shown across all three screens: the central 4 x 4 digiwall and a 14' x 10.5' Screenworks soft screen at either side of the stage, with rear projection from Barco 8000s. It depicted a late night scene with an owl flying from the left, into the centre and out to the right, along with a sequence of the boys running through trees, and at different times focusing on one member mouthing the words to 'Steam', the opening number. At the end of the sequence, the boys came together in a graveyard on the centre screen, the image exploded, pyros were set off on the blacked-out stage and the boys stepped out from behind Gothic owl statues to a rather warm welcome.

Pete Barnes admitted that the Gothic owl concept was more than a little *Spinal Tap*-esque, but explained that given the theme, it was probably one of the only ways of successfully getting the four boys to the front of the stage in the blackout without the audience seeing them.

Tour manager Phil Byrne commented: "The show was put together in January 1996 and we started in Europe in April. Pete has been involved in the design and construction of East 17's set over the last few years and after I became tour manager in December 1995, the two of us came up with the concept of integrating some of the elements that we had before with some new pieces. Video was always going to be a big part of it and the intro video sequence was dreamed up by Pete and I. We set up the shoot in and around the graveyard at the back of Knebworth House between 8pm and midnight, and by 1am Pete had the whole thing edited. The band's record company loved us because we shot it remarkably cheaply, for about £12,000, so we are quite rightly very proud of it!

"PSL had put their new cube system together but unfortunately it wasn't ready in time for this tour, so we went for the Barco projectors and soft screens. The clarity of the digiwall is just amazing and PSL's professionalism is as superb as ever."

The increased use of video on the current East 17 tour, Barnes said, had much to do with his feeling that young audiences have seen most of what can be achieved with moving lights. "It's very hard to do anything new with lighting, with the tools that are available at the moment. So in looking at creating a new feel for the East 17 show, we concentrated on developing the video aspects further."

His way forward was to employ an ingenious MIDI system which, via musical director Simon Ellis's keyboard, cued video footage from two Sony CRV laser discs and two Sony Betacam 1200 machines, synchronised to the nine-piece backing band's music. The use of this new technology came together over four days during rehearsals at Elstree earlier in 1996.

In charge of the system was video systems technician Derek Burt who explained: "The system was pre-programmed before I got involved although I have since tailored and fine tuned it to the current set under Pete's direction. Simon's keyboards send a MIDI signal on XLR line drivers to an Apple Macintosh computer with on-board specialist Dataton software. The signal is then translated into a cue that looks for a specific point on one of the two video disc and Betacam machines. Via a switcher, these clips are sent to the digiwall in certain sequences depending on the music being played at the time. Even if the band are busking a song and it isn't sequenced, they can repeat a verse or a middle eight section and the video clip will be cued again. It's not a fixed thing where they are locked by SMPTE to a click track."

Barnes added: "Fortunately, the way in which this all works is very simple. As soon as the computer in the video racks receives this MIDI cue it knows which clip to run and it switches from live camera action to the video machine, then switches back to live output when that clip is finished. There is no separate keyboard for this purpose, but simply a separate MIDI output on Simon's sequencer. I just tell him in advance which note to hit on the keyboard and the computer does the rest. There is no added pressure on him unless he changes an arrangement. In which case, we just confer to make sure that the note he is going to hit corresponds with the cue I am expecting. Otherwise, he continues to play the songs as he would normally, and the cues are triggered automatically.

"Any problems we initially had with the MIDI system in rehearsals have now been ironed out. There is a little window that you can open on the computer which shows the MIDI notes coming in and the system status. When that window is open it is one more thing for the computer to do and occasionally a note would be missed because of the drain on the memory."

Burt informed that the recall time from the point when Ellis hits a note to when the image appears on screen was slightly faster than one second, while the Betacam machine, which was used only for the intro and outro sequences, ran a little slower. He said: "Having only learned to use this system from scratch a few weeks before the tour [in December 1996], I am having no problems whatsoever to re-programme and change timings. All I have to do is discuss things with Simon Ellis, and if the timings are not quite right on the incoming MIDI, he can trim it at his end. There are very tight timings in some places and sometimes there's a certain amount of delay by the time the image hits the video wall. So there is always some trimming to do in order to be in time with the music. It's just a case of pre-empting the clips."

The enabling software was, in fact, the third version of Dataton's package which was brand new for this tour and incorporated extra multi-tasking to allow more equipment to be run simultaneously. Burt said: "It's a beautiful piece of software to use. Until I started this job I had never heard of cueing from a keyboard. But really it is just a data stream that gets translated and this technology could be used in a number of different applications. You could actually run pyrotechnics, relays, motors and moving trusses from keyboard or desk cues, and I'm confident that its use will grow. In fact, we could get really carried away with it and have it doing a lot more than we are currently doing, but the art is discipline!"

Sat behind a battery of monitors and control equipment for the whole of the show was video director Blue Leach who, apart from overseeing the playback of laser disc sequences, was mixing source material provided by a total of eight cameras – three manned Sony 537s (one hand-held, two in the pit), and five Panasonic WVKS-152 minicams littered about the stage, fixed to the drums, keyboards, backing vocals, or wherever he pleased from gig to gig. When we spoke, Leach was looking forward to working on the last three dates of the tour with the new Barco 9100 projectors which he described as "quite outstanding".

In tandem with the tastes and techniques of some other contemporary video directors working in live situations at this time, Leach occasionally used a strobing effect on the live output – removing one frame per second – to produce a cinematic effect. Leach, who like Pete Barnes, Simon Ellis and other colleagues went on to work with The Spice Girls, said: "On one of the songs in the middle of the set I have a close-up of [singer] Brian Harvey in black and white, and strobe it for a liquid result. I'm also using some digital video effects (DVEs) such as wipes, spins and different patterns from my For-A VSP-300 vision mixer, and I'll probably use more as the tour progresses. I'd like to use some sepia as well, but it's whatever suits the show because there's no point in introducing DVEs just because they are available to you. They have to be appropriate.

"Sepia would translate well to the digiwall but even better on the Barco projections. The Barcos are there more for the cameras, while the digiwall is essentially for the laser disc output. Forty per cent of the show is all camera work, so in between the laser disc clips I tend to feature mainly close-ups on the digiwall while the Barcos display wider shots from the cameras. It's definitely a case of mixing and matching images, although there are also times when I have the same action appearing across all three screens."

As the lighting designer in a video-led show, Barnes attempted to light the stage in such a way that it would help the cameras, although he pointed out how difficult it is guarantee this to a video director in a live situation. Barnes, who was working on a *Smash Hits* pop tour immediately before going out on the road with East 17, said: "Being a live show, I am running the lighting board with more of a live approach than I would if doing a TV show. It's only reinforcement for the people that are in the venue, whereas if you have five million people watching at home on TV, what you do with the lighting becomes much more important."

For many years, Chris Mounsor was the logistical backbone of audio rental giant Britannia Row Productions. The two-day Oasis concert epic at Knebworth in August 1996, however, marked his last work with the company as he set off for pastures new in his new role as the head of PSL's Concert Touring Division. "Moving from Brit Row has been very exciting," he said. "As a sign-off, I couldn't have done anything bigger or better than Knebworth, so I left on a real high. I've now thrown myself into an industry that is incredibly vibrant and it's a great challenge."

Whereas video screens have been mainly linked with large venues over recent years, their use has widened as they have become less facilitating and more an integral part of shows. No longer do they exist to provide audiences at the back of a venue an enlarged view of the stage action. By the end of 1996, PSL was supplying to seven UK tours (including Boyzone and The Manic Street Preachers) and four tours in America (Alanis Morissette, Smashing Pumpkins, etc), and all of them featured creative footage that was a vital part of the production's overall look. The Manic Street Preachers' Everything Must Go show, for instance, was totally reliant on video clips shot specifically to add a further dimension to five of their numbers.

Mounsor commented: "Video is required now on more and more tours, and it is becoming the norm rather than the exception. It has been a long haul, but many production managers are now regarding video as being as important as any other element of a touring package. We are in a very fortunate position at PSL. Instead of there being thirty companies chasing the same work, as in sound, there are only a couple of players in this market and so we are able to pretty much stick to a standard hire price list. One of the reasons for the lack of competition is that the investment in video equipment is so high that it precludes new companies from entering the game, although costs are beginning to drop and these savings are enabling more bands to include video in their budget.

"Concert touring video is really only about four or five years old and Depeche Mode were among the first wave of bands to be handled by PSL. Being a new industry, there are no pre-conceived ideas of how things are done and so every new job is a fresh challenge, unlike sound where you had a twenty-five-year history to refer to and possibly be chained to."

As far as other elements of the production of East 17's Insomniax show were concerned, the sound at the Brighton Centre in particular appeared to suffer, although this had little to do with the efforts of rental company Wigwam, the sixty-four-box d&b 402 audiotechnik PA system and front-of-house engineer Mike Dolling – it was the hormonally-charged girls (and, somewhat disturbingly, boys) who were to blame! On this tour, Dolling was routinely subjected to insane screaming levels of up to 118dB (as measured at his desk), and this resulted in the listener's apparent loss of top end frequency recognition. As he explained: "Everything begins to sound very dull because the screaming shuts your ears down and you over-compensate by winding up the top end. It becomes a vicious circle."

When Dolling took the FOH reins of The Spice Girls a year later, his ears must have felt like they were on holiday. The screaming reached only 105dB at the desk. Oh, the joys of being a sound engineer for a kids' pop act.

The Who's *Quadrophenia* at the Hyde Park Masters Of Music concert, 1996

Eric Clapton at Masters Of Music

Mark Cunningham with Harvey Goldsmith CBE

Chris Hey of sound designers Spencer-Hey Associates

Chuck Crampton of Unusual Services

Clair Brothers engineer, Dave Kob

Final rehearsal on the eve of the show

Soccer legend Pele meets Ronnie Wood
and son backstage at Masters Of Music

Set designer
Jonathan Park

Mick Double,
production
manager

John Entwistle

Screenco's Anita Page and David Crump

Hyde Park "luminaries": Skippy, Tony Panico and Tom Kenny

Zak Starkey – the nearest thing to Keith Moon since Keith Moon?

Pete Townshend

The Who repeated
Quadrophenia on tour
in 1996-7

Roger Daltrey

Bryan Adams: 18 Til I Die at Wembley Stadium

Mark Cunniffe
(foreground) – controlling
the lights for Adams

The kids wanna rock!

It was the
summer of 96

Monitor
engineer Glen
Collett

Dean Roney
and Jeff Lilly of
Vancouver PA
company Jason
Sound

Hell Froze Over for The Eagles

JD Brill

Spoilt for choice? Don
Felder's axe stash!

Chris Lantz on Eagles monitors

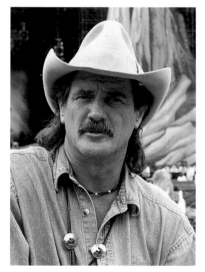

Stetson logic: production manager
Chris Lamb

Lighting director Richard "Nook"
Schoenfield

Shed Seven at The Forum, Kentish Town, London

Pete Sarson lighting the Sheds with the Celco Ventura 1000 controller

East 17: Insomniax at the Brighton Centre

Video director Blue Leach

East 17 tour manager Phil Byrne, Chris
Mounsor of PSL and production manager
Jimmy Innes

The Brit Awards 1997 at Earl's Court

Mick Kluczynski

Toby Allington in the Manor Mobile

The Bee Gees collect the Lifetime Achievement Award at the Brits 97

Recording engineers Mike Oliver and Dave Porter

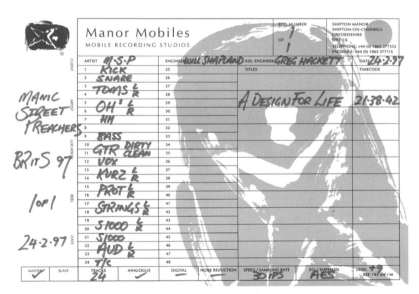

The Manor Mobile's channel sheet for the recording of the Manics' 'A Design For Life'

Sheryl Crow – a Brits highlight

Derrick Zieba and Bryan Grant

Sound engineers Chris
Coxhead and Steve Ludlum

Left and below: two views of Supertramp in rehearsal in Acton, West London for the It's About Time tour

Sound engineers Angus Davidson and Johan Schreuder at work

Cue sheets for Supertramp classics

CHAPTER THIRTEEN

The 1997 Brit Awards

Throughout the Nineties, February has been a red letter month for British pop music fans and television audiences. With the exception of the deaf, dumb and blind, no one living in the UK is able to escape the magnificent media hype which preceded the annual Britannia Music Club Awards, otherwise known as the Brits, the industry barometer for the success of all British pop artists.

In 1997, Earl's Court was the venue for the second year running and all eyes were fixed on the gleaming Bill Laslett-designed stage in the hope that a controversial incident might once again make the news. The previous year bore witness to the hysterical scenes involving Pulp singer Jarvis Cocker's "gatecrashing" of Michael Jackson's performance of 'Earth Song'. However, apart from a brief four-letter outburst from award presenter Elton John and some nonsensical utterance by Kula Shaker's would-be mystic Crispian Mills (neither seen by the TV audience), the show was comparatively mild. If anything, comedian host Ben Elton's normal wit was disappointingly tame.

After a frustrating delay, the event got off to a blistering start when the nation's favourite female act, The Spice Girls were accompanied by copious pyrotechnics for 'Wannabe'. They were followed, in between award ceremonies, by a string of diverse and mostly outstanding performers. Namely, Mark Morrison, Jamiroquai and Diana Ross (singing 'Upside Down'), Skunk Anansie (with an unexpected cover of The Undertones' 'Teenage Kicks'), The Short Bloke Who Was Christened Prince Rogers Nelson (aka The Artist), Fugees, Sheryl Crow,

Manic Street Preachers (who stole the show with their stunning 'A Design For Life') and finally The Bee Gees who, as recipients of their lifetime award, saw fit to play a medley of hits stretching back over thirty years – a sure reminder of their songwriting genius.

While record industry execs and hopeful artists dined at the cost of £350 per head, and other spectators coughed up £100 to sit in the Gods, the truly privileged gained a fantastic view of the proceedings on the front-of-house mix platform...stomach empty but wallet intact. It was here that "the few" jostled for position in between *six* consoles, while engineers Steve Ludlum and Chris Coxhead got on with the frenzied task of balancing the sound for all of the acts, five of which were completely live, the others singing live to playback.

Former Pink Floyd roadie and production manager, Mick Kluczynski seriously burned the midnight oil coordinating all the behind-the-scenes elements of the Brits as the event's production supremo. He pondered on the differences between the demands of this show and non-TV orientated multi-artist festivals. "There are radical differences because anytime that you introduce the element of television, you are immediately working to another discipline altogether," he insisted. "On a festival you are dealing with a show as it happens, in front of a finite audience, and your eye for detail is trained to observe other aspects. Even if there are television cameras at the festival, they are only recording what they see happening live. But this show is driven by a TV director working with a TV set designer who together have the final word about everything. They are God!

"This show is unique in that you have a very important live audience – the record industry – who are ultimately funding it. The most important consideration is what we are delivering to Carlton Television [part of the ITV network] to broadcast the next day. What we are trying to create is the live element of rock 'n' roll in a controlled environment or, if you like, rock 'n' roll that is designed to suit television. In a festival situation, we would be looking for the biggest stage that we could create in a field because we want the guy at the very back of the audience to get a feel for what's happening. At the Brits we are tailoring a very exclusive, five star, luxury environment combined with the freedom of a festival and it must look good on a TV screen. In essence, we are using rock 'n' roll technology to create something special by combining two disciplines."

Derrick Zieba of Dimension Audio, the audio rental company hired to provide all of the sound orientated services since 1993, said that his first contact with the BPI (the show's governing body) was in the previous October when he was made aware of the forthcoming event's venue and date, and an outline of Dimension Audio's involvement and preliminary budgets. He said: "We generally know who the performing bands are about two weeks in advance of the show itself, and sometimes the lead time on detail for those bands in terms of line-up, miking and special requirements can be a just a few days before the event. Obviously the show is a topical one and the organisers want it to be as up to date as possible, so they leave it to the last moment to announce the performers. That gives us the greatest possible problem, because we are estimating everything. On top of that there are lots of politics which govern the way in which we operate. Nevertheless, we still come through!"

Seventy-two hours before showtime, the sound requirements for The Artist were still a mystery to Zieba and his crew. He said: "He is rehearsing tomorrow but we still do not know what he needs from our mics and desk space. But this is the normal pattern for the Brits. We currently have as much information as we're allowed and have estimated how we might cover the performance. We've run it down to two possible scenarios of what he wants to do and how he might stage it: one is a very live affair, the other is where there may be lots of dancers." It turned out to be the latter.

The pattern and style of the Brits has changed from year to year. Owing to a shortage of rehearsal time in 1996 there were a number of technical problems which marred the occasion, and the original intention for 1997 was to have a large percentage of performances to playback, in order to minimise risk. Following a dramatic increase in pre-production time, a reverse decision was put into action. "The live element is very good for the excitement it generates, but having all the necessary information so late in the schedule is not the ideal situation for us. It certainly keeps us on our toes," admitted Zieba.

Rehearsals and soundchecks took place over the weekend prior to the Monday night show. Each band was given a two-hour slot to rehearse their moves while the engineers noted mix positions and TV director David Mallet assessed various camera angles for broadcast purposes. Said Zieba: "Sometimes if it is a particularly complicated set-up, as it is for the Manics with their string section, we will extend that time forward and attempt to make up time in advance. The Manics are coming in early on Saturday and their complex stage set (which combined both live and abstract video footage) will have been pre-prepared before the band and their string section start rehearsing. By and large it is still quite a tight rehearsal schedule. We will get through every band over the weekend and have a final dress rehearsal on Monday which we'll use to go through all the aspects of the show in running order. It's a staggered run through and although we won't go through every number we will rehearse the changeovers."

It was extraordinary to find that even though the event was not to be broadcast to the nation until the following evening, it was run almost wholly without pauses – as if it were being aired as it happened. "Because of the lack of editing time overnight before broadcast on Carlton TV, we all have to treat it as a live event. In the case of two particular acts in the programme, there are just three minutes and six seconds to get one act totally offstage and the next act in place, set up and ready to perform. All this madness happens while awards are taking place on the same stage. That is quite a feat."

Although Dimension Audio was no stranger to the awards, 1997 marked its first tie-up with Britannia Row Productions who were sub-contracted to supply a highly substantial Turbosound PA system. Ironically, it could be argued that Dimension "stole" the Brits contract from Brit Row, who serviced the show up until 1993. Said Zieba: "The size and nature of the event at Earl's Court last year determined that we had to sub-hire an enormous amount of equipment from various sources to add to the core system and contract additional crew. In any show where you are sub-hiring to that degree, clearly not all the equipment you have will be up to your desired standard. There were also problems with interfacing different boards and processing from different suppliers.

"Knowing that it would be a longer event this year with more acts, I felt that my time would be better spent on the audio design, and interfacing with the crew and television personnel. So I've booked the engineers and am overseeing the whole sound effort, while Brit Row have supplied and installed, and are servicing, the entire PA."

Apart from additional load-in/-out hands, Zieba's hand-picked crew consisted of two front-of-house and two monitor engineers, four people on stage to look after the miking and setting up, and Brit Row systems technician and troubleshooter Gerry Fradley. "The arrangement has worked absolutely brilliantly, and all the crew get on very well together," Zieba explained. "We've got the best of both worlds: Brit Row don't have any of the hassle of dealing with the TV company or trying to get information out of bands. I deal with all of that while they deliver all the show's requirements. Because they are such a big rock 'n' roll company, Brit Row have everything that's needed in their warehouse, and so everything interfaces well together first time and consequently this year is a much easier ride. If I'm involved in the Brits again next year I will certainly go down this route and hopefully, with the relationship that has been forged between Dimension Audio and Brit Row, we will use this arrangement on other big shows of this kind."

Walking into the empty auditorium on the Friday, one was immediately drawn to the high-spec PA which was noticeably more complex than that of The Who in the same cavernous venue only two months before, even though the audience was considerably smaller this time around. The system was designed around a BSS-amplified flown Turbosound Flashlight rig, the configuration of which was determined by the television-led nature of the event. With cameras ruling the roost and no space in which to stack sub bass or front fill cabinets, Brit Row's Pete Brotzman organised for the subs to be incorporated into the flown clusters – an unusual technique at the time. In total, the front clusters featured eighteen Flashlight and sixteen bass cabinets, four underhung highs and two underhung mids per side. These clusters were flown at an incredible height to prevent the PA from obstructing camera views of wide stage shots. The side "hangs" for the tribune were four Floodlight boxes and two underhung mids per side; infills consisted of eight Meyer UPAs and four Turbosound bass cabinets per side. Delays in the upper balcony were catered for by four Floodlight per side, while the total of cabinets, left and right, in the main delay clusters amounted to sixteen Flashlight and sixteen bass.

But why this sophistication? Zieba explained: "Firstly, this is not a rock 'n' roll show. Although it contains rock 'n' roll acts, it is primarily an awards event and therein lies a big difference. I organise the sound for a lot of these types of shows and unless the audience are interested in what is being said and which awards are being handed out, you lose those people and this had been happening with the Brits over recent years. It is a very difficult task to control the level of audio on the bands as well as having the presenters' speeches well heard and well covered in the hall.

"When I got involved, one of the principles that I developed for the show was to use a delayed sound system for speech, so that everybody could hear every word of what was being said in the awards ceremony and get fired up by the ad lib quips by people like the Gallagher brothers that may otherwise be lost. That kept the audience's attention and it made for a much better camera cut away to the audience who were obviously excited. For that reason, we have designed this system to operate in a similar way. The delays, underhung speakers in the balcony and gallery throws all guarantee that the award sections of the show are exciting to hear, regardless of the live music."

Sure enough, the system worked brilliantly for both the live music and the presentations, although Ben Elton's voice did fade into the background at times. Despite being capable of bone crunching volume levels, as Oasis fans would readily testify, the Flashlight PA's output was kept to a polite minimum for the benefit of the diners. Zieba said: "We don't want the levels to get out of hand down the front. Of course, it's a massive auditorium and so the idea is that the delay system gives the engineer on the mix platform something to mix to and allow him to generate a decent level rather than one which is uncontrolled at the front. Our aim is to keep things as even as possible throughout the hall."

The lion's share of the mixing duties fell on Steve Ludlum and Chris Coxhead. The division of their responsibilities was very clear: Ludlum mixed most of the live bands, and in cases where bands had their own engineer (such as Jamiroquai's Rick Pope and Skunk Anansie's Dave Ramsay) he "babysat" the desk to ensure everything went smoothly. Ideally suited to the event, not least due to his experience in both rock 'n' roll and award shows, Coxhead was mixing all of the live vocal to playback performances, the walk up "stings", VT inserts, presentations and sections of the show when Ben Elton moved from his lectern for some hand-held mic banter.

"We might assume that most of the acts will bring their own engineers, but it isn't always the rule," said Zieba. "Two years ago when we had Madonna, we were pretty certain that Trip Khalaf would be coming from the States but he didn't arrive, so I mixed Madonna instead and John Roden did the monitors. She was very pleased too! We're never 100% sure until the day of the show exactly who is doing what. But we are well prepared for any situation."

At front-of-house, four Yamaha PM4000 consoles took care of all the acts with the exception of Jamiroquai/Diana Ross whose sound was controlled from a Midas XL3 and an XL3 sixteen-channel stretch board. They were all bussed together into one main console which formed the output for the system. A similar scheme was followed backstage in what could only be described as "monitor village" – a mound of flight cases behind which lay five interlinked XL3s, manned by monitor chief Alan Bradshaw and Gareth Williams. Bradshaw said of the XL3: "It's extremely silent, but in a situation like this one has to make sure that all the inserts on the boards not in use are out and that everything is switched on at the right time. It's not as foolproof as it may seem!"

Both up front and backstage, every artist's requirement in terms of outboard rack equipment was adhered to, especially where graphic equalisers were concerned. Rarely had there been so many BSS FCS-960s gathered together in one place outside the Hertfordshire factory! Other notable toys of the trade in evidence in the two engineering territories included Klark Teknik DN-360 graphics, dbx 160A compressor/limiters, Drawmer gates and compressors, Lexicon 480L digital effects, Eventide H3000 Ultra Harmonizers, a Roland SDE-330 Space Delay (used exclusively for the Manics), Lexicon PCM-70 digital effects, Yamaha Rev 5 digital reverb and Summit DCL-200 dual compressor/limiters. They couldn't go far wrong, could they?

Turbosound wedges were out in full force, although The Bee Gees and Mark Morrison had also requested Garwood in-ear monitors which, Williams said, also proved useful for non-musical applications.

"The in-ears are also used for our shout system which is used during line checking by the front-of-house guys, myself and the Manor truck in between bands. There are two engineers on stage with systems that share one frequency on the Garwoods. It's now a standard Brit Row festival policy to use in-ears for line checking, but for this type of event this kind of system is invaluable because it is so silent and discreet."

He added: "We regularly do festivals where we have two desks and we are operating on the same principle here, only there are five. Whereas at a festival, each band will perform for about an hour and the engineers can get into it, here the performances are literally one song in length and the changeover times are so short. So it might seem that we're putting in a lot of effort with little to show for it. That's why there is so much control backstage, because there is no time to spend on resetting a desk."

In previous years, Dimension Audio specified the pencil-thin, television industry-standard AKG C747 microphone for show presenters. In hindsight, Zieba firmly believes that this was not the right tool for the job. "What we are dealing with are presenters who are used to rock 'n' roll and familiar with a microphone with a head on it," he explained. "We often suffer from instances when because someone didn't know where the mic was or where they were meant to stand, they've actually gone right down on the mic and created havoc with sound systems both in the truck and in the hall. This year we have gone for a different approach which is to put some Neumann KM-140s on goosenecks with pop shields so that the presenters see a mic which they will definitely recognise. We hope the visual aspects of the mic will be reasonable for TV and it will certainly give us an improved audio result."

Whilst not overtly apparent in the hall where most speeches were clearly audible but a little on the thin-sounding side, it was noted that the mic really did deliver the goods for TV when viewed the next evening. Blindingly obvious was the excellent quality of the AKG WMS-900 UHF wireless radio mic system of which eight channels were in use for singers with AKG Tri-Power C5900 hand-held transmitters. By 1997, the system had encouraged the support of many leading names, notably Mick Hucknall, Rod Stewart and Wet Wet Wet's Marti Pellow, but it really came into its own when it saved the 1996 Brits from certain disaster.

Derrick Zieba took up the story: "Through the bands' own choices we supplied Shure VHF radios with Beta 58 heads last year, and as expected they worked perfectly throughout rehearsals and during every single artist warm-up. At about 6.30pm on the evening of the show, however, every microphone was suddenly blighted by interference. The trouble occurred when the doors were opened to let the audience in along with TV crews doing interviews with the artists and following celebrities around. Because the radio frequency spectrum in this country is so tight, they were using equipment that was on the same channels as our hand-held mics. The net effect was such that we had to wipe out all of the Shure mics. Interestingly, the only mics unaffected by this interference and which worked without a problem were the three AKGs we had been loaned by Harman which Mick Hucknall insisted on using. They were his main mic, a back-up and a spare, and we did every single band that needed a hand-held with those."

Needless to say, Zieba's choice for 1997 was enormously influenced by this reliability. "I would have been foolish to have gone with anything other than the AKG WMS-900 equipment," he insisted. "They sounded great for broadcast, they suited the rock 'n' roll side of the show and Harman was kind enough this year to send down one of their engineers, Ian Oakland, with a rack of those mics for us to use. So every hand-held seen on TV, as well as the headset mics used by some artists, are all from AKG. Otherwise we go by all the bands' traditional microphone spec for drums and guitar cabinets, and follow their riders one to one. We don't interchange instrument microphones; as soon as one band is finished, their mics are put away and another set brought on for the next act."

Microphone nursemaid Ian Oakland explained further about the system: "The eight hand-held mics run in TV channel 69 and we actually have the capacity for twelve mics although this would mean a fair amount of doubling up on frequencies. The way Dimension Audio have worked out the frequency allocation and plotting has allowed plenty of spares to be available at any one point during the show. The presenter will always have a spare. When The Spice Girls come on with five mics, the presenters' mics will become spares for them. The receivers are stored in a rack behind the fourth monitor desk and there is an active omni antenna either side of the stage."

In conjunction with Mick Kluczynski, TV expert Bill Laslett designed an imaginative set around a ring theme. While the stage infrastructure was built by StageCo and the rigging supplied by Unusual, all of the elements that created Laslett's set were assembled by Blackfriars. Central to the stage was Screenco's largest JTS-17 JumboTron available, supplied through Black Pig. Measuring 11.76 metres wide by 6.25 metres high, the screen was suspended from a specially-built structure which raised and lowered it depending on set changes during the show. Video screen director was Screenco regular Dick Carruthers who had worked on one of the company's big 1996 highlights: Oasis at Knebworth. As on that show, the video feeds for the Brits came from Creative Technology's 16:9 digital OB truck. CT also provided three cameras and several TV monitors for backstage viewing.

Kluczynski commented before the show: "As well as allowing the audience at the back to see what is happening on stage, we're using the video screen as a creative backdrop, especially in the case of the Manics who have some very interesting footage behind them."

A man with much experience in television lighting and camera work, Brits LD Micky Sutcliffe hired most of his rig from CPL and LSD. The rig comprised eighty Icons, sixteen Golden Scans, eighty-four Robocolors (from Entec), eight Troupers, five Panis on the back truss, 157 VL5s, four Lightning Strikes, two 4kW Sky Arts and around 200 Par cans. The main artist lighting was controlled from an Icon board which also handled the Vari*Lites via DMX. All the architectural lights on the set rings and towers were cued from an Artisan desk, while an Avolites Diamond ran the Robocolors, Scans and conventional lights.

Sutcliffe said: "In working with the JumboTron we have to turn the screen down to minimum brightness because we have the cameras fairly wide open. We have a colouriser on the screen this year so we can turn the brightness down even further this year than Screenco would normally have it set." Screenco's Anita Page advised that the screen brightness was set on level one out of a possible sixteen.

So no Jarvis-like antics in 1997, but the spin-off advantage of such an absence gave all the more emphasis to the attention-deserving music which, when you remove the hype, is what this event is supposed to be about, after all.

CHAPTER FOURTEEN

Supertramp

It's About Time – 1997

They may be casually dismissed in some quarters as rock dinosaurs, but there is a timeless charm about Supertramp's music which filled halls around the world in 1997 as they went on tour for the first time in nine years to promote their album *Some Things Never Change*.

Fans and historians will remember their boundary-breaking Crime Of The Century tour of 1975, one of the first to feature a full production, and the 1979 Breakfast In America shows which represented the band's commercial peak. Nearly two whole decades later, the previews of the 1997 It's About Time tour, witnessed during rehearsals at Black Island Studios in Acton between 9-23 April, made it clear that they had not lost any of the presentation values that set them apart from most of their Seventies peers.

Of the classic Supertramp line-up, only founding vocalist, keyboard player and songwriter Rick Davies and long-term members John Helliwell (sax) and Bob Siebenberg (drums) remained, but the spirit was intact and fuelled by five additional crack musos including bassist Cliff Hugo and former Crowded House keys and guitar man Mark Hart, the replacement for Roger Hodgson who left the band in 1983. The set for the It's About Time tour featured nine songs from *Some Things Never Change*, amongst a twenty-four-song repertoire which naturally included 'The Logical Song', 'Bloody Well Right', 'Goodbye Stranger', 'Give

A Little Bit' and 'School'.

Both Brilliant Stages and Black Island's neighbour Light & Sound Design (London) were involved with the respective staging and lighting supply, meeting designer Roy Bennett's ever discerning specifications. John Gittings of Brilliant was handling the set logistics, concerning himself with the 28' tall x 8' deep brushed aluminium-faceted fan "cones" at either side of the stage. Each of the three musician risers was adorned with an ultra brilliant white paint to reflect the large numbers of moving lights on the show. The production was also notable for Creative Technology's projections of specially commissioned video footage, as well as "Floyd style" random access graphics stored on laser disc. All of which were projected by a Barco 9200 on to an odd-shaped, 56' wide x 26' deep custom-made screen which formed the basis of the set.

Considering that Supertramp's history began in earnest when they were "discovered" playing in Munich in 1969, it was apt that the sound for this "reunion" tour was supplied by Westfalen Sound – the Emsdetten, Germany-based rental outfit formed in 1978, and which later became part of the large POOL production operation. Lars Brogaard intended to join the tour as production manager and although he fulfilled the role for some months during initial rehearsals, his external commitments with Diana Ross prevented any continuation. Instead, Bill Leabody stepped in.

When it came to choosing the front-of-house engineer, Mark Hart did not hesitate to suggest Aussie sound man Angus Davidson, with whom he worked for several years whilst touring with Crowded House and the Finn brothers in the early to mid Nineties. Davidson was more than happy to oblige and although he originally favoured either an EAW or a Turbosound PA for the tour, he took up Brogaard's faxed recommendation to investigate the extraordinary L-Acoustics V-DOSC product of which Westfalen had purchased twenty-four systems in 1996. Supertramp booked the system after evaluating it at the Zenith in Paris.

A sound system which typified the movement towards a new generation of sound reinforcement technology in the mid to late Nineties, V-DOSC (the French abbreviation of *Diffuseur d'Ondes*

Sonores Cylindriques – the "V" refers to the shape of the acoustic loading of the mid/high transducers) was designed by French nuclear physicist Dr Christian Heil in conjunction with Professor Marcel Urban in the late Eighties and first made available in prototype form in late 1992. However, the system had only made its way into the major rental market since 1996, on tours with Bob Dylan and Diana Ross.

Heil had studied conventionally arrayed PA systems and noted several disadvantages with the separation of multiple sources which were intended to create integrity in the sound. Davidson explained the virtues of Heil's curious alternative: "The principles of V-DOSC deal with many of the problems I have been trying to overcome for years. It is an incredibly precise system with a 90° horizontal/0° vertical dispersion pattern and it has been designed to create a cylindrical waveform. It is therefore very directional and phase coherent, and the sound source is extremely linear. However, because of these qualities you have to be very careful about where you point the boxes. If you position them in such a way that you miss some sections of the audience, they will simply hear no direct sound and just the secondary reflections of the room, because the sound does not travel in an expediential spherical wave and is very tight. The characteristics of the system are such that you are listening in the nearfield all the time because of the box design and the way that the drivers are mounted.

"Since it is a 90° system, as soon as you start playing in arenas you need to add on stacks which need to be regarded as a separate PA for audience seating at the sides. But you cannot place these stacks next to the main system because they will destroy the effect of the V-DOSC waveform sculpture technology. In Supertramp's case we are using L-Acoustics ARCS speakers."

The components in each of the V-DOSC cabinets are two 15", four 7" and two 1³/₄" drivers, and while the ARCS in the centre cluster and side fills carry similar drivers, they have a different horn and a 60° vertical/22° horizontal coverage. For the Supertramp tour, the main PA consisted of just sixteen boxes per side – a veritable dream for truck packers, set designers and sound engineers alike, although there were also sixteen Aura Sound 2 x

18" sub basses to consider. But how did this relatively small V-DOSC rig handle the demands of a middle to large scale venue? Westfalen Systems Technician Johan Schreuder said: "The big advantage of having a vertical 0° system is that the cylindrical wave field reduces the dB loss factor in distance doubling and the loss of coherent signals to a physical minimum. The effect of this is that the levels at the back of a hall are much louder than experienced with conventional systems, but to achieve this it does not require the sound to be uncomfortably loud at the front. Between 100 and 200 meters, the SPL only suffers a 3dB loss which I think is remarkable, and an almost weird feeling because your brain is telling you that this should not be happening! You have a very even spread on the horizontal axis even with pink noise because there is only one high end sound source, you do not experience any summing or filtering when you walk from left to right in front of the rig."

Schreuder added: "To be honest, I think V-DOSC is far and away the best system I have ever heard. The results are not achieved through clever tricks. It is simply the work of a mixer, a crossover, an amplifier and a cabinet that has been designed by looking at the subject of sound reinforcement from a completely new angle."

The V-DOSC system was also used for Mike Oldfield's live world premiere of *Tubular Bells 3* at Horseguards Parade, Westminster, in the September of the following year. Front-of-house engineer Gary Bradshaw was not completely new to V-DOSC, having used it on a few European festivals and shows with Simple Minds, Paul Young and Tears For Fears. He said: "I was very impressed with it even though I knew nothing about Christian Heil's principles. I just turned up and thought it sounded great. At one festival in Stockholm there were just eight flown cabs a side with nothing on the stage in a similar sized venue and it was really powerful. I didn't need to insert any system EQ, which was unusual, and it's definitely a system which suits Mike's music well. It looks so clean and neat either side of the stage, and makes a refreshing change from enormous PA stacks."

The Oldfield system, supplied in a joint effort between Westfalen Sound and V-DOSC Rentals UK, comprised twelve flown

V-DOSC cabinets and seven 2 x 18" Heil ground-stacked subs per side, plus two central subs. There were also two pairs of flown ARCS, running in stereo, under the stage canopy, two outfills for the sides of the bleachers, and four ARCS at the back of the stage pointing towards St James' Park.

For Supertramp, a JBL Smaart analysis system was employed as the caretaker for the delays. Said Davidson: "Because V-DOSC is such a precise PA, it becomes important to ensure that your time delays are set perfectly. Now, that may seem a terribly obvious thing to say, but any anomalies that might not be quite so apparent in conventional systems immediately become glaringly noticeable with this because it is so refined."

When Supertramp began their earlier rehearsals in Los Angeles, in-ear monitoring of the Garwood variety was discussed as a possibility, and John Helliwell and trumpeter Lee Thornberg were immediately enthusiastic. Davidson says: "Their instruments are on radios anyway and by introducing IEM their mobility is aided even further. When we arrived at Black Island to rehearse, more and more members of the band started to get in on the act, and so there has been a gradual shift towards the ear moulds."

Down at BSS Audio in suburban Potters Bar, software designer Mark Buchanan, along with Kevin Haggar, had been toiling away throughout the previous year in pursuit of the ultimate PC control package to drive his company's highly successful Omnidrive and Varicurve units. Named Soundbench, and out on the road for the first time with Supertramp, this software brought the front panel operations of these devices into Windows to give the engineer control of the units via a PC monitor. Rather than pressing keys on the actual units, tasks can be performed directly from this software interface at the click of a mouse – a boon for both live professionals and, potentially, the installation market.

Angus Davidson was using a beta version of this software – the final product became widely available towards the end of 1997. "It basically takes the control away from the digital domain and back into the old days of moving faders up and down," he said. "So if you're someone who has grown up using graphics quickly to gain an instant idea of what's going on the room, it's great to be able to achieve the same thing but with a mouse. It has a very fast response time and as you are moving it, the activities on the screen are pretty much reflected in real time. You can save a lot of presets, as is possible on the actual units, but one of the real benefits is that by having a bigger screen you can see your curves and other information much more clearly. It certainly simplifies my job a hell of a lot."

By the time the tour reached the UK in June 1997, Johan Schreuder was virtually operating all of his rack systems via the Soundbench set-up, running it in conjunction with the MIDI line driver. His long term aim was to drive all of the DSP rack units from one PC control station.

This BSS software was driving three Varicurves and two Omnidrives, including the new 1U rack size Omnidrive Compact FDS-355 – yet another BSS product making its debut with Supertramp – which boasted the extended EQ and filtering facilities that so impressed Schreuder. "The Compact is used specifically for the ARCS that cover the nearfield infills, and it is run without any external equalisers because we access the internal EQ in a 2 x two-way configuration. It's fantastic because there are some fifty points of EQ. If I configured it as a crossover and put in another six bands of EQ, I would still have nine EQ points left which is phenomenal."

Also on this tour was the PC-controlled Crown IQ remote controller which operated in conjunction with the Crown M5000 VZ amplification driving the PA. Essentially an ideal tool for monitoring the amps' performance and status from way back at front-of-house position, the IQ provided copious amplifier functions, such as basic volume controls, phase reversal on the inputs and outputs, and several internal controls.

Davidson mixed Supertramp on an automated forty-channel Midas XL4 and a Yamaha O2R digital console. At the outset of the project he was given the choice of either taking the fully automated XL4 or the automated VCA version, but plumped for the latter with ten VCA sub-groups. "I tend to run everything in unity and work off the sub-groups," commented Davidson. "Once I get to a point where I do need to change things, I have so much time now with the automation anyway and the fact that all the effects are MIDI-automated, that I would much rather have the final say dynamically and alter things on the channels as they come to mind.

"The O2R is automating all the percussion and the effects returns, allowing me to gain maximum control over the effects for each song. I actually specified two XL4s for this tour but I'm more than happy with this arrangement, a by-product of it is, of course, that it leaves a bit more room to move around on the mixing riser!"

The sound of the Supertramp shows throughout 1997 proved to be one of several reference points for the shape of things to come in live audio. For many people it was their introduction to the V-DOSC system, which was later put into practice with Italian star Eros Ramazzotti, Rod Stewart, Deep Purple, Van Morrison, Metallica and the stunning, all-star Music For Montserrat benefit concert organised by Sir George Martin, and featuring Sir Paul McCartney, Sting, Eric Clapton, Mark Knopfler and Sir Elton John.

To the audiences, the Supertramp show design was everything one would expect from the imagination of Roy Bennett, who created the visuals shortly before working with Jean Michel Jarre on the Oxygene tour. However, Bennett later described It's About Time as a production he would rather forget. "Supertramp was a big disappointment; a very frustrating tour for me for a number of reasons. There was a problem with their management understanding what it takes to make a show. I don't think they were very clever in how they used their time and people, and they were trying to cut corners where they shouldn't have. That really bothered me and I never felt that we achieved our aims. [Programmer] Guy Forrester was out on that tour and it was certainly nothing to do with him or anything that we had done as a team. We were simply never allowed the chance to get there. When things don't go to plan, I take it very personally and although I wouldn't say it was depressing, Supertramp's show did sap my energy.

"In general, you never get enough time in rehearsals. No matter how much time you get, you could always do with one more day, but that's creative people for you! That's why my operators are there, to develop a system. There's always a bit of frustration and I don't think I've ever walked away from a build-up and said, 'Yeah, that's great, I can go now.' Even in the rare instances when I'm out there for a whole tour, it's still never perfect for me. There's always a little something I could have improved."

CHAPTER FIFTEEN

U2

PopMart – 1997/98

On 25 April, 1997 at the Sam Boyd Stadium in Las Vegas, U2 performed the first show of their first tour since 1993: PopMart. The world's hedonistic capital of gambling provided an appropriate location for the tour's launch, for it was here that U2 committed millions to rewriting the text book on the staging of live shows. At the outset, the jackpot forecast looked good.

Throughout the preceding months, stories had been filtering through the industry about the radical complexity of the production, most of which were greeted with the normal amount of professional scepticism. They said that the "sci-fi supermarket set" would carry the world's biggest video screen. Oh yeah? A 35' high motorised mirrorball lemon will be transporting the band from the A to the B stage. And the whole set would be topped by a 100' golden arch. Were these the same four scruffs as seen at a Canning Town boozer back in 1979? Was this *Spinal Tap* revisited?

It was not until the three-week production build-up at the Sam Boyd that it suddenly became obvious just what all the fuss was about. Standing in the middle of the stadium with the burning Nevada sun against one's back, it was all too easy to become transfixed by the sight of a huge pumpkin orange PA cluster, flown centrally in front of, yes, the biggest LED video screen on the planet – all 150 x 50 feet of it. Such excess deserved to be launched in Vegas's adult playground. In the most grossly overstated way this production, costing upwards of $50 million, boasted the ultimate convergence of audio and visual technologies which aimed to steer the course of live rock 'n' roll in another direction. A far cry from the days of *Boy* and *October*, to be sure.

The tour, which reached the UK in August 1997 and returned to the USA for an indoor leg in October, ran to more than 100 shows over ten months. After a break for Christmas, U2 played a string of shows in South America before taking PopMart to Australia, New Zealand, Japan and the Far East, and finally ending up in Johannesburg for the last show in February 1998. A documentary movie of the tour received its first screening during the Edinburgh Festival in August 1998, and the long-form *U2 PopMart: Live In Mexico City* video was in the shops by the autumn.

Whilst technology was such a focus of PopMart, it rarely detracted from the band's music and particularly Bono's (and guitar hero Edge's) ability to loom larger than the big screen itself at times. The newer material from *Pop*, although condemned as too radical in some quarters upon release, was greeted with increasing respect as the tour rolled on, while 'New Year's Day', 'Pride', 'Where The Streets Have No Name' and other staple anthems regularly incited feverish responses from the consistent sell-out crowds – one's faith in the ability of stadium rock to reach out and move people was restored.

Around 80% of the 200 crew members working on PopMart were involved in the Zoo TV campaign of 1993, while twenty-three went back to the 1987 Joshua Tree tour. But there were some with an even longer association with U2. These included Jake Kennedy, who joined the organisation in 1979 as the band's lighting man and was ruling PopMart as tour director, a title that remained somewhat of a mystery to him. Like the audiences, he is constantly in awe of the band's ability to reinvent themselves, almost on an album-by-album basis. PopMart took such abilities to the extreme.

He commented: "U2 have never done the same thing twice, at any level. They're less afraid than ever to take things on and we were all concerned that this tour should deliver something radically different. Would we scale it right down and play half a dozen clubs in a ground level rock 'n' roll way, or would we attempt to be bigger than Zoo TV? Bit by bit it began to dawn on all of us that the mistake we were making was asking that question in the first place. The question we should have been asking was: 'What is the music telling us we should do?', and it became obvious that none of us wanted to do a small tour. Once we got over that first hurdle we never looked back at Zoo TV. It's good for us to have a new challenge; it keeps an edge to the whole business of putting U2 on stage."

In Vegas, the atmosphere amongst the friendly crew could be best described as one of guarded calm as they prepared for the First Coming Of The Band. Much of the fabrication and construction work was still in progress up until just a few days prior to the first show, with many of the elements manufactured in places as far flung as Belgium, Nottingham and Pennsylvania. All was going smoothly until two weekends before opening night when, right in the middle of the set-up, the stadium played host to a Monster Truck event which forced the evacuation of the front-of-house control hut and the hasty erection of a barrier in front of the stage. Production director Steve Iredale mentioned the possibility of U2 buying out the event to prevent the interruption, but with the large car park areas available at the rear of the stadium for workspace it proved unnecessary.

Richard Hartman, who headed up the pre-production engineering teams on Pink Floyd's Division Bell tour, the Stones' Voodoo Lounge and U2's Zoo TV, was once again involved with U2 as project manager, acting as a conduit between production engineering and design, and working with specialist firm Atelier One. (This was the same man who designed the original Hartman Towers trusses which American roadies introduced to Britain via the Rainbow Theatre in the early Seventies.) Whilst Hartman worried about hiring the right fabrication and welding teams for on-site duties, Steve Iredale was going to bed at night dreaming of trucks and load-in/-out logistics, and the leapfrogging of duplicate structural elements from venue to venue.

Iredale said: "There are three sets of steel for the sub structure and scaffolding of the towers, and the top and bottom of the arch, plus two sets of other production elements, such as the cladding that covers the arch, motorised rigging for lights and sound, and PA support structures including one that has been custom built to achieve the 'wrap' of the cluster. Everything else we just have one of. We have about twenty-eight production trucks connected directly to the U2 organisation. Eight of those are advancing the A and B systems, with the remaining twenty travelling universally. There are fourteen trucks per steel system, giving us a total of about seventy trucks. On top of that we will have the catering, merchandising trucks so at the end of the day we are looking at around eighty, as opposed to forty-six on Zoo TV, so economically it's not something to be proud of because you have to spend half the night loading and unloading!"

Two staging companies were involved: StageCo from Belgium, supplying and building the tower system, and Upfront from Austin, Texas handling the decking. Between the three travelling systems the steel weight was around 840 tonnes. But even more weight was added by twenty-four tonnes of water which was used as staging ballast. Said Iredale: "The arch is capable of withstanding 135km per hour, but we can increase that tolerance by about another 15km with the ballast which may well end up being critical. This is all way past what we needed to know years ago, but as productions become more complex it is critical knowledge."

In detailing every aspect of the PopMart production, one feels compelled to begin with the set design and other visual elements which influenced everything that moved on the show. Willie Williams, whose experience with U2 dates back to their 1982/83 War campaign, set a new precedent even by his own standards when he conjured his new design in association with set architect Mark Fisher. Working to the same A and B stage template that lay at the heart of Zoo TV, the performance area of the main stage was 80' wide x 30' deep, within an overall set of over 100' high, 200' wide and 50' deep. Seventy-five feet from the lip of the main stage was the 24 x 12' B stage which the band visited twice in their performances. But it was the physical attributes and not the statistics that impressed the most.

Williams, who first suggested the PopMart name, explained the origins of his creation: "With all things to do with U2, the various concepts come from dialogue with the band although an awful lot of ideas are suggested by me. February 1996 was the first time I saw the band for a few years and it was then that we started to talk loosely about this tour."

But exactly how much creative input does a band like U2 have in the production design? "The band's involvement is everything and nothing," said Williams. "They are certainly not like David Bowie who can talk to me about lighting in technical terms. He can almost say, 'Let's put a 6 x 12 there,' but U2 will talk about the type of mood and feel they want rather than anything specific. I've found that because I've worked with U2 for fifteen years and have understood the progression of their work, they really trust my instincts. Even though they are not involved in the step-by-step process, their spirit is in every part of what I do. It has also helped that U2 are not difficult people, or if they ever are it's for all the right reasons because they want everything to be the best. Nearly good enough is nowhere near good enough.

"Somehow we have ended up designing the biggest tour in rock history. Apart from the fact that they're Irish, the great thing about U2 is they take their work seriously but they're not prepared to make their shows into monolithic events. The set pieces we have are pure fun. It feels a little bit like the teacher has left the room and we're left alone to write rude words on the blackboard. That's where all the madness comes from, by thinking about what the most ridiculous we can take out on the road might be. It's good for them to have found a way of delegating whilst remaining involved with the overall germination of the design. For me, this is the kind of creative relationship I've always dreamed of, where they appreciate what I'm doing but they're not breathing down my neck."

At the outset of the project, Williams was discussing possibilities with a number of designers, including Gerard Howland, the theatrical designer with whom he collaborated for the Atlanta Olympics. But it was Fisher's ideas which particularly captured Williams' imagination. Fisher said: "The books of ideas that Willie presented to the band had sketches by both Gerard and I. Gerard was producing some neo-classical baroque ideas while I was putting forward more modern, minimalist concepts, and eventually I hit on some of things which became major features of the show. There were times when we were in despair because the band were being quite boring, wanting to do stuff that we thought was dull. We were looking for that elusive moment when we could finally put something in front of them that they suddenly appreciated and understood."

"One of Mark's early architectural drawings of the stage looked a bit like a petrol station, and on the roof it said 'U2000' which was a title we played with for a while," recalled Williams. "But Bono said it looked like a supermarket and that immediately suggested taking a similar kind of a building on tour. So I did a little sketch and for the want of a better name I wrote PopMart on the drawing, and by September, Mark went one better with one of his great front elevation sketches which ended up in the *Pop* CD booklet which was very gratifying!"

Maintaining the supermarket theme (the tour was announced to the US press at a conference held in a K-Mart store), the omnipresent shopping trolley logo was created when Willie Williams was searching for an image to use as a header for fax communications with the band. "It just kind of stayed and everyone accepted it," explained Jake Kennedy. "The supermarket is an honest reflection of the rock 'n' roll business because what we are doing is selling enjoyment, selling albums, T-shirts or whatever. So why not be open about it and play in front of something that resembles a supermarket? We're not saving the world here; what we are really doing is making a living. Just like a shopping mall, we are providing an environment for people to have an enjoyable day out. There's a lot of humour in this, obviously!"

Rising from stage level to the very top of the set was a 100' high Golden Arch, referred to in the production office as the Banana. It would have been naive to even suggest that it resembled one half of a certain fast food chain's logo, but it was almost impossible to drive around the Sam Boyd without developing an appetite for a Big Mac! Mark Fisher leapt to the arch's defence: "It might look familiar but arches have been around a long time. It's a very particular shape of arch – thicker at the top than anything I've seen. This one is formed from various forms of composite honeycomb panels that have been made by two British companies: William Osborne who make lifeboats and SP Offshore who manufacture cabins for oil rigs. It's so high that we're having to put a red or blue light on the top of the arch for aircraft safety. We did something similar on Zoo TV and we're even higher this time."

The crew's lifting into position of the upper arch – in tug of war style – took the best part of an hour and, in the face of a stiff breeze, was an amazing sight to behold. There were debates about which type of crane should be used (sixty, eighty or 120 tonne) and the physical techniques involved. After a gust of wind had everyone biting their lips, the process went smoothly and Steve Iredale breathed a sigh of relief. "When we were getting the arch in place there were no receivers welded into position so we had to spend time fabricating the receivers in situ. Until that point, no one had any idea about what the arch might do at 100' in the air. It could have behaved like a giant sycamore seed in the wind! Eventually, the yellow upper arch cladding will extend all the way down from behind the PA grid to stage level and the lower cladding will be fixed to the rails along the towers. That's all in Los Angeles having rope light fixed to it to give the visual profile and then we will erect it along the same lines as we've done for the upper arch. The arch is on a track system. Each panel is a metre high by 2.4 metres wide, and to slot in place they will follow each other up the arch on custom built carriers and slide up on two sets of Unitrack." Manufacturers Triple E had to reconfigure the track so that not only did it curve on a different plane, but it could be constructed and de-rigged without the use of hand tools.

Audiences decided for themselves whether Williams' idea to feature at stage left both a 35' high mirrorball lemon and a huge olive speared by a 100' "toothpick" as part of the set was the work of either a genius or a madman. He took the acclaim or the criticism in his stride, because for him and Mark Fisher it all represented enormous fun...with a large budget. Said Fisher: "We think we've designed the world's largest lemon. If not, then it's certainly the world's largest mirror ball lemon that can carry four people inside it, and open and shut." The lemon was also internally lit with yellow fluorescents and even spewed out lemon scented fog at key moments, thus proving U2's will and financial means to play out the role of rock's jesters, whatever the cost.

Approximately the size of a regular London terraced house, the lemon was built by Brilliant Stages at its Greenford, Middlesex base. MD Charlie Kail had seen some outrageous designs pass through his company before, but during the lemon's outdoor construction, he often had cause to rub his eyes when he looked out of his office window to check on the progress!

It was a hot and dry Saturday afternoon in the desert wasteland behind the Sam Boyd when a dedicated crew unpacked the fragile one and a half tonnes' worth of mirror panels and began fixing them to the lemon chassis. To remove the lemon from the truck at each venue, a system was devised to use a petrol-driven engine. Once driven from the car park and into the venue, it transferred to an hydraulic operation which ran the lemon on a track system. The hydraulics, organised by Michael Tait of Tait Towers and Charlie Kail, provided a leverage for the central stem which raised and lowered the top half of the lemon.

To the strains of a remixed 'Pop Musik' (M's 1979 classic), a small trap door allowed the band to enter the lemon as it moved out along the B stage. A computerised staircase appeared, and the top of the lemon was raised to reveal the band and as they stepped out on to the B stage. "Lemon entry, dear Watson!" was the standing joke amongst the crew.

Williams glowed with fruity pride: "I love the lemon and there's this special moment in the show every night when the four band members of U2, the same four who were at school together in 1976 and became this huge success, are in this small room with just a couple of wardrobe assistants, totally isolated from the audience and road crew. The lighting's bright as hell and all the walls are revolving, so the experience is like riding to work inside a cement mixer!"

Whereas the lemon icon had been a part of U2 culture since they recorded their song 'Lemon' for the *Zooropa* album, the olive (about the size of a VW Beetle) was totally new. Exactly how was this to fit into the set? "On a cocktail stick, naturally!" laughed Fisher. "I drew that on when I was playing around with an idea to include a planet with orbits, like a generic Fifties piece of decoration. I became aware that we were pastiching Fifties styling, the type found in LA and Miami coffee bars and motels, and I started looking further. In that same period there were lots of space age designs entering all areas of life. I originally drew a spike on the edge of the stage with a planet and an orbit, then Willie was sitting in Miami sometime before Christmas and as he gazed into his Martini he suddenly thought, 'Hey, it needs to be a giant stuffed fibre glass olive!'" But of course.

Having successfully introduced the B stage concept to U2 on their Zoo TV tour, Williams and Fisher moved it from one side of the stadium field to the other for PopMart. Said Jake Kennedy: "I met a lot of people, particularly musicians, who really liked the B stage and felt that it was the part of the show that meant the most to them. The band were in the middle of the audience performing a mostly acoustic set and the barrier that naturally existed between them and the audience in a stadium show just disappeared. That's always a challenge to U2 – they are very conscious of reaching the crowd and try to overcome those perceived barriers. So the B stage was automatically incorporated into the set design; it was something that didn't really require much discussion apart from asking ourselves how we could maximise the use of it."

Of all the progressions on this tour, it is the startling SmartVision LED video screen which will live the longest in the memories of the audiences. Built by Montreal-based Saco Controls Inc and Lorrymage Technologies (the Belgian company behind the Zoo TV video cubes), and measuring 150 x 50' (750 square metres), it was at the time the largest video screen in the world for a live music application. What it absolutely represented was the beginning of a new generation of video screen systems that not only kick-started a race among manufacturers for improved image resolution within the LED technology genre (as seen the following year on The Spice Girls' SpiceWorld tour and also Janet Jackson's Velvet Rope production), but it also began to influence radical departures in set design.

At an early stage in the discussions about PopMart, it was decided that a large screen would act as a backdrop for the band. However, existing screen technology was either too bulky or too expensive. Once Mark Fisher discovered that recent developments in LED technology would at last afford images of a useful quality, and that a lightweight surface consisting of aluminium tubes could be manufactured, it all began to look possible. "Willie and I were talking about various methods, and I'd seen LED screen demonstrations [in 1996] in New York and had the idea of taking what was basically a high resolution screen, then expanding it so that the pixels were further apart. The main difference between this and other screen formats is that LEDs are not affected by reflections, so what you are seeing is a pure image with very solid colour. From the day we first saw LEDs and realised what we could do with them, the screen took four months to design and build, which is quite remarkable."

Whilst Lorrymage Technologies constructed the screen at its Torhout factory, Saco Controls designed its video processor and LED electronics. Key to the quality of the images was the recent availability of the new blue LED. Saco's Fred Jalbout commented: "The travel of video data in real time on a 50' high surface is not easy, so Fredric Opsomer (Lorrymage project manager) visited our company to find the right LED for the project. By having the blue in high intensity and also a true green LED it helps enormously to produce a full colour screen with 16.7 million colours. The LED we have chosen is a very low-current LED, with high brightness and a high view angle. At 180° from the centre of the screen you are able to see the colour without any colour shift. We have positioned the LEDs in a triangular pixel formation in such a way that the quality of image is constant whether a person is seated on the left or right of the stadium.

"The more LEDs you have mounted within a square metre, the brighter the surface will become. In daylight, you don't see the information because of the gaps between the pixel tubes and the fact that there is not a black backdrop to the stage. The tubes are gold [and red if you counted the painted-on PopMart logo] and therefore the sunlight reflects on them. You cannot compete with the sun for brightness!"

Ten pm on the evening of Thursday 10 April was a landmark hour for the production team, as they gathered en masse in the Sam Boyd to see the screen up and running, and showing a full demo of video sequences for the first time. Despite the absence of several pixel panels which were still to be fitted, never before had so much brightness been emitted from a screen in a concert venue. In the centre of the screen was a high resolution area which carried a higher pixel count than the remainder of the surface. This portion's brightness was measured at 8,000 candela per square metre – approximately four times brighter than the low resolution area (2,100 candela). (It was possible to switch the whole surface to a low resolution output so that it acted in unison.)

Three video processors with NTSC and RGB inputs, and twenty-four-bit digital output, each processed the images for one-third of the screen, and there was the ability to either divide an image in three or send a single full screen image to the entire surface.

When faced with the challenge of designing the screen's mechanical construction in relatively breakneck time, Fredric Opsomer was concerned that because of its 50' height, the end product should be simple to rig. He said: "These extremely lightweight aluminium tubes are easily removed from a flight case. There are 4,500 tubes mounted on to 175 panels and our biggest problem was to make sure that when we folded those panels together, the LEDs did not connect. So we designed a special locking double hinge to give space between the LEDs so that the panel always stays at 180°."

Economically, the screen was a winner all the way. On Zoo TV, U2's 100 square metre digiwall cubes required nine trucks. The new SmartVision screen, however, was neatly packed in just two. Power consumption was another major issue and one-third of the screen drew only ten amps/380 volts, which in the grand scheme of things was small potatoes for this field of application.

But as far as image quality was concerned, there were many critics. By the very nature of LED technology on such a grand scale, if one was stood at the very back of the stadium, the overall picture was simply stunning. However, the closer the audience is to an LED screen of any type, the more the images will pixillate, but that was not a concern to Willie Williams. He commented: "The images turn into *Blade Runner* or an electronic painting because of that wonderful pixillation. I even enhance the pixillation at times because there's almost a disappointment that it's too clean, amazingly. I had to commission all the video pieces before I saw the screen, so I was mostly guessing what the resolution would be like. Being as it is LED technology, it has a different look to everything else in rock 'n' roll right now and I've been really surprised at the way the screen has reacted to certain kinds of material."

Williams pondered over the readability of the camera pictures on the low resolution area. As live images, they are not post-produced and it is difficult in concert situations to achieve optimum lighting angles. He said: "I thought that would be the ultimate test but the camera pictures read wonderfully, as do a lot of the simple graphics. Others don't and I've found it has a lot to do with movement and familiarity. Camera pictures are complex but they are very recognisable. The more complex images are, however, the more you lose the ability to read them because they're overpowering.

"A lot of my hunches were right. It's such a different experience and restraint will be the key. You can have the most wonderful visual thing in the world, but if you overuse it from the start of the show, the audience might get a little bored by the second half."

With a surface this large to work with, the last thing on Willie Williams' mind was to fill it with bland material. In fact, most of the video footage was hard-edged, abstract material from strange and interesting sources. The curator of the video imagery was Catherine Owens, a New York-based Irish artist who worked on Zoo TV and whose firm grip of the U2 aesthetic prepared her well for the demands of PopMart. A valued reference point for contemporary art, Owens spent five months scouring the globe to amass a colossal range of footage from college students and new, unknown video artists to such acclaimed sources as Roy Lichtenstein (who died during the tour, aged seventy-three) and the Andy Warhol Estate.

No one was more delighted with Owens' treasure trove than Williams. He enthused: "Because we wanted to have an energetic Nineties take on Pop Art concepts and not be backward looking, Catherine paired off Sixties Pop artists with Nineties animators and the results have been startling. A lot of the material is animated due to the resolution of the screen. We thought that a mix of computerised and old-fashioned painted cell animation would be an interesting way to go, and she found that most of the people we wanted to use were in London. You can put just about any soundtrack to a piece of animation and the two elements will gel brilliantly.

"It was a great buzz to animate some of Roy Lichtenstein's pieces, like the jet fighters. Similarly there is an Andy Warhol piece [Monroe imagery] that the Warhol Foundation gave us, and we also have the only piece of animation that Keith Haring ever made. It's been sitting in a vault for years and has never been seen until now. So this is a very exciting area to be working in because it's not being done by anyone else at the moment."

In contrast to Zoo TV, on which video sequences were shot and precisely edited for specific songs, the more free-form PopMart approach was influenced by Williams' experience of a previous REM tour. He says: "If you go to see a Broadway show it's the same every night, but there is something about rock 'n' roll that incites an expectancy of spontaneity. But the script is actually a pretty good idea and U2 have found some middle ground by sticking to a set list in essence. As a designer, however, you kind of wonder what would happen if you let go of the reins and that's what that REM show was all about. They played a different set list every night and my brief to the filmmakers was to make an unedited piece of film which we mixed around each night with varying degrees of success. My brief to the artists and animators was that even if they had specific songs in mind they should not edit to music, and as such there are only a couple of points in the show where video is precisely synchronised."

Video director Monica Caston began her touring career in 1984 and became an assistant director after working on several corporate projects. San Francisco-based, like Williams, she collaborated with him on numerous tours, including the Stones' Voodoo Lounge, David Bowie's Glass Spider and Zoo TV. In addition, she directed Michael Jackson's show for the Sultan of Brunei in Jeradong Park in the summer of 1996. "I've tried to look for projects that are challenging but short term," she said, "although PopMart is anything but short term!"

Presiding over a battery of PSL-furnished equipment, Caston's main control tool was her a twenty-two-input Grass Valley 250 console with two fadeable mix effects (ME) busses and two aux busses. Her two types of DVE sources were the four-channel Abekas DVEOUS from Sytex and the Snell & Wilcox Magic DaVE, both of which offered typical manipulation such as image stretching, positioning, colourising, strobing and posterising, in addition to creating star fields, shadows and light boxes.

Caston commented: "I've used the Grass Valley 250 before and I needed the different ME busses for fadeability, because the transitions of getting the pictures on and off the screen are critical. Once you tie material up with DVEs and you are going direct to screens, you don't have control over the fading. There is no master fade to black on the screen so you have to be very careful about the images you put up there. There is certainly an awful lot of stuff to keep track of."

All of the images, including those collected on tape by Catherine

Owens, were stored on two ProFile hard disk drives from Tectronics, one of which acted purely as a back-up. At the speed Caston recorded the material, the ProFile was able to store up to three and a half hours of images. Supporting the hard disk medium were two Sony Betacam BVW-75 VTRs and a Sony SVO-9600 S-VHS HiFi recorder, all of which formed part of a large editing system to prepare clips for dumping to hard disk. Caston said: "Three and a half hours will be enough material because on Zoo TV we had nine hours of video stored as fixed items on laser disc, which was a bit of a nightmare. What's so good about the ProFile is that if something doesn't work you can go in and re-record over it, and all the images have a fantastic digital quality."

The show was blessed with six brand new Ikegami HL59W cameras which switch between normal 4:3 TV aspect ratio and the more filmic 16:9. Caston required this switching feature in order for her camera operators to quickly change to wide angle shots and therefore place more information on the screen at given times. She used two long lenses in the house – a 70:1 lens at the front-of-house mix position, and a 55:1 in front of one of the delay towers at house right. On stage were three hand-helds – one at stage right, one at stage left and one upstage near the drum riser.

Caston also had a Jimmy Jib boom. She said: "We currently have it in the front pit but we might actually have it on stage, because I need it in the best position to cover my basic Bono shots. He likes his microphone tilted and that makes it difficult to get a good angle on him for face shots. It's really down to me to do the best I can with what is comfortable for the band. Where I am positioned in the front-of-house tent, it's nice to be able to see the whole screen clearly. I try to look at the screen as much as I can while hitting the console switches. Even though I have very good cameramen in place there might be something else happening on stage that I notice should be covered. I like to experience the overall effect of what's going on, so that I can time the dissolves correctly and know that the video is working in the way it should. If the audience is going absolutely insane, maybe the crowd reaction is the thing that should be on the screen and not the video footage. That's obviously an aspect that will change from show to show."

The video team also incorporated a wireless miniature CCD chip camera into a headset device and a pair of glasses for Bono to wear for one or more songs. The aim was to simulate a "night patrol" view of the audience and stage which was colourised for added effect.

Video sequences for the PopMart show were pre-programmed with all cues locked into a main computer which recalled effects on the switcher and DVEs. The enabling software, designed by ARTI (Advanced Remote Technologies Inc) of Campbell, California, was previously used by Caston on Voodoo Lounge, and together on-site with ARTI chairman Michael Short she developed her own personal files for the show. She said: "You load in each cue and everything you need, like router points, the effects or switcher direction, can be preset instantly. It'll also programme chains of cues that may be recalled in one song, but my assistant director will be handling all that while I am tied up with directing the cameras."

The ARTI networking software so beneficial to PopMart was the fruit of over a decade's work, and basically employed the same principle as that used on several American TV game shows, such as *Jeopardy*. Michael Short essentially designed the system for production and post-production applications, and although it relied on standard computers, the software was production orientated.

Short explained: "The underlying backbone of the network needed to connect into the servers, the VTRs, the DVEs, the routers and video switchers, lighting systems and MIDI instruments, so it became a problem of translating and interpreting protocols and synchronising all this together. We grew up in this world where you're only given a month to develop something specific for a distinct end user and get it working, but on Academy Award shows you often have only a couple of days. So in some ways I guess we've been fortunate with PopMart.

"This software handles all the mix effect recalls from the Grass Valley switcher and if Monica is mixing on ME1 to a portion of the screen, I may be programming ME2 under computer control, so we are sharing the resource. We have a Leitch 32 x 32 routing system which allows us to route signals directly to the screen at any time, and we're also interfaced to all of the processors on stage for the screen itself and can determine the brightness, colour, picture sizing and contrast levels."

Short was on hand throughout the production build-up and rehearsals to train the video team in the use of the system. The network software remained in place for the whole tour until it was necessary for the video hardware to be changed, at which point Short re-programmed it by remotely connecting to the touring system via the Internet or dedicated land lines.

It was not unknown for U2 to alter their set list at the eleventh hour, and although there were limitations with Caston's system she was able to cope with the re-assigning of accompanying video material. Even the impromptu extension of guitar solos didn't cause a problem. "My job isn't really affected in those cases because I simply wait for that solo to end and then hit the next cue," said Caston. "The Edge is actually triggering video material through the MIDI rack, so if hc triggers early, it just all happens early. Some people use MIDI as a computer signal output or MIDI is converted to SMPTE time code to which the video equipment responds. It is triggered on stage by either a keyboard or foot switch and if a cue is set up at 00:00:00:00, I pre-roll everything two frames forward so that when either Edge or Des Broadbery [Edge's guitar tech] hits the key everything will roll precisely. It's rather like lighting where you build a lot of macros and sequences, and in this case it might be cueing up some video to playback or recalling an effect on the switcher and setting up a DVE to squeeze something into the corner of the screen. You can do all that at once as a macro and then slide it into the programme whenever it's required.

"One of the effects of U2 pushing the limitations of technology is that they are always willing to let you be dangerous, but you can always step back. If I couldn't do that and didn't have this technology and a crew that will go to the limit, then it wouldn't be fun. And if it's not fun there is no reason to leave home! But all of us are aware that even if the lights went out and the video stopped rolling, U2 would be able to keep the audience on their feet just on the merits of their music alone. They are the reason the audience have bought their tickets, but one thing is for sure, they are going to get their money's worth this time."

The integration of video is a continuing facet of live rock 'n' roll, but even on Zoo TV where it was adopted as an art form rather than for pure reinforcement, it remained quite separate from lighting. PopMart, however, witnessed the first real merging of these two disciplines. Owing to its slats and protruding LEDs, it was possible to light the screen like a cyc and shine lights through it from behind as well as showing video pictures. Together on one canvas, the combination of the moving image with lights – supplied by LSD – made for compelling viewing.

Appropriately for a man who began his career as an LD, Willie Williams took on the responsibility of both the set and lighting design. He predicted enormous potential for the video/lighting marriage: "If you light somebody from the side so that their face is sculptured in black, you can put the image up on the screen as an outline of that person. Where the person is lit you will see perfect flesh tones, but where it should be black, you can insert psychedelic patterns and perform a kind of live chromakey. Many of these patterns come from the generative computer art programme Bliss. You give it the parameters that you want to work within and it generates its own vivid images. You can also light the image from the back and we have a whole bunch of Maxi Brute Par 64 nine-lights behind the screen which deliver an astonishing effect as they poke through the picture."

As ever with his lighting, Williams' intention was to steer clear of an overly complex approach, but with a show of this scale even the most simple design required a large volume of elements to cover the set. "It became obvious that some kind of colour changer light was going to be necessary and I was most surprised to find that High End Systems had the winner with the Studio Colors. I'm not a major Vari*Lite user but I thought this might be an opportunity to take the new VL5Arcs on board because they were smaller and less clever-looking. I'm more interested in achieving motion in the lighting without doing it through physical movement, and whether that is by colour rolls or subtle chases it doesn't matter as long as I can get the feel of motion. I did three shoot-outs between the two products in various indoor and outdoor conditions, and the Studio Colors put out more light and just had what it took. I had never really taken High End seriously as a company before now, especially their Dataflash product, so it just shows you!"

LD Bruce Ramus was equally impressed by High End's Studio Colors, which made their debut in premier league touring with Metallica. He commented: "The Studio Colors are operating brilliantly. We've been beating their colour mechanisms to death and they still work fine. There are 190 of them all tolled – 112 in the air as wash lights, and for colour strobing and beam shaping, and eighty on the ground which mostly light the arch and sides of the stage."

Like everything else in view, the lighting positions were dictated by the architecture. Under the roof rig there were sixty Studio Colors, whilst three 70kW Lightning Strikes provided typical looks. Eight-light cells focused on the rear of the PA and nine-lights lined the stage at floor level. To underline the bottom of the screen, there were standard stadium issue sports lights which ran all the way from left to right. There were eighteen follow spots – eight 1,200 watt Star Flights on stage, three 2kW Xenon short throws under the PA and seven 3kW Gladiators in the house. Ramus said: "We have manually-operated spots on the arch that poke out of holes in the cladding. Willie and I both like the fluidity that comes of random manual movement, so there was a conscious decision to not use any of the automated spots."

Custom-made for PopMart by Wynne Willson Gottelier's Peter Wynne-Willson (the lighting expert behind Pink Floyd during the Sixties psychedelic era) was a new product called the Razorhead – a light which evolved from the 360° x 360° two-axis revolving head concept he designed for the Coemar NAT light. It included break-up and multi-colour change layers, and several of them were positioned in the house, spinning large 27" elliptical beam heads on 7kW Xenons. Additional Xenons, with dousers, remote strikes and focus capability, ringed the stadium. When all were firing endlessly skyward, they made even a 50' high screen pale in comparison and were particularly effective during the B stage segments. This stage relied on key light spots and underneath its perspex disco floor [just right for the song 'Discotheque'] there were eight Molefay lights and strobes to add what Williams described as "gratuitous nonsense!".

He added: "The house lights bring the show into the audience, and you need that to provide some form of relief from the big screen. I felt the biggest compromise on Zoo TV was with the stage set. As the tour went on, more and more of the staging elements disappeared, largely to pay for the video! I really wanted to address that balance because you can only take so much visual information from a video screen and I wanted more physical gags in the show to strike a balance."

Of the remaining lighting elements, perhaps the most noteworthy was the one and three-quarter miles of Crystal fluorescent rope light in the arch, the PA and, well, everywhere it seemed. Williams specified this not just for its kitsch value, but also because in certain scenes it looked so graceful. "I suppose you get two gags for the price of one because you can have a very still and lovely look one moment, and then you can chase it and it becomes a piece of comedy. I realise we are sometimes teetering on the edge of it being either incredibly great or fantastically crap, but that's for the audience to decide!"

Bruce Ramus, whose association with Williams dated back seven years, was driving the light show from the same Avolites QM500 180-way console that U2 purchased way back in 1984 for the Unforgettable Fire tour. "It's been a real workhorse," Ramus admitted. "We output analogue to analogue through an Avolites analogue rack, and run analogue to digital via an interface that runs all the house Xenons that I can strike remotely. We also have relays for the sports lights and flexiflash. Analogue is as good as ever. You hit the button and see the light...it's dead simple but it knocks you out every time."

Working behind Ramus was Icon board operator Tom Thompson who took specific charge of fifty-four Terra Strobes, the periscope heads and all of the Studio Colors. The latter were run through LSD's newly-developed Universal Guest Luminaire Interface (UGLI) fixture control modules which translates Icon language into DMX language. Thompson commented: "UGLI is brand new for this tour and the way in which it has been designed has avoided a lot of patent infringements." The Icon man used an Apple Newton think pad to download cues and climbed atop the PA cluster to focus the lights on the top of the arch. "On a rig this size you can't see half of your lights, so it's a great opportunity to use this kind of technique."

Almost from the moment that Mark Fisher was poised with pen in hand to make the first sketches of the PopMart set, the traditional formula of stacking PA cabinets at stage left and right was under threat. Fisher's drawings dictated that not only would the PA be based around a single, centrally-flown cluster, but also that it would contain a minimal amount of boxes...all coloured orange! The central cluster concept was not wholly original. Back in the Thirties, Altec Lansing's whole system was based on this principle, and in the early Seventies The Grateful Dead's system contained a central vocal cluster in front of their legendary "wall of sound" columns. More recently, it became the norm to have a centralised PA at London's bowl-shaped Royal Albert Hall. But for stadium tours on U2's level, this represented a brave new world.

As Willie Williams so eloquently put it: "Getting rid of the PA bookends is a great and glorious victory for the human race as far as I am concerned, because for the first time you are actually taking possession of the whole of the end of the stadium and there are no blank areas filled by speaker cabinets."

For Mark Fisher, it fulfilled a long-time ambition: "The biggest dominators of the live rock 'n' roll landscape are the two symmetrical PA wings. It's been in my mind for years to try to change that but there has always been a political obstacle. For a start, you have to work with a band that will actually consider such a departure and, instinctively, the PA companies' necks are on the line so they will tell you it can't be done. It's not in their interests to experiment so why would they say anything else? It involves greater cost, uncertainty and responsibility without the opportunity to test it, and I understand all those problems very well. So they are being squeezed when someone like me comes along and is working with a band that likes the idea of implementing a major change to a conventional PA arrangement."

As the man ultimately responsible for ensuring top results whatever the colour and shape of the PA, Joe O'Herlihy was understandably cautious: "To a certain extent set designers have ruled all the territories of live performance for a long time and given a free rein, they will normally forget about the PA system when they are drawing up their plans. My good friend Tony Blanc went to a production meeting for David Bowie's Glass Spider tour and everything was hunky dory with everyone saying how wonderful the set design was until Tony said, 'Well, where does the PA go, boys?' It took a few seconds to translate that in everyone's minds, by which point everyone looked at the drawings in utter disbelief. 'Ugh!' He got a quick wink and a nod from David. 'Nice one, Tony! I guess it's back to the drawing board.'"

Finding the right sound rental company to take on the job was not straightforward. Clair Brothers Audio was automatically in the frame, having served U2 since 1984, but with the re-evaluation of all of U2's touring vendors on the cards, the audio contract was far from cut and dried, and a shoot-out between Clair Bros, Britannia Row and SSE ensued. Brit Row's involvement came as a result of Fisher setting the cat among the pigeons. He said: "I drew the first PA cluster in the sky as a Brit Row Turbosound PA just so that everybody would be able to see what it look like if it wasn't a Clair PA. In fact, I originally sketched the PA on two twisted, post-modern antelope horns. It's true that for a considerable time, Clairs said that what was being proposed would be impossible which did create rather an odd situation. There were people who were willing to do the most wonderful things but Brit Row appeared to be the only vendor either able or willing to deliver what we were looking for, because of the size of the boxes. They effectively put the squeeze on Clairs because they were the ones who said they could accommodate our wishes, and therefore Clairs were manoeuvred into a position where they had to either decide they could also do it or lose the gig.

"Eventually, Roy Clair had a crunch meeting with the band and came away with the account, most probably because his company was so familiar to U2 and that it may have been too much of a risk to change suppliers in such a crucial area of something this big. I'm sure Bryan Grant wouldn't have liked painting the blue Turbo boxes orange, but my guess is that he would have done to get the gig! [Grant later admitted he would not have outruled the prospect!] What Clairs have done works perfectly well which is blindingly obvious to anyone in the business of sound because U2 have always mixed their sound in mono to a certain extent. It's all to do with this business of trying to advance the science of presenting live rock shows that look interesting and give good value to the public."

Clair Bros crew chief and assistant front-of-house engineer Jo Ravitch took pride in his company's ability to conduct customised work, but this rig presented an almighty challenge. Originally, the cluster was to feature sixty standard Clair S4 P-type cabinets in six rows of ten (this JBL-loaded box, introduced in 1975, just won't go away!). A test hang on a grid in a Nottingham steel mill in February, however, showed that when the cluster was pulled back to form the desired wrap, the corners of the bottom row boxes collided. Whilst the top five rows were all long-throw boxes, the design called for the remainder to be short-throw trapezoidal cabinets, but the non-existence of such S4s meant that a special set of cabinets with tapered sides had to be built quickly.

Ravitch said: "I don't know of any other supplier that would have either the desire and technical ability to do that if they were faced with a similar situation, but we saw it as a real test of strength along the way to getting the job done. Fortunately that was one of the things that we had the most lead time on. The decision to paint the boxes orange was made much later and it was a very specific shade of orange that was required [Pantone Orange 21]. Painting a black speaker orange isn't simple. The coating process took quite a while, with the intermediary primer stage before the orange went on. It'll have to be touched up every day when we fly it."

With the cluster at a 45' trim height from the stage, there was theoretically nothing in its path to stop it directing sound to all four corners of the stadium. Supplementing the "Flying Pumpkin" were two side columns of eleven S4s at each side of the stage which tucked in to the ends of the screen to direct sound into seating areas which would not otherwise be covered. There was a cluster of eight P4s centred underneath the front thrust of the stage and another four per side off stage for corner coverage. Out on the B stage were another eight P4s to help the band gain a feel for their performance. Meanwhile, forty-six blue subs, driven by seven Crown Macrotech 10000 amplifiers, formed a line across the front of the main stage. These subs were, in fact, old S4s. Clair Bros' policy had been to convert damaged S4s into sub basses, and whilst the crew were a little anxious about the low end capability of the system as a whole, the ninety-two 18" drivers on the bottom end delivered the traditional U2 clout – or so it was promised. All the rest of the PA was driven by Crest 9001s and 10004s, except for the delays which were handled by

Carver amps.

For the Sam Boyd opener, the PA included four delay positions, but on larger American stadium events with capacities of around 70-80,000 there were anywhere between six and eight delays. The delay tower count rose to ten when U2 performed at 120,000-capacity green field shows around Europe later that summer. Each delay tower carried four clusters of six S4s and a custom horn cluster that sat on top to deliver additional punch.

The Clair Bros crew (notably Brent Carpenter) were using the Sam Berkow-designed JBL Smaart real-time and analysis package to set up sixteen different delay times. In this situation, the Smaart system was employed in three ways: a) aligning the delay clusters with its integral Delay Locator; b) setting EQ; c) documenting venue acoustical characteristics.

Jo Ravitch explained U2's application: "The cluster is half a sphere with the sub basses in a straight line below and in front of it. As you move further away from the centre of the cluster to its edge, the distance and time between the flown cabinets and the subs increases, and you have to break that line of sub lows up into five different delay times. Even when you have two adjacent speakers on different delay times you really can't identify the fact that there is a time alignment. But overall, when you step back from it, the speakers are tightened up tremendously and it forces the whole system to wrap electronically, just like the cluster.

"The Delay Locator allows you to assess a comparative distance, compares the board output to a microphone output at any given location and then does a mathematical calculation to figure out the difference in time between the two. What you look for on the monitor is a spike which is the delay arrival. Everything is aligned to the centre of the cluster. The sub lows start at 31ms in the centre and the largest delay off stage is 61ms. The side columns are around 12ms and the front fills are 30ms. The Sam Boyd is a very short stadium and the delays are about 125' and 75' apart. In others the delays will be moved further downstage which won't be a problem considering we have more than five miles of cable on this show!"

Ravitch agreed that whilst JBL Smaart would never take the place of checking delays by ear, it dramatically reduced the length of time needed to achieve optimum settings. "You get this system demonstrated to you in a perfect acoustic environment where there isn't anything else going on. But in an outdoor situation there can be some very nasty reflections from seats and the ground, there are people making noise and the wind is blowing, so in reality things aren't as cut and dried as you'd like them to be. You might have to run the same analysis five or six times at various times to get a good chunk of information that makes sense because if you get a gust of wind that alters the signal it can change the figures tremendously."

When the nuts and bolts issues regarding the PA design were first tabled in June 1996, there was naturally an equal proportion of both doubt and excitement in the mind of Joe O'Herlihy, U2's long time front-of-house engineer and head of sound. His main fear was that the drive towards an outlandish set design might belittle the importance of audio. O'Herlihy, who after five years as Rory Gallagher's sound man joined the fledgling U2 crew on 9 September, 1978, said at the start of the tour: "Willie Williams and I have very close communication on audio issues. We appreciate each other's territories and I thoroughly accepted the audio challenge that has been thrown down here. Audio has always been the mainstay of U2's shows and I suppose what we are now dealing with is a different approach. The decision to change from a left/right system meant that we took a good look at the audio bible for the last time, then tore it up, threw it away and began work on something that was very adventurous and futuristic, with the power to deliver. The system we have ended up with offers us fantastic coverage and it is a blessed relief because it seemed that it was playing second fiddle to design, and yet the audio quality on this tour is second to none."

This fragmented, distributed system helped to comply with the environmental laws around the world. "Even in America where legislation has not been as tight as Europe, it is stipulated that SPLs should not rise above a given level," said O'Herlihy. "It's no longer a case of throwing gear on stage and turning up the volume; there's a lot more science involved now. It's something that we have to acknowledge and the use of a distributed system is the best way we can deliver a powerful sound while keeping within the law. You can fly things out on several independently controllable fixed matrices with a view to channelling audio where it needs to be, so you won't be dealing with vast amounts of hot spots. I feel confident that this is the way forward."

However, not everyone shared O'Herlihy's enthusiasm about the quality of the PA's sound. Chris Beale of SSE Hire for one: "The design of the U2 show was so catastrophically appalling in terms of the effect it had on the band's sound, that somebody should have realised it before it went into production and said, 'Okay, it's a fuck up...let's change it before it's a terminal case.' But no, they ran with it for the whole tour and I don't know one person who genuinely thought it sounded good. That can't be good for the band."

Huw Richards, who mixed Oasis when they supported U2 in Los Angeles, also had his reservations. He said: "I was shocked at the lack of power in the sound system. I found it unbelievable that U2 chose to work with that PA. It not only looked like a pumpkin, it sounded like a pumpkin! The first night was quite a battle. I understood the reasons for having the big cluster, because of the LED screen, and I loved the idea of the big production. But when you looked at the stage from the front-of-house position or on any of the TV monitors in the backstage area, all you could see was this bloody great pumpkin in the way of the screened images. Either side of the arch was okay, but face on it was a major obstacle, with people's heads cut off on the screen. I still think it would have been far better off putting a left and right system up and letting the central image be uncluttered."

Later to become The Rolling Stones' front-of-house engineer, fellow Irishman Robbie McGrath sprang to O'Herlihy's defence, whom he felt had received a raw deal from within the industry about the sound of PopMart. "Joe has a loyalty to Clair Bros that most PA companies would only be able to dream of from their own staff, and it must be incredibly difficult to come in a month after Willie Williams and Mark Fisher have designed a set that the band love, and then ask where the PA is going. It must have been like telling a child he can't play with his fucking train set! So instantly you have to come up with a solution that hopefully heads somewhere in the direction of the desired result, but sometimes we get it wrong. Then all of a sudden you notice that people in the same field of work, who you expect would understand the sort of problems that Joe is up against, are dumping on the guy. I wish these people would try to put themselves in Joe's shoes and shut the fuck up!"

O'Herlihy had a chance to respond himself when PopMart reached Wembley Stadium four months into the tour. He raised an eyebrow and said: "The sound has worked out exactly as I hoped it would – what's all the fuss about? We operated in America with low-profile delays on a shorter stem, but then replaced them with larger, taller stacks to achieve an elevation of the sound which also helps sight lines. Power has been an issue – U2's SPL on previous tours has always been calculated off 144 S4s, so the SPL is obviously going to be quite different with such a smaller system, but we are trying to get the centre cluster image as close as we can to that in the context of it being in mono.

"There are various arguments as to whether it works or not. The main difficulty with the system is about the effect it has on the band playing directly underneath it. At times it's not a pretty sight for them and invariably it's a challenge. [At Wembley] we had a 101dB ceiling at the console and we didn't get many complaints. The sound impressed David Gilmour and Peter Gabriel sufficiently for them to come by and compliment us."

At the beginning of 1997, when considering his control gear for the then rapidly approaching PopMart, O'Herlihy shortlisted the Midas XL4, Amek Recall and ATI Paragon as his possible front-of-house mixing consoles. He eventually picked two sixty-four-input XL4s. So what did this desk offer him that the others did not? "I'm always looking for the least difficult solution, and that was really the factor which inspired my choice," he said. "On the Zoo TV tour we had an ATI Paragon and a Clair custom board, with three people doing hands-on, multi-faceted performance mixes every night, flying things in and out on the faders, making cues and everything that was necessary. It was as good as it could be from a cue point of view; it was always trial and error, and there would often be things that were missed. On a tour as technically complex as Zoo TV, it was bordering on a nightmare every night and we'd all leave the gig shattered. In the intervening time I went out with REM and again I used the ATI Paragon which is an exceptionally good console, so it was definitely going to be in the frame for PopMart. But technology has moved on in leaps and bounds, and so we looked at a variety of new consoles for this tour, from the perspectives of physical design and automation. Simplicity was the watchword and we didn't want to get into the situation where our minds were so boggled with getting cues right that we couldn't mix the show properly."

O'Herlihy considered the Amek Recall a "wonderful product", but from a practical point of view it threw up a number of concerns when he compared it with the XL4. "Ninety-nine per cent of my time would have been spent looking at the console monitor and, to me, that is not mixing the show. I could have had Jo Ravitch track it but because I am the main engineer I would ultimately have to look at the screen at times and I'd be wondering if it was doing what it was supposed to, which is not an ideal scenario.

"The Midas XL4 gives you the best of both worlds. Firstly, it's a computer-assisted console rather than computer-driven, and the terminology speaks for itself. The audio passes through no matter what happens, so if the computer decides to wave goodbye and lock off, you're into an immediate hands-on situation which I can live with, having worked that way for more than twenty years. Because of the vast amount of cues and intricate elements of the band's material, there is a huge amount of fader movement, treatments and effects going in and out all the time. To be able to pre-programme that is a great asset. For production rehearsals we have about forty songs locked in, and there may be a minimum of two to three scenes per song, and some of them have as many as eight which may be different treatments or different elements of the same treatment. They are not going to play forty songs every night, but we know that whichever set they choose, all those cues are pre-programmed into the XL4 and it's a nice cushion to have. That's what I've been busy doing over the past two months in studio rehearsals in Dublin but it's all academic until you're in the stadium and doing it for real."

The man whose heroic beard is almost as long as his career has been a Midas fan since his early engineering days, when he and his colleagues yearned to get their hands on one of the company's products. He said: "This time they came back with a product that the industry is going to take on board in a big way as the engineer's choice, and inevitably the XL4 will find its way into a lot of sound companies across the world."

Compared with virtually every other element of the show, the front-of-house treatments and effects employed by O'Herlihy were incredibly straightforward. Summit compressors were used on vocals and bass, while his other main outboard weapons included Lexicon 480L reverbs, PCM-70s, Yamaha SPX-900s and Eventide H3000SEs. Nothing out of the ordinary there, but his main aim was to reproduce the flavour of the *Pop* album. "There is a lot more MIDI control on this tour, mainly because the album is a genuine major progression and it embraces technology to an extent that the band have never done before. It's no longer 'three chords and the truth' as Bono used to say, but people don't make the advances in technology without the artist taking it on board and using it rather than abusing it."

Assisting O'Herlihy in a loose fashion was record producer Flood (aka Mark Ellis) who began working with U2 on the *Achtung Baby* album, in partnership with Brian Eno. His influence on the band's studio creations grew significantly during the Nineties to the point where his occasional presence – and also remixer Howie B's – on the PopMart tour was necessary to guarantee the new music's smooth transition from the studio to the live stage. Jake Kennedy commented: "At heart, U2 are a live band but the aural changes that were happening in the studio made everybody a little concerned with the live reproduction. Flood, as the main producer of the *Pop* album, was the one guy who would be able to instinctively understand these changes and given his great relationship with Joe O'Herlihy he would also be able to understand Joe's job as the front-of-house mix engineer. He has an intimate knowledge of every aspect of the new music, and also where the new influences are affecting the older music, and he'll be coming and going throughout the tour to guide us as required."

Prior to Zoo TV, U2 were strictly a floor monitor band, but with the PA now situated above their heads and with a wider stage for them to negotiate, the most logical way forward was for them to use in-ear monitoring. This decision was especially vital for the B stage sequences in the centre of the stadium where hideous sound reflections would otherwise make accurate time-keeping virtually impossible.

The system of choice was Garwood, while the actual ear moulds were supplied by Futuresonics. Monitor engineer Dave Skaff of Clair Bros had worked with Futuresonics' Marty Garcia for several years and efforts were made to ensure that Skaff's own sets of moulds matched the band's to guarantee that the sounds he heard were identical to those monitored on stage. He said: "Bono and The Edge have sealed moulds because the amount of ambient noise will be pretty substantial even with a tiny pin-hole port. As the holes get bigger for the ports, the bottom end increases tremendously, which is why Larry and Adam are using ported moulds."

For the dress rehearsal and early dates, U2 were using Garwood's standard Radio Station system. Together with Nashville-based Clair colleague Steve McCale, Skaff designed an innovative switching system which solved a nagging problem associated with in-ear mixes. "We found that having fixed frequency transmitter units that are fixed to either one or two frequencies can be a bit limiting, depending on where you're at and what you may be doing. If you have three to five people listening to in-ear monitors, you end up trying to prioritise the best-sounding units from an RF standpoint and you may have to constantly re-patch things in order to make things happen. So to give us all the quality in-ear mixes we needed, we developed a rack which takes all of the IEM protection limiters, and a set of Logitech ten input x two output stereo switchers is placed in front of each one of the Radio Station transmitters.

"At the moment we have six mixes running for the main stage and we can switch any mix to any one of the Radio Stations at any time, all on the fly. We could have everybody on the same mix if required, and accommodate a guest artist on Bono's mix by punching that Radio Station into his mix."

A few dates into the tour, Garwood despatched to Clair Bros six units of its top-of-the-range IDS system which replaced the original Radio Stations. The Radio Station IDS not only covered the full range of legal frequencies available in each country, from 517 up to 862 mHz, but it was also arranged in bands of frequencies dependent on the country. Its foolproof LCD display allowed Skaff to set the frequency by the country's two digit abbreviation, such as GB, US and D for Germany, and thereby effortlessly stay within the law.

Skaff was first interested in the IDS when equipment for the tour was being specified, however, there was a difficulty that needed attention. "After the switcher rack, the signal goes into the Radio Stations and then into a combiner. It then goes into a linear which brings it back up to Garwood's rated output for each unit. Without that method, when you combine signals you will suffer dB loss every time you add a unit to the rack. We're just using the one antenna but there is a directional antenna which we can aim wherever we want and that makes a big difference in achieving gain. The IDS system that we had for consideration was not capable of doing that because it had the transmitter located at the end of a cable that just carries audio and control, and we couldn't physically combine that into a linear without modifying the unit." Which, after Skaff discussed the matter with Garwood's MD Chrys Lindop, is exactly what happened. The active transmitter electronics were installed inside the IDS processor to give a standard antenna output which could then go into the combiner. This, however, did not constitute a standard feature on the IDS, but a specific modification for U2.

With so much attention given to the set design, it was somewhat surprising to note the appearance of floor wedges "spoiling" the stage landscape, especially when one considered the presence of in-ear systems. Making their debut on a major tour were sixteen of the new Clair Bros 12AM Series II 1 x 12" wedges and twenty-two 2 x 12" models, while sixteen 18" sub-lows were also available on stand-by. Skaff: "On Zoo TV, Adam was into a lot of low end, so there was a side fill that consisted of six 18" boxes and one mid/high. In keeping with the rest of the band, Adam wants to decrease his monitoring this time and although we have plenty of subs, we won't be putting them all out unless we need to. We also have some subs and 12AM Series IIs for Larry, but they will only be activated if there's an in-ear problem because Larry is committed to not using wedges."

Skaff EQ'd the wedges on stage with the tc electronic 6032 remote controller for the 1128 graphic equaliser. The 6032 controlled twenty-three 1128s – eighteen of them dedicated to individual wedge mixes and the remainder existing for specific patching purposes.

With assistance from Ed Conrad, Skaff shared the monitor mixing duties with Clair colleague Donovan Garber who was exclusively covering Larry Mullen Jr's and Adam Clayton's mix requirements, while Skaff handled Bono and The Edge. The need to send any input to any monitor at the drop of a hat determined that four (yes, four!) fifty-two-channel Yamaha PM4000M consoles would be used, with most channels full to the brim. "The amount of mixes that need to be derived, including ten for effects, and the segregation of the in-ear monitors and floor wedges means that a lot of channels are quickly consumed," explained Skaff, who also used a Yamaha ProMix 01 "side car" desk to inject stadium ambience into the in-ear mixes, care of nine AKG 460 mics on the main stage and a pair of stereo mics at front-of-house. "Sometimes the EQ for the floor wedge mix doesn't work at all for the in-ears. If you try compressing a standard vocal mic into a loud set of wedges you come up with nothing but problems, whereas you need to compress or at least peak limit a vocal mic when it's going into in-ears to smooth out the RF over-modulation problems.

"Des Broadbery has his own local Turbosound Impact monitors for his keyboard and sampling rig and we also send him a global mix of drums, bass, guitars, vocals and talkbacks. At some points in the show there are eight channels of keyboards running that have been segregated down for mixing purposes as a left and right composite feed of keys, a sampler left/right and also a left/right feed of percussion. With two stages to consider, the band generate a lot of channels on their own and we have also set aside channels for satellite link-ups, the video soundtracks and Internet audio because there are vague plans to send and receive postings live on the Net. [This occurred on a number of dates, including Rotterdam and Wembley.] I have this vision of Cyber Hell with Cyber video and audio feedback going through a Clair PA. We have a couple of channels allotted to pure creativity because these guys certainly like to do strange, spontaneous things!"

The five backline technicians charged with maintaining U2's instrument requirements were Sam O'Sullivan, Fraser McAlister, Dallas Schoo, Des Broadbery and Stuart Morgan, the latter going out on the road with The Corrs immediately following the U2 tour. In every U2 show, most of the musical focus has naturally fallen on Edge, whose unique guitar sound has always been the backbone of the band's music. The crew referred to his substantial set up as the Edge Orchestra, but Dallas Schoo, the former Prince guitar technician who had worked with U2's guitar hero for twelve years at this point, described it as the Garden of Allah!

For PopMart, Schoo spent six days with a Hollywood designer and three assistants to replace every cable in Edge's rig and rebuild it from scratch. He said: "Edge wanted to use some of the effects that he used on the *Pop* album and that was the decision which initially forced the rig overhaul. I've changed the sequence of events according to his effects. The signal path has been altered following the last tour and we have inserted an additional computer at his pedal board. In the past, all six amplifiers that he uses in the show were accessed by me via presets. But the additional computer now allows him to access those amps directly while he is performing, as well as engaging an additional amp besides the one that was programmed into his past presets.

"Edge uses an average of three sounds per song and has the capability of five preset sounds, although he could actually directly access all the effects in his rig at any time. He can now either allow his dry signal to come through on the effects, or he can mute his direct signal through the rig, so that he gets a 100% wet effect sound from his effects. He has been experimenting during soundchecks with various ratios of wet to dry. We have also organised for his delays to trail through to the next song in a segue approach.

"We are using the Bradshaw switching system which is very reliable and I am using an additional system underneath the stage where I am situated because Edge is leaving his area quite a bit to interact with Bono and the crowd. He is essentially relying on me to change his sounds for solos and other periods of songs when he is away from his main performing area."

The featured guitar part on the recording of 'Staring At The Sun' was textured with a classic Leslie rotary cabinet sound. This was recreated on stage with a Rocktron Replifex box, although Schoo considered a more organic approach. "We discussed calling [Pink Floyd tech] Phil Taylor to ask for the contact details of the guy who made David Gilmour's Doppola rotary speakers that I saw backstage on the last Floyd tour because they really sounded fantastic. But

Edge's rig was already so complex and he only uses combo amps, so I really didn't want to introduce anymore outboard pieces. I presented the Rocktron device to Edge and if he didn't think it would do the job, then I'd get on to Phil. We did the first show with the Rocktron and I thought it sounded okay. It's up to Edge as to whether we continue with it."

Effects in The Edge's rig were a combination of old favourites and those specific to *Pop*. "The Eventide H3500 is used quite a lot for octave pitch and it has an envelope filter in auto mode that is a major part of Edge's sound. The tc electronic 2290 is his main delay effect source which is MIDI controlled, although his oldest delay is the Korg SDD-3000 that has its own character but is unfortunately no longer in production. It's analogue and because I cannot address it with MIDI commands I have to make those moves myself to bump up the various preset delay time programmes. That was a bit of a thorn in my side but it has the most pleasant delay tone for Edge, and if he could do the whole show with that one unit he would. However, the range of material now played by the band demands a variety of effects sources.

"For the new songs, Edge uses a Lovetone Big Cheese overdrive which delivers a very broken sound, but for his really big distortion he still uses the small FET pre-amp and his Electro-Harmonix Big Muff. The Digitech 2112 can also produce some quite offensive-sounding distortions which seem like they are coming from a closed 4 x 12" cabinet with a Marshall head. His shimmer effect on 'With Or Without You' and 'If God Will Send His Angels' is achieved with his old AMS digital delay. He's using a lot more wah-wah than ever and he has a custom envelope filter box that Bobby Bradshaw made for the *Zooropa* album. I have also given him an expression pedal through which he can address the Eventide and control the extent and output of the unit. I've introduced a Dunlop Multi Wah system which has parameters of EQ and that has been experimented with in soundchecks to see if it presents a better direction than we've had before."

Edge played through six combo-style guitar amplifiers which included four 1960s Vox AC30 Top Boost amps, one of which provided the power behind the recordings of all the U2 anthems. Said Schoo: "Edge uses that for almost 80% of the show and combinations of the other three AC30s are activated at different times. They each have extremely different tones because of the variety of speakers inside them, and in soundchecks we have experimented with miking up each speaker. The range of sounds we pick up that way is quite extraordinary."

Added to the AC30s were two Randall RG180 1 x 12" combos which Edge acquired from Joe Elliott of Def Leppard. Each Randall was set with a completely different EQ. "Those amps provide the real crunch on songs like 'Last Night On Earth'," Schoo commented, "but they are also used for the very straight and dry guitar sounds."

And so on to the actual source of Edge's sound: his guitars. His mainstay guitar for the tour was a 1976 Gibson Les Paul Gold Top reissue which, along with two Gretsch Chet Atkins Country Gentleman guitars (1965 and 1967), provided the sounds for many of the new songs. The standard issue black Strat continued to be used on 'Where The Streets Have No Name' and 'Pride', and an Eric Clapton Signature model Strat was modified by Schoo to give a hotter output for 'The Fly', a number which found its way into the set later in the tour. Meanwhile, Edge's favourite Rickenbacker, the 330-12, was played on 'Real Thing' and 'Gone', while 'End Of The World' featured the man on a 1972 cream Les Paul.

Out on the B stage, a Fernandez Sustain guitar or a mirror-plated Les Paul (depending on the leg of the tour) was played by Edge during the "lemon" sequence of the show which featured 'Discotheque'. As the summer wore on and some acoustic numbers were added to the B stage set, Edge also dusted off his trusty Washburn acoustic.

With so many guitars flying around during the show, Schoo, who has also worked as a guitar tech for Pearl Jam's Eddie Vedder, was often seen cooking up a sweat. He said: "The amount of changes makes things quite dangerous. I've been with Edge for twelve years and we've done a lot of complex sets but this one is a bit mashed up at the moment, so we're going to sit down together to see if we can possibly simplify and reduce the changes. Each guitar has a different level of output, so for each change I have to make an adjustment on the guitar system so that the rig always receives the same input and the effects respond accordingly.

"I'm changing the sounds on the computer, I'm tuning and switching between five belt pack transmitters, which is a lot in itself. But Edge demands new strings not only for the soundcheck but also for the show. He uses very heavy gauge strings (.011" to .054") and because the band tunes down a semitone to protect Bono's voice it adds more of a problem to the stretching time required to get the guitar tunings stable. So I get nervous because I want to do my best for him, but I often get only two hours to re-string, tune and re-tune six guitars. To also remember that each single guitar needs to have its own output regulated can sometimes stretch me a little too far and it was pretty mad on the first night in Vegas! But as we progress through the tour and get a pattern going I will get a firm handle on it all."

Guitar freaks constantly ask Schoo about the ingredients behind the Edge sound. The end results, he said, have mostly relied on the extraordinary lengths of time spent by the guitarist analysing his sound. "This man puts so much time into perfecting his sound and it is also venue-specific. I have a whole dossier of notes pertaining to different venues around the world which tell me about the slapback delay measurement from the stage at, for instance, Wembley Stadium to the back wall.

"Edge will not accept that the sounds for one show will work for the next and will think nothing of spending hours working on things with me, a long time past the band soundcheck, when the others have escaped to catering or wherever. But the longer he stays on stage perfecting his presets, the less time I have to change the strings and stretch them sufficiently. So I get my dinner brought to me while I'm re-stringing! At the end of every U2 show, I really feel like I have been a part of the performance, which I cannot honestly say for a lot of my other employers. Edge truly relies on me and you just don't want to let the guy down."

Complementing the Edge guitar orchestra on PopMart was an extensive range of keyboards, sequencers and samplers that aided the faithful stage reproduction of the new songs from *Pop* and updated versions of classics such as 'I Will Follow' and 'With Or Without You'. Des Broadbery, who handled much of the keyboard programming on the Dublin sessions for *Pop*, was put in charge of the keyboards and sequencers that Edge either physically played or triggered on stage.

Broadbery explained his duties: "In some parts of the show I am responsible for a large chunk of the sound delivered from the stage. There is a lot coming from me at times and very little at others. On the last tour, there were no keyboard or sampled parts incorporated into the B stage set, but there will be this time because the whole emphasis is on that part of the show being very different to Zoo TV.

"I am using eleven keyboards and a couple of Akai S1100 samplers which are being replaced by an Emu and an Emulator 4, none of which Edge has access to on stage. He triggers the sounds via a Roland PC200 controller which is MIDI linked to my world next to the monitor control area under stage right to make things a little neater up there. The Roland is a very small keyboard and we're using it because it is so discreet and we can throw it on and off stage with great ease, MIDI linked to my world next to the monitor control area under stage right to make things a little neater up there. Edge plays piano via that Roland on 'Gone' and 'New Year's Day', and he basically has access to whatever he wants to play but the majority of the sounds, like the synth lines for 'MoFo', are sequenced. The idea of being in that under stage area is good but I'm not sure how it will work for the shows because there's not a lot of space.

"Having programmed the keyboards for the *Pop* album it does make life a lot easier having immediate access to all those sounds. However, for several of the songs we are either adding or removing bits and pieces. There is a lot going on and as much as possible we try to keep things simple, although in some cases because the music has grown to be more complex we obviously can't. But musically, Edge tries to cover everything in spirit, likewise with all the guys."

Musician gossip suggested that the impressive sound for the sequence of 'MoFo' was apparently sourced from a Novation Bass Station but Broadbery was sceptical. "It was one of those sounds that kind of arrived in the studio one day and we never found out exactly where it came from. Quite a lot of things happened like that. My guess is that it was sourced from a Nordlead."

In his hideaway during the warm-ups at the Sam Boyd Stadium, in amongst a tower of hardware, Broadbery was spending most of his waking hours completing his remaining programming work before the final band dress rehearsals. Along the echoey stone backstage corridors, the robotic strains of the 'MoFo' sequence must have been heard more than a hundred times. "There's a little editing work to be done to some of the sequences and there are still some sounds to be sourced," he said, three days before the debut show. "The building of the rig has to be completed after being torn apart over the past few months, and we are also finalising the equipment that we need for the road as opposed to being static in the studio and in rehearsal. Everything in my rig is designed to be put up and taken down in twenty minutes flat because I need to have as much time as possible for preparation before the gig. The rig contains three working keyboards with a desk on top, two Macintosh computers to run the sequencing software, and a rack of samplers and modules."

Broadbery worked alongside software guru Tony Widoff, who created material in another part of the programming that Broadbery looked after for the synchronisation between the visuals and the music. "We basically use SMPTE to start each video sequence in time with the music. That is written in a programme called Max which is designed by Opcode, the same company that designs the sequencing package. Tony knows how to write in this MIDI language which is a very different way to normal programming.

"In a bid to achieve a cleaner signal path we have chosen a Mackie SR 32•8 desk. I'm up to something like fifty-six inputs and the Mackie is great for what I need. The older Mackie gear had a reputation for being a little noisy but it's a vast improvement on the previous desk I used for Zoo TV. I have a monitor mix coming to me through a pair of Turbosound Impact 80s and also a video monitor so that I know where the band are at and I can see if there are any problems occurring."

Although Sam O'Sullivan's technician role began with the 1987 Joshua Tree tour, his association with U2 dates back to their early days. A keen drummer himself, Sam was not only maintaining Larry Mullen Jr's kits but also took overall responsibility for the entire backline operation in a similar vein to Steve Jones, Phil Collins' drum technician and backline crew chief.

He said: "Each tech is assigned their own band member, so I watch out for Larry first as my priority and then keep an eye over everyone else. In truth, we all look out for each other anyway. If I'm in a position where something goes down in somebody's else's area, I just jump down and fix it.

"The job starts with the load on to stage for me. I make sure that the backline is set up properly in the space allocated and deal with the stage managers to make sure they give me enough crew to help with our equipment. In the order of loading and rigging, we're kind of last on but first off, so everybody's either knackered by the time they come to us or really fresh and bouncy, depending on which end of the gig it is! So my job is to make sure that everything is up and running, and in the correct position, see that the risers are lined up in place and that carpets are laid. I check with the Clair Bros sound crew to see that the miking is done correctly and the mics are firmly locked on to the stands. Then we work with the monitor boys to get the stage sound right.

"It doesn't really matter whether it's the drum tech or the guitar tech who has the additional role of backline chief. It has nothing to do with the instrument you're looking after. It's a progression for me – a position I like being in because I like knowing what's going on and that things are getting done to schedule."

Mullen Jr continued to prefer Yamaha drums above all other brands, but in the spirit of the PopMart stage design, he ordered a brand new type of kit – multi-coloured and sparkly. Said O'Sullivan: "Yamaha designed it especially for him but it will be on the market soon for the general public to buy. It's a new metallic custom thirtieth anniversary kit and all the badges have Larry's name engraved. We decided to take all their range and incorporate it into one kit. So there is a gold bass drum, a red rack tom, two green floor toms and a wood-shaded snare. On the B stage there will be a white sparkle kit which will look marvellous under the lights. Larry has played bodhran [traditional Irish drum] on albums but never live. This time I've brought one with me so that it's there if he wants to use it and I've also got various percussion items like tambourines and bells.

"On the road I will be carrying two kits of the multi-coloured drums and there will just be the one white kit. If I should need extra gear, Yamaha can have a new kit sprayed and delivered within two days. We've experimented with a few shells over the past few years and we've come back to the maple beech. The Yamaha quality has improved over the years, shell-wise. They are incredibly reliable.

"Larry uses Paiste cymbals. He's been with them for a long time and he's very happy with the Signature Series which sound beautiful. We went over to Switzerland once and he went into a cymbal room and personally picked out the sizes. After a few minutes of playing the cymbals there you have to leave and come back in because the sound is so intense. We've never had any problems with Yamaha or Paiste; they've always been tremendously supportive."

As O'Sullivan explained, the band's move to in-ear monitoring was particularly valuable to the drummer. "Larry now likes a very controlled sound in his ears. You can hear the sound of the shells now because there are no longer any wedges pumping sound back down the mics. To hear drums sing is beautiful, whereas before you were concentrating on the sound of the drum with the monitor box creating the sound as an effect. It was always a big sound with the wedges, and the enormous low end was almost moving him off his seat. But since the advent of the ear monitors it's much more controlled. We do have a drum fill available but we won't start with it; we'll begin just with the in-ears and only bring out the stage monitors if Larry desperately needs the extra reinforcement. I hope he won't because he's getting enough low end in there to satisfy him. There are side fills on stage for Adam and Edge and hopefully he'll get enough rumble from there.

"I wear the in-ears as well for reference and I can hear almost exactly what he's getting. It's a proven fact now that it's not dangerous to wear these in-ears and we both agree that this is the best direction to go. The damage that can be done to your hearing just by walking past a speaker that's feeding back is quite horrific. You won't get that with in-ears; it's very safe and the sound is fantastic. Larry doesn't want to go deaf, so it's important for him not to ask for more level. For me, that's a great hurdle we have jumped. Some drummers don't care, they just want more and more level until it is seriously threatening. But Larry is aware of what that would do to him within a few years."

On the Zoo TV tour of 1993, Mullen Jr occasionally played electronic percussion linked to an E-Max sampler to enable him to recreate the explosions on 'Zoo Station'. However, such tools were ruled out for PopMart. "Larry has been using shaker click tracks in his ears since the band first used sequencers on the Joshua Tree tour. He was on closed cup cans then until we eliminated them and brought in a pair of JBL Control 1s hung on mic stands for Zoo TV. Now it's just the ear moulds."

Joe O'Herlihy, Dave Skaff and Don Garber decided on the microphone plot for the entire stage between them. "For Larry's toms we are using Shure SM98s which clip on to the drum shells," said O'Sullivan. "We used them in the studio for the album and also in rehearsals, and they sounded great so we've gone with them for the tour. The snare will have an SM57 top and bottom. There has been a lot of experimentation with the bass drum mic and we actually have three in there! We've tried the flat SM91 which sounded good in rehearsal but they want to try it out with the big PA before committing themselves. The normal routine is to put a PZM in there and something else, because the PZM doesn't normally give you a lot of the slap but it will give you a good bass sound. You then put another mic in there to pick up the slap of the skin. I'm always interested in what the sound boys do and if I don't like the sound or think Larry won't like it, I'll let them know and they are normally very cooperative."

Originally straightforward when he joined the crew for *The Joshua Tree*, Fraser McAlister's job as Bono's guitar tech has increased in complexity with each tour. It was a crew position for which there had been no predecessor. He said: "I used to work for Adam and also look after Bono's guitars when he just played one or two songs. Gradually, Bono's use of guitars became so busy that I physically couldn't handle the responsibility for both guys, so we got Stuart Morgan in as Adam's tech and everything has been fine ever since. On Zoo TV, Bono played on about five or six songs on average. This time, out of the twenty-two or so songs in the set he will be playing for about half of them. And when I say he is playing, I mean it. He's not just wearing the thing around his neck as a prop and filling in a few chords, he's actually holding songs down now and fulfilling a true rhythm guitarist's role to support Edge. He's pretty proficient as a guitarist now and he certainly keeps me on my toes.

"His choice of guitars tends to vary in that he might play

something different each time on a particular song. Last time we used a few Gibson ES175s which he liked the sound of and the big body shape, and we had the Gibson Hummingbird acoustics which we had made in custom colours for the B stage performances of 'Angel Of Harlem', 'Stay' and songs like that. This time around, the set is more electric orientated and there are very few acoustic songs. There are, of course, the gentler numbers like 'Staring At The Sun' that he plays acoustic on. Outside of that it's pretty much full-on electric stuff and he'll play Les Pauls, Fender 1972 Candy Apple Red Telecasters and the bright orange 1958 Gretsch 6119 Chet Atkins that he particularly loves. He also has an early Seventies Custom Telecaster with a humbucker and a treble pick-up on it. We also looked at getting some custom coloured guitars that match Larry's drum kit, because everything is going a bit colour crazy on this tour, rather than standard rock 'n' roll black. They are basically good guitars that have a solid sound first and foremost, but the colours will be a secondary issue for show purposes."

With his frontman vocalist routines occupying his mind almost totally, Bono assigned all of the guitar effects switching to McAlister who operated them from his bunker at stage left where he lived with a pedal board and a rack of various MIDI effects. "Each song has different sounds going all the way through it. The verse, chorus and rhythm that Bono plays behind Edge's solos all have a different setting and it's all remotely activated by me. That allows him to traverse the stage on his wireless system and concentrate on delivering a show. The whole show is wireless and we're using Sony radios as we've always done. We have two older Sonys that we've had for years and we have upgraded to one of the newer multi-frequency switchable diversity tuners that we need now because of frequency licensing around the world. On Zoo TV we had so many frequencies in operation but it was in the days when switchable multi-frequency systems weren't available to us. Between radio mics, wireless in-ear monitors, guitar transmitters and comms on both the A and B stages, it added up to a hell of a lot of wireless signals and frequencies. You started taking hits on everything so you had to carry spares and double up on everything just to safeguard the show.

"Bono's guitar sounds are fairly straight compared to Edge who handles all the mad, effected, multi-layered parts. Having said that, Bono does play a few interesting things. To recreate the new stuff live you could really do with ten guitar players but between Edge and Bono they manage to strip the parts down to something meaningful that puts over the spirit of the songs.

"Primarily I use the Korg A3s which I find handy for reverbs and tremolo effects for things like 'Miss Sarajevo'. But I really like going back to the old analogue pedals. We have the purple Roger Mayer Fuzz Mongoose which is a really heavy-sounding fuzz pedal; there's no digital flavour about it at all. The Lovetone Meatball is another straightforward analogue pedal and I'm using a Custom Audio Electronics Super Tremolo system for vibrato and tremolo settings. The Digitech 2112 is a multi-effects unit which is very hands-on. When you look at the front screen you can see where your chain is, and what you're going in and out of. I use that on 'Staring At The Sun', 'With Or Without You' and 'Gone', but nothing is ever 100% set in stone with U2 so things could very easily change.

"I use the Bradshaw Switcher which cuts between the two amps and gives the facility to add more amps on if desired. At the moment we have a Mesa Boogie Maverick 2 x 12" dual channel amp which is wound up for the more kerrang-type rock sounds, and a Vox AC30 with top boosters for cleaner sounds. We have a broad selection of equipment."

Aside from minor adjustments, the show ran exactly to plan until it was finally laid to rest in Johannesburg after ten glorious months. The initial caustic reviews in America and temporary system glitches caused by inclement weather were long forgotten. PopMart was a triumph and that big Vegas gamble had paid off like no other.

As the tour reached its end, a tired-looking Jake Kennedy said that it had been mostly disaster-free: "We still have the lemon and the olive, and for the most part the screen has behaved very well. The efficiency level of how the set comes together and dismantles is far better than I expected, with load-out reduced from six to four hours. In Washington we were hit with a phenomenal rainstorm that dumped five inches of water in the area and the screen took a battering. However, the band went on and played brilliantly, and the *Washington Press* review still mentioned the screen in glowing terms.

The screen has continued to occupy our attention and it is more labour-intensive than we reckoned for, but I think that's the nature of the beast." [The screen was the centre of attention for the mainstream press when, at the band's Edinburgh show on 2 September, the giant image of Princess Diana, who had died only two days before, was shown in tribute and naturally provoked an overwhelming emotional reaction.]

Was the longevity of the set icons an issue? "After America we flew the screen back to Lorrymage in Belgium where some new internal electronics were added and some replaced, then they re-assembled it in time for Europe. We did the same during the next long break. Because the screen is the only one of its kind in the world and that it's essentially a prototype, operating every second day on average, one expects there to be a certain amount of constant maintenance. Similarly with the lemon, after America it was returned to the Lemon Hospital [Brilliant Stages] to be overhauled although it was mechanically sound. There were mirror panels falling off it because the glue that fixes the mirrors in place wasn't reacting well to the rain. As quickly as we put the mirrors back on, another lot were tumbling off. You don't take a 35' mirror ball lemon out on the road and expect it to be in pristine condition halfway through the tour. Even standard, off-the-shelf items like guitar amps can fail."

For the first time in the band's history, U2 used one promoter for an entire world tour. In amongst a number of tenders from competing promoters, TNA of Canada (previously CPI) put forward the most attractive proposal to Principle Management and immediately started the ball rolling. TNA effectively bought the tour and guaranteed U2's fee per show, just as it would do with The Rolling Stones. This was clearly an arrangement which found favour with Kennedy and the band. Kennedy commented: "The agreement hasn't affected the audiences as much as it affected our turnover through not dealing with several promoters all over the world. I always believed that having one promoter worldwide was the most sensible move. I think the marriage of two strong personalities is always going to be difficult and there have been a few financial battles, but we've all dealt with this sensibly. It certainly took the pressure off the band who after each show were no longer concerned with how much they made, because it's all pre-determined.

"On a lot of the shows that the press claimed were badly attended, such as Phoenix, we actually sold more tickets there than we did on Zoo TV. It's a difficult audience in America. They're...jaded would be too strong a word, but they have so much else to entertain them. If it's not sport, it's home videos and computer games, and we've been in competition with some very glossy things. But the exit polls clearly stated that the audiences believed this has been quite a stupendous tour. Overall we've been very pleased."

The planned Dublin show at Lansdowne Road in September lay in doubt for some time because of the Irish authorities' delay in granting permission. For an Irish band of such immense international standing, this must have caused a fair degree of embarrassment. Kennedy commented: "The Paddy joke was on us and we could only deal with it through good humour. The authorities seem reluctant to make things law, because immediately that makes them responsible. We can play shows in Sarajevo without a fuss which makes this fence-sitting at Irish authority level look ridiculous. It would be understandable if it was a licence issue, because all we'd do is go through the motions and give certain guarantees. But this situation is wide open to subjectivity. If it had been any other major band, they'd have just said, 'Stuff it.' But U2, being who they are, had to see it through."

CHAPTER SIXTEEN

Jean Michel Jarre

Oxygene '97

Jean Michel Jarre has been active in the professional music world since 1967 when, at the age of twelve, he followed in his father Maurice's footsteps and recorded music for an obscure Gallic film. It was his later discovery of the synthesizer which sparked his late 1970s rise to prominence as a self-contained keyboard genius who made albums to be consumed in a distant galaxy, and designed special one-off concert events that employed whole cities as venues, with apartment and office blocks used as canvases for extravagant light and laser displays.

The charismatic Frenchman enjoyed something of a renaissance in 1997 as he celebrated the twentieth anniversary of the release of *Oxygene*, the album which launched his international career. Taking a leaf out of Mike Oldfield's book (another solo instrumentalist who marked the twentieth anniversary of *Tubular Bells* by rearranging the melodies and issuing *Tubular Bells II*), Jarre had recently released *Oxygene 7-13* – seven new synthesized gems which continued the 1977 "concept" – and saw fit to undertake his first-ever tour of European indoor arenas. A bit of a come down from playing huge chunks of Paris, London, Houston and Hong Kong? Well, not exactly. The audiences may have been microscopic in comparison to the hordes who attended his *La Tour Eiffel* spectacle in Paris in 1994, but the scaled-down quality of presentation left little to be desired, even though on the first date of the UK tour, at Birmingham's NEC Arena, some aspects of the production were a little rickety.

Jarre's performance opened with the white-gloved maestro playing his trademark laser harp – a cluster of green laser beams focused at the front of the stage which, when touched, send MIDI signals to one of his keyboards. Painfully, this did not always go to plan and as a result of a MIDI glitch, several notes were embarrassingly absent. Standing on the mixing platform, his charming Irish assistant Fiona de Montaignac shook her head in annoyance and jotted down the first of several comments in her Big Book. Observations which would surely be reported to the boss at a later post mortem. Damn lasers!

Clearly preoccupied with the technology at his fingertips, Jarre took great pains to give his audience a little background behind a number of his toys, including his newly-renovated Mellotrons and the amazing Big Briar Theremin which required some roadie attention before he was able to coax any life out of it. Once its sci-fi signals began to pour from the PA, the effect was awesome and his mad professor hand movements made for compelling viewing. All of the lead melody sounds for 'Oxygene 4' were programmed into just one keyboard, the new Nord Lead 2, which, if his introductory speech was anything to go by, appeared to be his latest fad.

The set performed by the six-piece band (including Jarre) was drawn largely from both *Oxygene* albums and the original's 1978 follow-up *Equinoxe*. Not surprisingly, the recognition by the audience of these "greatest hits" was high. However, the show lacked emotion in part and relied on the impact of the visuals, but what does one expect from a vocal-less synthesizer act, regardless of its unquestionable musical skills? What was apparent was Jarre's passion for his music, and the audience loved him for it. With Kraftwerk going down a storm at Tribal Gathering earlier in the year, and the reinstated enthusiasm for Jarre's work clearly in evidence, the tour helped make way for a major synth pop revival, and the inevitable resurgence of interest in early Eighties pop culture...unfortunately!

The impressive lighting and set design for the tour was undertaken by the uniquely talented Roy Bennett, fresh from his Supertramp "experience", who devised his ideas and finally thrashed them out with the star. The set itself relied on the interaction of its contents and the way they took light. In short, it was a rather strange beast. Most of the surface viewed by the audience was formed from a rubberised,

U2's PopMart in reality (above) and how it was originally presented to the band as a Mark Fisher CAD drawing (right)

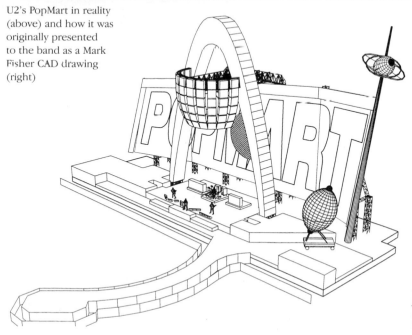

Above: PopMart in California
Right: the PopMart LED screen was
a production landmark

Willie Williams

U2's catering team from Flying Saucers

Manoeuvring the arch at the Sam Boyd
Stadium in Las Vegas

Assembling the mighty "lemon" in the
Nevada desert

Bono and an LED Edge

Building the PopMart B stage

Jake Kennedy

Bono at large

Joe O'Herlihy

The seven ages of shopping

Backline crew chief Sam O'Sullivan

U2 guitar tech Dallas Schoo

Bono axe minder Fraser McAllister

Mark Fisher

The two Freds:
Jalbout and
Opsomer – the
men behind the
Lorrymage/Saco
screen

U2 video director
Monica Caston

Roy Clair

Courtesy Clair Brothers Audio

Close up on the LED panels

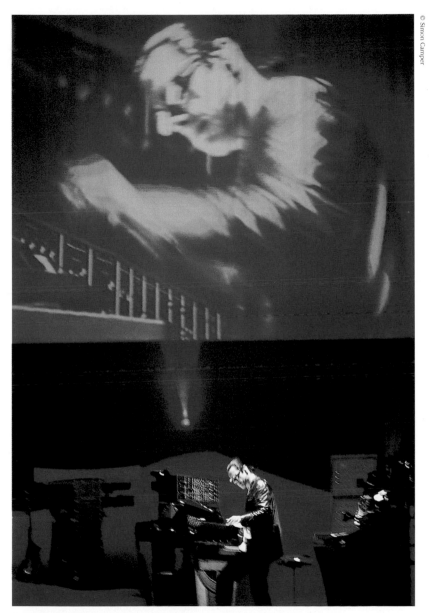

Jean Michel Jarre at the NEC, Birmingham on his 1997 Oxygene tour

Jarre's triple screen visuals

Playing the laser harp

JMJ with the author

Last minute synth checks at the NEC

Mellotron UK's John Bradley and
Martin Smith

Roy Bennett

ArKaos fan Jesse Deep

The French keyboard maestro and (below) his flying cadavers

The crew from Audio Rent/Clair Brothers Europe

Lighting director Wally Lees

Korn in Toronto on the Lollapalooza tour, 1997

Lollapalooza mostly visited tented
"sheds"

Video guru and part-time juggler
Dick Carruthers

Artificial Joy Club on Lollapalooza's second stage

Side show distractions at Lollapalooza

Tricky's FOH mixer,
Jon Burton

Orbital

Smoother Smyth and
Jack Alexander

Lollapalooza's
video crew with
Malcolm Mellows
(ex-PSL USA) in
the driving seat

James – not necessarily urging the crowd to "Sit Down"

A candid shot of James from the wings

Video technician Matthew Askem

The stage is set for INXS at Wembley Arena

INXS toured in 1997 with JBL's HLA sound system

FOH engineer Stuart Kerrison

Michael Hutchence –
his last ever London
concert appearance

Sean "Motley" Hackett
– the INXS LD

inflatable material which wrapped around the band members like a huge bloated snake.

Bennett said: "Jarre's been a breath of fresh air because he's very creative, a brilliant guy. A lot of the ideas came from me, in fact it was all left up to me which was interesting because he'd been using the same team for a very long time. But this was new and they had never ventured into arenas in all the time since the original *Oxygene* album; it had always been huge outdoor productions. So Jean Michel was very nervous. Because I'd done so much in arenas, they looked to me to come up with a way to portray the essence of his big spectacles within the boundaries of the arena. To me, it's all relative to the size of the venue. You can light an entire city but you can achieve the same impact when you are inside a building of any dimension. The production, therefore, had to be on a grand scale but it didn't need to be over the top."

Lighting director Wally Lees filled in the detail. "Jean Michel refers to the stage as 'the living organism' because it does look as if it's breathing sometimes, especially during the second number, 'Oxygene 2', and also later on. The effect of lighting the material from the inside and overhead makes it appear like it is an organic membrane or a shifting sand dune, whereas in truth the stage is not moving at all. Finding someone to produce the set was a real headache but at the last minute we discovered Daniel Dorleans of Voileries Dorleans who could manufacture the set at very short notice. The only drawback of this set is that once it is inflated it makes access very difficult because it is virtually impossible to walk on it without falling over!"

Stationed in the roof rig were five dummies, or, as Jarre insisted, human cadavers. During 'Oxygene 4' (the single which kicked off Jarre's widespread fame) these cadavers descended on motorised wire winches to about 20' above the deck, hovering over the seemingly pulsating set. Even the cadavers, which were controlled by the set carpenters, appeared to be breathing – they each wore oxygen masks and the lines on which they were suspended seemed to contain rising air bubbles. It was just another of several abstract looks which could only have been conjured by an eccentric mind.

The cadavers were also Bennett's brainchild. "We used something that was a little more sedate compared to our original idea," he grinned. "I have an movie industry acquaintance in LA who has helped with construction on Nine Inch Nails, and he had access to actual moulds of cadavers which are used in films. But he had moved on somewhere else and I didn't have the time to look him up so we dropped it and came up with these other figures. I'd thought about doing something like that for Slayer. It was all linked to things that relate to oxygen, whether that was the air, breathing, leaves or how it makes things grow."

The set took light brilliantly – its texture seemed to suck the light in yet put out a startling beauty. Fortunately, the three video screens at the back of the stage did not cause any problems for Lees; they did not pick up any glare from the set owing to the stage being more absorbent than reflective and Lees was able to be creative without interfering with the clarity of the video projections.

Lees controlled twenty-four VL4s from an Artisan and twenty VL5s were run DMX from an Icon desk, along with forty LSD Icons. At the NEC, Vari*Lite technician Richard Gorrod was pushing the Go button on the Artisan while Lees activated the Icon board. Later on down the line, the desks were MIDI-linked to enable Lees to operate as a one-man band. He commented: "Technical rehearsals were so short and bringing the MIDI in is a gradual process. Doing things this way will take someone else out of the loop and remove the need for two sets of timing."

Lighting was supplied by both LSD and Vari*Lite. Aside from some conventional fixtures for cyc lighting, the rig was totally automated and designed to be as "clean" and easy to manipulate as possible. Said Lees: "If we had to we could easily break it down into a smaller rig or expand it to form a larger one, and being fully automated the diversity gives you much more to play with. There are so many toys up there that if you had enough time you could spend hours getting beautiful stuff out of it without repeating yourself. The combination of the Icons and VL4s and 5s is extremely potent. There are seven multicolour Icons upstage that have a number of interesting gobos on them which contribute to the moving looks on the inflatable set."

Those who witnessed more than one show would have noted that Jarre's aim was to slightly alter the visual presentation each night. "Jean Michel wants the show to evolve as the tour progresses to see what he can get out of it artistically, which is why the video projections change and that also affects my job, because I'm reacting to songs in different ways all the time," said Lees. "We change the lighting looks to accommodate the differences in video presentation – it all depends on the colour textures on the screens, and also the amount of set-up time we have prior to each date, of course!"

Whilst Vari*Lite supplied its own branded products, LSD looked after the strobes and Icons, as well as all the hardware, D-type trussing and cabling. At one point this was going to be the first rock 'n' roll tour for the Irideon AR5 lights, but the product was not quite ready for the road. Lees: "We were going to use them to add more light to the band members, and to be honest I think we could really have done with them because lighting the band from the air with VL4s sometimes takes away from the clarity of what you're trying to achieve throughout the rest of the set, due to spill. When you really want to highlight them but leave the set dark we face a minor struggle, so the little AR5s would have been ideal for picking out the keyboards and people without affecting other areas of the big picture."

Rising up periodically at the very back of the stage was a full stage width screen manufactured by Atmosphere-Concept, the company which also made the silk curtain that fell at the front of the stage at the start of the show. For cyc lighting, Lees used seventeen four-cell Par 36 cyc units and four eight-cells, all with Molemag colour changers, and a seventy-two-way Avo DMX dimmer. "We were going to project on to that big screen, and we do show the occasional image on it, but the general feeling is that it works better as a canvas for lighting, leaving the three cameo screens to take the projections. I do believe, however, that the screen will be more widely used as the tour goes on."

The rig also featured fourteen MiniMags on twin Diversitronic 3000 strobes that were placed all over the set and ganged together in pairs to produce maximum intensity. "You can control the rate and power of the strobes which is great for me," said Lees. "There is one point in the set where Jean Michel and the band appear to be animated, as if they are in an old-style, fast paced movie, and that is all down to the strobes. On a normal strobe, you just hit a button and it will flash on and off with consistent speed, but with this particular version of software you can crank it up and the strobe will decay beautifully."

Another interesting effect was afforded by forty Kino Flo fluorescent tubes which descended from the roof at a couple of points during the show. Roy Bennett's co-lighting designer Gary Westcott dreamed up the idea of a slinky-looking unit which could deliver various permutations of fluorescent light along moving bars – the angulation and configuration of which could change during any number. These units were on half tonne motors with a blend of 5600 and 3200 luminaires which gave a difference in colour temperature between the bars. Each set of four bars was on six motors, and they were activated just over halfway through the set to provide a totally new look.

"They don't exist to light anybody or anything, it's just an electrifying effect," stated Lees. "We wouldn't want to overuse them, and in fact they only appear in three numbers maximum. I love them because they change the whole visual aspect of the show and provide a bit of a stop gap for the performance."

In terms of audio, there were twelve channels of radio (RF) in total, but that number increased through the video crew's use of RF. For most of the show, Jarre wore sunglasses with an integral wireless miniature CCD-chip video camera which sent images of whatever he saw, such as his keyboard rigs, to the video screens. The camera itself was a Russian invention, formerly used by the KGB for surveillance and was one of four sources which supplied video director Laurent Bertho with the images required for the three 6 x 4.5 metre screens which dropped into place behind the band at key moments in the presentation. The other three sources were CDV, a manually-operated Betacam in the pit and a remotely-operated 360° Robocam on stage.

The video equipment supplied for the tour by E/T/C of Paris included three new Barco 9200 projectors which also served a small oval-shaped screen on stage, used occasionally throughout the show for cameo images. At these points, two stage hands came on to manually move the screen to different angles – surprising, really, considering the technological prowess otherwise demonstrated.

To create the mind-blowing range of imagery projected on to the screens, Jesse Deep, who worked under the outlandish title of "abstract image operator", used the ArKaos X-Pose software he had been developing over five years to manipulate the visuals provided to him by Bertho. He said: "I am dealing with real-time graphics, and the video for each show looks totally different. I assign image samples to a variety of notes along a keyboard and I play them with the flow of the music. Those images are projected directly to the screens and Laurent is also mixing different sources, so between the two of us we are responsible for the video show. Laurent chooses the best image sources for me to integrate into my video mixes. I grab those images and apply some real-time effects to fade, posterise or distort shapes. I try to follow the beat and almost act as if I am another member of the band, only I am outputting visual and not musical signals."

Wherever Jarre travelled on the tour, he carried a small Canon digital camera to take photographs of anything that might look interesting on the screens. Prior to each show, Jarre passed the camera to Deep who downloaded the pictures to his hard drive and into an Adobe Photoshop program, and then manipulated them before adding them to his library. One example was a strange-looking door which captured Jarre's imagination at Glasgow Station. Sure enough, giant-sized snatches of the image cropped up in triplicate behind the French combo. And to think it was all being controlled from a small table amidst a tower of empty flight cases backstage. Smart stuff.

Complementing the video towards the end of the show were 35mm movie projections of extremely abstract footage operated by Didier Robin of Flash Production from behind the FOH sound and lighting desks. The footage was projected directly on to Jarre during 'Oxygene 12' and provided a stimulating transition into the last two encore numbers. Jesse Deep said: "It's a very novel piece of film with some great photography that is a brilliant accompaniment to the music. The movie is so abstract that almost every member of the audience will have a different perception of its meaning, which was exactly what Jean Michel had in mind when the idea for using the footage came about."

Deep later began working with Steinberg to develop a new video system which would have applications in this field of work. Up until then, Deep was using Steinberg's Cubase MIDI sequencing package to ensure perfect synchronisation of the images. Being linked to the general SMPTE network employed by the sound crew allowed Deep to trigger the instant appearance of images via one of Laurent Faucheux's electronic drums. "It's a great explosive effect which works brilliantly with the sound of the drums. It really fills the screen with a mad intensity for a brief moment, a moment loaded with drama. That's what it's all about for me."

Despite the use of what was essentially a standard Clair Bros S4 rig, as supplied by Audio Rent (Clair Bros Europe), the PA concept was unusual owing to the bulk of the boxes being hung at the sides of the truss, approximately one-third back from the front line. This was only possible because of the non-vocal music and, naturally, Audio Rent systems engineer and sound crew chief Willie Williams would certainly not endorse such an approach on a vocal-orientated show. Said Williams: "Because of the inclusion of video screens, the show design team wanted to remove any risk of the back of the stage being hidden from the audience. So we have to fly the PA high but there is the advantage of flying deep at the sides which has given us a distinctive edge for the sound we are trying to create, because a five-deep column in a vertical array reproduces a wonderful bottom end. That is aided in part by a line of eight Servodrive subs which are mostly used as an effect at certain moments in the show. Renaud Letang, our front-of-house engineer, is typically forming a kind of acid house-flavoured mix with very solid low frequencies, so this configuration is perfect."

The main touring rig consisted of forty-eight Crest-amplified, JBL-loaded S4 cabinets, with eight long throws per side which projected straight down the hall and into the corners, while underneath them a number of regular S4s provided cover to the sides. On the inner stack there were pull-back motors to angle the boxes towards the front of the audience, however, due to the boxes being positioned further back and the distance between the speakers and the audience is small, the pull-back angle did not need to be so acute.

"For delays we run a 12' bumper with six S4s up high in front of the truss, angled down at the general body of the hall and also pointing towards the back," said Williams. "There are P4 pistons rigged up above the mixing platform just to add a little extra horn top end for the people on the bleachers. As far as I can judge the distribution of sound is as widespread as it needs to be and we are more or less managing to maintain optimum phase coherence and time alignment, despite the fact that the NEC Arena is a difficult venue. Actually, the hall isn't that bad...I've played a lot worse than this, believe me!"

In spite of new technological developments geared towards ensuring absolute accuracy when tuning delay systems, Williams preferred to use more traditional, manual methods. "Without the modern technology, but with my beloved t.c. crossovers, a tape measure, a pen and paper, and a well-trained pair of ears, I can plot the delay measurements accurately enough to not rely too much on electronics. Being forced to hang at the sides has actually proved beneficial to the kind of effect we are trying to get. Our long vertical columns are at the back so we don't cut anybody's sight lines and they work well. I'm fortunate in that I don't have to take out the extra delays and crossovers; it just wasn't necessary."

Being Jarre's first indoor arena tour, in terms of the audio challenge there were obvious technical differences to his famous outdoor events. With those one-off shows, one did not need to design a sound system with a view to repeating the formula every night for a couple of months. However, for this tour Audio Rent had to modify all the aspects that Jarre would normally demand, to enable the crew to comfortably incorporate them on every date. This, Williams explained, required much effort in the rehearsal studio before his team could guarantee the desired level of consistency.

In his dual role as systems engineer and sound crew chief, Williams demonstrated enviable skills in both technical and people management departments, and the buck stopped with him when it came to rigging the PA and ensuring good dispersion in every venue. For him, working with Jarre was a genuine pleasure. He commented: "The tour is proving to be very satisfying, technically-speaking. It's been an interesting exercise because I was invited over to Paris to meet Jean Michel way back in January and discuss with him the concepts he wanted for the diffusion of sound. He had always performed in a tight box situation, with the stage at one end and all the audience in front. But at the NEC our audience extends around to the sides, and so it was necessary to find a way whereby none of the information in the music would be lost. We solved that by a relatively simple method of splitting the signal in the stacks, so that anyone in the middle of the hall would hear the signal left and right, but to enable those at the sides to hear a balanced sound we reversed the left and right channels in the outer stacks. As it is instrumental music you would be very hard pushed to notice the difference!

"I've never known a star to be as involved in sound design as Jean Michel, and take that much care and interest in what people like myself are actually doing in the pursuit of the best possible sound. We discussed various aspects of our speaker concept and unlike a normal band's use, he is using the entire frequency range. Apart from the subs on the ground, all of the sound is coming from the same place, up in the air. So as you go down the octave on the keyboard the sound doesn't suddenly travel from the flown cabinets to the grounded subs."

Freelance FOH engineer Renaud Letang worked with Jarre on his previous open-air European tour and also the huge *La Tour Eiffel* show in Paris on 14 July, 1994. To the right hand side of his Midas XL4 console (with forty-eight mono and four stereo channels, plus sixteen effects line returns) were two Revox open reel tape machines which were Letang's principal effects sources. They came into play on the older, vintage keyboards for delays and also to help achieve a spacious stereo image. This was something that Jarre insisted on, having used Revoxes for exactly the same same reasons in his private recording studio.

Commented Letang: "You can't achieve the same effect with digital processing. The Revox method promotes a much warmer result and an entirely different sound. I have four speed positions which give me different delay timings and my choice depends on the tempo of any given song. When you are mixing electronic keyboards and there are no guitars, vocals or brass, all the sounds are so one-dimensional and there is no acoustic coloration, and so it is very difficult to give depth to the sounds in the PA. But the Revox is fantastic at giving a kind of lively, organic reverb and echo flavour to these instruments, but also preserving the vintage quality."

An admirer of the XL4, Letang considered the on-board EQ to be "second to none", although he found a need to additionally work with a Summit EQ and Tube Limiter to gain extra control of the bass keyboards. "The music changes all the time and so the sounds for each song are quite different," he said. "So although I prefer to mix live for most of the show, there are certain layers of keyboards and scenes that I have automated to help me survive the gig, otherwise I would be frantic, and the XL4 has to be the greatest automated board I have come across in terms of user-friendliness and functionality."

Above Letang's desk at every show was a pair of nearfield monitors, an approach born of a previous Audio Rent client's request, as Willie Williams explained: "There was a studio engineer who wanted these monitors added just in case he was placed in an awkward position when working live. I kept incorporating those monitors and found that other engineers liked them because they are time-aligned and rather than listen to something on cans, they can solo a channel with the rest of the show going on in front of them. They then only have to revert to cans if there's a real problem with one of the channels. I just think it's a very sensible and practical idea which looks like it could become another Clair standard."

Over in Xavier Gendron's monitor cockpit, the total number of inputs rose to seventy-eight hence his requirement for two Midas XL3 desks. Together with Remy Blanchet, he was responsible for ensuring the vital smooth operation of two Tascam DA-88 machines (plus two spares) which ran the SMPTE time code, band cues and a click track for the drummer. This system was also synchronised to video and a Yamaha O2R console at front-of-house which mixed digital tapes containing sounds and effects which could not physically be played by the six guys on the stage.

In discussions with Jarre, Gendron felt that the style of the music and nature of the show suggested the need for the band to employ in-ear monitoring. He was using a total of eight Garwood IDS units including two spares, one of which was used for special guests later on in the tour. Everybody using the in-ears was on wireless systems except the video crew who use hard-wired M-Pack versions. "In-ear monitoring appealed to Jean Michel in that everybody would hear the music in stereo and the very clean sound that you can achieve is highly appropriate to the flavour of the performance," commented Gendron.

"This isn't like a traditional rock show; it's a very subtle production with interesting, futuristic sounds. Jean Michel actually helped me to persuade the musicians to give the system a shot because few of them had ever tried this technology. Also, two of the band had never played any concerts inside arenas, having only worked with JMJ on the big open-air shows. So during the first two weeks of production rehearsals, we had what I assume to be the normal problems associated with the familiarisation of in-ear monitoring, such as getting used to the different acoustic feel experienced through the ear moulds. But after two or three weeks everybody remarked on how well it was working. The good thing about it for me is that certain sounds do not get lost in the big wash that you have with regular stage monitors."

The tour did, however, carry monitor wedges as a back-up, mainly to cater for drummer Laurent Faucheux whose fill consisted of two Clair 12AMs and an ML18. "He plays electronic d-drums and he wanted to approximate the natural feeling of a real acoustic kit," said Gendron. In addition, one ML18 sat underneath the set behind the bass/keyboard player Christophe Papendieck's riser to provide a little more low end and four of the latest generation 12AMs exist for guest artists.

Apart from a few percussion items, every instrument on stage was electronic, and therefore only a few microphones were required because of the proliferation of (forty-five) Countryman DI boxes which Gendron found "very solid and reliable". Alongside the modern keyboards, the charismatic vintage instruments provided Gendron and the crew with an endless source of fascination. A major aficionado of all things analogue, Jarre had been a long-time user of the legendary Mellotron, the forerunner of digital samplers such as the Fairlight CMI, and it was a sight to behold when he played it on 'Souvenir Of China'.

The Mellotron was conceived in the Midlands in the early Sixties by Les Bradley who sadly died in January 1997, and it became an instrument synonymous with the psychedelic era – The Beatles' 'Strawberry Fields Forever', Manfred Mann's 'Ha Ha Said The Clown' and 'Hole In My Shoe' by Traffic were just a few of the hits to be adorned with the Mellotron's grainy flute and string sounds.

It was a joy to see an original 1964 vintage Mark II model on home ground gracing the stage at the NEC, accompanied by John Bradley (Les's son) and Martin Smith of Mellotron Archives, the company set up in the mid Nineties to service existing 'Trons. Its appearance attracted the attention of BBC Television who interviewed Jarre about the instrument prior to the show.

How did the Mark II find its way on to the Oxygene tour? Martin

Smith said: "Back in January, I heard that Jean Michel had been using an old Mellotron on the new *Oxygene* album and I contacted him through a French keyboard magazine. It turned out that he was really keen on getting hold of a machine that was sufficiently roadworthy for this tour. Fiona, his assistant, told us that it "had to be spectacular" and so we suggested a Mark II and designed a lighting pack to go inside it to make it glow green and red. We removed the cycling [which activates a completely new bank of sounds] so that all the tape mechanisms were fixed and therefore nothing could go wrong on stage.

"Jean Michel wanted two specific sounds to access during the shows: 'Jarre Orchestra' and 'Jarrotron', the latter being a half-speed Mellotron string sound with a Leslie effect. So he sent us a DAT and we had to prepare brand new $3/8$", three-track tapes for the instrument, which was the first time we had ever needed to do this. John and I then delivered the machine to his studio and while we were there we renovated his Novatron which he also uses on stage."

The down side of using antiquated instrumentation is, of course, noise. Something that Gendron was clearly on top of. "For the most part we are dealing with very clean signals, although the older, more funky keyboards groan a little and emit strange noises, which is why we are using noise gates on every set of keys. With so many keyboards on stage it can present a few problems with RF interference, so I have Remy with me for the whole show. He helps me with the running of the tapes and assists with RF aspects, making sure that all the frequencies are clean and moving the antennae. But since we took on the Garwood IDS systems we haven't had too much to worry about because you can change frequencies very quickly, and legally too because the software makes it very difficult to use illegal bands!"

When addressing the audience, Jarre used a Sennheiser SKM-5000 radio mic and also had a small AKG mic on a belt pack to pick up his megaphone which triggered the Vocoder effect on 'Revolution'. There were also mics on the hi-hat (451) and four Shure Beta 57s for overheads. Gendron: "The PA is hung on the same line as the musicians, so we have to ensure that the mics we use on the drums will not feedback and the Beta 57s have pretty good rejection. I also have two Sennheiser shotgun-type ambience mics to capture some hall sound and inject it into the musicians' mixes which is a very important thing for all in-ear monitoring engineers to do. It is also sometimes very important to heavily process the in-ear sound to achieve depth, and my tools for the job in question include the t.c. M5000 with remote, and three M2000s, plus a full cage of Aphex Expressor compressor/limiters."

The Oxygene European tour concluded at the end of June and another of Jarre's classic open-air spectaculars was held in Moscow on 6 September as part of the Russian city's 850th anniversary. The following summer of 1998 witnessed the synth star's return to the Paris cityscape when, on 14 July, the anniversary of the French Revolution, he staged his free Rendezvous '98 Electronic Night, performing in front of the Eiffel Tower alongside many of the day's cult dance heroes.

Coming just two days after the French soccer team's World Cup victory, and in the same location which played host to the pre-Final Three Tenors Concert, Rendezvous '98 saw the Eiffel Tower bathed in a series of E/T/C image projections and LSD lighting, ranging from stripes of yellow and green through to a patchwork of candy pink. It was the perfect climax to what had been the most thrilling month in the annals of France's twentieth century cultural history.

CHAPTER SEVENTEEN

On The Road With Lollapalooza

Toronto and Buffalo – 1997

Since 1969's epic Woodstock event, promoters the world over have sought to recreate a similar magic, and line their pockets, with a vast range of themed, open-air summer festivals. In the UK, the most popular annual event of its kind since the early Seventies has been the Glastonbury Fair, occasionally known as the Great British Mud Bath, depending on the kindness of the weather across Somerset. In Belgium in 1977, promoter Herman Scheuermans established an interesting long-running formula, whereby two separate bills of artists "flip-flopped" between sites in Torhout and Werchter across two days. This package proved to be the blueprint for Virgin's V96 festival in both Leeds and Chelmsford.

Over in North America, the sheer expanse of the country influenced the birth of a new kind of festival in 1991: Lollapalooza. Originally devised by ex-Jane's Addiction frontman Perry Farrell, Lollapalooza was unique not only because as a festival that from June to mid August steamrolled through American cities on a daily basis, but because the range of artists that it brought in its wake was arguably the most diverse to ever be experienced in one place. Almost as off the wall as the audience.

The 1997 tour began in West Palm Beach and arrived (with yours truly in tow) at the Kingswood Amphitheatre in Toronto on 4 July, departing the next day for Darien Lake in Buffalo, New York. Although the bill altered slightly later on in the tour, with Devo, Prodigy and The Orb jumping aboard at various intervals, the main stage at this time featured the reggae of opening act The Marley Brothers (sons of Bob), the clever English pop of James, the eclectic sounds of Tricky, hard rockin' Korn, crass rapper Snoop Doggy Dogg, the searing guitars and crunching rhythms of headlining US heroes Tool, and Orbital who, despite being faced with a high proportion of Tool fans in both audiences, won the crowd over with their incredible audio-visual production which crossed the boundaries of both techno and rock.

Backstage, a luxurious tour bus was home to the Lollapalooza production office and, in particular, tour director Stuart Ross who had been on the festival team since 1991, when Lollapalooza began as Jane's Addiction's farewell tour. "Perry Farrell wanted to go out with a bang and tour with six opening acts, arts and crafts, and some cool food stalls," explained Ross, who then operated as the tour accountant. "Perry named the show after an archaic American term which before World War II was used to describe a huge event or party. And this party turned out to be an enormous success, so we decided to form a company to repeat the formula. In 1992, we had The Red Hot Chili Peppers, Ministry and Pearl Jam whose enormous popularity helped Lollapalooza become quickly established."

By 1997, a number of copycat American touring festivals had taken their lead from Lollapalooza, namely HORDE (Heaps Of Rock Developing Everywhere) and the all-female Lilith Fair, launched in 1997 by singer-with-a-mission Sarah McLachlan. But Lollapalooza was quite literally in another field.

"With other festivals in the United States you don't get this huge entourage travelling from city to city," said Ross. "We were the first people to be stupid enough to try and tour a festival! And in a production sense this is a big tour because we are carrying 350 people. We're not just talking about the main stage production; everything, such as the Brain Forest rave tent and extraordinary sideshow activities on the concourse, travel with us. We own and transport the big, fold-out second stage which sets itself up with hydraulics, and we've spent six figures on the site artwork alone. It's not as if we throw a few food booths and video games out there and say, 'Hey, go enjoy yourselves!' We believe that the kids who come to this show for eleven hours deserve some quality entertainment outside of the main stage live music."

Surprisingly for someone with an accountancy background, Ross made an effort to tour in the most expensive way possible. "There are several areas in which we could cut costs, but we'd be compromising the quality. We always book great hotels for the bands and entourage, but we always get good deals because we book a lot of rooms, spend a lot of money and the hotels tend to want us back every year."

The diverse artist line-up had many people baffled, so how did the central committee of Ross, Farrell, Ted Gardner and Peter Grosslight choose the entertainment? "We start meeting on this in November every year. Perry probably has the most input regarding which acts to book and he informs us of the musical direction in which we should be heading. He was very insistent that world music and techno should be seriously represented, which accounts for the opening and closing acts this year. The main stage is a very tough stage to book, and inevitably there are a lot of back and forth negotiations about positioning on the bill, although the second stage is a breeze. When we started booking second stage talent we had a list of 350 acts that were submitted and it was simply a case of picking the most credible ones."

Among them were James, whose guitarist/violinist Saul Davies remarked on Lollapalooza's individuality. However, he admitted to having a few reservations about the tour when James arrived for the first date. He said: "It felt really corporate and not very welcoming but after two dates I started really getting into it. We toured with WOMAD for about twenty dates around America and that was much more shambolic than this. I've found the organisation behind Lollapalooza to be very well-oiled. I don't think we would have a tour like this in Britain with such a mad range of artists playing on the same stage. We go back home soon to play Reading with Suede and Cast, and we fit in snugly with all those bands, as far as the audience is concerned. But this must be incredibly confusing for the people here, most of whom have mainly bought tickets to see Tool."

The show loaded in every day at 6am, the doors opened at noon and the show started at 2pm. It was all over by 11pm and, with an identical schedule to follow the next morning, it was essential that the last of the seven trucks was cleared by 1.30am. With such a strict regime, Ross insisted that efficiency was the most desirable factor. "If we're unable to leave before 2.30am, we'll arrive at 7am, the show will start late and we'll be playing catch-up for days. It constantly amazes me that we are all rigged and ready for every show on time. We're not operating a typical tour where you can load in at a reasonable hour, wait for the band to show up at 4pm, soundcheck, have dinner and start the show at 8pm. We don't have that luxury and we don't do soundchecks. There are fifteen to twenty minute set changes and there are no options, so packaging and efficiency mean everything and they are the key aspects which help us determine which vendors we invite to do the tour."

The main service companies for the 1997 tour were Delicate Productions (PA), The Obie Company (Lighting) and PSL (Video). California-based Delicate was no stranger to Lollapalooza, in fact it handled the sound (and lighting) for the very first tour in 1991 and in many ways helped to define the standard of audio demanded by the festival committee. Ross explained that all production services were subject to an open bid that was "restricted to A-level vendors who we are sure will have their bid taken very seriously". Touring schedules prevented Delicate from supplying the festival between 1992 and 1996, but Ross was delighted that things worked out with the company for 1997.

"All of the companies who have done sound for us, such as dB Sound, Delicate and Electrotec, are all terrific companies who are absolutely qualified to do the tour. The headlining act normally has some say in which PA they would prefer to work with on the main stage, and that was definitely the case with Tool. Metallica played last year and their preferred system was the EV MT-4. Prior to that, The Red Hot Chili Peppers wanted Electrotec. Tool were already working with Delicate, but I'm pleased to say that all of the other main stage bands are also very happy with the way things are sounding."

The founder and owner of Delicate Productions is Chris "Smoother" Smyth, an Englishman who re-located to the United States in 1976. Delicate's flagship Martin Audio F2 rig was put into action for Lollapalooza. Mixed at front-of-house on two sixty-channel Yamaha PM4000 boards which flip-flopped between bands, the 120-box touring rig was configured as a long-throw system, designed to push effortlessly through the covered area of the venues and out to the rear lawn, without the need for delay speakers. (When the desk meter read 110dB, the measurement on the lawn indicated a hefty 104dB.)

On the outer columns of the flown rig were boxes containing long-throw highs with 2 x 2" drivers and 3 x 1" drivers, and 3 x 12" mids. On the very top row there was a vertical array of the mids and highs to achieve a throw of approximately one mile. At the centre was a four wide column of bass cabinets.

Although the full rig was in place at the Buffalo show, a trim height restriction dictated that the ground stack was a few boxes short. Scotty Scherban, Delicate's crew chief, said: "Normally, the ground stack consists of a four wide bass column and on the outer sides we then use full range, front fill boxes that we call combis – a combination of a 12", 2" and 1" driver. I then stack ten subs underneath, two on top of each other. It's a pretty large rig and by the time we're done, it's a good 28' of PA." The system is driven by eight racks of seven Crest 7001 amps and, for the subs, four racks of three 8001s.

One of Smoother's goals for the summer was to gain some well-earned respect for the F2, at a time when a handful of new PA developments, such as JBL's HLA and L-Acoustics' V-DOSC, were proving to be a distraction. "I don't think F2 gets the credit it deserves and that could be because it is rarely used to its full potential," he said. "In Europe there is more of a trend for rental companies to latch on to new boxes, as if they are scared to be seen with the older products. But the F2 has been around for about the same time as the EAW KF-850 and came out just after Showco's Prism system. Clair Brothers are now into their umpteenth version of the S4 and people in the States don't seem to be as paranoid about using a box that has been doing good business for several years. Why should I change?"

One or two production managers had confided that the F2 was just a little too heavyweight for modern touring requirements, and yet this had never posed a problem for Smoother who, with the F2, ended up with a lighter load than the Clair S4 – his basic reference point for system weight. "It's about packaging an awful lot of components into a box in combination with physics to do the job well. Having a good sound is a good place to start when you're designing a system, and if set designers and accountants are joining the bandwagon, then it's a sad day for audio."

On site was Jack Alexander, who was soon to leave Martin Audio's US distributor TGI and join Martin itself. He had been a fan of Martin systems since he saw the first bin and horn rigs roll into the States in the early 1970s, and was convinced that F2 was as relevant as ever. "If you're presented with a large dance floor and the accountants are watching progress, and you need to achieve x amount of SPL with x amount of bandwidth, I submit that F2 is still ahead of its time. A properly set-up F2 rig with some of the new control platforms like the BSS Omnidrive or the XTA DP-200 will still be state-of-the-art. It continues to set a standard by which other manufacturers define themselves."

In general, the engineers on Lollapalooza who normally toured with other system brands were extremely satisfied with the Martin rig. Even Mickey Mann, Orbital's FOH engineer, who had originally doubted its suitability. He said: "I've unfortunately had some bad experiences with the F2, which probably had more to do with the concrete venues I used it in, like the Bierkeller in Bristol. I found it difficult to control the mid range. But the F2 has been performing very well on the Lollapalooza dates and my attitude towards the system is now completely different."

For Tool's engineer, Monty Lee Wilkes, mixing on this festival felt like a homecoming. "I used to work for Southern Thunder Sound in Minneapolis and their proprietary system, built by a genius called Art Welter, was very similar to the F2. So every time I sit down to mix on an F2 rig it feels just like mixing with what I grew up on. It's certainly giving me what I want in terms of the Tool sound. The F2's detractors will claim that it's just a bin and horn system, and you can't disagree with them, but as far as bin and horn systems go, it's hands down the best one out there."

As far as new audio technology was concerned, Lollapalooza was notable for the first major use of Shure's Personal Monitor System, one of the newly-emerged alternatives to Garwood's in-ear monitoring market champ, the Radio Station. The exclusive user on this tour was James singer Tim Booth and it was interesting to discover that both he and monitor engineer Eddie Mulrainey preferred it to the competing Garwood model. "There are a couple of features that set the Shure product apart," said Mulrainey. "I think the peak limiting is a lot more friendly to the wearer; the volume control is more easily accessible on the body pack, and Tim is able to design his preferred stereo balancing." After working with a prototype version on the band's previous UK tour, James were equipped with a completed wireless production model and were just one of a string of bands, including The Rolling Stones, to take it on board before the end of the year.

Monitoring was divided into two "flip-flop" systems, each controlled via a Midas XL3 desk. There were twelve Martin LE 700 wedges on stage, two in each monitor control position for cueing, and the rest distributed along the front line. Eight of the older LE 600s were upstage. The side fills consisted of two F2 bass with F1 mid high per side, and drum fills had an F1 1 x 18" folded horn bass and F1 mid high.

Mickey Mann started his engineering career in 1986 with the band who would later become The Shamen. Since the early Nineties, however, he had been working for Orbital and was on top form for Lollapalooza. The techno duo operated a highly sophisticated synth and sampler rig on-stage and sent composite stereo channel pairs to Mann via two Mackie desks, a 32•4 and a 16•4.

Mann's job was made complex by the nature of the performances. He said: "The songs vary within themselves and I'm constantly doing a lot of graphics work. It's a very fluid experience and I have to pre-judge anything that comes my way. The sound alters so much that I can't set everything up and just babysit the mix. If I take my hands away from the desk, one minute everybody's jumping around, and the next thing you know, they start getting distracted. So I have to get back on the case and play the desk like an instrument."

Many of Orbital's numbers featured a slow 808 kick drum and on every fourth beat Mann inserted a dbx sub bass unit to fill it out. He needed to apply caution here as an absence of subtlety may have destroyed the clarity of the basses. Quality DIs were therefore necessary weapons. "I always use DIs because you get a better, cleaner bass response and I find the Countryman boxes we're using here are very reliable. I put a -20dB pad in to give me a lot of gain control. Some desks, particularly the old TAC Scorpions, have a bit of a sweet spot on the gain and when you have level changes like we have, you end up chasing the gain around to get the best sound. But when you move up to Midas, Yamaha, Ramsa and Gamble, they're all fine and you can set them pretty much on one gain and ride the fader."

As their music suggested, Orbital's low end was undoubtedly more potent than that of any other band on the bill – the result of Scotsman Mann's tinkering with the system EQ. He said: "The system is set up with Varicurves but there's also a set of graphics which no one seems to be touching. In some of these shows there have been some really tight decibel restrictions, so if I find one or two frequencies in the bass area that are upsetting the meters, I just pull them out a little. That allows me to boost the level while retaining a controlled sound."

Meanwhile, Monty Lee Wilkes, formerly the FOH engineer with Live and The Sneaker Pimps, was enjoying having control over Tool's various experimental sounds. The song 'Sober' featured Danny Carey's extraordinary drum solo – yes, drum solo! – which was enhanced by guitarist Adam Jones' use of...an Epilady! Said Wilkes: "Adam makes all kinds of noises with strange devices held over the pick-ups while Danny goes wild. The drum stuff is left fairly untreated but he also uses a very old Simmons SDX pad system that triggers various samples from glass breaking to nice percussion sounds, and I receive a stereo feed from the Simmons brain."

Fourteen AKGs, forty Shures, seven Sennheisers, four EVs, one Beyer and five Sony UHF wireless hand-helds (with Beta 58 capsules) comprised Delicate's microphone inventory, which accounted for just about every band's needs. However, Wilkes informed that Tool's preference for Audix mics meant that the band brought their own trunk full of goodies. Lead singer Maynard Keenan used an Audix OM7 vocal mic and apart from the Shure SM91 kick drum mic and AKG 414s on the hi-hat and overheads, Audix was present everywhere on the Tool stage, with D4s on the floor toms, D3s on rack toms, D2s on the snare, and a mixture of D2s and D1s on the guitar and bass. "Maynard claims that Audix produce the best mics on the market, but that's a subjective view," said Wilkes. "Audix approached me about using their stuff and I'll try anything once and twice if I like it, and I've really been knocked out with the products."

Among the weird and wonderful tricks that Wilkes occupied himself with at the desk were some vocal effects. "We have two vocal mics on stage, one of which is purely for vocal effects and it has a switch on the cord. That mic does not route to stereo – it is fed straight into an SPX-900 with a chorused distortion setting and because it isn't a direct signal we are getting a much better gain before feedback. I give that mic a little sweetening at the top end just to enhance the razor-like sound. When it's working correctly, it really sounds bad, which is the desired result! On 'Eulogy', Maynard is singing into a slightly modified Radio Shack megaphone which stands out as an amazing distortion effect. The crew broke off the megaphone horn and put some female velcro inside the phase plug to reduce the horn sound, and the resulting sound gets a 150 millisecond delay."

Both Tool's and Orbital's sets were augmented by stunning video sequences, using three of the latest generation Barco 9200 projectors supplied along with all the necessary processing and monitoring equipment by PSL Inc, the American subsidiary of the pioneering international audio-visual company that is part of the global Gearhouse Group.

A simple but effective system for both bands was overseen and managed by video technician Matthew Askem, who made his debut with PSL on a Suede UK tour in 1994. His career, like the implementation of live video itself, had come on leaps and bounds in the intervening years (his credits include Smashing Pumpkins, Eternal and M People), and the smooth-running of this particular aspect of Lollapalooza relied heavily on his expertise.

The control rack contained three Betacam VCRs with remote control, two Panasonic MX-50 switchers, and preview monitoring and distribution. The Tool video projected on to a 93% solid, 15' high x 80' wide cotton weave cyc situated above a 10' high black – all of which was mounted on runners.

In between the two sets, Askem could be seen ferreting around behind the scenes, preparing for Orbital. He said: "The three Barcos are on a truss. Two of them are moveable on a turret frame which allows me to move them through 50° or 60°. At the end of Tool's set, the cyc runners go back and we put Orbital's three 12 x 16' screens up on the festival truss and lift that up. I go up in the truss and re focus the 9200s on to those screens, and re-patch to Giles Thacker's [Orbital's video director] video processing. In front there are two 7 x 5 foot screens that are the side stage cameos.

By the very nature of projection, direct sunlight played havoc with the images, which was probably why only the last two bands carried video production. However, by the time Tool kicked off mid evening in Toronto, the stage was in deep shadow and all was hunky dory. Buffalo was a different story – it wasn't the sun that posed a threat, it was the wind. Being open at the back, the stage became a wind trap by late afternoon and a decision was made to drop the rear screens on both sets, and only use the two cameo screens for Orbital.

Considering that Giles Thacker and Tool's video director Jerry

Rodgers were using virtually the same equipment, it was interesting how vast the differences were in their approach. Orbital's video show was much more considered and rehearsed, where as Tool's was designed on the fly and more manually operated. It all appeared to be dictated by how Rodgers was feeling as he sat in front of the controls and listened to the band. Askem was particularly impressed by Thacker's work: "Giles is really dedicated about what goes up on the screens and tries hard not to use footage that anyone's seen before."

Orbital's images were strangely abstract – the video that accompanied their hit re-working of the 'Saint' theme featured close-up stills of everyday office appliances, and gave one the feeling that Thacker was viewing the world with different eyes to the rest of us mere mortals. He said: "The video images stored on the three VCRs were shot by myself with Orbital's previous LD, Luke Losey, and we edited them on an Avid system to S-VHS format. We spent hours and hours filming typewriters and phones, and all kinds of things. Another recurring image we project is an oscilloscope. We take sound feeds from the FOH mixing desk and film the soundwaves on the oscilloscope read out with a camera."

Their Lollapalooza shows were not typical Orbital performances. "They change their set around a lot depending on the nature of the show," said Thacker. "Here, we are playing for an hour, straight after a heavy metal band, so we've spiced up the show with faster tracks than we'd have on a regular performance. We were worried that we'd be playing to the wrong sort of audience and that's why we've tailored the show in this way, to have a faster, rock edge to it. We have video material for about twenty tracks and we kind of pick and mix, and form the most appropriate set."

Matthew Askem said that most of Tool's imagery was created by guitarist Adam, although one number featured extracts from a recent single promo. "Most of what they use is what we call fractal footage, with images of tunnels, patterns, psychedelic colours and other computer-generated graphics."

PSL Inc was launched as a service centre in California with an Ozzy Osbourne tour in January 1996, initially with former British lighting designer Malcolm Mellows at the helm of the Concert Touring Division. He was replaced in 1998 by Bob Higgins, as PSL's parent company Gearhouse began to spread its net across the world in a bid to acquire small operations, and thereby creating a network of audio-visual services. By the summer of 1998, Gearhouse, along with the Production Resource Group and Vari-Lite Production Services, represented the "big three" worldwide event production service groups, all sharing plans for further expansion.

At the time of Lollapalooza, Mellows believed there were considerable differences between PSL's UK and US operations, not least ease of transportation. "Supporting tours in the USA is easier because the infrastructure for shipping equipment quickly is in place. None of PSL's stock is ever more than two years old so we are always dealing with the state-of-the-art. Over in America, people have been used to equipment that is considerably older than that. So it has been interesting to see people's reactions when we turn up on tours with sensibly packaged and easy to rig equipment. They are simply not used to it!"

Orbital started incorporating video into their set when Thacker joined them in 1994. Although the services of Quadrant and Creative Technology had been hired on occasions, the band were booking PSL for around 75% of their shows, always using the projection format. "PSL is the best video company I've used," said Thacker, who underlined Mellows' every word. "We've used other companies who do okay, but you can always rely on PSL to provide absolutely pukka kit and crew who know exactly what they're doing."

Delicate provided lighting on the very first Lollapalooza, followed by LSD for the next five years. A new supplier came into the picture for 1997: LA-based The Obie Company. Arguably one of the top five rock 'n' roll lighting rental firms in the USA, Obie handles much US trade for products such as Telescans and the Coemar Nat, as well as touring with Michael Jackson, Janet Jackson, Paula Abdul, Neil Diamond and Michael Bolton.

According to Stuart Ross, Obie's top ranking in the bidding war was helped by its new proprietary CTS rigging system that was not only extremely practical but also saved on truck space. "The sides of the lighting truss slide up and form a gantry. The crew call it the catwalk truss because you can walk along it when you're working. Obie designed it to carry Vari*Lites so that if they ever tour with hundreds of Vari*Lites on it, instead of having a truck full of lights with boxes, the boxes are already in the truss so you're saving a fortune in trucking as well as installation time. Our budget is not infinite, so if we can fit lights in one truck as opposed to two, we're deliriously happy."

This was lighting technician and programmer Adam Burton's first tour as part of the Obie team; he put the show together in an impressive three days. The original spec included a Whole Hog controller (Burton's favourite), but in the end he opted for a High End Status Cue. "There was the option of either controller, but none of the bands' LDs knew the Hog, so the choice was easy to make," he commented. "Trying to programme the show and teach someone the board is impossible when you're working festivals. But the Status Cue (a Windows-based package which runs all fixture types) is pretty simple to use."

Based on the general wish lists of the bands' LDs, the Obie rig contained twenty-two High End Studio Colors, thirteen Cyberlites, sixteen AF-1000s (DMX), a total of thirty-six four- and eight-cell Molephays with colour changers, eleven ACL bars, eight 6' MR16 strips, fifty-eight Par 64s, four F-100 smoke machines (DMX) and two DF-50 Profusion crackers. Orbital's Jonny Gaskell, the only LD on this tour who actually programmed the lights to move off the stage, felt he had fared well considering his band were not technically the headliners. "Tool's LD [Mark Jacobson] just uses the rig for standard rock 'n' roll looks, pointing the lights at the drum kit or whatever. So what we do makes a huge difference to the whole feel of the show. We introduce some high level drama and it gives me the opportunity to show what this rig can really do."

Although Gaskell was happy with the rig, he felt compelled to bring along a few extras. "We've added some Optikinetics specials, a couple of Solar 575s and four Clay Paky Astro Raggies which are balls that fire out beams to fill out everything along the level below the screens. I had a lot of difficulty finding them until we discovered that AC Lighting had some in their warehouse and that the only gig they'd done with them was the Eurovision Song Contest! Since we bought them we've had a great response to what we've been doing and it has been very satisfying to design my light show around such a fantastic video production."

CHAPTER EIGHTEEN

INXS

Elegantly Wasted – 1997

In 1997, only a few months before singer Michael Hutchence was found dead in his Sydney hotel room, INXS were playing live in Europe, following the release of *Elegantly Wasted*, the album which unknown to them would mark the end of an era.

The "New Sensation" on this tour was JBL's newly-developed HLA (Horn Loaded Array) Concert Touring System, a PA rig recently purchased by Belgian rental company EML. The Belgians seized the contract for the INXS tour after supplying a Martin F2 system for one of the band's club promo showcases that spring. EML had listened to a shoot-out between an EAW system, Meyer MSL-5 and JBL's HLA, and, as account manager Wim Despiegelaere explained, the company took to the latter without hesitation and placed an order. What followed was strangely ironic, with EML servicing a major arena tour with HLA, partly as a consequence of a small club gig with F2!

Just three weeks before the arena tour began, Despiegelaere took an INXS party to the JBL factory in California to sample the new system, and production manager Chris Hey was convinced on the spot. He said: "We looked at every rental company's proposals [including those of Brit Row, SSE and Concert Sound] but it was primarily EML's investment in HLA that influenced me to give them the contract. It's the best system I've heard in a long, long time."

So what sparked EML's investment after so many years of loyalty to Martin F2? Despiegelaere said: "We still love F2 and use those speakers as INXS' sidefills, but we have faced a growing problem on tours

217

because it is quite a heavy system to fly and takes a fair amount of rigging time. All those disadvantages are non-existent with HLA and it's possible to fly a full arena system within an hour. Although it's a big box, it's still compact and you don't need many boxes for an arena show. If we tried to achieve the same reinforcement with Martin F2, we would need one and a half trucks full of boxes; we can now do the job with just one truck."

Arena configurations for HLA were varied. With round-ish venues like Wembley Arena, the system was flown six boxes wide and three deep. For a long venue, it was recommended to fly it four deep and five wide, and depending on the angulation of the boxes (the drivers can be angled within the boxes), the system could be either long or short throw.

Another benefit applauded by Despiegelaere was the headroom of the system, run on the tour with BSS Omnidrives. "We have the factory crossover points as designed by JBL, but the bigger the array you make and the more coupling you have with the 14" boxes, the lower you can go with the crossover points between those and the subs. That means plenty of headroom but you do not change the sound of the system, which is the best aspect of it. It's the first system I've ever heard on which you can change the crossover points without affecting the sound."

He was also impressed with the incredibly even dispersion of the cabinets. "It's a horn-loaded system but it sounds front-loaded which is unusual. I think it's going to shake up the industry; it's one of the best innovations in touring technology for many years. There are plenty of good-sounding systems in the world but there are so many logistical and practical aspects to take care of. My feeling is that HLA has an advantage in the design considerations to practical use."

Stuart Kerrison started as INXS's FOH engineer in April 1997, and although he was among those invited to the JBL factory, the first time he actually heard HLA in an arena configuration was on the afternoon of the first show! A bit of a gamble? "I was thinking, 'This had better be good, otherwise we'll be up the creek without a paddle!' But not only was it good, it sounded fantastic and I was really happy. The system that lets me quickly achieve the sounds I'm hearing in my head is going to be the one for me. I want to hear the band loud and clear, and with depth and colour. HLA does that job."

The efficient sub-bass section of the PA was a revelation to Kerrison. "We are using only eight HLA subs per side, but they are delivering the same SPL and quality as the last time I worked at Wembley with a total of twenty-eight Meyer 650 subs. It's loud, but there's absolutely no distortion at all and my belief is that as soon as your brain detects a square wave, you automatically think that what you're hearing is too loud."

Kerrison was raised in Australia but moved to England in 1984 where he took up with Orchestral Manoeuvres In The Dark as their FOH engineer. A Midas XL4 user with INXS, he found that as he became better acquainted with the board's automation, he increasingly relied on it. His long-time wish for a reliable automated mixing aid appeared to have come true. "You could never leave the faders in a row with OMD if you wanted the sound to be big and dynamic, because with so many different keyboard sounds and velocities on each channel, you had constant movement. I've engineered a lot of bands like that [including Erasure] and have been used to working like crazy to reset the desk for the next number.

"Naturally, I've been saying to people for some time, including Midas, that I need some kind of automated recall facility to help me relax! When the XL3 came out it was a fantastic board, but I commented that all I needed was to have this desk with some moving faders and my dreams would come true. They told me that the XL4 would have that facility, so when it came out and I heard I was going out with INXS, with all the sequences involved in their music, I knew I had to use it."

It was difficult to connect with INXS's performance, even though the opening two numbers (including the *Elegantly Wasted* title track) promised great things. The set design was often more inviting to the eye than the preening, posing Hutchence. The concept – a kind of sci-fi wasteland scene in front of a silver gauze backdrop – originated from the mind of drummer Jon Farriss, but it took the further input of Chris Hey, crew chief Dave Edwards and, especially, LD Sean "Motley" Hackett before becoming reality.

"My initial understanding was that the set was going to reflect the street scene of the [*Elegantly Wasted*] album cover, so we were looking at having a bridge across the stage and some street lights," said Hackett. "That got blown out and I was then looking at a kooky, sci-fi space lab kind of thing. Multiple drawings came from different angles and there were things that looked like they came out of *The Jetsons*. Jon was influenced by the film *Barbarella* and wanted something silver and shimmering. It's turned out to be really funky because we've got these bullet things which look a bit phallic. We've used the old Brilliant Stages set from the last tour and painted it silver and got Supotco to dress it differently. There are a couple of UV stars around the place and we have these things we call 'socks' which are 3' diameter vertical tubes [the 'Plasma Drives'] dressed in white gauze material. We light those from the bottom with a Colour Changer and from the top with an Icon Washlight which I can move and twirl inside to create some amazing effects."

The "Hellish" rig was supplied by LSD – an Icon system with seventeen Icons and eighteen Washlights, with everything controlled from an Icon desk except for Colormags which were run from a dedicated Colormag console. "I just have a thing about running colour changers from a separate desk. If everything's gonna go wrong, at least I'll be on the right colour!" commented the LD.

Hackett designed the rig such that there were large gaps in between the lights. "I've tried to make every Icon sit so that there are no two Icons in front of or next to each other. I find that if you put two lights together it doesn't necessarily look too much bigger, compared to when you position them further apart. I did think about fixing them to T-bars at varying heights but with budgets and crew to think about, we decided against it.

Initially afraid that with a silver backdrop, the stage would turn into a giant reflector for the lights, Hackett was relieved that everything worked out perfectly. "If I don't light it, it's very dark, but if I do it takes colour very well. Everything on stage is grey with silver glitter sprayed all over. When people look down on the stage, as the lights change the stage shimmers. Once the set came in it became this big symmetrical thing although the lighting was, by design, a total mess. I wanted the rig to look like it had just fallen down from Hell." Beelzebub himself would have been impressed.

CHAPTER NINETEEN

Michael Jackson

HIStory – 1997

The crowd looked on in near silence. Accompanied by only the percussive tapping of his gently walking feet, he approached the high stool upon which he rested the curious suitcase. The audience was hushed in wonder. The suitcase was opened. Out of the shadows, he revealed but a single silver glove. Instant recognition gave way to a deafening eruption which at once filled the borough of Brent. This was the near-deified King Of Pop...this was Michael Jackson, delivering the unique, theatrical brand of show that only he would dare present.

An average of 86,000 besotted worshippers gathered on each of the three dates at Wembley Stadium in July 1997 to see Jackson's HIStory show in the flesh – a true measure of this living legend's everlasting popularity. And yet while it was easy to become wrapped up, or even distracted, by the size and glamour of the production, to those who took a really good look around them the whole experience felt rather empty.

Disillusionment set in before the star hit the stage. Knowing that each member of the audience had paid no mean price to see their hero, it was sickening to watch walkabout merchandising sales people hawking cardboard tube periscopes at £5 a time, in order for the height-challenged amongst the crowd to be able to see their hero. The sight of thousands spending most of the gig looking into these tubes instead of the actual stage was all too much to stomach. Was this really how low top grade rock had gravitated?

For hours before Jackson stepped from the wings, one pondered on the set. Masking the PA at either side of the stage were scrim frontages with an architectural design that was meant to represent the Temple of History, and pretty soon the audience were sent back into the mists of time as the artist regaled them with hits by the score, yielded from a catalogue which started in 1970 with 'I Want You Back'. The show itself began with an ingenious opening sequence which married lighting effects with a screened computer graphic ride through space, at the end of which the spaceship crashed through the back of the stage and Jackson emerged looking every inch like one of the Cybernauts that regularly appeared in *Doctor Who*. Cue the screams...now where were those ear plugs?

Yes, this was pure pop theatre, bordering on the most expensive Vegas cabaret show ever created, with production values that would have made Cecil B de Mille and Busby Berkeley beam with pride. And Roger Waters would have been flattered if he'd have seen 'Black And White' with its Floydesque tumbling wall of guitar cabinets, followed by pyromania and the sound effects of a buzzing helicopter.

Every move, flinch, "ad lib", gesture to the video cameras, and especially every vocal line was being repeated with precision night after night after night – strictly choreographed right down to Jackson's long-winded displays of emotion. Sympathy and respect to the crew – the boredom factor attached to a long-running tour on which each show was a carbon copy of the last must have been virtually insufferable. When Jackson uttered on more than one occasion "Love you...England", it was mightily impressive – he could have been anywhere.

The third Wembley date was Clair Brothers' front-of-house engineer Trip Khalaf's thirty-first show as a sound engineer at the Stadium, seventeen years after his first arrival during Fleetwood Mac's Tusk tour. His CV by this point listed such names as Madonna, Stevie Nicks and Queen, for whom he produced their *Live Magic* album. "I am told by Wembley officials that I hold the record and no one comes close," he revealed.

Khalaf was quite visibly taking it easy at Wembley, to the point where, at times, he was sitting back and resting his feet on the corner of one of his two Midas XL4 consoles. "All the hard work for me on this tour is long passed and I'm just swanning around now," he explained. "With the automation on the XL4s in place I barely need to show up, and there's probably a few people on the tour who'd be glad if I didn't! One of these days I hope to be treated just like a lighting designer, someone who earns a huge amount of money, but you never see them!"

Khalaf had to be admired for trying to have as much fun as he could muster, against all odds. A fascinating, dry-witted, and controversial character, he oozed cynicism at every juncture but with a smile that made every comment utterly palatable. More often than not, that cynicism was levelled at his audio responsibilities. Take the Clair S4 PA system, for example, which on this tour was not a standard stadium configuration, thanks to the demands of the set design.

"I really stuck my neck out on this one," Khalaf grinned, Jack Nicholson style. "Usually we fly nine high by eight or nine wide, but these guys wanted to put the JumboTrons in the middle of the sound wall. I got that director's look that said, 'You're gonna do this?' So I thought about it for a while and stuck my neck out, and to tell you the truth it's great. The PA configuration is now four wide and nine high, with a 14' gap for the Sony JumboTron, and then three wide and nine high off stage. It has actually got rid of that huge low end lobe that goes out at about 20° from the stage, and it's very even all the way across. Would I ever do it again? I think not. Would anybody ever want to pay for the extra 16' of staging and truck full of crap it takes to do this? Nah!"

The front-of-house sound was augmented around the stadium by the resident ElectroVoice house system that was installed by Shuttlesound back in 1989. However, the Clair crew erected high frequency drivers on delay poles to re-establish some of the high end and maintain some intelligibility at the back of the pitch. Much of the equipment for the European leg was shipped by Stacks & Racks, while monitors and other elements of the rig came from the USA, straight from rehearsals in Los Angeles. "[Clair Brothers'] Bob Weibel came over to Europe a week early to sort through all the boxes and supervise the packaging and shipping of the systems from Audio Rent, so at least when the crew turned up they'd know where everything was," said Khalaf.

Khalaf says that EVI's Bob Doyle "talked him into" taking his two XL4s on the road for HIStory. But there was just one thing..."Of course, Joe O'Herlihy uses automation on all of his faders with U2, but the difference is that I work for the sound company. Joe turns to Clair Bros and says, 'Well, I really think that I need full automation on every fader...' Troy Clair replies, 'Okay, Joe.' I ask for something similar and Troy turns round and says, 'No!' 'I just thought I'd ask...' So I'm just using the VCAs and it's no problem. As long as you have kick, snare, vocals, bass, keyboards and guitars, boom, you're done!

"This whole show is built around different musical styles and sounds, and from song to song it's almost as if you are listening to a different band. The hardest part is actually getting ready for the next tune and you really had to be an earthmover when doing the same things on a Yamaha PM4000 – I could never really concentrate on what was really going on. With VCA automation you can be set up in an instant. The wonders of modern science! Of course, I'm convinced that one of these days I'm going to hit the button and nothing's gonna happen. Bob Doyle'll be the first to hear of it!"

There was much speculation in the mainstream press at the time of the Wembley shows surrounding the integrity of Jackson's vocal performance, with some journalists claiming that for most of the heavily choreographed numbers (which accounted for the lion's share of the show), the singer was relying on playback. This accusation was once also aimed squarely at Madonna. In Jackson's defence, the desk channel strip was clearly labelled with the singer's headset and hand mics, although it did seem rather inconceivable that on several occasions he was able to walk in front of the Clair PA rig wearing a live headset lavalier mic and not cause feedback. Each to their own.

Khalaf was fairly graphic about his approach to mixing between mics. "We're using a Shure Beta 87 capsule on Michael's hand-held radio mic. One of the propeller heads in my office at Clair Bros built an antenna distribution system which I am sure handles extra-terrestrial signals as well as Michael's vocals. It's great, like a giant combining network for all of the radio systems on stage, including the in-ear monitoring gear. Michael also uses a headset mic, which I think is the worst idea that anyone ever came up with for live rock 'n' roll. But we do the best we can," he sighed, eyes reaching skyward. "Michael was using an omni-directional capsule for his headset mic, but on this tour he's using an AKG cardioid because there needs to be a lot more rejection, and it does sound much better. He has a tendency to hold the mic nearer to his mouth. What am I supposed to do? Whack him on the head and say, 'Mikey, don't do that!'?"

He also reserved a little criticism for some of his engineering contemporaries: "Listen, the only significant outboard I use on Michael's voice is a dbx 903. I've seen too many engineers put a vocal signal into a limiter, out of a limiter, into a de-esser, through some vocal stabiliser, downstairs into the basement, bring it back up and...it sounds like shit. All the numbers are right, so it must sound great. But you end up chasing your own tail. For me, it's got to be the mic, the equaliser, and then the speaker, that's what it's all about. The number one criteria for me is to mix a show so that the audience can understand what the artist is singing about. Except for some of the newer bands, that is. If you can actually understand the vocals, the artist's manager will tell you to turn the vocal down. Why is that?"

Following a mystery phone call from Clair Brothers, John Roden joined the Michael Jackson entourage in April as monitor engineer, replacing Randy Weitzel who went on to work as a Yamaha sales representative on the US West Coast. Said Roden: "I was in New York, working with The Spice Girls as their monitor guy for a string of TV appearances, all of which were using Clair monitoring. Greg Hall rang me to say that a 'major client' was without a monitor engineer for a big tour, and asked if I'd be interested. It was hard to make a decision because Greg wouldn't divulge the artist's name. Eventually I got it out of him and, of course, I had to accept the job. It certainly looks nice on the CV! This is my first outing working for Clair Bros and I like the way I'm being looked after."

Rated at a mammoth 120dB between the sidefills, the sheer volume coming from off-stage at Wembley, as at all the shows, was incredibly loud. Roden himself said: "I wouldn't want to stand where Michael is for too long. It's harsh enough for me behind the desk! Because it is so loud I can just turn off my local wedge and mix off the sidefills. It's the first time I've ever really been able to do that."

Surely, this on-stage SPL posed a problem for Khalaf at FOH? "Yeah, let's say that it adds some interesting colour to the sound in the house, and it influenced the decision to leave out the front fills – we didn't need 'em! There's nothing I can do about it because that's the way Michael wants it and I have to deal with that as best I can in my own sweet way, given the circumstances! If he wants his head beaten, who am I to argue? Luckily, most of that volume is all downstage of the band, and most of it is direct anyway [with Countryman DIs and real-time triggered drum samples a-plenty]."

In real terms, how did he deal with this dilemma? "Oh, I just go on stage and kill the monitors, and do two or three shows while they try to replace them." But seriously..."I've watched this thing gradually grow and grow. I'm lucky because we are doing stadium shows, but if I tried to put that kind of SPL on the stage in an arena, we'd be dead in the water. We are talking about the possibility of an arena tour in the US and the idea is scaring the hell out of me. Here, I have half a million watts staring down my throat, so the monitor situation isn't worrying me that much, but I can still hear it coming from the stage even though I'm halfway into the stadium."

Assisted by Scott Appleton, Roden used two Yamaha PM4000M boards, running a total of seventy channels between them, including back-ups. Several of these channels were devoted to wireless in-ear monitoring for four members of the nine-piece band: backing vocalists Kevin Dorsey, Dorian Holley and Fred White, and shock-haired guitarist Jennifer Batten – the latter, along with her bass and guitar-playing band colleagues, also having mono mixes in Clair 12AM Series II wedges. The Clair-owned Garwood systems in use were the new IDS models, of which Roden said: "It's great to have so many frequencies to choose from, because you normally have to carry a couple of spares and change them depending on which country you're going to. But with these, we can be up and running instantly."

Jackson himself continued to abstain from ear-worn monitoring. "IEM was never an option for Michael and to my knowledge he doesn't like the idea of using that technology," said Roden. Although the front of the stage was free of wedges, the sidefill cabinets covering Jackson's working area were substantial in number, with five Clair R4s and five ML18s per side – a total of twenty 18" speakers – delivering a phenomenal amount of low end!

Roden concentrated on giving Jackson a full mix, with all monitoring EQ'd with the t.c. electronic remote graphics system. "Michael likes the on-stage sound to be hard and tight, drum and percussion heavy, and I notice that is what he's moving and dancing to. That seems to please him. The sounds he and the band hear are by nature wet-sounding because of the stadium venues we are playing. The slapback that's coming from the house makes it fairly lively on stage, although I have two Lexicon reverb units, one of which I have on the backing vocals, and another which I dial in just for Michael on a couple of occasions."

Drummer Jon Moffett had two ML18s and a pair of 12AM Series I wedges, while both the keyboard players had stereo mixes in Clair 12AM Series II wedges which Roden claimed had improved bass response and sounded "a bit sweeter" than the original model. Crest amps were assigned to the sidefills and the house system, and the Carver amps originally specified to drive the 12AMs were replaced in rehearsals by a rack of QSC Powerlight 2.0HV amps, in conjunction with TOA DP-0204 digital processors/crossovers.

Explained Roden: "In rehearsals I was clipping the Carvers all the time. The Carvers see a square wave very quickly and I was causing a lot of damage to the wedges which was no surprise, considering the volume. I just rang Clairs and said that the Carvers weren't cutting it, and they immediately replaced them with the Powerlights which have completely solved the problem. These amps have been balanced by the engineers back at Clair Bros to give the optimum output to run with these wedges. Despite the fact that I'm running the Powerlights exactly the same as the Carvers, I have yet to see them clipping."

Under Kenny Ortega's direction, design consultant John McGraw of Planview (who worked with production manager Chris Lamb on The Eagles and Madonna) designed, engineered and manufactured the set structure. It was McGraw's idea to split the JTS-17 JumboTron screen at upstage centre and incorporate the stage thrust, while Michael Cotton was credited with the general visual appearance of the set, including the "Temple of History" scrims. Most of the lighting crew on HIStory had worked with lighting designer Peter Morse at some time or another in the past; lighting director Michael Keller's association with Morse stretched back more than fifteen years, during which time they built up a healthy rapport based on a clear understanding and appreciation of each other's roles. Morse was present during rehearsals for this tour in California and also attended some of the early shows. Although the cooperation between Morse and Keller had been close, the famous designer was absent from much of the tour. Keller, instead, explained a little about the visual side of the production.

Three specialist companies supplied the lighting of HIStory: Light & Sound Design, Vari-Lite and The Obie Company. In his dual role as Lighting Director and Operator, Keller ran conventional lighting with colour changers from an Avolites Diamond II console, of which he said: "The Diamond II is a great board, although we are not utilising anywhere near the full amount of features on it; it's just there for colour changers. I was coming in to replace someone who had been with Michael for twelve years and I wanted something that could be labelled for easy operation so that I could address it as well as possible, and the Diamond II couldn't be bettered in my view."

Benny Kirkham operated the Vari*Lite system from an Artisan Plus, while Ryan Nicholson took care of all the Obie lighting from two Whole Hog IIs. "Between the three of us we have just about every type of lighting you can think of, and then some!" laughed Keller. "It's a virtual travelling LDI show!" A glance at the exhaustive equipment list bore out this tongue-in-cheek description: Vari-Lite supplied thirty-seven VL2Cs, twenty-four VL5Arcs, twenty-seven VL6s and fifteen VL4s, while the remainder of the rig included Intellabeams, Cyberlights, five Martin Professional PAL 1200s and seven MAC 1200s, twelve Studio Colors, Coemar Nats (twelve 2500s and nine 1200s) and five Obie XeScans.

It was interesting to note how particular groupings of lights were "showcased" during certain parts of the show, almost to the point where it resembled a demo for Vari*Lites, then Intellabeams, and so on. At other times, it seemed as if it was all hands on deck, with every element in the rig attempting to outperform each other – a trademark of Morse's work. The live re-creation of the classic mock horror scenes of 'Thriller', for instance, was a big Vari*Lite moment, whereas the vibrant 'Blood On The Dancefloor' demonstrated, well, everything.

Obie operator Ryan Nicholson seemed impressed with the features on the latest version of the Whole Hog II effects generator – he used two boards. "The focused preset effects and dynamic graphics, like circles, spirals, are fabulous," he said. "The algorithms are already built into the board, and so the focus just happens on single key strokes, which is really nifty. You assign that and change the parameters, and change the actual size of the focus. It's one of the best boards you can lay your hands on."

The most impressive visual aspect of the show was the upstage back wall containing a large grid of Obie-supplied Intellabeams which formed the basis of many lighting looks. "I've never seen I-Beams look so good," claimed Keller. "Everything else might seem to be straightforward, it's just that there is so much of it that the rig is like an effect in itself. The VL6s do some pretty creative stuff, and the VL5Arcs we have here are an upgrade on the incandescent arcs we used last year. All of those add a factor to the show, but the most visually entertaining elements from a dynamic point of view are those I-Beams. Man, they're really something!"

Video formed a major part of the production, with live camera images magnifying Jackson's every move, and a mixture of promo clips, graphics and archive footage providing a distraction between several songs. Two different screen systems were in operation. The portrait format screens referred to by Trip Khalaf were three modules high by six wide, approximately 4.5m wide x 7m high. These two JTS-80V Sony JumboTron screens were personally owned by Michael Jackson and were the same type as the ones used on Genesis's Invisible Touch tour by Screenco.

Jackson purchased the screens for use on his Dangerous tour, following which they were configured into one screen for use at his Neverland ranch in California, presumably for viewing his home movies! Reconfigured yet again, they were dragged away from Bubbles and his pals for this tour, and were operated by San Francisco's Nocturne, the video contractor for the tour.

Providing a high level of hospitality in the Mezzanine Bar on all three nights at Wembley was David Crump, MD of Screenco, whose company also assisted the production by installing a newer generation JTS-17 JumboTron upstage centre which split in half and tracked on and off as two screens at various points in the programme. When in use, the overall screen was four by four modules; when off stage, it was invisible to the audience. Crump said that the screen tracked in a similar way to that of the Screenco system at the Masters Of Music concert in Hyde Park. "It is hung from a very accurately computer-controlled tracking system devised by Steve Colley at [Hertfordshire-based] Ocean State Rigging. The one at Hyde Park was done by Unusual and was fairly crude because it was done for a one-off show, whereas this is a lot more sophisticated and able to withstand the rigours and demands of touring – it certainly goes in a lot more quickly."

It was quite noticeable when viewing the two different generations of JumboTron technology side by side just how much better the resolution was on the newer JTS-17. Although used primarily for the video inserts between numbers, there were some portions of the show where the central screen carried live images. "Although effectively two screens, it is run as a single screen, with a single image controller assigned to it," said Crump. "We've had to put together boosters because we have very long cable runs of up to 70m between the image controller, which is buried in the stage underworld, and the screen. Because of the way the cables have to route, we have a very sophisticated cable management system through the roof. The screen system goes in and out now in under an hour, and really is completely trouble-free. The JumboTron crew [including Screenco freelancer Dave "Chalky" White] spend all their time keeping Michael's gear working and fortunately our JTS-17 just plods along nicely every night."

The camera production was handled by Nocturne, and Paul Becher, who had been Jackson's video director for the past three tours, continued his association with the star. Becher's team were switching with a Grass Valley 100 console. All the recorded images were played in from either laser disk or VT from a CRV player, whereas live images were fed to the video control zone backstage by four Ikegami cameras: one on a Jimmy Jib boom in the pit, one front-of-house, one on a tripod and one hand-held.

Crump observed: "For the camera crew it is a very conventional show; Jackson does exactly the same things every night and the dance routine is so accurately choreographed that after a couple of shows, the camera work goes like clockwork and you can easily cut a perfect show from that point onwards. The cameras are very focused on Jackson which is his request. After all, that's who the punters are here to see."

For a variety of reasons, the Wembley shows ranked among the most bizarre of recent years. The ending was a spectacular anti-climax – not so much an encore as a piece of video footage which was screened while Jackson retreated backstage, leaving most of the audience completely baffled. "Michael has left the building" would have been a useful announcement. Going into battle with the slowly escaping Wembley traffic, a snigger had to be forced back as one recalled Johnny Rotten's famous last words to the audience as he exited the stage at Winterland at the end of The Sex Pistols' farewell concert in 1978. Go figure.

CHAPTER TWENTY

Oasis

Be Here Now In Production – 1997

Knebworth Park, August 1996: 250,000 people attend Oasis's two weekend shows and become part of one of the cornerstone events in British rock's brief history. In past eras, this field in deepest Hertfordshire played host to unforgettable open-air concerts by Pink Floyd, The Rolling Stones and Led Zeppelin, but it has since become revered as hallowed ground by a new generation – those who helped Liam and Noel Gallagher and the band claim the Nineties as their decade.

For a while it looked as if it all might go wrong for Oasis. Less than a fortnight after the Knebworth shows, the band were forced to perform for MTV *Unplugged* without the troubled Liam. A few weeks later, burned out by the treadmill of constant touring and intense media attention, Oasis interrupted an American trip and suddenly returned home to the UK as speculation mounted that they were about to split. The tabloids went into overdrive, but the drama soon subsided with the announcement that the band had repaired to the studio to begin the recording of their "difficult" third album, *Be Here Now*.

And it was that album, released on 21 August, 1997, which revitalised the band and gave birth to a new touring production that hit Europe three weeks later before making its way around the UK where, amongst other venues, they played three nights at Earl's Court – the very same venue where, in November 1995, overwhelmed (and arguably over-excited) critics began to compare them to The Beatles.

With the Knebworth experience behind them, Oasis, and

specifically lighting/set designer Mikey Howard, deliberately scaled down the size of their visual presentation for the Be Here Now tour, but used the space within the set more creatively, relying on the involvement of Light & Sound Design and Vari-Lite, new set construction firm PW Stage Productions, trussing builder Total Fabrications, and, for video, both PSL and Screenco. Meanwhile, the live sound continued to be in the capable hands of front-of-house engineer Huw Richards and monitor engineer Gareth Williams, with a Turbosound PA and manpower provided by Britannia Row Productions.

In early August, the band were to be found deep in rehearsals at Music Bank Studios in South London, where live previews of the album suggested an even heavier, brasher Oasis – and that was saying something. The guitars were as unforgiving as ever. 'Magic Pie' gave the impression of a ballad until sixteen bars in when it kicked the idle listener in the face; songs like 'All Around The World' and 'Stand By Me' were football terrace anthems waiting to happen, and sounded incredibly powerful in a tried and tested Gallagher fashion. Even 'Wonderwall' had ceased to be performed as an acoustic number – at Music Bank its plaintive subtleties were replaced by a restrained aggression, with Noel preferring an Epiphone electric guitar and Matchless amp combination.

Rehearsals were relaxed. For the first week the band routined their material for around four hours a day, but soon broke the workload down to a single run-through of the set between 5.00 and 7.00pm every day and leaving the studio on a high, rather than playing the songs to death. After a twelve-day break, the Oasis crew reconvened at London Arena on 26 August for production rehearsals, where during the final four days before flying to Oslo for the start of the tour (on 8 September) the band rehearsed for the first time with Mikey Howard's set.

The UK and European tour took in a variety of venue sizes, with the 20,000 capacity of Earl's Court at one extreme, while other halls averaged at around 7,000. This was indicative of Oasis's liking for intimacy and also their sense of occasion. Fine, but in order to satisfy all ports of call, Britannia Row had to allocate more PA stock than would be needed on most dates.

Generally, the main Turbosound system coping with the majority of venues (including Exeter Westpoint Arena and Birmingham's National

Indoor Arena) consisted of sixty Flashlight highs, eight Floodlight highs, sixteen underhung Flashlight mid highs, twelve underhung Floodlight mids and sixty-eight Flashlight TFS-780L lows. The centre delay contained sixteen Flashlight highs and eight lows, with a centre fill of two underhung Flashlight mid highs, one underhung Floodlight mid and four Flashlight lows. Earl's Court, however, witnessed a much larger rig of around 300 cabinets.

Huw Richards commented: "At Earl's Court the PA is ten wide and four deep with underhung cabinets, infills and 100 bass bins on the main system. There are six delays along either side of the room covering the top balconies, with a main eight wide by four deep delay halfway down the room and a centre fill above and behind the mixing desk. All of this equipment is assigned to the tour whether it gets partly or fully used, and dealing with that financially is very difficult."

Richards' choice of FOH console remained a Yamaha fifty-six-channel PM4000, although at one point he was considering a Midas XL4 for its automation facility. However, he stated that because of the vast number of inputs being used by Oasis he would have had to resort to adding an XL4 stretch. He said: "There are twelve stereo positions in the whole XL4 desk but I believe they have to be designated – you can't actually move them around the desk which makes things very inflexible for me. With Travis and The Verve supporting on the tour, I don't really want loads of desks out there for fear of the mixing position being cramped."

The input count began to increase when, as a surprise to everyone, Alan White arrived at Music Bank one day with a larger drum kit. "That put a bit of a spanner in the works because everything had already been prepped," said Richards. "We laid everything out in rehearsals as it would normally be and we walked in the next day to be greeted with the sight of this double bass drum monstrosity! There are also another two toms and I'm glad that was all because the desk is pushed to its very limit. It was a single kick, snare, hat, two toms and overheads, but now we have four extra channels for kit. We also, of course, have our five brass players to consider, and we now have congas which Liam was originally going to play on 'Fade In/Out', but [keyboard player] Mike Rowe's handling that. The great thing about the PM4000 is that you can accommodate for most changes by removing mono channels and replacing them with stereo versions to create more space."

In the control racks were five BSS Omnidrives linked to Varicurves and BSS graphics, while the effects racks were stacked with items including Yamaha SPX-990s, a Roland SDE-330, t.c. electronic TC 2290, Eventide H3000SE harmoniser, AMS RMX-16 reverb, and Lexicon 480L digital reverb. Richards also chose Summit TLA-100s for the two main vocals: "It's actually a line driver as well as a compressor, which gives you a bit more control. The TLAs sound so good. I'm using those in conjunction with two of Amek's Rupert Neve 9098 EQs but I also have a new device that Jerry Wing built around one of the old original Cadac desk EQs. I also have Summit DCL-200 compressors on kicks and snares, and there is a Tube-Tech compressor on the keyboards purely because Brit Row ran out of Summits as I'm using so many!"

In addition, Richards employed two old, unbadged SSL compressors on the bass and across the whole system. "Al Smart designed the compression stage of the SSL desk at the time of the company's first digital products and these units are based on that compressor design. Jon Lemon [who was soon to engineer The Verve on their Urban Hymns tour] is also very aware of these compressors; we're both big fans of the sound."

One major difference on this tour was that the live string section in evidence at Knebworth and other Oasis shows in 1996 were replaced by electronics. Part of the reason for the change was financial, but from a practical point of view the use of the strings proved to be more trouble than it was worth. Said Richards: "Before I came on board in 1995 they had used a string section on *(What's The Story) Morning Glory?* which was great but they were inevitably expensive, and often not available for all the dates. When we decided to use strings on the tour we looked at another section who seemed to have great difficulty playing live with the SPLs that Oasis put out. That's when we introduced the Violectras for last summer's dates."

The Violectras – two electric violins, a viola and a cello – were custom-built by Dave Bruce Johnson in Birmingham and cost no less than £20,000. Although these instruments were feedback immune, it became evident from the show recordings that the musicians were still not playing in tune. "The band just had enough of these problems and on the new album they used live strings but sampled them and cut them about a little," commented the engineer. "On the recording of 'D'You Know What I Mean' they fed the strings through a Marshall 4 x 12" rig and distorted the sound. Of course, we can't do that live, so the only way was to play those sounds from a keyboard. That is ultimately cheaper. Orchestral sections are very expensive to hire and at Knebworth it cost £15,000 just for strings."

The two keyboard players appearing with Oasis were Paul Stacey (who handled all of the sampled string parts) and pianist/organist Mike Rowe who played with the band for the first time on MTV *Unplugged* shortly after Knebworth. Richards: "Our input requirements are further extended now that there are two keyboard players. But they both go through an electronic rack beside them, so they're not miked separately, and the inputs are kept down. We are getting a DI signal now which is great for the separation."

Keyboard tech Steve Honest was able to explain a little about the rig he took care of for Paul Stacey and Mike Rowe. "Mike plays a lot of analogue sounds and uses a Hammond XB2 and an old Wurlitzer of which we carry a spare at all times...just in case! The Roland A-90 is his main MIDI controller. In the rack there is a Mark Of The Unicorn MIDI patch bay which has a SMPTE clock generator that although may be useful in the future to lock to video projections is not being used right now – the console for the MIDI patch bay is on a PC so I can do all the patch changes from song to song on that.

"Paul uses a Korg T3 keyboard and his main controller is a Yamaha AN-1X, while all his samples are stored on both a Roland S760 digital sampler and an E-Mu E4X Turbo. He uses two Roland units – an MSE-1 and an MOC-1 – for string and orchestral sounds. Everything goes through a Yamaha ProMix 01 console which is totally blinding because you preset all the keyboard levels for each song and every time you hit the advance button for the next song, the desk will instantly recall those settings and it's a piece of cake. The mixer also drives Noel's main delay unit – a t.c. electronic TC 2290 – and changes his delay times for each song."

The rack also included a UPS power conditioner and cycle changer built by Robbie Gladwell at John Henry's to enable the system to run correctly in any country, regardless of the type of voltage. Huw Richards commented: "We put the building of the keyboard rack out to tender and John Henry's came through with the best proposal and cooperation, even though they were the most expensive. Our aim on this tour was to get everything built that would last us into the future, so at the moment there's a bit more gear than we really need but it will all be used at some point."

Despite Richards' interest in introducing a Yamaha 02R digital console for the mixing of keyboards and certain samples, he was, for the time being, sticking with just the PM4000. Obviously, replacing the strings with keyboards had done wonders in cleaning up the sound. "Saturation is a word that is bandied around these parts quite often. Strings, amazingly enough, are the easiest sounds to deal with because I focus more on the low end cellos that are coming from the keyboard player. That's an area that's reasonably clean. I'm still fighting to get certain subtle sounds heard, such as on 'Don't Look Back In Anger' where making the piano heard clearly is a bit of a struggle. You almost have to turn it into quite a vicious instrument to get it to cut through, certainly in the rehearsal room where it's stuck 6' away from a stack of Floodlight which isn't ideal. The guitars still are quite ferocious and fill up so much space. Guigs isn't a demanding bassist; sonically he's pretty simple and doesn't seem to need a vast amount of level on stage. In fact, I sometimes have to get him to turn up so that he can hear what he's playing, which is mighty unusual for a bass player. I've been lucky in that respect."

The vocal mics favoured by Liam and Noel – Shure SM57As – were retained for this tour. At Music Bank, Richards was in the process of deciding whether he would be using Audio Technica 4050 mics or AKG 414s on the guitar cabinets. He said later: "I tried the 4050s and they sound absolutely fine but they don't suit Oasis's style anything like the 414s. I think if you have a switcher system where you have four or five amplifiers that are being used for different types of sounds throughout the set, then that's fine and you can consistently rely on the signal you're going to get. But there are no switching units involved in Oasis's set at all – they are all flat out and the only thing that controls the uplifting of any of the amps at any one time is a simple overdrive in line with the amps."

Richards was also trying out ideas for the miking of Alan White's kit but was convinced that the small Audio Technica clip-on drum mic was going to be the way forward for the bottom snare and hi-hat. "We can get in very close and that's made a difference to the band on stage because I can get a much denser, more crisp sound from the snare which they have not heard before. You can actually get so close to the snare that it's almost touching, but you can EQ off rather than add EQ which is a much better scenario."

Monitoring at Knebworth was a big affair because of the number of people involved. It may have been plain sailing as far as the five members of Oasis were concerned, but when 'Whatever' kicked in with the strings, monitor engineer Gareth Williams's sub routing increased from nine groups to twenty-six! With the monitoring regime cut down for Be Here Now, Williams concentrated on a more straightforward rock 'n' roll band situation, using fifteen groups including effects which he said was more than manageable. "It's only eleven mixes at the moment but that will extend to fourteen or fifteen once the brass players come in for the final rehearsals," he said.

The amount of monitor speakers was similar to Knebworth, minus some of the side fills. The actual specification was for fourteen Turbosound TFM-350 wedges and two Funktion One FK1 1 x 15" wedges on stage, with six Flashlight highs, four Floodlight highs and twelve TFS-780L lows as side fills. Said Williams: "To obtain clarity in the open air, you need to boost the amount of Flashlight in order to really cut through, but indoors is another thing altogether. We're dealing with a 60' stage and the band are now much closer to each other. I'm able to fly two Flashlights per side for Liam and angle the boxes down at 45° to centre stage, and we also have a four-way mix in the side fills with a left and right mix for him, and a ground stack of four bass and two Floods per side for the band. I've discovered that it's much better for the band if I keep everything on the deck – by switching most of the speakers off in the air I found that there are fewer complaints about 'muddy sound', and that less was indeed more. Liam's monitoring might appear to be bass-light, but he is getting plenty of low end from the band's mixes."

Williams's control continued to be based around his forty-channel Midas XL3 console and sixteen-channel XL3 stretch which was the quad console used on Pink Floyd's Division Bell tour. He had a little more in the way of compressors (twelve channels of BSS DPR-402) and gates (ten channels of Drawmer DS-201) because of the larger drum kit, but overall Williams tried to maintain a minimalist approach.

Excessive volume goes with the territory when working as part of the Oasis team. One recalled the experience of standing close to Noel Gallagher during a soundcheck at Earl's Court in 1995 when the on-stage SPL reached 121dB. At Music Bank, it seemed as though the guitar amps were directly linked to the National Grid, making even some of the most notoriously loud thrash metal bands appear tame by comparison, although within all of the volume Noel had become more focused on achieving a cleaner sound.

Williams commented: "People just don't believe you when you tell them how loud Oasis are. When we were rehearsing in here for our support slots with U2 in Oakland there was a video crew and I came in with a bagful of sponge ear defenders for them. I said, 'Look, wear these, you're gonna need them.' They were just here to check the band out for a TV documentary that's going to tie in with the album launch [aired on BBC TV on 20 August]. The video people were saying, 'No, no, we're used to this, it's okay.' But as soon as Noel strapped on his guitar, and Liam shouted, '1-2,' down the mic, there was this scramble for the bag I'd brought in. They were putting these sponge defenders in their ears, up their noses and anywhere where sound could penetrate. It was so funny."

The man at the monitor desk was certainly taking no chances when it came to protecting his own ears. "I wear the Ultratech ER-15s for rehearsals because sitting behind Noel's amps I can't even hear my own pair of 2 x 15" listening wedges," said Williams. "The ER-15s cut out all the external noise without sibilance or EQ loss, which is ideal. They literally bring the whole thing down by 15dB and you can work in comfort. You get your ear canal moulded and the mould gets sent away to Holland for manufacture. There is a little valve in each ear piece – you can get a -25dB version made which in my opinion is far too great a reduction in level. They could do with producing a -5dB version actually. A lot of artists wear them, including Radiohead and Garbage, just to cut down the noise. They can still crank up the amps and get that warm, glowing valve guitar sound, but without endangering their hearing. The good thing is that they are so unobtrusive – no one would know you had them in. No one's questioned me about them, anyway! It would be professional suicide to not wear these when working with Oasis."

Never the most animated of performers, Oasis had long seemed content to rely on sheer volume intensity and a visual presentation that even Mikey Howard, their long-time lighting designer, admitted was effective but basic. The band's attitude towards set design, particularly that of their natural leader Noel Gallagher, now shifted dramatically towards "making more of a show for the punters" as Howard – officially wearing both the set designer and LD hats – propelled them into a new area of sophistication for the Be Here Now tour.

There was a magical moment in rehearsals at Music Bank Studios when all five band members were shown for the first time an animated CAD program of Howard's design which had been prepared by the Midlands-based set construction company PW Stage Productions. One could see from their varied reactions that they were at once itching to get it together on such a stage. PW's Jon Perry commented: "In our [Windows and Mac-based] design studio, you can participate in the realisation of your concept as a virtual model, and have it burned on to a CD to show the band, plus have engineering drawings for production. We have a reputation for delivering what we visualise – a virtual model created by people with years of practical workshop experience means what you see is what you will get."

As Oasis kicked off their daily set run-through, Howard gave an insight into the content of the CAD presentation: "On previous shows, the band have just been standing there and there hasn't been much of a set – just a few risers for the drums, brass and strings, and the harmonica player," he said. "The big twist has been to base the set around icons that are featured on the Be Here Now album cover, such as the telephone box, the Rolls Royce and a big clock. We've got Alan White's drums on top of the Roller and the steps that appear by the swimming pool on the cover actually go up to meet the kit on stage. There's even a Manchester City Council parking meter at the side – there's detail for you! It's all a bit of a laugh really."

Some imaginative people had remarked that a lot of these icons were veiled Beatles references. In reality, these were designed to evoke a feeling of the Seventies, and more specifically the band members' childhood. It did not take much, however, to imagine that if the Fab Four had still been operating as a live band, this might have been the kind of set they'd go for.

For various reasons, some of them fairly obvious, the band were keen to install a bar/keyboard pit (complete with Boddingtons and Ansells on tap!) as part of the stage decor. "We did it so that Liam would have somewhere to chill out and have a drink while Noel sang 'Magic Pie' and 'Don't Look Back In Anger'. The brass section appear on 'All Around The World' and they'll come out of the phone box and stand in front when they're playing."

The phone box idea was not wholly original, as anyone who saw Peter Gabriel on his Secret World tour would know. Mikey Howard, it should be pointed out, did not see any of those shows..."Everyone's told me about bloody Peter Gabriel! I didn't know that, and in any case it was dictated by the album cover. It's a different type of phone box – bigger, in fact, and sticking out of the stage at an angle. Dave Perry at PW made the Gabriel box and he's done ours as well, so there is a link!"

A major feature of the set which dominated the view and influenced everything around it was the curved trussing, a variant of Light & Sound Design's A-Type truss, which was built for the tour by Total Fabrications using its in-house CNC machinery. "I was sick of using straight trusses," said Howard. "Light & Sound Design had circles made for Eros Ramazzotti but they were built the wrong way round to how I wanted to use them, so we had to have what we wanted built from scratch. I've wanted to take this approach for a long while but there was never the budget to do it. Things have progressed in that area, of course, and we can build our own truss if we like. It's a great feeling."

Tapered to one end, each of the four arms of the truss was 32' long and from point to point on the outside it measured approximately 56'. It gave the appearance of the band standing in front of a large cage, although the truss was lit from within and clad in a unique aluminium mesh to make it look like a solid object. "Because I was having curved trussing, I wanted to follow that through with a circular pattern on the floor. That's when I came up with the red, white and blue design. It's like a distorted Mod target because Geoff Grainger at LSD came up with the idea of stretching it into an ellipse shape which fits in a lot better with the curves and helps to disguise the trussing. The blue part of the design falls off the stage and it all helps to create this image of a disjointed target. With everything else on top of it, the majority of the audience won't recognise it as a target until quite a way into the show."

When Oasis were supporting U2 in the USA in June 1997, Howard presented a number of his set ideas to Huw Richards and Mike Lowe of Britannia Row. One of these was to have the flown Turbosound PA rig painted in a red, white and blue checker board design. But after Howard saw the child-like, multi-coloured PA designed by Willie Williams for the Bryan Adams tour, he went back to the drawing board. "I thought that coloured PA was great, it's just that it had been done before, and I didn't want to rip off Willie, so I then thought we should go off on a different tangent."

As an alternative, he decided to colour code the on-stage monitors according to where they sat on the "target". He commented: "Noel's, Bonehead's and Guigs' monitors are covered in a lighter blue cloth, and Liam's are white. It should make them blend into their surroundings better than if they were to stay regulation Turbosound blue! Even some of the LSD Icons which are dotted around the stage will be painted red."

There was much consideration given to the interaction of the band on stage, but that was hardly surprising considering the input of the band themselves, as Howard explained: "The design mainly came from them this time. They've shown interest in the past but they haven't been too bothered about being involved or even using elaborate sets. This time, Noel put a lot into it. Noel came into it slowly and now he's really developed a sharp eye and feel for what I do.

"Most of the ideas, like the bar, the phone box and the Roller came from him through conversations with the band. It was down to me to weave them into the overall design, with a lot of support and assistance from Geoff Grainger. We went big at Knebworth with a massive rig and enormous screens, and I suppose there may be some people who are expecting us to go even bigger. But that's missing the point to some degree. I wanted to close it all in more and make the set more intimate, and by doing that you retain more focus on the band. The curves really help to achieve that."

One might have expected the set design to have been drawn up before the lighting plans, but in reality the reverse happened, with the set evolving over three months. LSD supplied all of the lighting requirements apart from Vari*Lites which were supplied direct from Vari-Lite Europe. Howard said that compared to previous tours, the lighting spec was somewhat reduced. "At Earl's Court in 1995 we had about eighty Icon washlights and I remember thinking at the time that we really didn't need that many. In the past I've tried to use lots of different things because they're new but I don't think you need to. I've also relied heavily on generics, but as they take too much time focusing, I'm only taking four bars of six Pars.

"This time we have brought the number of Icons down to around forty and added thirty-eight VL5Arcs and twelve VL6s. For control I am using an Avolites Diamond III and an Icon desk just for the Icons. On the Diamond III I'm controlling VL6s, VL5s and Dataflash strobes, as well as all the Series 300s, four bars of six Pars and four eight-lite Molefays, and in the house we'll have four front-of-house spots." The VL5Arcs he specified were retro-fitted models with liquid lenses and new blades and blade bearings which help to improve blackout. The positive reaction to this one-off modification following the use on this Oasis tour encouraged Vari-Lite Europe to retro-fit all subsequent VL5Arcs in this way.

Flanking the central video screen were two curved projection screens for the lights which were fabricated with a new metallic material from America. This approach resulted in interesting shafted, distorted patterns created by the material and the angle of the screens. The Icons were focused on to that surface for projections and also to colour them up at various points.

"It's a great design from an audience's perspective," said Howard. "Wherever you sit or stand, you still have lights shooting out from behind the band. If you are watching from the side at a regular stadium show, you just see the sides of the beams coming out, but this design is much more full frontal and in your face. There are only ever going to be four lights in a row that are on the same angle and at the same height; all the lights are meant to be at different angles. Even turning the lights on in any position, there's a look there straight away without even doing anything, just because of the angles they're all coming in at."

Howard also had a word or two to say in favour of his lighting supplier. "I might have come up with the practical design ideas, but everyone at LSD has been fantastic. People like Geoff Grainger, Robin Wain, Jo McKay and even Terry Lee have been very helpful. It took a lot of working out, with how the curved trussing was going to be put together and how it would stack in the truck. In the past I used to draw it all out but now I've developed a good relationship with all those people; they know how I work and what I want!"

Work on The Rolling Stones' Bridges To Babylon tour (which opened in the same month) prevented Oasis's regular video director Dick Carruthers from active on-the-road involvement in the Be Here Now tour. He was, however, a major part of the planning stage and in Mikey Howard's words he had "looked after all the production side, and decided what camera package we'd need, where the cameras will be positioned and which director [Chris Hilson] we are going to have." Howard added: "Dick does have his own style of doing things and we'll be following that as closely as possible. He may be out in the States with Mick and Keith, but his spirit will certainly be with us!"

The video projection, cameras and control package for the whole tour was supplied by PSL, but at the Earl's Court and Manchester shows, the set was bolstered by two Sony JumboTrons (probably JTS-17s) from Screenco – a rare act of brotherly interaction by two competing firms.

At centre stage of the set for all of the shows was a PW custom-manufactured 12' domed or globular video projection screen, mounted on a spinning device, and receiving images from two Barco 9200 projectors which were positioned on the front-of-house mix riser to enable even brightness all around the sphere – this would not have been guaranteed if the projectors were flown. The further back the 9200s were, the greater the depth of field was, and so focus was less critical. With an image throw from 90' to 110', the front-of-house mix position was ideal. At Earl's Court the amount of 9200s was tripled and PSL's crew needed to fly them because of a huge risk of movement caused by the vibrations of the audience.

The control equipment included the now infamous Magic DaVE DVE video processor which enabled the projections to be bent around the shape of the screen. All of the images shown on the central screen were stored on laser discs and accessed under Dataton control. Briefed by Howard and Noel Gallagher, the video software was produced by Dion Allen. On the Scandinavian and UK shows leading up to Earl's Court, Julian Hogg was responsible for "dropping in images" on the handful of songs requiring projection sequences, including 'Magic Pie', 'My Big Mouth' and 'All Around The World'.

Said Howard: "On 'All Around The World' we are showing footage of a revolving globe, which you can get hold of as standard stock film. There are various views available, like the world at nighttime with all the lights twinkling, and you can actually zoom in to any point on the globe, any country or any town. For the Manchester show, we were planning to zoom right in from space into Manchester and the actual venue at the end of the song, but we simply haven't had the time to sort it out properly."

Although playback material was screened on the JumboTrons when they were used at Oasis's 1995 Earl's Court shows, and also at Maine Road and Knebworth in 1996, this time around they were primarily reserved for live camera shots to complement the creative central projection. But there was an added twist – the JumboTrons, whilst being hung in landscape format, were masked off here to give the appearance of oval-shaped screens, reminiscent of the TV set next to the swimming pool on the *Be Here Now* album cover. Yet more curves! Howard: "They act purely as video amplification of the band for the punters at the back and we'll be giving the camera images the usual Dick Carruthers strobing treatment."

So what did Howard and the band have up their sleeves as a dramatic opening for the show? At Newcastle, he said: "There were a couple of ideas floating around, but we went for a Kabuki across the set with the clock and dice artwork from the album. In the past I've had problems with Kabukis or drape reveals because they can be a real nightmare, with the Kabuki coming down too soon. So I thought about this and chose the old Velcro trick, with two people pulling it from each side. My actual favourite idea for the start of the show was for the phone in the box to ring and there'd be an answering machine message with Noel saying, 'Sorry we can't come to the phone, we've got to go...' and suddenly they'd leg it out to the stage."

At Newcastle Arena, the performance started with set carpenter Dennis Brown assuming the role of doorman and opening the phone box to reveal the band (this guy had his own dressing room!). A very effective start to a show that marked a new phase for Britain's most successful contemporary rock band of the decade.

CHAPTER TWENTY-ONE

Songs & Visions

The Carlsberg Concert – 1997

Throughout the spring and summer months of 1997, it was impossible for patrons of British ale houses not to have noticed the hordes of beer mats and flyers confidently advertising what was going to be "probably the best concert in the world" – the Carlsberg-sponsored Songs & Visions show at Wembley Stadium on 16 August, the twentieth anniversary of Elvis Presley's death.

Upon the initial announcement that Songs & Visions would be broadcast either live or post-produced in sixty countries, the concert was described as a celebration of the classic songs of the last forty years, sung by a cross section of contemporary stars, and with each year introduced by archive video footage depicting familiar events. Much like a live concert version of BBC TV's immensely popular documentary series *The Rock 'N' Roll Years*, really.

There was no doubt that with executive producer and chairman of Tribute Productions Tony Hollingsworth at the helm, the involvement of the high priests of set and lighting design, Mark Fisher and Patrick Woodroffe, and an investment of $8 million, this was going to be a major spectacular. A unique evening was certainly guaranteed with such a glittering array of artists: Rod Stewart, Jon Bon Jovi, Chaka Khan, Steve Winwood, Robert Palmer, Toni Braxton, kd lang, Seal, Mary J Blige and, the ultimate wild card, Eikichi Yazawa, the "Japanese Elvis" who had sold more than 10 million albums in his native land, and whose appearance at Songs & Visions was allegedly influenced by the sale of broadcast rights to Japan's NHK television channel.

But there were mixed feelings of intrigue and bemusement – one's cabaret alarm bell ringing loudly with the fear that kd lang might attempt to bring a sassy respectability to Black Lace's holiday fave 'Agadoo'. Thankfully it was not to be, as Tony Hollingsworth confirmed in his board room at Tribute when he first explained the show concept. It was Hollingsworth's idea for Songs & Visions which gave Sensible Events' Andrew Zweck the perfect solution when approached by Carlsberg about a concert package that would boost the beer giant's profile in entertainment. Once the marriage between Carlsberg and Tribute was consummated, Zweck ducked out of the frame and Hollingsworth began the brainstorming.

He said: "We looked back at all the major international television music events and asked the broadcasters what they remembered about them. The most vivid memories were of the unique combinations of artists and the special moments that would never happen again. People remembered Bowie and Jagger at Live Aid and the fantastic Eric Clapton/Dire Straits set at the Nelson Mandela Seventieth Birthday Tribute, and international television wants that extra 'something'. We then decided to design a show where 50% of the programme would focus on special combinations. So what could we choose as a subject to get people to do a whole series of duets or trios? We settled on the greatest hits of the last forty years and decided to choose one hit per year, from 1996 back to 1956. To give it an extra televisual element we would put on the front of each number a set of iconic images that introduced the audience to that year."

The clear intention was to make great music for the benefit of the 70,000 at Wembley, and the estimated 500 million television viewers around the planet, but the old adage "you can't please all the people, all the time" inevitably came into play. Shortlisting, never mind finalising, the forty-song set list was always going to cause much pain and frustration, and many people aired their reservations about the inclusion of some titles. At our meeting, Hollingsworth stressed the importance of "divorcing the artists from their own material", and instead get them to perform faithful interpretations of the classics.

"Over the years, people have increasingly become locked into the idea that artists have to do their own songs. But if you look back at entertainment over the last 200 years, singers just went out and performed the greatest songs they could get hold of. There are some fantastic pop songs and voices, and we're putting them together. The important thing is that no one is performing in order to promote his or her latest single or album. Even though we are putting it on international television, we are doing exactly the opposite of any other television company which will normally buy finished acts, put them on the stage and record them. But we are creating something different which may eventually come out on record and hopefully last as a piece of television for over five years."

Sure enough, the show kicked off in style with 'Papa Was A Rolling Stone' (deliberately out of chronological order), as the TV cameras "explored the geography" of the music by focusing on each member of The UnAffordables, the aptly-named stellar backing band and thirty-two-piece orchestra led by musical director Stewart Levine. The song provided an excellent means by which to introduce the first group of artists before spinning back through the decades.

It was with the next number that the show shifted away from its original concept. The hit of 1996 was not an Oasis song as pre-advertised, but Toni Braxton's 'Unbreak My Heart', sung by...Toni Braxton. Okay, it would have been hard to imagine this soul diva performing 'Don't Look Back In Anger', but wasn't this missing the point? In fact, only one of the first seven "chronological" numbers – Rod & Mary J's version of 'Nothing Compares 2 U' – kept to this brief of "divorcing the artists" from their own songs. By the end of the show, more than a quarter of the forty songs had been sung by their original hitmakers. That's artist management pressure for you.

On reflection, there were a number of genuine highpoints. Seal and Steve Winwood gave a rousing version of U2's 'Still Haven't Found What I'm Looking For', Rod and Robert Palmer were tremendous on 'I Heard It Through The Grapevine', kd and Chaka divine on 'Every Breath You Take' and Winwood's own 'Gimme Some Lovin'', with that grinding Hammond organ, sounded every bit as electrifying as it did back in 1966 (not 1967 as the screens stated). And as for Jon Bon Jovi, it seemed as if his entire international fan club had just flown in to drool at the sight of their idol.

As a celebration of classic songwriting, the concert worked, but some irritating negatives could hardly be ignored. For a show which was so preoccupied with its historical theme, its indifference to the most important cultural landmarks of our time bordered on insult. 1976 was the year of Punk, and like it or not, it marked a total music revolution which continued to inspire the bands of the Nineties. At Wembley, the video screens may have shown a fleeting, token glimpse of some spiky-haired revellers, but there was no musical reference to this phenomenon. Instead, 1976 was represented by Rod's 'Tonight's The Night'. Similarly, the psychedelic watershed year of 1967 was celebrated by Mary J singing 'You Make Me Feel Like A Natural Woman'. Far out!

UnAffordables' keyboard player and one-time Paul McCartney band member Wix Wickens attempted to explain the dilemma: "The set list is a very subjective area because what might have been a million-selling classic in one country might not mean much in another. Ultimately, the final set depends on global recognition."

Two observations of Tribute's attention to historical accuracy led one to ponder over the intelligence of the show's researchers. Representing the year 1972 was Seal's version of Led Zep's 'Stairway To Heaven'...a song released in 1971. The screens also dared to cut one year off of Jim Morrison's already tragically short life. Production designer Mark Fisher's words dashed the nit-pickers. "The show traced pop history through songs which would be enjoyed by the masses, and achieving that is no mean feat. It was interesting to contrast it with U2's PopMart show, on which some part of the agenda is to make people think. Most people like to think in their own time and sometimes they just want to go out, sing and dance, and have fun. Songs & Visions was all about enjoyment and didn't pretend to be anything else. It was never about saving the world; it was about making people feel good about the popular culture of the last forty years and giving it value."

Prior to the show, the music took shape over two and a half weeks of rehearsals with the band, orchestra and singers at London's Olympic Studios. Stewart Levine's skill at coordinating the talent was amazing to observe, while rehearsal playbacks in the control room offered much promise for the eventual show. Not least due to the crack musicianship of drummer Vinnie Colaiuta, guitarists Mike Landau and Heitor Pereira, bassist Nathan East, Stones' keyboard player Chuck Leavell, and their colleagues.

Levine, along with arranger Jerry Hey, was the man responsible for researching all of the greatest hits of the last forty years to gauge which would accommodate certain combinations of artists. As a musician/producer who for over thirty-five years had worked on records for the likes of Hugh Masekela, Minnie Riperton, Joe Cocker and Simply Red, Levine was, in the mind of Tony Hollingsworth, the perfect man to keep the music and musicians in check, and a recording studio was always going to provide the ideal environment for this type of pre-production.

At Olympic, Hollingsworth said: "Tribute shows seem to be the only ones which consistently employ the directional talents of senior figures from the international recording industry. We had Bob Clearmountain on the first Mandela show, Phil Ramone on Guitar Legends, and Sir George Martin on The Great Music Experience in Japan. It demonstrates an attention to music that normal television or even live sound in general doesn't have.

"We're rehearsing in a more controlled way than might normally be the case for a live show. Stewart is getting everyone to rehearse but [engineer] Greg Jackman is also recording it as we go along. That has allowed us to send DATs of rhythm tracks to artists, so that they can get used to the arrangements or suggest key changes before they arrive at the studio during this final week. Hot session players like these guys are used to the producer being in charge, as Stewart is here, and they approach the rehearsals as disciplined as they would for a recording session."

The second week of rehearsals saw Olympic linked via ISDN to various international studios, enabling artists to remotely rehearse their solo numbers. "It only starts to get seriously expensive when I have to book all ten artists to arrive at Olympic for a full week," said Hollingsworth. "And it's now that we're going through the twenty songs that are either duets, trios or ensemble arrangements."

The studio method appeared to suit everyone from the singers to the musicians. Robert Palmer said: "It's super streamlined, which of course it has to be. Everything is worked out specifically before we come in, so it's not as if we're experimenting to arrive at a happy mixture of songs. Otherwise it would be nigh on impossible to even consider getting it done. It would be mayhem... you can't afford to be very flexible on a show like this."

Monitor engineer John "JJ" James noted that for certain shows, the recording studio was starting to find favour for pre-production. "I suppose it's still unusual but we did something like this with Cher in Trevor Horn's studio a couple of years ago with a similar monitor system to get a more controlled feel." Greg Jackman who, with assistance from Jay Reynolds, was recording the rehearsals on fifty-six tracks (Sony 3348 and DA-88), and also mixed the actual show for broadcast in one of two Manor Mobiles, had previously worked this way for the first Nelson Mandela show as well as numerous Prince's Trust gigs. He said: "I am trying to reproduce on tape at Olympic what is going to be heard at Wembley. I'm using very little screening so that the spill factor is fairly realistic, as per live performance."

Key to the clarity of sound heard by band members and singers in the studio and on stage was the global use of both wired and wireless Garwood in-ear monitoring systems which, along with radio mics, were supplied by Hand Held Audio. One of the supplier's additional responsibilities was to locate audiologists across the world and organise appointments for artists to have impressions of their ear canals made, which were then returned to London so that Hand Held Audio could order personalised moulds.

Several of the performers were first-time IEM users, including Steve Winwood, Mary J, Chaka, Jon Bon Jovi and Robert Palmer. "I haven't used IEM before but I'm delighted with it," said Palmer. "The sound is so clear and precise, to the point where you feel that you're listening to your favourite hi-fi system. It's not to every singer's taste: Chaka can't stand them; they're hurting her ears. But Rod, who's been using IEM for a few years, has been like an ambassador for the technology, helping some of us get to grips with it."

Apart from approximately six 1 x 12" wedges installed backstage to provide some "vibe" for the artists before and in between their segments, there were no monitor wedges in evidence at Wembley, which left room on stage for altogether more important things...like autocues. In fact, the show completely relied on IEM and thus contributed to the use of just about every frequency legally available. Those who were not using the ten wireless Garwood Radio Station systems, namely the fixed musicians and backing vocalists, used the sixteen "hard-wired" Garwood Outstations. JJ said: "The decision to go totally in-ear was influenced by the close proximity of the string section to everyone else. After all the pre-production, to go into the stadium and suddenly deal with a totally different method of monitoring at high volume would have been futile, especially with a band that has never played together before. This way, when they actually arrive at Wembley it won't sound a lot different to them on stage. Hand Held Audio have been wonderful – they got us out of some trouble by building thirty-two small monitor splitter boxes, enabling us to just send one global mix to the orchestra [each wearing generic Garwood IEM II ear pieces], although the individual boxes have a volume control so that each member can set his or her desired level." The orchestra IEM system was run off four channels of Brit Row's BSS amplification.

On the eve of the concert, the cast arrived at Wembley for a full dress rehearsal with everyone dressed exactly as they would appear the following night...and for good reason. Said Hollingsworth: "We're recording the dress rehearsal and the tapes act as the backup for radio and television for the next day. It was something I did for The Wall In Berlin and we needed it. The monitor stage sound failed three times and on one of those times I couldn't go to backup tape because when we filmed the dress rehearsal the night before, Roger Waters had gone up to the microphone and said, 'I'm not going to sing this one because I'm saving my voice for tomorrow.' I had no choice but to show the world that there was a problem, with Roger on his knees, praying!"

The main Britannia Row front-of-house PA system at Wembley consisted of sixty-four Turbosound Flashlight cabinets and sixty-four 21" Flashlight lows, with a combination of Floodlight cabinets for the front of stage infills and near fills. The mixing tower delay featured eight Flashlight and eight Flashlight lows, with a further four Flashlight and four Flashlight lows, left and right of the mix position.

Front-of-house engineer for the main show was Simon Honywill, who looked after the ninety-six channels coming from the stage with two linked Midas XL4 automated consoles, and whose experience with orchestras was considered essential. An Amek Recall console for the support bands (Posh, The Mutton Birds and The Bootleg Beatles) was controlled behind Honywill by John Garrish. On stage were four desks: firstly a support band Midas XL3, then for the main event JJ used a Yamaha PM4000M combined with a Soundcraft SM12 board which mainly sub-mixed percussion. Adjacent to JJ was Steve Lutley who mixed the orchestra down on a PM4000 and sent sub-groups to JJ and Honywill.

Brit Row project manager Mike Warren (later to join rival rental firm Capital Sound Hire) was extremely pleased about his preference of monitor engineer, saying: "I think JJ is probably the best choice I could have made on this because he has such a great adult temperament and doesn't appear to get fazed by anything. One might think that with the range of artists on this bill there would be a few personality clashes, but everyone involved has been great."

Another key choice was that of Accusound mics for the orchestra – Greg Jackman, a big fan of the mics, insisted on fitting them with B&K capsules and inserting them directly into the string instruments' f-holes. While Hand Held Audio provided ten Samson UHF radio mics with SM58 heads for the star vocalists, kd lang preferred a wired 535, and Yazawa used a wired Shure SM58. The backing vocalists, meanwhile, were on Shure Beta 58s.

For the first five numbers of the show, the vocals were struggling to be heard over the band. This, a senior member of the crew explained, was "a mix thing", which was surprising, given the full rehearsal on the previous night, and the existence of the XL4's automation. Toni Braxton's problem, however, had less to do with engineering than her mic technique. As the vocal penetration improved, a most bizarre explosion sound during Winwood and Chaka Khan's version of 'Superstition' alarmed the inhabitants of the mix tower. This was explained later by Hand Held's Nick Bruce-Smith as the result of a bizarre case of radio interference: "The very same thing happened at the same point in the set during the dress rehearsal. We heard this big bang and when we checked it out with a spectrum analyser, we found that an ethnic radio station was broadcasting right in the middle of Channel 69, the same channel occupied by the mics."

When asked about the integrity of the stadium sound at the event, Brit Row's Bryan Grant suggested that any failure to project the traditional Flashlight quality may have had something to do with the increasingly common "set versus sound" battle. "There was a compromise with sound from the beginning because we were presented with a *fait accompli*. The PA was pushed halfway up the stage and then they stuck [set motifs] in front of the stack but still insisted that it had to sound perfect. In reality it's actually quite difficult to project a good sound through several inches of plywood. But that's indicative of the sibling rivalry between set design and live audio."

The set itself was on a typically grand Mark Fisher scale, extending across almost the entire width of one end of the Wembley pitch, with Edwin Shirley Staging's Tower System roof heroically taking the strain of thirty tons of JumboTron video screens and around fifteen tons of lighting. There were three main visual motifs: a set of gold curtains to the right made by Blackout which were loosely based on one of the rooms at Elvis's Graceland; the large Brilliant Stages-manufactured zipper at the back of the stage was representative of The Rolling Stones' *Sticky Fingers* album cover (although for practical reasons the zipper on this stage was upside down); and, the red and white striped drapes to the left (again by Blackout) were another recognisable pop motif. Added to these items were two sets of gold torches from Brilliant Stages, which Fisher simply felt were "a good idea".

He said: "One could choose to intellectualise about the design and how it might or might not have fitted in to the pop history theme, or one might prefer to take the view that pop is not an intellectual activity and therefore the design doesn't really matter as long as it's fun and attractive."

Fisher, who has designed the sets for every Tribute show to date (including The Greatest Music Party In The World – see Chapter Six), said that he and Hollingsworth spent several long meetings looking at computer-simulated views of the stage before deciding on the optimum angles for television. "Just as Jagger is with the Stones and Gilmour and Mason are with the Floyd, Tony becomes a major part of the design dialogue. But the big difference is money. My discretionary budget for the Stones [Bridges To Babylon] is between $10-20 million which is being amortised over 150 shows. But Songs & Visions is a one-nighter, so I literally have about one-hundredth of the Stones' budget to work with. To arrive at something that looks as big in Wembley Stadium as the U2 set when you're only paying for it over one night is a major exercise in economics. It is a mammoth conjuring trick to make the project break even, and that is taking into account the sponsorship."

One of the most striking aspects of the set was the integration of the video material – a mixture of live camera images and historical icon imagery (eg newsreel footage and newspaper headlines) sourced and edited by Mark Norton of 4i, and displayed on five Screenco-supplied JumboTrons which created a interesting "wall" background for both camera shots and the general look of the set. 4i's images were fed to the screens by a BBC OB unit which sent signals to each of Screenco's four ICS controllers. Screenco's Anita Page commented: "It was essentially the BBC's show; our involvement was as simple as arriving with the screens and rigging them. They ran the cameras and provided the DVEs which dictated how the images looked on the three JTS-35 JumboTrons [hung upstage centre, stage left and right, and each measuring 5.04 metres wide x 7.56 metres high]."

Adding a further two 4.22 x 3.17 metre JTS-80s to the set only two days before the event, to aid sight lines at the front of the crowd, did not present any problem to Screenco which just happened to have enough stock in its Eastleigh, Hampshire warehouse to cope with the demand. "We had twenty-five modules of the Arsenal Football Club screen in the warehouse which was waiting to go out a few days later for The Prodigy's gig in Dublin. So it wasn't too much hassle; we just had to ensure that we had all the necessary cable." The extra screens faced each other at either side of the stage structure and were fed images from a variety of those relayed to the three upstage JumboTrons. "Because the DVEs were able to divide images, at any one time there could have been seven separate images shown on stage, although the actual maximum on the night was four," added Page.

Lighting a show for both a 70,000 capacity live audience and the television cameras is a skill that designer Patrick Woodroffe had carefully honed over several years. Whilst the television requirements had to take priority, the lighting could never be to the detriment of the stadium spectators and the atmosphere.

"We obviously needed a lot of lights just to light the scenery, but there was very little space to rig lights within the scenery because of the large screens and decoration, and one did not want to place big trusses in front of those. So the lighting was pretty high in the air and although the cameras could hardly see the lighting system, the pay off was that they were constantly seeing the video screens, scenery and great-looking backgrounds," said Woodroffe, who commissioned CPL to supply the bulk of the lighting hardware, controlled from an Avolites Diamond console, with a Scancommander driving the six Sky Arts at front-of-house.

In a televised stadium show, it is often difficult to achieve good close-ups because the key (spot) lights are normally so far away from the stage. On Songs & Visions, the eight 3kW Gladiator Xenon troupers were 200' away and were keying from one side only, which put the artists' faces mostly in half-shadow to create an unusual but attractive look for television. Another consideration for television was the big, wide shot of the audience and set.

Woodroffe commented: "We lit the audience in a very distinct way, lighting them from central mixing tower island. We also lit them from each side of the stadium roof with long lines of Par 64 ACLs [the system boasted 288 of them]. Over the top of those we laid forty VL5Arcs which are incredibly powerful units and keep very good colour saturation over a long distance. That was a big success because the audience always had a different look and it was easy to match it with the stage cues. I'd never done this before, but I would definitely use the VL5Arcs for this purpose in the future."

To bring Fisher's gold torches to life, Woodroffe installed simple Molefay and Molemag elements in two shades, amber and yellow, on two flickering circuits. The rest of the rig consisted of thirty-five Light & Sound Design-supplied Icons (controlled by an Icon desk) which delivered extreme punch from a distance of 50' in the air. "The Icons gave us the revolving gobo which was great for dappling the stage and back shots. There were also sixty-nine workmanlike VL5s and twenty VL6s which put colour in and painted the scenery. Dave Hill programmed the Icons and Vari*Lites at very short notice and with only about a day and a half to do the job. I think everyone was very happy with the outcome."

Most of the 70,000 at Wembley departed glowing with satisfaction. It's all such a subjective area, of course, and if Tribute had presented this show purely as a celebrity singalong, without the sometimes flawed historical link, then it may have sat more comfortably with the more critical spectators. Just a few weeks after Wembley, Tribute staged a mammoth classical spectacular in Moscow to celebrate the city's 850th anniversary. Tony Hollingsworth truly knows the definition of the word "big". He remains one of the bravest men in the business and, despite any negative observations about the Songs & Visions content, deserves much acclaim for the way he has expanded the concert medium far beyond the boundaries of the venue.

Michael Jackson made HIStory at Wembley Stadium

Clair Brothers sound engineer, fisherman and columnist
Trip Khalaf with Midas XL4

Wanna Be Starting Something?

Earth Song

On the lighting tower: Benny Kirkham, Ryan Nicholson and
Michael Keller

Jacko is hydraulically lifted into the
audience

Even the drummer got a tour souvenir

Evening Glory: Noel
Gallagher, Earl's
Court, November
1995

The Oasis
backline boys: (L-
R) Steve Honest,
Jason Rhodes,
Roger Nowell and
Spooner

© Simon Camper

Liam Gallagher, Earl's Court, November 1995

Oasis, Maine Road 1996

Setting up at Knebworth

Huw Richards and Mikey Howard

Oasis monitor engineer Gareth Williams

Knebworth 1996

Rehearsing at Music Bank Studios,
South London, July 1997

In the Oasis production office: Helen
Smith and Mike O'Connor

A CAD animation for the Be Here Now
set, prepared by PW Stage Productions

Oasis in real time at Newcastle Arena,
September 1997

Seal

Songs & Visions – the
mix tower at Wembley
Stadium

In rehearsal at
Olympic Studios –
Rod Stewart, Chaka
Khan, Steve
Winwood and Mary
J Blige

The sprawling Songs & Visions stage

Jon Bon Jovi and his fan club

Steve Winwood: Gimme Some Lovin'

Britannia Row's Mike Lowe and Bryan Grant (with Pete Brotzman in background) discuss audio essentials with Mark Cunningham

Che Guevara looks on as Mary J Blige takes centre stage

Greg Jackman and Stewart Levine in the Olympic control room

kd lang

All together for the Songs & Visions finale

The Rolling Stones debut the Bridges To Babylon show at Soldier Field, Chicago, September 1997

Brilliant Stages' now legendary bridge

Barry Dane of dB Audio and LSD's Nick Jackson

Jagger – who else?

The firework finale

© Diana Scrimgeour

Richards – rock 'n' roll personified

Robbie McGrath – five minutes before his first tour date with the Stones

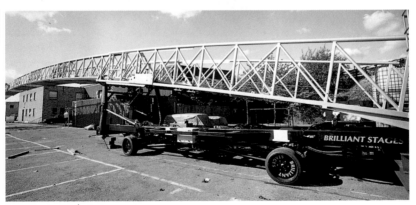

© Phil Dent

The bridge is completed in Greenford, Middlesex

McGrath's formidable Midas mix position

Dick Carruthers at the video controls

Electro-Voice's X-Array sound
system gleams in the Chicago
sunshine

Above and below: the elliptical Sony JumboTron screen was a focal point of Babylon

Back to basics on the Stones' B stage

A larger than life Mick Jagger

CHAPTER TWENTY-TWO

The Rolling Stones

Bridges To Babylon – 1997/98

When U2 began their PopMart tour in April 1997, audiences and professionals took one look at the hugeness of their gaudy but irresistible set design and naturally thought that it probably represented the concert industry's Everest. Nothing could get bigger. Well, arguably, not only was it surpassed on a number of levels, but the surprise was that it took just five months to do it...and by none other than The Rolling Stones, a band who even after more than thirty-five years are still capable of selling out massive stadiums and putting on the most sensational shows of the day.

Two years on from completing their then record-breaking Voodoo Lounge world tour, the Stones spent most of the late summer of 1997 routining new material in Toronto, before they and their heavyweight crew headed south for Chicago where, at Soldier Field on 23 September, they settled into familiar character and launched their Bridges To Babylon tour in front of 56,000 besotted fans – the first of a projected 100-date tour which reached most of Europe the following summer. Chicago was a perfect place for the kick off – the Windy City's blues legends, particularly Chuck Berry and other Chess label heroes, provided the band's earliest influences, and this was going to be one hell of a pay off.

The drama at the start of the show was intense. The sound of 56,000 people gasping as the Soldier Field house lights and intro tape suddenly shut off was almost deafening. Then, a confused silence. Emerging from the haze created by bank of DF50 fog machines and

JEM Roadies, a recording of "a lost tribe in the middle of the desert" gained momentum, until a solitary yell coincided with the sight of a cosmos on the JumboTron. Gradually, a meteor came into view and appeared to crash through the screen in a ball of flame, simultaneously accompanied by the ignition of forty-eight laser rockets and bursts of VL5 light from around the elliptical screen frame. On cue, Keith Richards struck the first notes of 'Satisfaction', and Jagger appeared on the horn riser as the audience retrieved their jaws from the ground.

From this stunning opener to the firework drama of the 'Brown Sugar' finale, the Stones oozed the same bad boy energy that epitomised them in the late Sixties and early Seventies, as the sexual references flowed in typical style – the peep show cartoon flick on 'Miss You' was but one of many sordid moments. They may have been in their fifties but when you can command a stage like Mick Jagger, the ultimate showman, and Keith Richards, the personification of rock 'n' roll with a wicked grin to die for, age becomes a triviality.

A local press review of the show criticised the band for including too much of the old and not enough new songs from their *Bridges To Babylon* album. At the front-of-house mix riser, this was not an issue. Oldies, yes, and plenty of them, covering the band's entire career span, but played with a refreshing spirit and engineered at front-of-house by Robbie McGrath in such a way that the Stones sounded unprocessed and as nature intended – a quality absent from their live shows for more than twenty years.

There was a smattering of new material, such as 'Anybody Seen My Baby', but the band seemed to have learned several lessons from the media's reaction to U2's repertoire on the early PopMart gigs, and risked little when it came to the set, thankfully. For those present at Soldier Field for the last few days of production rehearsals prior to the first show, it was a rare joy to see the Stones honing their set in such close proximity, and witness the nerve-wracking build-up as the sound, lighting, video and stage crews worked feverishly to meet the deadline.

In charge of these efforts was Jake Berry, Mr Production Manager, who broke off from a management flow chart exercise to explain his logistical battle, as he waited for the final pieces in the set jigsaw to arrive on site. "We're spending $4 million on this show," he said. "Everything here has been built in twelve weeks which is very tight for an arena show, let alone a stadium production of this size. Our trucks are multiplying by the hour – they seem to be breeding faster than the average rabbit! We haven't finished counting how many trucks we'll need, much to the annoyance of our accountants. But we know that the steel will require fourteen for each of the three [leapfrogging] systems, there will be around twenty-six for production, plus there are other vehicles carrying generators.

"For the first time in America we are actually transporting our own dressing room supplies and furniture in an effort to be a self-contained unit. So by the time we finish out there we'll run about thirty-two trucks from venue to venue, and the fourteen steel trucks every third venue. It's going to take a little while to get out of Chicago and if we get out in single digits [hours] we'd be really happy.

"When we built this stage set we had long talks with Brilliant Stages, Tait Towers and StageCo, and issued parameters to ensure that all the dollies would fit an ocean container, an American truck, an Indonesian truck, and the upper deck of a Boeing 747, because we realised that for most places we were going we would charter a plane so we've tried to make it all fit. All the stuff we had constructed was built for dollies, although there are a few exceptions. The other thing we tried to do out here is enforce the double utilisation of set carts. Instead of having a massive amount of set carts stored in some huge backstage area, we use some for spotlight gantries and platforms, and that kind of thing. It's all common sense, really." His, it has to be said, is no easy job.

What the Stones' set lacked in terms of lemons, olives and other such fruit and veg, was made up for with eclectic architecture, dripping with gold and riches, and flanked by exotic, statuesque, inflatable ladies, and even golden PA cabinets and light fixtures...all on a 177' wide x 85' deep x 82' high stage. The ever-present Mark Fisher was continuing to break new ground in this area, whilst within this landscape Patrick Woodroffe managed to weave his lighting spell to create a new, delicious ambience for every song, backed up by the ingenious use of the largest touring JumboTron screen to date.

Early on in the planning of the tour, the seven deadly sins was considered as the set design theme. Then came Babylon. "Everybody thinks it's very rational, but it isn't at all," said Fisher. "It's the result of an almost deliberately irrational dialogue mainly between Mick and myself about trying to find a visual theme based on what I thought they ought to do. Ideas were debated endlessly by Mick, Charlie Watts, Patrick and I, and whilst Mick doesn't have any preconceptions about these things, he instinctively knows what is right or wrong for the Stones."

Fisher aimed towards creating a very opulent setting and presented a number of proposals, one of which was titled "Gold" and supplied the key aspect of the eventual design, as physically built by Brilliant Stages and Tait Towers. "This was the sort of imagery of the divine power of kings; a vision of wealth, splendour, richness, and incredible opulence, using over the top decoration. In the process of trying to discover the visual language of that direction, I went through various sources like Iberian baroque-styled Catholic churches in Mexico.

"The set was going to be very three-dimensional and decorated in gold, and although that concept took hold early on in our discussions as being appropriate, the nitty-gritty of exactly what would be gold took a lot longer as we tried to get a foothold. Would it be a gold saint, a gold gargoyle? The seven deadly sins theme eventually went by the wayside, but we did in fact keep two of the figures, Sloth and Gluttony [the inflatables], as the thing evolved. Then we transferred our attention to the more opulent images."

At Fisher's invitation, Gerard Howland, the head of design at the San Francisco Opera, began to collaborate on the creation of sculptures for the stage set and suggested the futurist sculptor Bocchione as a baroque reference point. The eventual design was actually a collage borne of several different influences. "Gerard went on to design the two 'guardian' sculptures, and I really appreciated his insight. The fibre glass columns under the PA which have gold drapes painted on them [manufactured in the UK by Stephen Pyle] came from a Viennese image I was looking at. Some elements are Egyptian in style – the lion on the tour programme and album cover is an Abyssinian lion, and I've combined that with some Egyptian capitals which can be seen at stage left. Whereas over on stage right we have an Ionic figure which is distorted and stretched in the tradition of the eighteenth century.

"Looking back on it now, all this could be seen as a rich progression to a mythical fantasy place, but it is self-explanatory. We're no longer opening the curtains on a passion play about the seven deadly sins or a vision of Ozymandias in a lost city in the desert. It's a Rolling Stones collage with a whole lot of fantasy. What's funny is that people like to distil these things to one kind of image, and think that it must have a very simple explanation, but creating it has been rather like Mick and Keith writing a song. You have a whole lot of different, intuitive input from different directions, and then when you hear it, everybody tells you it sounds just like The Rolling Stones. Well, this set is very Rolling Stones, but getting there meant going through a number of detours, each of which led to something new."

The main band stage provided by Tait Towers was used, in a different form, on Voodoo Lounge. Said the company's founder Michael Tait: "It had been in storage for two or three years, but it has been reworked, redecked, and reconfigured, but it shares a number of identical components. We've supplied the elliptical frame in front of the JumboTron which also holds the Vari*Lites and strobes, and the upper and lower tracks for the main show drapes which block off all the set columns and JumboTron for the first part of the show. We also supplied all the platforming for the monitor control area] and Wives' World, which was originally going to be a viewing area for the band's wives and special guests, although it looks like it will be taken over by the support acts' monitor engineers and teleprompters. There's a hell of a lot that doesn't get seen, like lighting brackets, that doesn't look like fifty trucks' worth or whatever until you start loading it!"

The "Bridges To Babylon" album and tour title came from a core group of people looking at the set drawings. Fisher believed it was either Jagger or Stones friend, playwright Tom Stoppard who first coined the phrase "Bridges To Babylon", obviously influenced by the sight of the architect's distinctive, Egyptian-flavoured bridge. Sorry, did someone say "bridge"?

"The bridge is not here," said Fisher with hollow laughter, the "rabbit ate my homework" jokes wearing thin by this point. It's true – despite looking finished to those not as close as Fisher to the production, the set was missing several set pieces from the back of the stage in Chicago, plus the major mechanical set piece which makes the strongest connection to the name of the tour. Not even Monty Python could have topped this! The now-legendary bridge – 170' long when fully extended – did arrive in Charlotte around 10 October and worked perfectly first time, the band using it as the route to the centre stage, then returning on the runway. As Jagger has said: "Never make the same entrance twice."

Taking the bridge's absence to heart in the lead-up to opening night, Fisher said in Chicago: "It's a big disappointment to me because the bridge became part of the design a year ago, and it would certainly be a convenient way of getting to the centre stage, wouldn't it! There are a few people involved in building it but the ultimate responsibility for it not being here is mine. I'm the guy who sold it to the band and the one who said it would be here. So I had to tell them, rather painfully, it was going to be late, so I've been vacillating between feeling immensely pissed off and finding it incredibly funny because it's so out of control. The last thing anybody wants is the designer going around behaving like a raving asshole, although in my soul I am seriously aggrieved."

The explanation for the three-week delay was clear. Following tests during the final stages of its construction, the bridge was being fine-tuned by structural engineer Neil Thomas of Atelier One in London, under the watchful eye of Mal McLaren, whose responsibility it was to certify the bridge for use in the USA. The extra work included changing the rolling surfaces and mountings, and fitting additional bracing. In the absence of the bridge on early dates, the band moved to the centre stage via a temporary catwalk. Brilliant Stages' Charlie Kail commented: "There was the normal blood, sweat and tears you get from a disappointment like this, but we're all consoled by the fact that the bridge is without doubt the most spectacular thing to have ever come out of Brilliant Stages. It's the sort of job that would have taken the Ministry of Defence years to complete."

A few days after the bridge made its debut, a relieved Fisher was full of praise for Atelier One's Thomas, the engineer who made the creation of the unique arches from U2's PopMart and the Floyd's Division Bell staging, and the Stones' Voodoo Lounge "Cobra": "Neil's a very brave and inventive engineer who has never told me that any of my ideas are impossible. Neil had the balls to say that the bridge was possible, and then put his balls on the block to make it happen. The bridge will be remembered as the biggest effect in the show, and apart from those who have paid for it, he is the boldest contributor to its success."

Other companies involved in the supply of elements of the set included Air Artists of Norfolk, whose Rob Harries has manufactured all of the inflatables used on every Mark Fisher-designed show since the famous pig on Pink Floyd's 1977 Animals tour. Naturally, his work also includes the "Honky Tonk Women" and "Rabid Dogs" from the Stones' 1989-90 Steel Wheels tour, and Harries was now responsible for Babylon's 50' high brassy ladies, Miss Sloth and Mrs Gluttony, who were revealed seven songs into the show. "I always thought that the biggest set pieces would be inflatable because there's simply no other sensible way of doing it," commented Fisher.

Among the fabrication companies are SP Offshore who made the silver panels, Tomcat who handled much of the sub-contracted truss construction, and Triple E who provided Brilliant Stages with the Unitrack tracking for the heavy duty scenery carriers for the cladding which appeared on three sides of the PA towers. The 50 x 40' curtains, made by Landrell Fabric Engineering of Chepstow, were also a major part of the design – no previous concert production had used curtains on such a scale. Fisher said: "They used a fabric specially made in France that is very coarsely meshed, and I worked out all the pleating so that it looks freely swagged and will still look attractive in winds of up to 40 mph. They are held on working tracks at the bottom and top. The track we are using for this is designed for sails on high performance racing yachts, and was extremely cost-effective."

Fisher also spoke of his appreciation of the work carried out by the "very talented and hardworking scenery carpenters". He said: "Without their support and dedication, everything I've done, including The Division Bell, PopMart, Voodoo Lounge and Steel Wheels, would have been impossible. Too many people take them for granted."

A theatrical show in physical design, Bridges To Babylon was lit in a similar way to the grandest of operas. As on Voodoo Lounge, Concert Production Lighting (CPL) was the main lighting contractor, providing the lion's share of the equipment, including 148 Vari*Lite VL5s, fourteen VL5Arcs, sixty-two Molefays, forty-six Molemags, eight Lightning Strikes, thirty-six Diversitronics strobes, ten Sky Arts, and four 6kW HMIs. Joining forces with CPL was Light & Sound Design, whose eighty Icons were a crucial part of the design.

Nick Jackson of LSD's US operation said: "We weren't part of the last tour, but on the Steel Wheels tour we provided all the big Megamags for the lighting pods hung from the stage scaffolding, the main light source for that show. For many years, Stones tours have had a similar pattern as far as the production suppliers are concerned, and CPL's involvement has worked very well for the band. In return there's a lot of loyalty. So it's very pleasing for LSD to be here with the Icons in such a prominent position, working as one team with CPL.

"All of the Icons and Icon control have been supplied directly from LSD in the US, although it has been a joint effort with our UK base, and we've all been talking to Patrick Woodroffe and [programmer] Dave Hill about what we could do for them."

Whereas most of the automated lighting, including the VL5s, was controlled by Mark "Sparky" Risk from LSD's Icon desk, using two VMEs and five UGLIs [Universal Guest Luminaire Interface], all of the fixed lighting and some VL5s in the audience were handled by lighting director Ethan Weber with the CPL-supplied Avolites Diamond III. "Dave Hill has become very fond of the Icon controller, having used it on a number of shows," said Jackson. "He saw that the programming speed and the ease of operation of the desk was ideal for this show. He was quite instrumental in bringing the Icon benefits to the fore.

"Although Patrick had used Icons with The Cure some years ago, he hadn't put them on a truly major project until now. He saw that Icons had distinct advantages that he felt were right for this show, such as the brightness that you need on outdoor shows, and from the very beginning they were part of his spec."

It was probably the most elaborate and detailed set that Patrick Woodroffe, a Stones veteran, had ever had the pleasure of lighting. Given his wide portfolio, it's a bold statement to make, but none the less true. He did point out that the individual roles played by him and Fisher were not as cut and dried as they may have seemed; arriving at all things visual was an evolutionary process. "It was really a journey of discovery and from it has come this unique style," said Woodroffe. "Each of the last three Stones tours has been put together later than the last, and this was particularly fraught. However, the band say it's the best stage they've ever had, which is quite exciting."

Woodroffe ruled the roost when it came to directing the show's moving visuals, and there was a lot to keep him busy. "There are so many disparate elements – the lighting, scenery, video, fireworks, costumes, choreography – and they all have to be woven into a seamless whole, so it doesn't look like we're placing a load of special effects around the band just for the sake of it."

The Stones intended Babylon to be a journey for the audience, and in reaching that goal, there are four radically different scenes where the composition of the stage changes completely. Woodroffe commented: "That's a big advantage for me because I can light five songs one way and as soon as the scenery changes, the same lighting looks quite different. Mick and Charlie are the band members who have traditionally had a hand in the way the staging and lighting work. Funnily enough, we actually made a script of the show before we had a design of the stage. We ran a sort of impasse and it seemed the best way to push the process forward. We agreed on the very strong five-song opening which would be predominantly rock 'n' roll songs from yesteryear, before a big scenic change that introduced a more eclectic group of numbers including a couple from the new album.

"The centre stage set is lit very simply with white light to make the band appear as if they are in the intimate domain of the audience [and also give an appropriate feel to the Sixties set performed there]. Then there is a big production number for 'Sympathy For The Devil' as they go back to the main stage, before going for the home run. That was already established in our minds quite a long time ago, and it was a good vehicle for Mark when he was working out how he could apply his myriad set ideas. One's hope is that we can weave together all of these elements without it looking too self-conscious."

For all the expensive decoration, lighting and special effects, there was one prop that shone brighter than all of them, said Woodroffe. "I've always thought that the biggest effect on a Stones show is The Rolling Stones, because they project such enormous energy right from the middle of the stage that even the largest, most interesting set will be dwarfed by their personalities. As long as you're in tune with the music and the way it's performed then it's not that difficult to make the visuals fit.

"It's more about the areas in which the band are lit and we've divided the stage very specifically into the performing area right in the middle and then all the various scenic elements that are generally lit with wide washes from Molemags then cut with more accentuated detail from VL5s, wider gobo break-ups over them with Icons, harder accent lighting with a couple of different sorts of Lightning Strikes, some of them incorporating colourchangers, and then long and short throw Super Trouper follow spots. Because we've gone for a very open look, as on the last couple of tours, there is no specific position for front lighting. All the front light, apart from the follow spots, is from Gerard Howland's 'guardian' towers at the sides that hold eight Vari*Lites and some Molemags."

Although gobos were used extensively, it was not a gobo projection show. They existed to organically and geometrically break up the look of the curtains which responded to the treatment incredibly well. Woodroffe also set the difficult rule that the principal Stones and also the other musicians would be picked out and lit fairly evenly for most of the show. It was then the responsibility of the video department to decide which band members would be highlighted on the video screen, and allow the audience to choose who they look at.

"I'm happy to take on the responsibility of changing the dynamics and the look of the whole stage," said Woodroffe, "but I think the audience should have the privilege of deciding who they focus their attention on."

Using the audio delay towers as a site for long-throw lighting allowed for some powerful expression without spoiling audience sight lines. Also on the towers, and in the stage wings, were confetti cannons triggered by Jagger at the end of 'You Can't Always Get What You Want', sprinkling silver confetti across the entire crowd and, to the visible frustration of Robbie McGrath, the two front-of-house mixing desks!

MPA supplied all of the pyrotechnic services and despite Chicago's Fire Department clamping down on some of these plans for the opening show at Soldier Field, the pyro was spectacular. Drawing heavily on Le Maitre's stock, pyro had the biggest effect at the beginning of the show, on 'Sympathy For The Devil' and 'Jumping Jack Flash' (flame balls), and at the very end when the stage erupted with gushing fireworks.

Within all this, the stage underwent constant change. Said Woodroffe: "When the stage is all very purple for 'Sympathy For The

Devil', there are red emergency flares right back behind the stage. When the band come out to the centre stage we close all the curtains and while everyone's attention is on the band, we strike the backdrop and all the inflatable figures so that you are looking right through a 100' depth to the back of the stage with the big Sky Arts search lights coming down through the scenery."

The Stones were not purely performing to stadium audiences on this tour – the lighting, therefore, had to be multi-configurable. "We have a green field site festival system which is supplementing the big Xenotech Xenon head search lights and more lighting and video screens. Then there are US arena shows which won't use everything that's in Chicago. There will also be some 2-3,000 seater theatre shows where it all gets broken down again, and right at the end of the scale there's going to be some club dates where we'll just use whatever we can find, plus an MTV show. Variety, as they say, is the spice of life."

When video was first discussed for Bridges To Babylon, an LED screen was given consideration. Aware of U2's experience of the problems caused by rain ingress to their huge Lorrymage screen, however, the alternative CRT (Cathode Ray Tube) option was deemed more appropriate. The Stones were already happy with the superior resolution of the Sony JumboTron used on Voodoo Lounge, and this time around it was only going to be a question of increasing the size of that screen.

At the time, the new screen, supplied by Screenworks along with cameras and all necessary hardware by sister company BCC, was the largest portable JumboTron in existence. A JTS-35 model, it measured 33' high x 44' wide, weighed 44,000 pounds, and was around 60% larger than the one seen on Voodoo Lounge. That screen comprised of thirty-five modules; this time there were fifty-six providing what were claimed to be the cleanest images ever seen in a stadium show.

This JumboTron was attractively framed by a Tait Towers elliptical lighting truss, nicknamed either "the toilet seat" or "the doughnut" by some fearless members of the crew! In order to produce the desired screen shape behind the frame, Danny O'Bryen and his team at BCC calculated the weight factors and staggered the modules four columns of eight high, then two columns of seven high, two columns of five, and two of four.

Said O'Bryen: "This could have been done with [higher resolution] JTS-17s but once you are standing 100' or so back from the stage, the resolution would not make any difference and on a screen this size, you're better off with the 35s. There are four times as many CRTs on a 17 as there are with this, and they look their best when configured into small screen sizes, like 8 x 11s or 12 x 16s." On selected dates where audience viewing to the sides of the stage is restricted, such as Soldier Field, an 8 x 11 JTS-17 will be installed each side.

"When I was in Japan, I compared the 35s and 17s along with some LEDs, and the 35s looked better from a distance because they are 5000 NIT [brightness measurement] whereas the 17s are 4000 NIT. The 35 goes to a brightness of 16 and we have run it during daytime at 5, and at 1 during the night. We can't turn it down any further, so brightness has never been a problem."

Although most of the equipment was owned by BCC/Screenworks, the two companies took advantage of a close cooperation with Screenco, the Hampshire company with a minor financial interest in BCC. "We often trade equipment back and forth," said O'Bryen. "Michael Jackson took out a lot of Screenco's JTS-17s, so they have some of my 17s now. I own more 17s than Dave, but he has more 35s, so he has provided some extra 35s [and a number of Screenco's freelance camera operators] to help us out here. I could have gone out and spent another $1 million but it's better to pool resources, plus Sony has a sixteen-week lead time on delivering JumboTrons." Also included in the BCC package are six Ikegami HL-55 cameras, two three-chip Sony DXC-930 POV cameras, a Grass Valley 250 switcher, and Betacam and laser disk playback machines.

It was during a previous Jamiroquai tour that the effervescent Dick Carruthers hinted that he was soon to be working as video director on a major production "with the mother of all rock 'n' roll bands". Carruthers' new position came after he and production manager Jake Berry met on a TV show, and was subsequently offered the opportunity to submit a showreel demo for consideration. "I knew Patrick and Mark from previous jobs, and through my work with bands such as Oasis I suppose I qualified for shortlisting. My raw, gutsy and, some might say, street approach seemed to be in line with the way the Stones saw things, and I was invited to a meeting with Mick Jagger where I was asked what I would do in the context of the set design. It all soon fell into place."

Sporting a bleached blond, Cobain-esque hair style for the tour, Carruthers designed the video aspects of the show in consultation with Patrick Woodroffe, and he applauded the way in which Woodroffe and the band were receptive to new ideas. So many, in fact, that it took until two weeks before the first show to finalise the show introduction, which was arguably one of the most dramatic ever designed for live rock 'n' roll.

It certainly took some brainstorming before the meteor theme evolved as the correct intro formula. "One of Patrick's original concepts was that video would not be introduced until some way into the set, but in reality it has actually played a major role in the introduction," explained Carruthers. "You want to start with a bang but also keep something back, and the way we've approached things has meant that we have plenty in reserve for different pockets of the show. The JumboTron looks absolutely fantastic. At nighttime, if you turn a JumboTron on full brightness and give it a full white field, it's like the biggest flash bulb you've ever seen. That inspired the idea of beginning the show with a massive white-out to blind the audience into submission. But how we got to that point was the next challenge."

Whilst in Toronto, Carruthers met with the 3D graphics and compositing specialist company Extreme and commissioned the sequence of a meteor crashing down from a star system. "It was a perfect introduction to this world of the Stones and Babylon. My idea was to make a feature of the curtains opening by having swishing and clunking sound effects made by Crunch Recordings. Mark Fisher vetoed that on the ground that it was very Pink Floyd [presumably referring to the effect at the end of 'Welcome To The Machine'], and that was when we thought of having the sound of a lost tribe meeting at the gates of Babylon which, after 10,000 years, were suddenly opened at the sound of the high priest's yell. I'm sure that the guys at Crunch are probably in rehab now, having really gone through the mill to deliver what we wanted!"

The video production was a mixture of live camera shots and either animation or computer-generated graphics MIDI-driven by the ArKaos software package which came to Carruthers' attention through this author's coverage of the 1997 Jean Michel Jarre tour in *SPL* magazine. (To accurately cue each insert, Carruthers requested a delayed audio feed to his headphones, rather than act on the signal reaching him from the main PA.)

"The ArKaos people came over from Belgium to show me the effects and I thought, 'Yeah, I'll have it,' although I wasn't sure about how I'd work it into the show. In fact, I use it at the very end of the meteor sequence for a kind of polarised nuclear explosion before the screen totally whites out. ArKaos has lots of whizz-bang stuff which is very techno and I think it'll find its place. Just as Jesse Deep has done with Jarre, I've bought Mick a digital camera so that he can take photos of anything that takes his fancy, and we'll download the images into the computer and hopefully do a little slide show on the screen. People love those fly on the wall things. I've completely plagiarised Jesse, but the best ideas are there to be shamelessly adapted!"

Famed for his use of strobing in order to create a pleasing filmic effect, Carruthers observed that touring in the US has presented an annoying disadvantage. "I've found that the NTSC format in America doesn't respond to the strobe filter quite as well as in the UK. I'm sure that NTSC stands for 'Never Twice the Same Colour', but that's only because you can't get 'Total Load Of Crap' out of those initials! Because we are sending digitised images on to such a huge Tron, they look kind of strobed already. But I've wired one of the MIDI outputs of a keyboard such that I can insert the strobe filter at the touch of a key. I have a jittery strobe on 'Out Of Control' and if I also insert some posterising it contrasts better when returning to the full refresh rate."

Glancing at Carruthers' cue board, one was immediately intrigued the word "Kak" alongside the song title 'Ruby Tuesday'. Clearly, this was not a criticism of the Glimmer Twins' songwriting, but a reference to a video effect which Carruthers was keen to explain: "Kak is a cheesy, interference-type effect which I key with the black and white images we show of the band on 'Ruby Tuesday'. It creates some moodiness as well as establishing a Sixties atmosphere."

Looking at the titles of the video sequences – "Sex", "Blood", "Whore" – it was plain that, despite their fiftysomething age, the Stones continued to sustain a dangerous image. "Yeah, it's the fuckin' Rolling Stones, not The Smurfs, so let's have some sex!" laughed Carruthers, whose first animated sequence was on 'Bitch'. "I met a video artist called Barry Kamen who has a very individual style of painting on 35mm film and Telecining it at twelve frames per second to create a wonderful jitter. His sequence for 'Bitch' is titled 'Sex', and for good reason. There is a bridge of barbed wire which becomes a pair of spread-open legs and the 'camera' moves between them and up into the 'woman' where the journey to Babylon begins, and the Tower of Babel is portrayed as a big penis. It's sexy but very abstract, and very Stones."

'Sympathy For The Devil' was notable for its eerie screen image of an eye – this faithful rendition of the 1968 classic was introduced by a percussion sequence as the band returned to the main stage after their three-song centre stage workout. British production company Bug shot the 35mm close-up of the eye. Said Carruthers: "It represents the eye of the devil – the screen becomes an eye and because it's close up on a pupil, you don't realise it's an eye until it blinks. At various points in the song, I superimpose live cuts of Mick and the band into the pupil. I'm hoping that at some time on the tour I can get Mick to wear a glasses cam [small camera mounted into sunglasses] so that his own view of the audience can be shown in the 'eye of the devil', but it's an expensive process and we'll have to wait and see. It's an RF system and there's already so much RF on this show that it might cause a problem."

One idea which was implemented as the tour progressed was the fixing of a small RF camera on to the headstock of Ronnie Wood's guitar. This was being tried out during final rehearsals at Soldier Field, but was deliberately kept out of the first show. "I want to use Ronnie's guitarcam on his solo on 'Tumbling Dice'; he has already agreed to have the camera run on a cable if the RF is an issue. There are a few other effects with big price tags which I am pushing for. I think they will happen a few shows down the line but the band are more concerned with making sure the basics are right first, and they are quite correct."

Among the expensive gags on Carruthers' wish list was a Jimmy Jib boom at the front of the main stage, intended to capture roving images of the highly mobile frontman. Jagger was playing hard to get in the beginning. Carruthers: "The stage is Mick's playground and the jib can be an intrusion. He's a very experienced performer and accepts there will be big boom arms on TV shoots, but for regular shows he doesn't want to feel restricted or distracted. We were actually trying to keep it out of the way during rehearsals so that it wouldn't distract him, but then the shots from the jib were not so brilliant. The thing about a wide angle lens on a jib is that it only works dynamically if the artists are moving and you really fling the camera around. Scotty, our jib man, didn't do that in rehearsal because we told him about Mick's feelings, and that's why the shots looked a bit lame. But that's the irony of it all. The jib's back in its box for now, but twenty or thirty shows down the line, I'm confident we'll be able to bring it out again because it's a technique that was made for people like Mick and the Stones."

Carruthers later had his way.

Until the night before the first show, Carruthers had just one full rehearsal for video purposes, during which he was screening as many different images and effects as he could muster, in a bid to encourage reactions from the band. "Predictably, they told me that less is more. It's important to focus as much as possible on the Stones themselves, so when they first appear there are nice, clear close-ups of the band members for 'Satisfaction' and 'It's Only Rock 'N' Roll'. There are no songs where we only have video playback; we're constantly moving from VT to live camera. We introduce the songs with a bit of video, and cut to video from live images where the music dictates it, and then maybe round off a song with video before fading to black. It'll become self-evident when we've reached a happy medium."

For a band so long in the tooth, it was interesting how the Stones had grasped modern day information technology values and gone so far as to make a feature of the Internet during each show by holding a live "net surfer" song request vote via the Stones' official web site at http://www.the-rolling-stones.com.

"Mick and Patrick wanted an idea of how the audience could request a song without making it like a game show where you'd get someone up out of the crowd [à la Take That]," said Carruthers. "It also had to be completely genuine or the band wouldn't have anything to do with it. So I got together with Ted Mico from Virgin in LA and devised a method whereby people log on to the Net and click on icons to vote for their favourite song from a pre-rehearsed list of around twelve numbers that would not otherwise be in the set. We tap into the web site live and show the results of the vote on the JumboTron.

"We've actually gone further and decided to pipe the song that the

Net surfers have chosen down the line, so that they can actually see the Stones live, as it happens. To make that work, we've needed four ISDN lines to the venue: two for video, one for audio, and one for the return. Real Video is the company that's involved in making this wild idea a reality. It's not entirely original but it is a really cool idea which we'll be doing right from the first Chicago show. If it's a success it will be a feature of each of the 100 or so shows around the world." 'Under My Thumb' received the lion's share of the Web vote on the opening night and this particular segment was a highlight of every show.

The location of each show was further highlighted towards the end of the set by a video sequence which bore a striking resemblance to one idea used on Oasis's Be Here Now tour. Given Carruthers' association with both bands, this came as no surprise. Said Carruthers: "Just before the band come back for the encore, we show a map of the world on the screen and in Chicago it will zoom in to North America, the USA, Illinois, then Chicago, and finally a close-up of Soldier Field, at which point the audience will go mad! We'll be doing that kind of thing for every show."

The Bridges To Babylon tour marked a major change in the Stones' audio department, namely the appointment of rental company dB Sound and the aforementioned Robbie McGrath, whose new assignment was not so much the result of the luck of the Irish but the culmination of twenty years' worth of experience, most recently with Simply Red and The Pet Shop Boys. Chicago-based dB Sound, on the other hand, had the distinction of taking over from Showco, the Texan team which had been synonymous with the touring Stones since 1978.

This, of course, was no mean feat and, according to dB partner Barry Dane, it served as confirmation of everything he and his colleagues believed was possible when they (Harry Witz, Klaus Cramer and Olaf Schroeder) purchased the seventeen-year-old company's assets from their previous bosses and relaunched the dB name in 1995. He said: "We knew we could take dB from what it was and build it up to be what is arguably the most technically advanced sound company in the business."

Launching this tour in dB's hometown of Chicago was both a blessing and a curse, said Dane. "In some ways it would have been a lot simpler if it was in another city. It's been easier in one sense since we are able to pick up spare equipment from our warehouse very quickly. But because we are so well known here, it creates a problem with so many friends and business colleagues wanting to see opening night, so we've had to buy literally hundreds of tickets 'cause we can't say no! Overall though, kicking off in Chicago gives us the feeling that it was all meant to happen."

Key to dB's contract victory was its link with the ElectroVoice X-Array sound system which was chosen above a number of concert standards for service on Babylon, and decorated in gold paint [suddenly orange didn't seem such a good idea]. A feature of the system is its Ring Mode Decoupling technology, which maintains the integrity of EQ regardless of the volume level – something which had eluded the manufacturing industry at large for many years.

Dane had been aware of X-Array since its initiation as a nameless concept, but one which many felt was just what the marketplace needed. The technical involvement of Dane's dB partner Harry Witz, and Bob Doyle, Dave Webster and Mike O'Neill of EVI, coincided with the buy-out of dB Sound. "We knew that we would re-launch dB with a new PA system within a year. Two and a half years later, everything seems to have worked out perfectly, with the perfect band performing brilliantly through this great system," said Dane. "We were very confident that if anything was going to win the Stones' tour for dB, it was going to be X-Array."

For Robbie McGrath, X-Array was a system that he was prepared to stake his reputation upon, even though many people within the Stones camp were initially resistant to change. He commented: "Obviously, when you get the job they ask you what you want to use, which is fortunate because at the end of the day it's the FOH engineer who cops the flak if something doesn't sound great. With The Rolling Stones they ask you these questions because it's your balls on the line, and if anything goes wrong they certainly don't want you saying, 'Well if you didn't give me what I wanted, how can it be my fault?' So they're effectively maximising their ass-kicking power for when it all goes wrong, although when I was first asked I thought, 'Oh, how nice of them.' That's naivety for you!"

McGrath's association with ElectroVoice dated back to when he mixed AC/DC through an EV manifold rig. A strained relationship with

EV at the time led to him transferring his affections to Brit Row's Turbosound Flashlight system for tours with Simply Red. However, EV kept in touch with the Irishman and the relationship improved dramatically when Bob Doyle became part of the EV empire.

"I was introduced to the X-Array project very early on when it was simply a nice club system. It sounded good but it wasn't going to cut the ice at a higher level. However, I watched it develop and began to see what it could do. So when someone asked if I'd like to try it, I wasn't listening to a box from scratch – I appreciated what had gone into it, so it was easier for me to assess it. What I'm looking for is coverage – I want to be able to walk up the bleachers and clearly hear and feel the Stones wherever I am, and not have the sound going in and out of pockets. I want a low end that's musical, not just audio terrorism. I want to feel the notes in the low end, and not just have my chest caved in...although I'm not exactly averse to a bit of movement! So when we stacked up one side of the PA for the first proper tests in indoor and outdoor stadium array situations, after hearing all the other rigs available, I knew it was for me. For what we're doing right now, you can't get any better."

The front-of-house rig consisted of thirty-two Xb bass cabinets, forty-eight Xf mid/highs, forty-eight Xn full range boxes, and twenty-four Xds sub-basses, requiring more than 100 EV P3000 Precision Series amplifiers. Some of the X-Array cabinets in the flown rig were completely devoid of components. Did this represent a new form of invisible technology? "Oh Gawd, I've been sussed!" laughed McGrath. Mark Fisher appeared to have the definitive explanation: "The PA array was designed before the dB Sound was chosen, and so when we discovered just how efficient the X-Array system was and that fewer cabinets would be needed, it was decided to stay with the amount specified by the design but have around sixty dummies, just to make the rig accommodate the decoration. That PA certainly packs a terrific amount of punch."

To the side of each flown array, there was a vertical column of sub-basses which caused problems during early production rehearsals due to wind, but were later secured. "We had a thunder storm when we first arrived in Chicago," said McGrath. "I was standing on the FOH riser, undercover, when a massive bolt of lightning landed just behind the stadium although it looked as if it hit the stage. The crack was amazing and I've never seen lighting riggers jump off trussing so quickly in my life!"

McGrath had two automated Midas XL4 consoles at his disposal: one for the main stage, with "all the dancing faders", and another with just automated VCAs, strictly for the centre stage where a dedicated backline set-up was reserved for a pure rock 'n' roll set, which featured 'Little Queenie', 'Let It Bleed' and a brisk 'The Last Time' – twelve minutes of glorious intimacy. Two days before the first show, most of the pre-programming of McGrath's console cues for the song intros was complete, but his processing still needed attention.

"I've spent a month in a small room in Toronto and it's very nice to be able to get subtle reverbs going in such an environment, whereas it's an entirely different thing in a stadium," he said. "With a band like the Stones, everything's live and it's all down to what mood they're in. That has a major impact on how far you push a fader or tweak an EQ. Emotions come down the line at you when you're mixing, unlike machines. It's not like we're dealing with twenty channels of processed music. Sequencers don't have attitudes. So the XL4 recalls are great for getting you right on the money at the start of a number, but you're riding everything from that moment onwards."

The Al Smart compressor was earning its keep in the McGrath rig for general use. Elsewhere, Klark Teknik EQs were on vocals and the main system, and the rig also benefited from an Aphex Dominator II and a bank of BSS DPR-901IIs. A Spatializer was used to move the overall stereo mix and isolated channels around with a 3D feel. McGrath: "It's especially good when a guitar kicks in for a solo because I can lift it above the mix to achieve some sort of separation."

Next to his main stage XL4 sat a Yamaha ProMix 01 mixer which he used purely for effects returns, controlling levels from an Eventide H3000 and Lexicon PCM-70, two channels of each are on Jagger's vocals; two channels of H3000 on backing vocals; PCM-70 on brass, Yamaha SPX-90 and PCM-70 on drums, and a Yamaha Rev5 for general inserts.

Common to both McGrath and monitor engineer Chris Wade-Evans ("Wevans") were four BSS Varicurves which offered dedicated EQ processing for Jagger, Richards and Wood's various acoustics, from six- and twelve-string guitars to lap steels and Dobros – all of them with two pickups (neck and bridge) and run through a tube pre-amp system specified by Jagger's guitar tech, Pierre de Beauport. A Countryman DI was on the bridge pickup while a passive Sunrise was assigned to the neck. Each of these instruments had a different Varicurve programme setting which helped both engineers automate the guitars' EQ and presence in the mix. Said McGrath: "Rather than eating up desk channels on each of these radically different sounding guitars, we just have two channels of a Varicurve on each guitar with program changes to bring them in. It makes life very simple."

Each delay tower was equipped with four X-Array Xf mid/high cabinets and was forty-six metres from the main clusters. Delays were calibrated with a Klark Teknik DN6000, while the DN3698 hand-held remote controller was used to control the DN3600 graphics which were also utilised at the monitor position.

McGrath did what few engineers had been able to do for the Stones since the stadium became their venue of choice, and that was to make them sound raw and nasty...as they damn well should! "The one thing about The Rolling Stones that you really have to do is capture The Rolling Stones. It's a very simple statement but a difficult job in practice," he said. "The Stones are bigger than your PA or the best effects in your rack. They've been at it for thirty-five years and there's a recipe there that works, undeniably. You have to sit behind the desk and wait for those ingredients to start cooking. You can't run at it and start gating drums, and sticking your favourite gizmo on the guitars, because it doesn't work. I did that on the first night in this stadium and I sat back and said, 'Hey, that sounds great...but it's not The Rolling Stones'.

It might seem to an outsider that he was dealing with a very simplistic demand, but sometimes the most simple things in life present the biggest challenges. "One of the ways to win here is to just let the whole thing live and give it the reins, to a certain degree. You just listen to every bang, crank and wallop because it's all there for a purpose. They're a great rock 'n' roll band who have always lived on the edge of disaster, and they have a feel in their music that may sometimes sound ragged or like it's not going to work, but it really does work brilliantly if you allow it space and room to breathe. If you try to clean up the edges you run the risk of totally blowing it for them."

Simultaneously on tour with 1997's top two rock productions, Irish audio cousins McGrath and U2 engineer Joe O'Herlihy regularly passed each other as they wound their way around the globe. Both were working at the effect of a Mark Fisher set design, with the main difference that O'Herlihy had a mono central cluster to negotiate, while McGrath was faced with the more traditional left/right configuration. Did this make the Stones man happy? "Happy as a pig in shit, mate!" said a relieved McGrath. "That's a very tried a tested set-up, and the Stones do tend to be the types who don't fix things that aren't broken. Over the years, we've all tried to bend the laws of physics and some of it's worked but a fucking lot of the time it hasn't. I've been on the bad end of a few things, like centre stages and people performing in front of PAs, and it's not easy."

Whilst McGrath was a newcomer, Chris Wade-Evans had been mixing the monitors for the Stones for a number of years, and operated Harrison consoles on the previous two world tours, purely because they offered him the most flexible output configuration available. On Voodoo Lounge, however, he ran into a compromise when mixing for the "runway" portion of the set.

After the tour, Wade-Evans met the Cadac team from Clive Green & Co, and began discussing the qualities which would make the ideal monitor desk for modern touring. Time passed quickly and the engineer was soon presented with the prototype Cadac M-Type console.

Commented Wade-Evans: "The original idea involved having seventy-two busses, but the practicalities determined that we would narrow it down to twenty-eight outputs. I was involved with Cadac all the way through the design process of both this desk and the F-Type. Once we arrived at a product that had more outputs than the Harrison, it became apparent that this was going to be the desk for the main stage on the current Stones tour."

(Clive Green, the co-founder of Cadac, effectively started and ended his professional audio career with The Rolling Stones. As a studio technician at Olympic Studios in the Sixties, Green was present for many of the band's early sessions, and more than thirty years later, his company was responsible for changing the fortunes of their stage monitoring. That's karma for you.)

All twenty-eight outputs plus a portion of the matrix were used for the Stones, with Klark Teknik DN3600 EQs applied throughout, but outputs were not Wade-Evans' only concern. "Cadac consoles sound so good. The signal to noise ratio on the M-Type is phenomenal and it's so quiet. Although the automation is a real bonus, it isn't so critical with the Stones who, regardless of the fancy set trappings surrounding them, are essentially a live rock 'n' roll band, so it wasn't a factor in the decision. However, I am programming in some cues and using the automation to re-assign things, and it is very handy to control things from a single VCA."

Cadac's name is synonymous with the world of theatre, which is hardly the domain of the Stones. Wade-Evans believed, however, that the quality of the M-Type, and particularly its profile on this tour, would give Cadac a surprising breakthrough into rock 'n' roll territory. "In terms of what it brings to the Stones, it is by far the nicest-sounding mixing desk I've worked on. Everything about it is extremely professional, especially the EQ. I'm also extremely impressed with Cadac's back-up service because they leave nothing to chance, and they've even sent out one of their guys, Tony Waldron, to make sure that everything's running as it should."

Wade-Evans also had a separate console for the centre stage set – yet another XL4 – although an M-Type was being considered at one time. "I couldn't convince anybody that three songs on the centre stage was worth forking out for another Cadac. But the XL4 does the job very well and I'm happy with what I'm hearing."

The stage was littered with a total of 100 monitor wedges designed by Bryan Olson of Firehouse with Wade-Evans' involvement. The pair had known each other for several years, often meeting up at festivals to share monitor mixing duties. When Olson was in London with The Cure in 1996, they met to discuss the re-designing of Firehouse's wedges with a view to producing smaller, more efficient, flat-sounding F-12 1 x 12" and F-15 1 x 15" models, without electronic processing.

"I went to Firehouse in upstate New York for a couple of two-week visits and we went through all sorts of components before Bryan came up with these new wedges," said Wade-Evans. "For both models, we actually ended up using the same TAD 15" and 2" compression driver that he's always used, as well as a customised EVI horn. TAD doesn't make an appropriate 1 x 12" speaker, so we used a 600 watt JBL alternative. They weren't specifically designed for the Stones, but that's what we've gone for here – they're on balconies, above my head, out the back, by teleprompter people – everywhere!"

There were twenty-five different wedge mixes on the main stage, amplified by forty Crown Macrotech 36x12 amplifiers fitted with PIP cards – channel one of each amp drives the bass output in exactly the same way as a Crown 3600VZ, while channel two drives the high end with the equivalent power of a 1200 model. "The drum and keyboard fills are the EV 2 x 18" bass cabinets with Firehouse 1 x 12s on top, run three ways. The side fills consist of X-Array cabinets, with two of each of the sub basses, 2 x 18s, full ranges, and long throws, per side. We also have three full range X-Array boxes at the sides behind the runways as part of the runway fills."

Bridges To Babylon was the first major international tour to take on board the first-ever UHF in-ear monitoring system from microphone giant Shure, the PSM600 Personal Stereo Monitor, which soon piled pressure on technology frontrunner Garwood. Despite its appearance on the tour, getting the Stones to use the system proved difficult. They flatly refused to wear ear moulds on the main stage, and it was only after it was explained to them about the delay problems encountered when performing 150' away from the PA in the middle of the stadium that they relented and agreed to wear them on the centre stage. Well, some of the band at least...

"Mick, Ron and [bassist] Darryl Jones are wearing wireless Shures, Charlie wasn't keen so he wears a pair of Sennheiser HD-265 headphones, [keyboard player] Chuck Leavell has a hard-wired Shure system, and Keith just plays off wedges regardless of the distracting delay from the PA," said Wade-Evans. "No one's saying, 'Wow, this is brilliant!' They just accept that it's a means to an end for the short time they're out there in the middle of the crowd.

"The Shure system is the best IEM product I've come across so far, but it still has a very limited dynamic range and any singers I've ever heard using IEM immediately stop projecting because regardless of whether they're whispering or shouting, it comes back at them within this very small dynamic range compared to a PA or wedge system. So the band still have wedges on the centre stage because if you have at least a feel of some sound coming at you from the outside as well, it can help you overcome some of the dynamic limitations.

"There's a Klark Teknik compressor on each input of the in-ears so that I can visually monitor what's going on with them. But to ensure that we wouldn't run into radio transmission problems we decided to position the Shure racks out by the centre stage along with the amp racks for that system."

Taking care of the Sony 800 Series wireless mics for Mick Jagger and the backing singers was Ray Withers, MD of Raycom. On the Voodoo Lounge tour, the Stones became one of the first bands to try the prototype WRR-850 receiver, and this time they went the whole hog by employing a bank of five, along with WRT-867 mics which had Al Smart compressors inserted across their channels. Withers was also responsible for Jagger, Richards and Wood's Sony wireless guitar systems which worked alongside the Shure wireless IEM and bass guitar equipment.

As on Voodoo Lounge, Withers' other responsibility was frequency management. He said: "I'm the guy who sorts out which channels people can use for the main channels, back-up channels and back-ups to the back-ups, not just in the USA but everywhere else in the world, which can be a major headache! The back-up frequencies must work with the existing frequencies, and vice versa, so that there is no interference when a back-up gets used. So we are using a pilot tone on everything to prevent such interference. There are other wireless nightmares here because of the centre stage and we have to put another receiver out there with more antennae. Shows seem to be getting bigger and bigger, and the requirement for wireless systems over long distances are on the increase."

As well as guitar, Jagger played harmonica on some numbers later in the tour, and in order to achieve a more organic sound from his "clean" wireless Sony mic, Wade-Evans fed the signal through a Mesa Boogie Maverick guitar amp. "Mick doesn't have time to change to another microphone when he's roving the stage, so he stays with the wireless Sony. But because that sounds so clean, we send it through a compressor and then through the Boogie with a speaker simulator on the back of it, and the resulting signal is fed back as a normal channel. So when he plays the harp we just drop the radio mic level and bring this distorted, compressed, horrible amp noise in on top of it. It actually sounds great!"

Of the remainder of the mics, Wade-Evans said: "In rehearsals we tried out a very wide range of microphones and arrived at a choice that met both my and Robbie's requirements. We've ended up with a Beyer M88 on the kick drum and there are three mics on the snare. I specified a B&K [Danish Pro Audio] on the top snare, Robbie wanted a Shure SM57, and there's an RE-200 on the bottom. There's a 460 on the hi-hat and ride, and Audio Technica 4050s on the rack, floor toms and overheads, and all the guitar cabinets. Sennheiser 421s are on brass, Shure SM58s on cabled vocals, and Chuck Leavell's Leslie cabinet has an RE-20 on the bottom driver and SM57s on the high." In addition, Countryman DIs are used for bass and keyboards.

Across the two stages, the Audio Technica 4050 mics amounted to a healthy twenty. McGrath's fondness for the microphone had been well publicised, to the point where he featured in several A-T advertising campaigns. One might have taken a cynical view of his support, but he insisted his belief in the product was 100% genuine. "I'll be absolutely honest, if the 4050 didn't work I wouldn't have anything to do with it. It's the same reason why I'm not joined at the hip to any one sound company for any great length of time because I use those companies that give me what I need at any one time, and those needs are forever changing.

"Bands should start realising that if you can pick an engineer who isn't tied in with industry politics and whose sole aim is to provide for the band's needs, they're on to a winner. But the more mature the industry becomes, the more political it is, and the harder it is to keep that middle ground. It's still a relatively new industry; it's still growing."

Considering the extent of the monitor system, comparatively little outboard equipment was in use. Lexicon PCM-80s provided reverbs for vocals and delays for trumpets, BSS graphics were on vocals, Al Smart compressors were across the radio mics, and a TL Audio tube compressor was applied to Darryl Jones' bass. Drawmer gates were used on the drum kit, but as Wade-Evans pointed out: "The way Charlie Watts plays can be so soft that all the gates are doing is shutting mics off at the ends of songs. He's a jazz drummer at heart who plays with his wrists, and his sound is not the kind that screams out for the heavily-gated treatment."

Touring with the Stones for more than a year was obviously going to be an education for McGrath, even after twenty years in the game. Lessons, he said just an hour before the band's first show, had already been learned. "I've realised I should never take on a job as big as this again! Seriously though, with every band comes some valuable experience. Understanding equipment is one thing; we're way beyond the times when if you heard the bass drum and the vocal, you were a genius. Now you've got to capture the essence and get that feel. Stadium sound is always difficult and not just because of the bricks and mortar. Unfortunately, God comes along once in a while with a downpouring of rain, gusts of wind and all sorts just to make sure you're awake! You have to fight all that. Understanding music is a completely different ball game; every band has its unique musical imprint and ideas of how their music should come across to their audience. Learning that is the hardest part."

After Take That, Oasis, and the Manics, to name but a few headline acts, what did landing this tour mean to video man Dick Carruthers – apart from a new hair do? "It's the first time in my life that I've known what I'm doing for the next twelve months. My schedules are normally concrete for no more than three weeks at a time, but my situation suddenly became very appropriate for going off on tour for a year and if I go back to England, which I may not, I think I'll buy a boat and do something incredibly humble before my ego gets too inflated!"

1997 was remembered as one of the busiest years for the Mark Fisher/Patrick Woodroffe partnership which, within the space of a few months had been responsible not only for the Stones' tour, but also the internationally-televised Songs & Visions spectacle at Wembley Stadium and the Genesis tour, featuring Phil Collins' replacement Ray Wilson. Add to this list Fisher's work with Willie Williams on PopMart and it's clear who was the leading force in this area of the industry in the Nineties. "I've been very lucky to have been invited to design the year's biggest touring productions," said Fisher. "I'm not about to back this up with another major show. I'm like anyone else really – you have busy and lean periods. I don't take these things for granted, but the main thing is to take advantage of the opportunities that come your way. It does mean that you stick your neck out occasionally and it can be painful when things like bridges don't show up on time!"

The Stones' Babylon tour was due to roll into the UK in August 1998 for shows at Wembley Stadium and in Edinburgh, however, despite healthy sales of tickets the band were forced to postpone them until the following summer, blaming the Labour Government's revised tax laws. Until Budget Day in March 1998, British citizens working abroad were not liable to pay tax on overseas earnings if they spent sixty-two days or less in the UK per year. However, the Government's scrapping of the Foreign Earnings Deduction allowance scheme – which was planned to save HM Treasury £250 million a year – meant that if any paid work was undertaken in the UK at all, tax must be deducted from the entire annual earnings. With this background, the Stones would have faced an estimated £12 million tax penalty on their European tour if they proceeded with the British dates.

On behalf of the band, Mick Jagger commented at the time: "It's been a very difficult decision. I was tempted to bite the bullet but I am not the only one affected, and the Government turned down our suggestion to play the shows for charity. A Rolling Stones world tour is a two-year project and there are 200 [crew] involved. I am really sorry, especially for all those who will have to wait until next year to see the show."

As the news sunk into the industry consciousness, there were fears that other major British acts (and their crews) planning world tours would be forced to take up residence abroad. Robbie McGrath spoke for the Stones crew when he said: "Everybody's feeling the pinch on this one. If I came back to England, I'd personally earn much less out of the Babylon tour than I expected to at the start, and as a man with three kids to look after that's a real pain. There was a time when leaving your family to go on tour for a year was financially worthwhile, but for a lot of people that's all very questionable now." It was a gloomy pause midway through the Stones' most celebrated tour of the decade.

CHAPTER TWENTY-THREE

Phil Collins

Dance Into The Light – 1997

On his first tour since leaving Genesis, Phil Collins, whose 'In The Air Tonight' launched his sideline solo career back in 1981, had been circumnavigating the globe with his Dance Into The Light production for ten months by the time he surfaced at London's Earl's Court in December 1997. And quite a show it was: an attractive in-the-round presentation which Collins ruled with energetic, bloke-ish showmanship...and occasionally gravitated to working men's club level when he dragged his band around the stage in a kind of mock 'Conga'.

'In The Air' (and *that* drum break) still cooked live, and his other Eighties gems fuelled a warm glow, although Collins himself possibly feared his newer songs may have sat on the wrong side of the MOR fence. "Some of them you'll like...some of them you won't," he warned. You can't knock honesty, and neither could one criticise his vocals – judging by his "yodelling" at the start of each show, Collins's relocation to the fresh-aired Swiss mountainside had done much for him.

Ticket sales for his Dance Into The Light tour were as remarkably healthy. Which was more than could be said for his ex-band whose new production, thanks to a massive reduction in the budget, was a mere shadow of the original plan. Not that Collins' departure from Genesis has had any effect on their album and tour sales, and budgets. Oh no.

For Collins's tour, production director Robbie Williams (also the man charged with Genesis) hired the services of Showco, Brilliant

Stages, CPL and Vari*Lite, all of whom are linked by history and business structure. Collins and Genesis provide the ultimate link, having been behind the original development of the Vari*Lite automated luminaire, as debuted on the Abacab tour of 1981.

Continuing his role as Collins' live audio guru on Dance Into The Light was front-of-house engineer Rob "Cubby" Colby. On the previous Collins tour in 1994 [Both Sides], Colby was using a Midas XL3 console newly fitted with Out Board Automation faders. Whilst Colby still regarded himself a Midas fan, he had fallen head over heels in love with the Amek Recall. So why the switch?

"I'd wanted to change to the XL4 but production of the console had been pushed back and that's when I got interested in the Recall," he said. "It did everything I wanted it to do and more...and at a very fair price. I wanted to purchase a flexible console that would work as effectively for me on the road and in my recording studio, and it became a really wise choice, because of the time code, recall facilities, and virtual dynamics. Having all of those facilities in one board is an excellent solution. I was also impressed with Amek's operation and how responsive they were to what I needed to learn from a demo."

Although Colby mixed manually, all his scene changes were triggered by automation, enabling his mix to be in the ball park at the start of each number. "I mix right off the VCAs – all my lead instruments and voices are in the centre section of the board, so although there is still a lot of manual mixing involved I can spend a lot more time listening to the show. We're often going from a rocker to a ballad and they involve different gates which are loaded instantly by the MIDI facility when the recall kicks in. All the compressors, gates, limiters, expanders and auto panners are recalled instantly, plus all their groupings. The band is so consistent that very little attention is needed to trimming effects and limiting, so I'm left with very few things to adjust at the start of a song."

Outside of the Collins tour, the Recall offered great advantages to support bands and Colby was always on hand to help them make the most of his console. "In between tours with Phil, I went out with Bob Seger where there was a change of support act every few weeks, and their engineers loved it because I would just set up recall positions and suddenly there was time for them to have a decent soundcheck.

Production management love having the board because of the time saved and the small amount of real estate it occupies, and when you can afford time for support soundchecks it makes for a much better vibe. I'm a real advocate of looking after support acts."

On this tour, as well as automatically adjusting effects settings, the Recall's MIDI operated a Yamaha ProMix 01 mixer to Colby's right which existed purely for Collins's drums. "I'm running a total of sisty-six inputs from the stage, and then I have six stereo returns on the console. In addition to Phil's kit, the ProMix handles his concert toms in two positions on the stage and a piccolo snare that Ricky Lawson plays on 'Just Another Story'."

For almost the entire band, Colby and the Showco crew used a full arsenal of Beyer mics – the exceptions being Audio-Technica 4050s on the guitars and Crown CM311 headset mics for vocals. "I find that to be the best headset mic I've used to date," said the engineer.

No surprise was the choice of Showco's Prism PA system – a cluster of twenty cabinets (five wide, four high) at each of the four "corners" of the in-the-round stage, all driven by Crown amps, and supported by an ever-changing ground stack, depending on the venue size. A new underhung box helped with this staging scenario when the audience were standing and blocking the ground fill – the low mids, highs and tweeters were still able to direct down to those people closest to the stage.

"Everywhere you sit in the room there is stereo imaging," said Colby. "But because there are two lefts and two rights, I don't do a lot of heavy panning. That the PA is closer to the audience [only a 120' throw to the back wall at Earl's Court] means that we don't need a delay system and they get the full impact of the sound. We try to compress it and keep it within the restrictions of the room."

There can be few engineers in the world who have had more exposure to the Prism system than Colby. What was his verdict? "The PA is quite unforgiving because it is so responsive. It has a very well thought out driver system and Showco has spent a great deal of time in its R&D. The curve of the PA graphics have remained remarkably consistent throughout this entire tour, mainly because I have used compression in the troublesome bandwidth areas to achieve what I've needed. If it's a hard, glassy room I will compress the high mids more and I can open up that compression if the room is warm and full of padded seating. It's a one-knob operation and it couldn't be more simple."

On monitors, Peter Buess operated two Yamaha PM4000Ms. Collins and his band all relied on wireless Garwood in-ear monitoring, supplied by Marty Garcia at Futuresonics five years ago – the only wedge was at the side of Collins' kit to add weight to his mix. "Because we are in-the-round, IEM was inevitable," commented Colby. "We started out with wired packs on horn positions, but as soon as we got to full band rehearsals in Switzerland and realised how much ease of movement we needed to allow for, the only way was to have everyone on wireless in-ears with wireless mics."

Designer Mark Fisher's idea for the nautical set – entirely built by Brilliant Stages – was to create something which, whilst in-the-round, still established a rich, inventive background against which lighting designer Patrick Woodroffe could create a range of moods. Said Fisher: "The stage also had to feel modern – Phil did not want a gothic or baroque look. Being in-the-round, there was limited scope for scenery which would obstruct sightlines. In the end, I imagined the stage set as a cross between the deck of a steamer and the verandah at Raffles Hotel, Singapore."

The 50' diameter stage was planked in 8" wide decking, with the 60' diameter stage canopy constructed from timber louvres. These eight "legs" above the stage each consisted of three panels which moved on half ton motors, controlled by a Hoist Commander and run by Nick Evans.

The stage concealed a whole range of quick change and sitting out areas, and also three large hydraulically-elevated risers for drums and keyboards – the centre piece rising for Collins' kit. The under stage corridor, which ran all around the stage, was covered with a further series of timber louvres which marked the transition between the main levels. Viewing an animated video sequence of the original design, it appears that the only items missing from Fisher's initial scheme were "ship's ventilators" and a banner drop.

"Patrick does some nice lighting, streaming it through the louvres like sunshine," commented Fisher. "And the louvres move into various shapes – all simple stuff, but effective."

Lighting crew chief Scotty Duhig said: "It's a very complicated show to run and there's a lot which could go wrong. Fortunately, apart from some minor problems with the hydraulics earlier in the tour, everything has gone ship shape."

Whereas Vari*Lites were a major part of Collins' Both Sides tour in 1994, it was Meteorlites who was the main contractor. Dance Into The Light, however, saw CPL take over this responsibility and the interaction of the "Greenford Mafia", namely CPL, Vari*Lite Europe and Brilliant Stages, appeared to have overcome any potential difficulties. As Vari*Lite's Matt Croft said: "It's now a Vari*Lite package in the broadest sense, with all of our associated companies working together. That came through Robbie Williams who does virtually all his projects with us and there's a lot of mutual satisfaction. He's just looking for a very straightforward honest deal and he knows his needs can be addressed under one roof, and therefore do away with handling separate bids. Any internal disagreements between the various parties can be ironed out within the same building, and no one need ever hear about it!"

A total of 128 Vari*Lites (fifty-six VL5s, forty VL6s and thirty-two VL2Cs) were controlled by Vari*Lite operator Tellson James from an Artisan board. As well as calling the spots, Vince Foster ("the lighting jostler") used a Wholehog II to run generic lighting and specials – these included two Lightning Strikes, sixteen Cyberlights, sixteen four-lamp bars with ACLs, twelve MR16 twenty-cell batons, Par 36s for key lights and twenty-four Diversitonic strobes.

Said Foster: "There are 742 active bulbs in the set itself and they are programmed from the Hog to give twinkly chases and enhance the edges of the set. In the mother group there are some 2Cs above the louvres which are the main part of the lighting rig. It's a very clean looking stage which helps to minimise the complications of playing in the round.

"The Cyberlights wash the stage – they are just too far away to become key lights. The musicians are on the inner part of the raised circle and they are lit by VLs which is difficult because the rig moves about eight times during the show and it means there's a completely different focus for Tellson on all his key lights. Phil spends about 70% of the show in the middle of the stage on the raised risers, just so that everyone can see him. He's a very good person to light – he's always in the right place at the right time, and it's very rare that he'll miss his cue."

Duhig interrupted the conversation to make mention of Charlie Kail's underwear. Charlie Kail's what? "Brilliant Stages came up with what we call 'Y-Fronts' which appear as a great effect on 'In The Air'," he said. "They're actually four electrically-driven Genie Tower masts which rise through the stage and form a 'Y' shape, and the VL6s on each of them provide some eeriness in the dark atmosphere of the song." Also of note was an exclusive stacking truss system, produced by Tomcat, which stacks on top of itself for transportation and saves on valuable truck space.

The crew took an interesting approach to focusing prior to each gig. "It was easier to focus from the stage as opposed to doing it at front-of-house," said Foster. "So we've taken our spare Artisan and Hog on to the stage after rigging to focus from there, rather than involve even more people to stand around and give instructions. It's very quick and I think I'd probably do that again."

Whilst in residence at Earl's Court, Rob Colby spent his mornings and afternoons in Studio E at London's Metropolis complex, mixing live tapes from the tour for a future live video. He undertook an identical task for Collins' *Serious Hits Live* album and also Genesis' *The Way We Walk*. "I've been helping Phil identify the best performances and working with engineer Nick Davies. Everything was recorded on fifty-six tracks of Tascam DA-88 and I just try to bring my live input to these projects," said Colby.

CHAPTER TWENTY-FOUR

Texas

White On Blonde – 1997

When the shimmering slide guitar of 'I Don't Want A Lover' launched Texas's career back in 1989, the smart money was on a long and healthy stay at the top. But whilst their success on the European continent remained consistent, by 1992 UK audiences had all but abandoned the Scottish band, fronted by Sharleen Spiteri. The spring 1997 release of *White On Blonde*, however, catapulted Texas back into the mainstream consciousness, with tracks such as 'Say What You Want' merging street cred hip-hop signals with familiar Texas musical territory.

Naturally, with two million units shifted, their winter 1997 tour of Europe was heavily subscribed, and audiences universally warmed to Spiteri's enthusiastic live performance. True to their roots values it was a family affair with the singer's father Eddie Spiteri responsible for the set.

An oriental influence presided, as suggested by the decoration of a performance of 'Halo' on BBC TV's *Top Of The Pops* and also the Hong Kong environment in which the single's promo video was shot. Lighting designer Steven Marr, from the main lighting contractor Total Quality Lighting, explained: "We developed the idea to use three Cantonese symbols [Kanji] which translate as 'White On Blonde' and they appear on a set of drops made by Hangman. They were made so that we could rear light them, so that we didn't have the Chinese look all through the show.

"In between the drops are hooped Chinese lanterns which are made cheaply from calico and look very good, especially when I project various colours and spirals on to them with Clay Paky Golden Scan HPEs from Northern Light. Above each lantern we have Solar 250s which are lovely old lights, and they have custom made discs with artwork of birds and oriental images created by Ronnie Heaps, who colour photocopied them on to acetates."

After the Chinese look was established, a set of silver mirrored blinds was installed in front of the Hangman drops and Icons (subbed from LSD) bounced off the mirrors to create yet another startling effect. This tour was Marr's first experience of working with an Icon desk, and LSD's Rob Lancaster, then training operators on all aspects of the desk, said that Marr had been extremely quick to grasp its fundamental operation.

On most European dates, video – supplied by Creative Technology – played a major part with travelogue-style sequences filmed by Marr and projected by Barcos on to twin 10m x 5m cream Rosco screens in front of the mirrors.

Handling the live sound for yet another Texas tour was Liverpool's Ad Lib Audio. On the last outing, Ad Lib fielded its proprietary, Dave Fletcher-designed PA cabinets, as it has done for other key accounts such as Space, Del Amitri and The Bootleg Beatles. However, this tour revealed the company's recent investment in a Martin Audio Wavefront 8 Compact system which featured the newly-launched W8CS sub-bass enclosure.

Front-of-house engineer and Ad Lib founder Andy Dockerty explained the purchase: "Despite our own cabinets sounding fantastic, not having a name brand amongst our inventory was a bit of a drawback when dealing with acts that are new to us. So when looking at the market, it was plain that the Wavefront offered us the best solution, and my friend Richard Rowley [Martin applications engineer] was very persuasive. I wouldn't say that the W8C was the most revolutionary cabinet but with our own experience of designing and building, we know it's the best deal available. We've had a very busy two months and with our own limited resources we couldn't turn enough of our own boxes to meet the demand anyway."

The PA configuration used throughout Europe varied from venue to venue, mostly featuring twenty-four W8Cs run with the W8CS subs and Ad Lib's own DF3 1 x 18" folded horn enclosures. This rig was amplified using C Audio RA 3001s and 4001s for the tops and mids, SRX 3801s for bass, and Crown VZ 5000s on subs. As the DF3 shared a similar footprint to Martin's 1 x 18" WSX sub, Dockerty confirmed that Ad Lib would be investing further with Martin to replace some of its older DF1 subs to update its hire stock. "The Martin system complements our own because the cabling is pinned identically, so we don't need to change amp racks."

The sell-out, 17,000-capacity Palais Omnisports de Bercy show in Paris was expected to conclude the winter tour, however, an extra date with a stripped-down production was added at the Brabantsal in Leuven, Belgium. Due to demand, the promoters decided to increase the capacity of the modular Leuven venue from 2,500 to 6,000 with just forty-eight hours' notice. On Texas's larger arena shows, the Wavefront was supplemented with a larger Martin Audio F2 system, sub-contracted from Capital Sound Hire. However, at the Brabantsal, operated by promoter and EML Sound & Light Productions' owner Herman Scheuermans, it was deemed a more economical move to bring in EML's F2 stock as a temporary measure.

"Capital have been fantastic," enthused Dockerty. "The manner in which they've done the business has been outstanding. They haven't imposed themselves on us – they've helped us achieve our aims rather than force a way of working down our throats."

At the heart of the FOH audio set-up was the forty-eight-channel Soundcraft Series Five live production console, for which Dockerty had become somewhat of an ambassador since becoming involved with its design. After taking the prototype on the road with Texas in April, Ad Lib purchased a Series Five through LMC Audio Systems, and Dockerty reported great progress with it on the winter tour.

He said: "Soundcraft had spent most of 1996 canvassing the opinions of hire companies in the UK and USA [including Showco, Audio Analysts, Concert Sound and Wigwam] about what would make the best product, because they desperately wanted to make this right. I was very impressed with how committed they were to the product, and how necessary they felt it was to approach companies like Ad Lib. We gave them as much input as we could, and there are quite a few features on the board that I'd like to think were suggested by us.

"Speaking as a sound engineer and a rental company director, it's definitely one of the best boards I've used to date. It has every feature of a Yamaha PM4000 plus a little more because I prefer the EQ. There are A and B input facilities on every channel, so if you are working with a support band, rather than having to do dramatic amounts of re-patching you can actually patch two lines into one channel and flip between them.

With four stereo returns, twelve aux busses, ten matrix outputs and incredibly good headroom, it's a very heavyweight desk."

Dockerty, who worked with Ad Lib colleague and systems engineer Dave Kay on the tour, saw one of the Series Five's main advantages being the user-friendly layout – one which would benefit up and coming engineers. "If a young engineer can walk up to a board and understand it at first sight, it's going to encourage them to use it on a long-term basis. A lot of them may have started with a Soundcraft 200B and if they can use a 200B, they can use the Series Five without any problem. Desks like the Midas XL3 are great products, but they can be daunting. That's why I see the Series Five becoming a prime choice for festivals, as well as theatres and fixed club installations."

Marc Peers mixed the monitors from another Soundcraft console – an SM24 – and fed to Ad Lib's own (15"/2"/60° x 40° horn) wedges, driven by a selection of Crown 2400s and 1200s, and C Audio RA 3001s. Significant to the on-stage sound was Peers' use of the BSS Audio FDS-355 Omnidrive Compact. Dockerty, who purchased four units for the tour, said: "Just being able to do simple things like time-alignment between the 15" and 2" gave us amazing results, and helped to get rid of the phase cancellation around 1-3kHz that always bothered us. The monitors can now sound so correct before you even touch the graphics, and the only reason to adjust the EQ is because of the venue acoustics. In that way, we've achieved 4dB more gain before feedback."

Peers added his confirmation of the Omni Compact's effect: "We physically measured the driver alignment and dialled it in exactly with the Compact, which really put the monitors right in the band's face."

Most interesting was the use of one Compact on the sub-bass section of the drum fill. Inputs A and B took conventional monitor mixes from the console and fed two outputs each for bi-amp wedges. Input C was the separately-derived sub feed, sent through a low-pass filter to the sub cabinet. The other Compacts were set with two monitor mixes feeding bi-amped wedges as before, with two FDS-355s coupled to provide an extra two-way monitor send. For this application, input C on each of the two units was fed with the monitor send from the console, and one FDS-355 provided the low-pass output, while the other provided the high-pass output to the wedge. Thus, from four FDS-355s AdLib Audio derived nine wedge feeds – as well as the drum fill sub.

CHAPTER TWENTY-FIVE

Ocean Colour Scene

A Moseley Shoals Special – 1997

Earlier in 1997, in February to be precise, Eric Clapton's absence from the Royal Albert Hall made room for a new kind of guitar-driven music. Enough of the champagne and strawberries, it was time to dig the new beer 'n' skittles breed, and celebrate the deserved ascension of Ocean Colour Scene whose one-off gig within the great domed auditorium proved to be a genuine special event. The signs were already in evidence before the first note was sounded: backstage in the Artists Bar, Noel Gallagher and Paul Weller traded muso banter, both of them mutual friends of the Birmingham band and prone to the odd impromptu live jam. This night would not be an exception.

A seven-man camera team linked to the Manor Mobiles recording truck was in place to capture this concert, a landmark in Ocean Colour Scene's career and one that drew to a close an amazing twelve months during which they supported The Who on their Quadrophenia tour of the States. No one was more surprised than the band members themselves when *Moseley Shoals* became one of the biggest-selling albums by a British act in the Nineties.

Formed in 1989, they struggled for recognition for several years, before guitarist Steve Cradock's sideline association with Paul Weller encouraged fans and record company executives alike to seriously investigate the band's considerable songwriting and live performance qualities. And those qualities made an earth-shattering impact at the Royal Albert Hall, the venue which they had always dreamed of playing...one day.

Supporting OCS were cellist Rosie Wetters, Liverpool indie veterans The Real People (who at one time were regularly supported by Oasis) and Paul Weller in a rare second billing. Then came the main event. Wearing their late Sixties/early Seventies influences proudly on their sleeves, OCS ran through a blistering set which mostly covered the best of *Moseley Shoals*, including the hits 'The Day We Caught The Train', 'The Circle', 'Riverboat Song' and the Stones soundalike '40 Past Midnight' – all of which were present and correct on the band's previous UK tour in the autumn of 1996 – plus previews of new songs from *Marchin' Already*, their next album.

With the quasi-psychedelic 'Get Away' completing the main set, Steve Cradock climbed up to the Albert Hall's legendary pipe organ (bet he always wanted to do this!) to accompany singer Simon Fowler on the first encore number, 'Robin Hood'. Then virtual hysteria set in when Weller returned to the stage with Noel Gallagher (fresh out of the bar) to join the Scene for a frenzied finale which climaxed with The Beatles' 'Day Tripper', the final chord thrust coinciding with a freak sound system power failure. Most other bands use pyrotechnics, but these guys were a law unto themselves.

Several of the band's crew members were long-term friends whose loyalty was rewarded as OCS grew in stature. Among them was LD Pete Wilson who had worked "on and off" with OCS since their formation, and whose commitment was repaid by a seat on the bus for their first major tour. His task was made easier by the close working relationship he had built up between supplier Neg Earth Lights and Avolites, the manufacturer of his Diamond II console. He said: "I did some training at Avolites a few years ago on the QM500 and returned later to train on the Sapphire with Steve Warren. When we started putting everything together for this tour, I was offered the Diamond II and I've found that it makes the operation of moving lights a lot easier, because everything is so accessible. Although it shows 180 channel outputs on the console, the whole thing is capable of over 3,000 output channels on DMX. We are using 120 channels on moving lights and a further sixty channels on generics."

Wilson, whose experience included working for many years on Glastonbury's acoustic stage, said that the significant advances in lighting technology which had occurred over recent years were instantly apparent when he came to specifying the OCS rig. "It's been a hell of a learning curve for me going into the moving lights scene. Fortunately I have had some expert assistance and now the show is up and running I'm very happy. Obviously, you never get to use all the effects that are available on the ten Golden Scan HPEs I'm using."

The HPEs on the front truss were used for front light positions but mostly for projections on to the two round screens positioned above the band. Rear HPEs were reserved for audience swirls and other effects. Other than the scans, Par cans and strobes formed the basis of the rig, along with a few floor lights dotted around the drum kit and some bars of ACLs which gave colour washes to the back and front in true rock 'n' roll style. Wilson said: "I also have two Source 4s, which are very similar to Leko profile lights, and I'm using them from the front truss to act as cyc lights for the two circular screens. I have colour changers on those, with ten different colours available to fire at the screens as well as the HPEs. There are also four Molefays with colour changers to act as cyc lights for the square screen at the back. It's a basic box truss up top and my aim has been to make the rig as simple as possible to set up."

All of the band members were vocal about certain elements of the lighting design and as the previous tour was about to begin, Wilson was required to run around at the last minute in a furious attempt to meet their demands. "They were keen to have an interesting opening sequence which is very simple, but it involved a lot of travelling on my part, backwards and forwards to DHA with bits of artwork for gobo cutting," he said.

This particular sequence began with a projection of the band's logo, the "Splegman", which appeared vertically at first and then slowly tilted on to its side to reveal the initials 'OCS'. This was followed by the more recognisable Ocean Colour Scene "targets" which span against darkness as the band came on stage. Added to these gobos was a photographic glass of the *Moseley Shoals* album cover photo which was again made by DHA for Wilson to project at the very end of the show.

It was through his work at Glastonbury that Wilson became acquainted with Neg Earth, on whom he lavished much praise. "Our budget has been pretty tight and so I asked for quotes from five different companies. I'm very glad that Neg Earth won the deal because I rate their back-up service as being second to none and I've always been impressed with the way they look after their equipment."

Wilson said that apart receiving complaints from the band about the heat of the lights (so touchy, these rock stars!), his job on recent shows has been a smooth ride. There were, however, a few sweaty brows when the crew loaded into Manchester Apollo: "The flight case containing the Diamond II was left upright in the rain on the way to the venue, and upon opening the lid we discovered that there was water pouring out of the hard disk drive. The chances of getting a replacement desk on a Sunday afternoon were pretty slim, but we managed to solve the problem with a few hairdryers!"

Providing the PA system and technical back-up was the crew from Capital Sound Hire, headed by Keith Davis. Notable for his long-term preference of Martin equipment, Davis decided that rather than use the F2 system which accompanied the band on their autumn tour, the OCS show might benefit from the use of Martin's latest generation Wavefront 8 Compact PA – the system which scooped the Best New Audio Product accolade in the 1997 Live! Awards.

Flying high above the stage and driven by Crown 2400 and 3600 amplifiers, the PA cluster consisted of eighteen Martin Wavefront 8 Compacts (W8C) and six W8S sub basses, and at ground level were four WSX folded horn sub woofers and four W8Cs with W2 two-way infills. Davis's instinct proved to be as keen as ever and after the show many agreed that it was one of the cleanest sounding they had heard in the venue.

Said Davis: "My decision was influenced partially because Capital Sound had never used Wavefront in this venue and this was a good opportunity to try it out because OCS are a great band to work with, and their tour manager Yaron Levy is very understanding. Bands are now beginning to ask for Wavefront and the main artists using the system so far have been Gary Glitter, Worlds Apart and Crash Test Dummies. We are very pleased to be using a system of this quality with OCS."

The designer behind Wavefront Compact was Bill Webb whose objective, it seemed, was to formulate the warmest-sounding, most transparent system possible, whilst not forgetting the most important reason for the very existence of the equipment: the music.

Webb said: "Until now, a lot of manufacturers have experienced real difficulties in terms of packaging and in most cases their systems have simply been too big. Most systems in the world have the same compression drivers for the high end of the vocal range, and they are the frequencies which hurt your ears although if you are a good engineer you can tame that. The F2, for instance, uses compression drivers and you can make it sound as loud and nasty as you want, but you can also make it sound pretty good. A compression driver inherently produces 30% distortion at high levels, and you can't run them when they are distorting, so you have to use a lot of them but this was an area I wanted to steer away from.

"The idea behind the 6.5" mid/high horn in the Wavefront 8 is that you can actually listen to it at high levels. We even use AC/DC records to demo the system, and you could not do that with a system that uses a compression driver – it would just tear your head off! We think we've moved the argument on a little and in years to come the Wavefront 8 will be seen as a major turning point in sound reinforcement development. I certainly won't be going back to the old ways."

In terms of packaging, the W8C is a very small and efficient box, and upon its launch confidently represented the direction in which the industry was now moving. Most importantly, it was also a friendly system and straightforward to use. Said Webb: "It is compatible with the Martin MX4 and MX5 analogue controllers although it's generally run with a BSS Omnidrive and there is a very good reason for that, being a fully horn-loaded system. There is a tweeter with a horn length of about 3" and right down at the other end of the spectrum there is a bass horn of 7', and ideally one needs to time align all those elements. The only precise method is by digital means and the Omnidrive is in my opinion the best digital controller.

"The Compact and WSX were launched at Frankfurt in 1996, and I've been very pleased with the way they have been received. I honestly think there is nothing on the market to touch it, and the Live! award for Best New Product helped to substantiate that theory."

After their autumn 1996 tour, a shift of power in the OCS camp resulted in Yaron Levy abandoning his dual role of monitor engineer and stage manager to become tour manager and General Overseer Of All Things. In his place, former Town & Country Club (later The

Forum) house monitor man Gerry Wilkes assumed control of the forty-channel Midas XL3 at the side of the stage and also inherited the stage management responsibility. Having already accumulated experience in both areas for Teenage Fan Club, he was used to the sometimes clashing burdens. "As long as soundchecks and the switching of bands all run to schedule, I'm as calm as a cucumber," he said with a slight twinkle of panic in his eye.

On stage were sixteen Martin LE700 monitor wedges (which feature a proprietary 15" diameter 4" coil bass driver and a 1.4" compression driver) and two side fills consisting of F2B bass cabinets and W8Cs.

The Albert Hall show was the fourth show of the month for OCS, following dates in Galway and Dublin's Olympic Theatre, but Wilkes' association with the band dated back over a year. He commented: "I actually mixed monitors for OCS before Yaron, around March 1996. They were due to play in Europe but couldn't afford to take me along so I then accepted an offer to do a tour in the States. In the meantime, they had some trouble with a house monitor engineer in Scandinavia and although I was tied up I put them in touch with Yaron who quickly sorted them out. I'm loving every minute of these dates. Yaron is a very hard act to follow and coming into a job like this when they have been so used to dealing with Yaron would be difficult for anyone, especially without rehearsals as was the case for me. To play things as safely as possible, I'm doing exactly the same as Yaron did in terms of the eleven mixes between the four band members and the various effects that happen from time to time."

OCS had a reputation for rivalling their Oasis buddies at times for on-stage volume, but things appeared reasonably tame at the Albert Hall – the only way to behave at this venue. Wilkes sent a total of eleven mixes around the stage and as one might expect, bassist Damon Minchella enjoyed a rhythm-heavy wedge mix, majoring in kick, snare and hi-hat. Adjacent to his Ampeg SVT rig was one side of Steve Cradock's Marshall JCM 800 stack which the bass player adjusted in volume to suit his own guitar monitoring requirements. Cradock's own needs were mostly a guitar and vocal-orientated mix, and naturally Fowler's mix concentrated on his own vocals which, it must be said, were then among the most powerful the UK had to offer. In addition to a wedge, Oscar Harrison received a BSS DPR-402 compressed mix of his backing vocals through his hard-wired Garwood in-ear system, which he used for the first time on the autumn tour.

The stretch Midas console to the left of the XL3 was there purely to give engineer Jon Ormisher a number of extra channels when he mixed the support bands' monitors. Effects for monitoring were purposely kept to a minimum, with two Yamaha SPX-990s delivering reverb for Fowler's vocals, and a richer reverb shared by Cradock's Leslie cabinet and drummer Oscar Harrison's backing vocal mic. His kit used six channels of Drawmer DS201 gates and a dbx 160 was inserted on Minchella's bass. One outboard item which travelled everywhere with Wilkes was his Klark Teknik parametric equaliser, of which he said: "I invested in it a few years ago to help me out particularly if I'm abroad and not using the same system every night. You never know what's going to be in the rack when you arrive at the venue, so it's best to be safe than sorry! At the very least it helps to achieve some kind of EQ consistency every night."

The secret of being a good and successful monitor engineer lies in being able to provide an intelligent balance of sound across the stage, whilst trying to avoid raising the master volume fader so high that the front-of-house mixer cannot cope with the spill into the mics. A simple enough task, one may think. But add 'difficult' personalities to the equation and a nightmare begins. Said Wilkes: "You have to develop a pretty hard shell in order to last the course, but if things do go disastrously wrong it can still affect you. There have been one or two occasions when, for some strange reason, I haven't got on with one of the band members and although I have gone to great lengths to get a good sound on stage for them, they have not been happy. Of course, they do not mind letting you know their feelings in the most colourful ways known to man! That's very hard to deal with."

A mild-mannered grizzly bear is how Steve Cradock described OCS guitar tech Dave Liddle, the fellow who in October 1977 found himself doing the same job for Paul Weller in the early days of The Jam. His relationship with the Woking wonder continued through until 1996 when Weller took a break from touring and OCS offered him twelve weeks on the road. Since then, Liddle had been looking after Simon

Fowler's acoustic guitars and Damon Minchella's bass gear.

Liddle commented: "Simon has just started using a Martin D35 with a pick-up in the bridge, along with his Takamine EN-40. As from this year we are feeding his acoustic via a DI box into a black face Fender Twin with the tremolo on for two songs and it works really well. He could use a tremolo pedal but Boss stopped making them."

Although he preferred the Martin from a traditional construction point of view, Liddle acknowledged the practical live performance benefits of the Takamine. "It actually works on stage a little better than the Martin. It's just a case of getting used to the Martin which has a great natural sound but it makes tuning difficult. The Takamine has a built in pre-amp so you can tune it backstage even when it's noisy. But you're dead on the ground with the Martin because someone only has to shout and the tuner will pick it up through the guitar. Simon requires a D tuning on that guitar and it can be a nightmare because I have to run a mile from the stage to tune it in a quiet corner."

Minchella used two Jazz basses: mainly a 1977 Fender with a maple fingerboard, and a Squier model in reserve. "He has Di Marzio pick-ups in the Fender and it's a killer sound, probably a bit too powerful for the stage at the moment! The backline level is quite loud out there, even with the acoustic guitar which rings out solidly from the side fills. Even so, Damon's not quite playing at half the volume capacity of his SVT rig so he has plenty of room to spare if he really wanted to kick in. But we try to keep it down so that the front-of-house engineer has something to do!"

Liddle confessed to feeling a little strange about working at a gig where he was not taking care of Weller's equipment. But old habits die hard – Weller's bass player Marco Nelson collared the tech during the afternoon to ask if he would tune his two vintage basses: a Gibson EB2 and a Gretsch Tennessean, as "used" by The Monkees! Said Liddle: "I have a standard saying that I don't do support acts, but I suppose I'll have to make an exception for once!"

A regular feature of the OCS set was the appearance of Cradock's guitar tech Kevin "Ewok" Rowe, who joined the four-piece to play piano on '40 Past Midnight'. At other times during the show, Ewok kept an eye on Cradock's main guitar, a 1968 re-issue Gibson Les Paul Gold Top which he played for most of the evening. "It's a real survivor, having been through a flood and God knows what!" said Ewok. "He also has a green custom Les Paul which has been constructed from various models and a Gibson SG which has a dropped D for 'Get Away'. That SG has a nice bite to its sound which is absolutely perfect for that song.

"We have a few others out there for him, like a Strat and the Gibson 335 that Paul Weller gave to him, and he may call up for them at any point, but it's all down to the mood he's in. Everything is so spontaneous with this band and there's so much space for improvisation, unlike a lot of others who will strictly choreograph their set and act like metronomes. Of course, Dave and I have to be prepared for what is going to happen as a result of whatever vibe is going down on stage and in the audience."

Liddle added: "Simon might just turn around and stop playing his acoustic halfway through a number so that he can play blues harp, and I've got to be on the case otherwise he'll just lay the guitar down on the stage. You've got to have eyes at the back of your head with these guys!"

Cradock employed a simple set-up and rather than use copious effects, he chose to shape his guitar sound from the natural tone of his instrument. "Very few guitarists do that today and instead spend all night tap dancing on their fuckin' monstrous pedal boards!" laughed Ewok. "Steve will only use the occasional effect literally as an effect to fatten a solo and not as the basis of his entire sound. He has a Small Stone phaser, a wah, a Marshall Blues Breaker, a DD5 delay and a Yamaha Rev 7 reverb, and everything goes through his Marshall JCM 800 rig. We've played around with the JMP stuff in the studio but for live work we still can't find anything to beat the JCM 800s."

After eight years away from the music business, Tony Keach (a former recording engineer for UB40) was persuaded by OCS to return to his front-of-house engineering role when, in 1996, the band's heightened profile demanded all hands on deck. "OCS are an amazing band to work for and I wouldn't have come out of retirement for anybody else," he proclaimed.

For this show Keach was assisted by one of the UK's top engineers, Gary Bradshaw of Pink Floyd's Division Bell tour fame. Keach mentioned how the duties split between them: "Gary is assisting me on this gig, mainly because he is used to the Albert Hall and I've never worked here before. He has done all the miking up and line checking, as Capital's Dave Bearman [later to join Peavey Electronics] did on the last tour, and I come in to work with the band in the soundcheck to re-EQ and get the final mix position. Gary has a hell of a pedigree with his work for Pink Floyd and Eurythmics, and while I can't claim to have a similar track record we work well together.

"Everyone was telling me that the Albert Hall was going to be a difficult gig from an engineering perspective but I've been really surprised how relatively easy it has been to get a good sound. I think a lot of that has been down to the Martin Wavefront PA which has a fantastic crystalline feel to it. Martin equipment was always a favourite with live engineers but it was always a pain to tour with because of the amount of boxes involved. This system, however, is a whole different ball game."

While the support bands' engineers shared a Yamaha PM4000, Keach got to grips with his favourite Midas XL3 forty-channel desk. "I think it's always better to get instruments to sound good at source rather than spending time applying lots of EQ," he commented. "I'm quite a fan of minimalism where EQ is concerned, but I must admit that the Midas EQ is very good, probably the best on a live desk that I've ever come across. It certainly beats the Soundcraft 100 Series board I remember using when I started in this business many moons ago."

Where miking is concerned, Tony Keach generally stuck to the classic tools of the trade, although he was also not averse to trying new and unorthodox products. He employed Shure SM57s on Oscar Harrison's hi-hat and (top and bottom) snare, AKG 451s on overheads and AKG clip mics on the toms. Inside the kick drum was a Beyer M88, although Keach's traditional choice for this application would have been an AKG D12. "The band like that 1960s sound, but that mic is rarely available on hire. Because OCS are so loud on stage, the top end of the kick can bleed through into the front mix, and I don't like a lot of click on the kick drum at all so that always requires a lot of attention."

Placed left and right on the rotating tweeter of Cradock's Leslie speaker were two Shure SM57s. Inside the band's occasionally used Kawai piano, meanwhile, was a C-Tape transducer system and a degree of signal processing was required due to the instrument's temperamental nature. Keach said: "I have a stereo Klark Teknik graphic on it and because I wasn't getting an even balance on the C-Tapes, I have to use a BSS DPR-402 compressor as well to even everything out and it sounds a lot better for the effort."

An Electro-Voice ND457 was originally specified in the autumn for Harrison's backing vocal, not least due to its superior rejection of drum kit spill. When Keach noted a significant presence peak he was lured instead to the Shure Beta 58, as used for all the other members' vocals. Said Keach: "Simon has a very powerful and distinctive voice, and I rarely have trouble getting him above the band, especially when I insert the BSS dynamic compressor on his channel."

One aspect of OCS's live sound which occupied Keach's mind throughout the show was the faithful recreation of their recorded material. He said: "It's mainly the guitar effects that we are recreating. In 'Get Away' there is a one-second delay on just one snare beat and that has to be inserted at just the right moment. That can sometimes be difficult to catch, especially if the desk is a long way from the stage and there is time delay to consider. There isn't time to put on a pair of headphones because that snare beat comes within a very busy point of the song where there are lots of things happening with reverbs on the harmonica and guitar.

"I'm also doing a lot of stereo panning with Steve's guitar at that and other points in the set, so I have my hands very full. When we were on tour in America with The Who, their engineer Dave Kob remarked that what I was attempting to do every night was pretty tough work. And he should know! I use a Roland SDE-3000A DDL for that snare delay and the return signal is also fed to a twelve-second reverb so that the repeats sound incredibly cavernous. That recreates roughly what was done on the album, although it was a Grampian spring reverb in the studio which, of course, would not be a practical choice of equipment in a live situation! Another piece of outboard that is essential is the Eventide H3000SE Ultra Harmonizer which helps to smooth out the spiky bits in the mix."

When asking Keach which tool he used live to reproduce Fowler's distorted vocal on 'The Day We Caught The Train', the Law of Sod stepped in. "Oh, we're not bothering to do that live. We did it for the album by plugging a microphone into a Marshall Blues

Breaker pedal and took a line out to the desk via a DI box. We could attempt to do it live but it only lasts for a few bars and it's not really worth risking the feedback." It would have been interesting, though. Another time, another place?

CHAPTER TWENTY-SIX

Roni Size & Reprazent

New Forms – 1997

When Bristol's Roni Size hit the headlines as the winner of the prestigious 1997 Mercury Music Prize, the future of drum 'n' bass as an all-conquering musical form appeared to be set in stone. Together with his band Reprazent, Size's ascent began at that year's Tribal Gathering event, followed by the release of his acclaimed album *New Forms* and a sell-out European tour which secured a bright future for this innovative musical genre.

Size's UK dates in October 1997 were notable for a number of firsts, including the early showing of the new Turbosound TFM-330 monitor wedges, and an improved THL-4 cabinet.

In a world where the often aggressive marketing of major system rental companies tends to preclude the involvement of small-time, but nonetheless skilful, operators on tours by new stars, it was encouraging to note that the sound for Roni Size was supplied by Wayne Barker's WE Audio.

Front-of-house engineer and production manager Laurie Brace said that it was Barker's commitment to Turbosound Floodlight in the shape of a £60,000 investment that earned him the tour in the face of strong opposition. "There were seven rental companies up for doing the tour, including some of the largest in the country," said Brace, a major Floodlight aficionado. "Basically, Wayne's price fitted our budget, but had he still been running his previous Court system, he wouldn't be here now! It's going very well with Wayne – it's not often that the owner of a PA company will come out on the road, muck in with the crew and get his hands dirty."

"We were invited to pitch for this tour only six weeks after taking delivery of the system," said Barker. "It was a heavy race between the big boys and a small guy from nowhere, but our confidence won us the deal. Turbosound helped us to design the system that Laurie was most happy with, and I've been absolutely stunned at the quality we've been able to achieve."

The Turbosound system used on the tour included eight TSW 21" subs, eight 2 x 18" cabinets and sixteen Floodlight tops, mixed by Brace from a Midas XL200 desk. "I prefer the XL200 for drum 'n' bass because it has a much warmer sound. The combination of the XL200 and Floodlight is incomparable."

This system was configured five-way, making use of one LMS-700 for four-way control, and another to run the subs. Brace insisted that Turbosound was the only brand capable of delivering the intense high and low frequencies involved in Reprazent's music. "It's a very loud band," he said. "I've been hitting 132dB but the intensity is mainly at the bottom end. Because the Floodlight is so smooth, it doesn't actually sound that loud at all and I can still talk to people on the FOH riser. The double 18" and 21" subs really come into their own – with some of the really low-frequency bass samples [going down to 12Hz], we are moving so much air that that the room just runs out of air."

But it was not just the low end that impressed the engineer. "I find that the Floodlight top end is superb for what I want. It handles the very fast transients of the samples extremely well, which is another reason why it's completely suitable for us. Because of the nature of the samples, they are quite heavily compressed. Some of them have quite nasty frequencies in there and the use of compression helps to smooth them out. I've tried loads of systems for Reprazent, but Floodlight is the best by far."

After meeting Steve Lutley at the Mercury awards, Brace knew that he had found the perfect monitor engineer for Size and the gang. For Lutley, mixing for Reprazent (on a Midas XL3) was a constant challenge. He commented: "Their music is forever evolving, and no two nights are ever the same. They're all DJs, so they're changing levels on everything and bring new samples to each gig. It took about ten gigs before I could get into it properly and understand what they needed to hear on stage. I don't get any advance warning – they perform as they feel it, so I have to be working by the seat of my pants every night, which is really quite exciting."

Amongst the monitors were two of the new Turbosound TFM-330 wedges. Lutley said: "The TFM-330s cut through a lot better to what I've been used to with this band. It's a far more efficient wedge and I'd like to have more of them. [WE Audio took delivery of twelve TFM-330s in early 1998.] Along with regular THL-4s with subs for side fills, we've also got the new, improved prototype version of the THL-4 which we're using as a drum fill and it's serving us very well. The band have noticed a positive difference, and that's where it counts."

As well as being a key development for WE Audio, the Size/Reprazent tour was an opportunity for lighting designer Dan Hardiman to display his own talents. Using an Avolites Pearl 2000 console, Hardiman controlled a rig containing six Golden Scan Mk IIIs, three Dataflash AF1000s, six Martin Pro 400 colourchangers, ten bars of six Pars, and an array of floor cans.

Apart from one show, Hardiman had been handling the lighting for the band since (and including) Tribal Gathering. The brief, he said, was to shroud Size and co in an "air of mystery" until the very end of the set. "It involves a lot of silhouette and underlighting work, along with walls of strobing. I also try to bring out rock elements of the music with Par cans, hence there's quite a large Par can rig. There's also a jazz element in songs such as 'Heroes' and 'Jazzy' which have more club-like connotations. Every member of the band has their own song, and gets introduced one by one as the set evolves. I attempt to bring out each person with a particular mood to match that song. There are some theatrical moments, a lot of full-on rave moments, but without making it too cheesy and all out strobe hell, which I'm not too keen on. At the end of the set, you basically see all of the band."

When off the road, Hardiman was cuing the lights for the Full Cycle (Size's home record label) events at London's hip club The End, and it was there that he got into the new music. He said: "I mainly used to do raves of assorted types, including hard core, the angrier kinds of jungle, and trance and techno. I understood the audience's need to feel enveloped by the sound and lost in their own worlds. You don't actually require many lights for drum 'n' bass in a club environment, otherwise it becomes too much of a distraction. It's just a case of picking out all the nice, ambient twiddly bits with big moves, rather than constantly having the rig working hard."

Furthering the production values of Reprazent was something occupying Hardiman's thoughts, as he anticipated larger venues in the future. "The capacities of the venues we've been playing vary quite a bit, and we've only used the full rig on a few gigs. The kit I've brought is designed to be chopped and changed around depending on the venue. I've got a lot more production ideas in store, involving inflatables and projections, especially the Toy projector that was launched in Glastonbury's Dance Tent by my lighting design company Total Herbal Confusion [THC – a partnership with Dave Farmer who has been touring recently with Daft Punk]. It's an add-on projection effect that can be used with Barcos, and it responds very well to music as well as to live operations. It manipulates images and you can use any light source on it. I intend to utilise that with the special frequencies that we get through this music, with video images as opposed to conventional lighting images."

The lighting for this tour was supplied by Utopium Lighting in Bristol, with whom Hardiman worked at Glastonbury. "We consider Utopium to be THC's sister company, because they own the lights and put them in the venues, and we go in to design and operate the lighting. It's a partnership that works very well. Utopium purchased the Avo desk especially for me to use on this tour, and I've worked very closely with Avolites in order to get the desk up to the version it is now. I took an experimental version of the desk around Europe in early October, and I've been the only person using this software."

"Roni's is a great tour to land," said Wayne Barker, who after ten years of struggle in the difficult world of rental was now finding his feet. "This tour is now completely sold out; they've been turning queues of people away at the door. The feeling is that the future of drum 'n' bass is potentially huge and Reprazent are moving mountains as the band heading up this new genre."

CHAPTER TWENTY-SEVEN

Yes

Open Your Eyes – 1997/98

Yes are a band who have probably survived more "definitive" line-ups than any other. In late 1997, almost thirty years after their formation, these progressive rock space cadets re-grouped once more to record a fine album, *Open Your Eyes*, and storm live venues across North America, Europe and many other territories with a show which not only underlined the grace of their enduring music, but also witnessed the rise of a new generation of Yes freaks.

With only keyboard wizard Rick Wakeman absent, the line-up was virtually classic Yes, featuring Jon Anderson, Chris Squire (whose fiftieth birthday was celebrated when the tour reached London in March 1998), Steve Howe and Alan White, together with keyboard substitute Igor "Ivan" Khoroshev and back-up guitarist Billy Sherwood. 'Roundabout', 'Siberian Khatru' and Eighties gem 'Owner Of A Lonely Heart' were all present and sounding fresh, with Anderson's high register warbling holding out admirably in the face of instrumental dexterity. Turning their backs on superficial Nineties values, Yes even had the bare-faced gall to perform, in its sprawling entirety, the twenty-two-minute 'Revealing Science Of God' from *Tales Of Topographic Oceans*. Standing ovations – or maybe deafening sighs of relief – often followed for up to five minutes. One cannot argue with that.

The main focus of Yes's presentation was the Jonathan Smeeton-designed "tent" which surrounded the band as a backdrop canvas for some outstanding kaleidoscopic lighting effects. John Broderick was originally responsible for the lighting design, however, at the end of the American leg, he was obliged to return to the Metallica fold for the Poor Touring Me project and left Yes in the capable hands of lighting programmer Ben Richards of Texan manufacturer High End Systems. "John designed the type of rig which would be sufficiently compact to allow us to do all these back-to-back theatre dates with maximum ease. By the time he left us, he condensed it down to a one-truck lighting situation," said Richards, whose familiarity with Yes's back catalogue played its part in the effective programming of the show.

"I re-listened to all of the Yes music that I've loved for years, and started charting every song right down to every drum fill [the chart was *very* explicit!], so that I would have my bag ready when I showed up. We kind of got fooled into doing four days of production rehearsals before the first official US date, and we came out of the starting gate looking pretty darn scary. When you've got songs of around twenty minutes' length in some cases you really need to spend a lot of time programming the lighting to keep the performances looking fresh and alive. The only way of making sure that we had a good light show for the first date was for me to operate it live. The Status Cue controller's capabilities are such that you can operate lights live if you know your way around groups and positions. Knowing the music was a tremendous advantage at that point because time was tight and I was able to hold the whole moving light show together."

Although Light & Sound Design supplied the rig for the tour, the Status Cue was leased from Lighting Technologies in Atlanta. Richards complimented Broderick on hiring a second Status Cue to control conventional lights and scrollers, and thus simplifying the job over two different people. Greg Maltby handled the conventionals and spot calling until Broderick's departure, after which Yes's management decided to narrow the lighting operation down to one Status Cue and one person. Namely, Nick Sholem, the English LD known for his work with Sting and The Eagles, and who was about to take over the Yes duties in full from Richards at the end of March. "We have the best qualified person in Nick and will be in very safe hands," said Richards, who went on to handle the programming for Metallica's 1998 tour.

"It's a nightmare show for one guy," said Sholem. "I've been through all 1,200 cues and it's like Ben is handing me the keys to his Ferrari! The Status Cue is fine and I'm getting my head round it. It's a very in-at-the-deep-end learning process. Like all these things it's very hard to take over someone's job – much harder than designing an Eagles or Sting show. But slowly, the penny drops and once I'm comfortable it'll be great." He could not have said a truer word.

Yes frontman Jon Anderson had long been known for keeping a firm grip on all of the band's visual aspects – from album covers to set design and lighting. At various points throughout the Open Your Eyes shows, he made a point of wandering the stage to see how the lighting "played" the stage, and was a frequent visitor to the front-of-house for in-depth discussions with Richards and Sholem.

"I consider Jon to be a co-director," said Richards. "For the first three weeks of the tour, Jon would check on how I'd programmed certain songs. I was taking on board all his comments and interpreting them as best I could. I think that whatever was happening was sparking his confidence in what we were doing, and it all helped him to relax. When Jon realised that this light show could do some pretty interesting things, because Yes music is very intense as far as different time signatures and dynamics are concerned, he said that he wanted the lights to feel everything the band plays. The lighting follows every rhythmic accent and that is no small embellishment.

"This is all-out visualisation, and every song has a theme of its own with the tent really coming into its own as a fantastic canvas for the fourteen Cyberlites and glorious patterns. We keep it different all the way through, which is an achievement for such a long show. Each Cyberlite has its own area on the tent to make it not quite one big picture but more a collection of the same images everywhere. It's kind of keystoned a little so you're not seeing big circles that are obvious except for the centre one which is the feature gobo most times. With the help of the sixteen Studio Colors we can wash the whole tent into one colour or multiples to get it grooving with whatever the band's doing. It's definitely an interesting way of going back and forth between imaging or solid colour washes either on the band or on the cyc, and you really don't get the feeling that you've seen the same thing six songs ago."

As well as featuring the Cyberlites and Studio Colors from LSD's inventory, the compact system contained 48kW of Par cans and colourchangers in the rig and on the front truss. At one of Yes's two shows at the Labatt's Apollo in London, Nick Sholem commented: "This is turning out to be a very exciting tour – one of the most enjoyable I've worked on for ages. The guys at High End are incredibly helpful, especially Bruce Jordahl who we love! The shows are selling out all over the place and the whole entourage, band and crew, are just a very happy bunch of campers."

One of whom was FOH sound engineer John Robbins who was working with Yes for the first time on this world tour. Clair Brothers had serviced the band's live audio requirements since the Seventies and a (Crest-amplified) twenty-four-box S4 system, complete with a flown fill for balcony coverage, formed the standard PA for most of the theatre-type gigs on this tour. Said Robbins: "Yes are a very stereo band. The idea is to put as much S4 gear as we can in all of these venues, and we achieve pretty much a hi-fi sound in these environments."

Robbins mixed from a Midas XL4, using the switching functions to get him from song to song. He pointed out his dislike of moving VCAs, and added: "I'd need 5,000 scenes for all the minor changes that I make with this band, and I feel happier doing it all live, so that I can react to the music. I'm still scared of automation in a way, not that there's a reason to be – it's just the way I was made! Yes are a delicate-sounding band and depending on the songs, which are extremely varied, it's difficult to know how to approach the mix. Should I focus on the power or try to highlight the melody? It's a hard choice and in some way I have to find the sweet spot between the two extremes, because Yes are known for both qualities."

Selections from Steve Howe's immense guitar collection in view at stage left gave an insight into the difficulties of Robbins' job. (Howe's tech, Shooz, had forty-five guitar change cues.) "Keeping the guitars in check is the biggest job for me...they all sound different," Robbins commented. "There are eight different acoustics, including a Portuguese twelve-string, and Billy Sherwood also has a bunch of different acoustics. It's the EQ changes that I have to remember between numbers, because I'm often sharing a channel between three guitars. Being a theatre tour, I had to cram as much as I could into the one XL4. Normally I'd have up to sixteen more channels, with all the keyboards, so I'm leaving it up to the keyboard tech to give a nice, balanced mix that comes to me as a stereo pair."

One of the more impressive sonic elements of the show was Chris Squire's bass sound: melodic, voluptuous, rich and arguably the most powerful signal ever to be projected from the stage of the Apollo. Still playing his coveted Rickenbacker, Squire milked his 'Fish' solo for all it was worth; it was to Robbins' credit that despite the velocity of the bass sound, every note could be enjoyed with studio-like clarity.

"Chris has a number of effects that are so old now, but they provide the guts of his sound," Robbins explained. "I take a DI out of his FX board, there's a 100-watt Marshall that's miked twice with EV RE-38s for the 'thrak' crackle and an Ampeg SVT that I mic [again with an EV RE-38, the mic also used on all of the guitar rigs] for the mids, and then a DI straight out of the guitar which gives me the real low end. Then there are the bass pedals which trigger E-Mu samples of the Moog Taurus sounds Chris used so many years ago. It all goes through Summit compressors – it's the only brand I've used which can faithfully retain Chris's sound."

Monitor engineer Ed Dracoules manned a Yamaha PM4000, sending mixes to the regular Clair 12AM wedges, as well as Futuresonics in-ear monitoring systems for Jon Anderson, Alan White and Igor Khoroshev. "I wish everybody was using the ear moulds," laughed Robbins. "Not only do we have a really loud stage but they also have in-ears, which could be construed as defeating the object of the in-ear exercise! Chris Squire doesn't care whether he's playing to twenty people or 20,000, he still needs to hear the rig the way it should sound. And it's certainly sweet when it's wound up to ten!"

The Open Your Eyes tour may have brought the pipe dreamers and earth mothers from out of their respective closets, but it certainly served as a reminder that the combination of virtuoso musicianship and tight vocal harmonies within the framework of intelligently-written and accessible melodies is a blissful experience. If only Lancashire-born Jon Anderson could have left that dreadful mid Atlantic accent in his dressing room and featured 'Time And A Word' in the set, the experience would have been even better.

CHAPTER TWENTY-EIGHT

Space

Touring On A Tin Planet – 1998

T he Kinks' Ray Davies meets the Ecstacy generation? Well, that may be a simplistic way of summing up the songs and sounds of top Liverpool band Space, but nonetheless accurate.

In the spring of 1998, three years after rising from their original stamping ground of local clubs, such as the Lomax, Space were purveyors of a fine Number One album (*Tin Planet*), with a sold-out tour of mid sized venues across the UK and Europe behind them. All along this weary but ultimately fulfilling route to the top, Space's crew had largely remained intact. Ad Lib Audio, and particularly engineers Dave Kay (Texas, Del Amitri) and Roger Kirby (Gun, The Real People), had been in evidence since those early club days, and it was a two-way loyalty that continued to pay dividends.

At the Forum in London's Kentish Town on 8 April, it was fully expected that, like the majority of visiting acts, they would use the house d&b audiotechnik sound system. However, an arrangement between Space and Kula Shaker – the following night's act – led to the "penalty" payment of £850 being split down the middle to allow the temporary removal of the d&b rig and the installation of each band's own touring system.

In the case of Space, the rig was Ad Lib's proprietary Dave Fletcher-designed PA, consisting of eight DF2 high packs and eight DF3 folded horn 1 x 18" subs per side, and powered by a rack per side of C Audio 3001s (top end), SRX 3801s (mids) and Crown VZ 5000s (sub/bass). For processing, much reliance was placed on BSS Audio's Omnidrives and Varicurves. As Dave Kay explained: "It's the configuration that we tend to load into most mid range, theatre-type venues of around 2-3,000 capacity. We're carrying a small amount of flying gear so that we can get speakers up on house bars. But we have no flying frames or motors because it's a one-truck tour, and we have to keep the size of the production down to a workable minimum."

Systems engineer Kay started the tour mixing monitors, but moved aside when the band's regular on-stage man Marc Peers (also of Texas fame) returned from promotional gig duties with Therapy?. The monitor rig here was virtually identical to the one which went out with Texas at the end of 1997, but with one interesting addition...

"We've been having some great success with the new Sabine ADF-4000 anti-feedback and processing units, two of which were loaned to us by [UK distributor] Fuzion," said Kay. "We've now invested in them because they really help us control the loud on-stage sound that Space like to maintain. Space are a very energetic band and they need that volume to drive them along, but getting the vocals on top of that requires a lot of work. The Sabine unit is so versatile – it combines graphic EQ with feedback circuitry, compressors, limiters and gates all in one package, and we have a number of them inserted on the vocal channels on stage."

The monitors are twelve of Ad Lib's own 15"/2" RCF-loaded wedges, while the DF2 system also forms the basis of the two side fill stacks. Kay: "We've got even more sub bass on stage. As all the musicians are situated on risers, there are sub bins on the keyboard riser and drum riser. The drum set-up is virtually shaking the whole riser, especially when he [Leon Caffrey] hits the kick drum! Franny Griffiths, the keyboard player, has said the sound is so intense that it's like playing with slippers on, when he slides down the keyboard for those bass notes. The subs we are using are very compact 2 x 15" enclosures that we built ourselves to create a very loud noise within a short distance. In that situation you need something that's going to do the business within two feet of you."

While Soundcraft took care of the Series Five front-of-house and SM24 monitor consoles, and Klark Teknik the DI box, Shure provided the mics, with Beta 58As on the lead vocals shared by guitarists Tommy Scott and Jamie Murphy, SM57s on guitar cabinets, and 91s, 98s, 57s and 81s all over the drums. To ease Griffiths' mobility on the keys, he wore a Shure headset mic which both Kirby and Kay praised to the hilt.

With a sophisticated and diverse record production style – from all-out rave rock ('One O'Clock') to an eerie, modern-day spin on vaudeville

('Female Of The Species' and 'The Ballad Of Tom Jones') – transmitting so many variables in a live scenario made big demands of Kirby, especially with the varied keyboard sounds taking up more than half of the band's FOH channels. Some of the keyboards were compressed individually, and compressed again as a composite group to help smooth out the mix. Said Kay: "There are a lot of keyboard samples triggered live from an Akai S3000, which is one of the reasons why the monitoring set-up needs to be so poky! Fran needs to have a good band feed, especially as he is triggering sounds and sequences in time with the drummer."

Performing the big hit single of the moment, 'The Ballad Of Tom Jones', a real live vocal duet between Tommy and Catatonia's Cerys Matthews, caused a major logistical problem owing to Cerys' commitments with her own band. Her absence was filled by the use of an ADAT backing track linked via time code to a video disk carrying specially-recorded footage of her apparently singing to the Space frontman. These images were shown on a Barco video monitor at each side of the stage, and on a large rear screen/cyc behind the band – all the domain of "videographer" Stan Talbot, on board since the previous summer.

"They asked me to work with them at the Sundance Festival in Norwich," he explained. "They really liked what I'd done and a few months later they were back on to me."

Assembled by Talbot, the Space video system was a low budget but comfortable affair. In addition to the two Barco monitors there was a Sanyo 200P LCD projector, two VHS video machines, a VHS camera at the back of the hall for wide angle stage shots, and a digital mixer. Around two-thirds of the set featured video. "Towyn Roberts [LD] and I get together to decide which video images are needed, and set about looking for clips and see if we can work up any graphics on the computer," Talbot said. "I've got thousands of video tapes and come up with all kinds of things – on 'Mad Days', for example, we show a clip from a psycho-thriller. I've also just bought a new Canon digital camcorder and SLR combination for recording close-up shots of guitars being played and I manipulate those on the computer for certain scenes. Because of a lack of budget for all this everything's on VHS which is very unstable, and hit or miss. So with a bit of luck we'll be upgrading the kit later on. What we have, considering the cost, is pretty good although we have experienced problems with the lighting washing out the video here and there."

Not surprising for a band whose career was built up in venues popularised during the rave era, Space favoured the huge projection bias of Roberts' designs. His main arsenal in this respect consisted of Optikinetics K1s (five on the front truss) and Solar 250s which provided a dynamic range of looks on the cyc and a different visual personality for each song. He specified two controllers – an Avolites Pearl for moving lights, and a Jands Event for generics and strobes.

Bryan Leitch's company Art Of Darkness supplied lighting for this tour following the band's previous relationship with Liverpool's Mr Fantasy. For movement, AOD were asked to hire eight Vari*Lite VL6s and six VL5s. "The VL5s are all on the floor for band positions and audience sweeps," said Roberts, "while the VL6s are used for a lot of sweeping and some of the cyc stuff. There are some iris chases to give a kaleidoscope effect, surrounding the centre of the cyc onto which the video is projected. It's like a keyhole effect that pulls your attention right in.

"I've also been using two Clay Paky Golden Scan HPEs in the rig. They do the sweeps really well and you can get some movement on stage without it being chaos. You just put a rotate head on and it gives enough movement without spoiling the show. I did have four but there's only so much you can do with them, and getting them on the floor is a bit of a problem. I just wanted to have more moving lights because the positioning is so much easier."

Roberts also "auditioned" the Martin MAC 500 on one show, and reported great potential. "They looked like they were going to be really good. I was going to take them out for the rest of the tour but we ended up going for the Vari*Lites. I think that I may be choosing the MACs next time, because I can do so many different things with them – for cyc looks, sweeping, and strobing."

Like Talbot, Roberts was plagued by a lack of funding but looked ahead to rosier days. "Working within tight means has been a problem all the way along, and it's made even worse by not actually having a tangible budget – I've kind of 'felt' my way through." Talbot added: "If I had loads of money to spend, I think I'd have four Barcos and four LCDs for the small screens. I do see some really good times ahead – I think the rewards are coming. With the new album doing well, it'll be nice to think that the budgets can be increased to allow our creativity to grow and take the band's production ideas to another level."

Phil Collins dances into
the light

Collins with front-of-house engineer
Rob "Cubby" Colby

Texas in Leuven, Belgium

A slick performance from Sharleen Spiteri

Ad Lib Audio's Dave Kay (far left) and Andy Dockerty (far right) parade the Soundcraft Series Five desk with Texas members Ally and Rick

View of the Texas stage from LD Steven Marr's Icon board

Ocean Colour Scene's Simon Fowler

Paul Weller and OCS bassist Damon
Minchella

Steve Cradock

Martin Audio's Martin Kelly and Bill Webb
with Keith Davis of Capital Sound Hire

A Martin Wavefront 8 rig flies from the roof of the Royal Albert Hall

Paul Weller and Noel Gallagher guest with Ocean Colour Scene at the RAH

Reprazent

Wayne Barker, Laurie Brace and Steve Lutley

Roni Size

Sizing up the lighting in Brighton: LD Dan Hardiman

(Above and below) Yes – Open Your Eyes at the Labatt's Apollo, Hammersmith

The Yes lighting team – Ben Richards of High End Systems and Nick Sholem

Chris Squire's FX

Space at The Forum, Kentish Town

Marc Peers, Dave Kay, Stan Talbot and Roger Kirby – four Space boys

Tori Amos at the Royal Albert Hall during the Plugged tour

The Nexo Alpha PA array at the Albert Hall

Behind the Amos sound: Rob Van Tuin, SSE's John Penn, Mark Hawley and (seated) Marcel Van Limbeek

The Spice Girls on their SpiceWorld tour, before the split with Geri Halliwell

Another new generation of LED screen technology from XL Video made its mark on SpiceWorld

The SpiceWorld production was enhanced and enlarged when the tour climaxed with two sold-out Wembley Stadium shows in September 1998

Céline Dion at the National Car Rental Centre, Fort Lauderdale, Florida

Dion and her impressive video production

A close-up of the "video floor"

Lighting and set designer, and Compulite console user, Yves Aucoin

Denis Savage at
his Soundcraft
Broadway console

CHAPTER TWENTY-NINE

Tori Amos

The Plugged Tour – 1998

With her most diverse album to date, *From The Choirgirl Hotel*, doing a roaring trade, American pianist-singer-songwriter Tori Amos took the brave step of ditching her previous scaled-down solo approach to live performance in favour of taking a band out on the road for the first time on her Plugged tour of 1998.

On a continuous quest for live audio fidelity that would leave most of her contemporaries standing, Amos' attention to, and knowledge of, technical detail reached an almost obsessive level on this tour. Given her enthusiasm, it was probably no coincidence that the man she chose to marry in the February of that year was her front-of-house engineer, Mark Hawley. Along with monitor engineer Marcel van Limbeek, Hawley was invited to join the Amos team by tour manager John Witherspoon in 1994. Since then, the pair had an increasing influence over the Amos sound both live and in the studio, being the technical brains behind the *Choirgirl Hotel* album.

Even four years before when Amos was beginning to break big with *Under The Pink* and the hit single 'Cornflake Girl', she broke all the rules for a self-contained solo act when her discerning needs meant that instead of renting in local services, Birmingham's SSE Hire was called on to ship an entire PA over to the States for a long-running theatre tour. The relationship with SSE grew further when the company advised on and supplied equipment for the *Boys For Pele* album sessions, on location in Ireland.

Formed in 1976 as Sigma Sound Enterprises by John & Heather

Penn, and based in the former Birmingham bus garage it shares with Light & Sound Design, SSE's role as the hardware supplier for Plugged was essentially the same as with any other tour, with Hawley and van Limbeek gaining advice on the equipment specification and how the package should piece together. MD John Penn was keen to point out that the two engineers, being "real audiophiles", had driven the project from day one, but admitted that SSE's efforts removed much of the stress from their hands-on engineering job.

Much of this combined expertise reached fruition with the design of one of the most sophisticated monitoring regimes ever to grace a four-piece band. An entire Midas XL4 (with an XL3 stretch for effects), operated by van Limbeek, was dedicated to the singer's own mixes, while behind him sat Rob van Tuin, mixing for the band on an XL3. Although the amount of signals being routed was a complex matter, the design of the modular line system allowed the link-up to be performed simply. The interface between the stage boxes, the consoles and racks was achieved using 100-pin multiway connectors, all terminated to XLR patch boxes. Once the system was patched at the start of a tour, set-up for each show was quick and simple, with just the multipins to plug in. This created much interest amongst The Verve's crew when they rehearsed next door to the Amos band at the Depot in North London.

As John Penn said, the recording sessions for the *Choirgirl Hotel* album dictated the way forward. "When I went down to the Cornwall studio in February to hear the album mixes, it was suggested that they'd need two monitor desks for the tour, and I didn't really believe it," he admitted. "But they started getting very specific, encouraged by Tori's demands, and Marcel has to completely mix her show. There was no way he could cope with Tori and simultaneously mix for a band because he can't take his eyes off her."

Van Limbeek explained the mixing approach: "We're handling two things simultaneously, reproducing a virtually complete mix of what's happening on stage, including effects, while I'm also riding Tori's vocal fader to help her singing. I know when she's getting tired. She's listening to four mixes; two are dedicated to the vocal plus effects, and the other two are full instrumental mixes."

But wasn't two boards and a stretch like taking a sledgehammer to crack a small nut? "Not in this case, because of the amount of channels coming in and also the amount of outputs we use. Tori uses only four mixes, but there's a lot of effects. Rob operates more as a traditional monitor engineer for the whole band and to make his life easier, I'm giving him quite a few sub-mixes. I have more effects returning on my board and I'll make sub-mixes for him which costs more outputs that I send from the XL4 to the XL3, and by the end of it the desks are full up."

The XL4s used by van Limbeek and (at FOH) Hawley featured automated VCAs and mute switching. This mix-friendly automation was further enhanced by a Macintosh-based Hypercard MIDI computer programme, written by van Tuin and christened "Bob Deluxe" (!), which realigned the whole monitor system, effects and desks at the start of every song. Said van Limbeek: "Before the show, you type a set list in and as the performance is going on you flick through the songs and every parameter of the VCAs, channel mutes, and effects programmes, and levels automatically adjust themselves. If Tori changes her mind about the set order at the last minute, we can very easily adjust the order on the lap top.

"Amongst other processing, Tori has a BSS Varicurve parametric EQ and a Focusrite inserted on her vocal that changes from song to song, and also at various times within the same song. Sometimes she likes more mids or more lows; on other songs she likes the vocal to be very bright, and those changes occur automatically via the computer."

During a break in the Albert Hall soundcheck, Amos offered her own slant on her monitoring needs. "There's a lot of detail in the music," the singer said. "It's the frequency of every bar of music that matters. Sometimes, because I'm moving so fast between the piano and Kurzweil keyboard, and triggering samples from the MIDI rack, and it requires so much breath control as I sing, I need different kinds of mixes around me to help me sing with accuracy. I have my monitors tweaked in a way that I'm hearing certain details, but I wouldn't say that the sound up there is pleasurable – it's purely a reference point. Marcel is working with me on every aspect of my personal monitoring. Meanwhile, Mark is trying to shelter the audience from what we're hearing. We're working with our clothes off up here. But people look much more attractive with their clothes on, and Mark makes sure that we have nice audio clothes for the audience.

"My whole monitor set-up supports how I can delineate sound. People have been commenting on the quality and subtlety of the sound at the shows, and that's a real compliment to Mark. Somebody's got to give, especially in rooms like the Albert Hall, and the audience has to win. Unfortunately, most bands don't learn that lesson. Mark is vicious but fair, and he'll say that we have to work off the FOH. He'll tell us to kill the on-stage volume, otherwise people will start throwing stuff at us! Sometimes we're pumped up, thinking that we're having a certain effect on the audience, whereas it isn't necessarily the case and we just have to work that bit harder with the stage sound."

The processing power on this show was quite astounding, and again driven by the album sessions. Hawley added: "We were mixing the album knowing we would have to do these songs live and so we came up with practical, alternative solutions to achieving studio effects. It became increasingly clear what the equipment spec would be for the tour, and around 75% of the rack contents are a direct copy of what we used for the recording."

Firstly, a t.c. electronic graphic EQ was applied generally to all of the various SSE-designed bi-amped monitors – 12PMs surrounding Amos, Betamax wedges for guitarist Steve Caton and drummer Matt Chamberlain, and MB3s for the bassist Jon Evans – and set up according to each venue's acoustics. Then, for the vocal and each instrument there were various dedicated FX units forming a neatly stacked bank behind each of the monitor men.

Van Limbeek commented: "The vocal has the Lexicon 480L, which is basically two machines, and I can flick between one with a short reverb for the verses, and the other which has a longer setting for the choruses. On the drum kit, we have a Rev 5 and a PCM-70, and on the bass and guitars we have dedicated SPX-990s, and the piano and Kurzweil each have a PCM-70. On the vocal there's an Eventide H3000 which gives me a chorus effect; there's an SPX-990 and a Roland SDE-330 which is set on a very simple delay pattern that I tap in here and there. Also, I have an SPL Vitalizer to make the high end a little more crispy and add some harmonics."

Tori Amos has turned the use of compression into an art form, and it was as present on tour as on the album. "It's our main tool in delivering the kind of controlled sound that is equal to the record," said Hawley. "It was the first time that I'd experimented with anything more than just a little compression. I learned so much about it in the studio that putting it into practice live is quite interesting. I've been putting a Neve 9098 over the drum group and that works wonders."

Van Limbeek, meanwhile, raved about the BSS DPR-901 for the vocals. "It's a frequency conscious compressor which particularly aids her performance because she can sing fairly low range one minute, and then really scream the next without pinning the meters."

"We really talked about using the effects and compression as instruments," Amos explained. "Not just whop it on, but actually design the way it's used. Four or five years ago, I was a little nervous of compression because it's the opposite, but I've since found a way of vocalising around the effect, especially valve compression which sounds so warm. Most of the time, the reverbs are all done manually on the Lexicon 480, and Mark and Marcel work for hours and hours to perfect it all the time.

"Even though I produced the record, Mark and Marcel have different gifts. Marcel is very much an EQ and effects freak, while Mark is concerned about the balancing. It becomes a very holistic thing. We'll argue but having a three-way debate means that sometimes the two of them will say to me, 'We know you want to achieve this sound or effect, but you can't do it this way,' and I defer to their judgement. It's like sonic geometry – we're always working on the shape of the music."

SSE's outboard rack flightcasing was designed such that it required little time to set up and de-rig. What with the extensive processing, and the need to facilitate the digital recording of every show for a live album, van Limbeek believed that without SSE's attention to detail, the tour may never have been possible.

"The way SSE have configured it all is quite amazing," he said. "They're our heroes! It just shows you what a rental company can do when it applies some thought. All the mic lines are coming off stage and end up in an SSE stage box where the patching is done into the multis. From there, you would normally get your traditional run to FOH and monitor board, but we feed all the lines to sixty channels of Focusrite mic pre-amps and twenty-four channels of Behringer pre-amps which go out to BSS active splitters, and every channel is split four ways [one to FOH, one to monitor desk 1, one to monitor desk 2, and the fourth went to a Tascam digital rack which was recording the shows on forty channels]. So the system really is a dream! By switching the multis around it's possible to review and mix last night's show on my monitor board, which is something Tori loves! That's good for designing new effects without the band being there."

Few artists use expensive Neumann mics on tour, but Tori Amos was an exception. "When Tori was touring with *Boys For Pele*, a very open-sounding album, it was all about using the best possible mic for the job," explained Hawley. "We had U87s in the piano, and other Neumanns for the vocal. With more of a rock 'n' roll line-up, we're not so purist anymore and aren't afraid to use SM57s in places. But for the vocal, we're staying with the Neumann KMS-140 [with a hypercardioid capsule to minimise wedge spill] which is the best vocal performance mic in the world for my tastes. It's another extension of us being in the studio. For the piano we're using two AKG 414s. The best piano sound you can get is with an open lid and two U87s, but playing with the band, the 414s are a bit brighter."

One of the biggest weapons in the SSE armoury was its heavy investment in the French-manufactured Nexo Alpha sound system, a move which represented the largest financial commitment of any single Alpha user. Powered by Crown amps, the rig sounded sublime at the Albert Hall, especially to Hawley. He said: "It's been strange because Marcel and I have been in the studio for a year, so hearing a PA system of any kind is always a bit of a shock. But I think the Alpha is the most present PA system I've ever heard, and the most smooth in dynamic range. That's important for Tori because hers is such a dynamic band. When it's quiet, the system is very coherent, and when they play louder it doesn't transgress into sounding shit!"

At the Albert Hall, there was a central mono Alpha cluster, flown seven wide and five deep on a independent grid using the house motors. The aim was to gain as low a trim as possible to achieve the shortest distance to the audience without spoiling sightlines. By doing this, it enabled the removal of boxes which would normally point at reflective surfaces. Added to the cluster, and producing a wonderful stereo spatial quality, were left and right effects clusters flown two wide and three deep, plus a number of Betamax speakers in the gallery.

After using the Electro-Voice MT system for several years, why was SSE persuaded to jump ship? Director Chris Beale said: "SSE's a company that likes to go its own way and develop its own systems and packaging – it's just something we find interesting. The point at which the MT had run its course as a competitive system came when we were looking at a product that we could have some involvement with. L-Acoustics' V-DOSC had been a possibility but at the time the HF performance wasn't that good, although the company later resolved this issue.

"Alpha was then very much in its concept stage. There were some boxes in existence but nothing like those we now use. It seemed a good idea to do something with Nexo, and provide a touring company's input into their system. This turned out to be a lengthier process than we first envisaged, but it's been interesting and very creative, and it's given a user an insight into the way a manufacturer works, and vice versa. The two modes of thought could not be more different and it's a reality check on both parts."

Once the partnership was agreed, Beale and Nexo's technical director Eric Vincenot began to burn the midnight oil and "almost killed each other" before mutual satisfaction was reached over each other's CAD drawings and ideas. "We linked computers over the Net and it meant that I could work on ideas from Birmingham while he stayed in Paris," recalled Beale. "We developed the crossbow rigging system and some of the box ergonomics. Nexo very much came up with the final design and the acoustic characteristics of the cabinet, and then we had big arguments about tuning and voicing, as one might expect! The flow of ideas was very healthy and exciting.

"We always wanted to have a completely integrated flying system with the cabinet, rather than having a third party manufacturer offering an existing flying system or a modification of the same, and not having all the virtues a truly homogenous design could offer. It therefore made perfect sense for us to design a new flying system alongside the development of the box, which is what happened. It proved very efficient, although we later made some modifications to enable easier manufacturing. After which, the system more or less worked straight out of the box and did exactly what we wanted it to do. I would say it's still the lightest and most compact integrated flying system out there right now; it's certainly the least complicated."

Of course, what sounds good in the lab doesn't necessarily hack it out in the brutal real world. Alpha's first outing was at the 1997 Torhout festival in Belgium – where the paint was still drying as the boxes were rigged! "It didn't work to 100% capacity but it was pretty good," said Beale. "Following Torhout we made some changes and added the B1 bass cabinet because we wanted to integrate bass systems into the rig rather than have all the mid highs in the air and all the bass on the ground. It then went out with Wet Wet Wet, Sepultura and a whole bunch of festivals, and it's been consistently reliable, and efficiently looked after by the people at Fuzion [Nexo's UK distributor], and it remains a really neat and compact system. More importantly to us, it has provided us with a building block for techniques that we could never have explored with the MT, not only because of its physical size and weight, but also because it was a fixed entity that EV was never going to develop any further."

Alpha soon became part of a small, elite club of top flight touring systems, competing with the likes of Turbosound's Flashlight, d&b, V-DOSC and Martin's Wavefront 8, with more than 1,000 units shifted within the first twelve months of its launch. What set these systems apart from each other was not always the internal components but the people working with them. "In an on-the-road situation, the success of the product depends on much more than what's flying in the rigging," observed Beale. "What actually makes the sound right, apart from the band's performance, is the expertise of the company that's installing it and the talents of the sound mixing engineer, but they are often the elements which receive the least attention in a production."

The Plugged tour was Simon Sidi's third as Tori Amos' lighting designer. "It's much easier with the band," he said. "Until this tour, there were always restrictions with the amount I could do with the lights, because of the noise they made. When it was just Tori and the piano, I couldn't do lots of big movements because it created too much distracting noise – the mics on stage would pick everything up. Even motor wind photography was banned. So we had to be very careful and clever how we lit the show. But this is a different ball game altogether and I can do whatever I want because they're just like any other noisy band!"

Two asymmetrically-positioned mirror balls came into play during the show, whereupon the whole production really took off. "They're separately controlled with different speeds, and we have a rotating gobo focused on them," he explained. "I like the fact that they come from different angles. One is on the floor stage right, and the other is in the truss. It's very easy to make mirror balls look tacky, but like a lot of old technology, it's how you use it that makes the difference, and you have to listen to the music to gauge the right approach."

Supplied by LSD, Sidi's rig consisted of eighteen Icons, eighteen washlights and ten mini Molemags, six eight-light Molefays on the floor, photo floods and Par cans, all controlled from his Icon desk. Thirty High End Studio Colors were later added for the USA tour. "I try to design a rig that will be as variable as possible. Ultimately it doesn't matter where the lights are coming from, it's what they do and how they do it, for me anyway."

Although Sidi was prepared for any eventuality, and decided on the set list with Amos, the set often changed mid show, according to the singer's mood and the vibe coming from the audience. "I've had bets with John Witherspoon about which song would be next, and we even had our money out on the console," Sidi revealed, "but we've both been wrong!"

The last word came from John Penn who clearly delighted in creating the best audio environment for this most welcome client. "Tori may be treated like a goddess by her fans, but she's a warm, down to earth person, who knows what she wants but is so very courteous about it," he said. "Just like the rest of her crew. It continues to be a pleasure to assist her tours and the world would be a much better place if all artists shared her attitude."

CHAPTER THIRTY

The Spice Girls

SpiceWorld – 1998

In every decade since the Sixties we have seen a number of pop acts attempting in vain to become "The Next Beatles", not coming remotely near the impact of Liverpool's finest whose seventeen Number Ones will probably never be surpassed. But in the late Nineties, thirty-five years on from those first scenes of Fab hysteria, there was more than a faint rumble of familiarity about the success pattern of Ginger, Posh, Sporty, Baby and Scary – aka The Spice Girls.

Since July 1996 when their first hit 'Wannabe' burst onto the airwaves, their records routinely occupied the Number One slot, and in December 1997 they released a movie which almost every kid under eleven years of age must have queued to see.

The fortuitous timing of the Girl Power phenomenon capitalised on every marketing and merchandising strategy formulated for today's pop world. No Brian Epstein oversights for this fivesome – every opportunity to earn a buck from advertising and sponsorship was exploited in an act of total control and confidence. In Istanbul in October 1997, The Spice Girls gave their first live concerts accompanied by a media frenzy. SpiceWorld: The Tour was the natural progression and this was where the scale of their popularity hit home.

Two dates in Glasgow, four in Manchester, eight at Wembley Arena and six at the Birmingham NEC, were all completely sold out through the fan club, without a single ticket ever being offered to the general public. It was a UK-only experiment which paid off big time, and fuelled confidence in staging at least four UK open-air stadium shows in September. Not even the well-publicised departure from the line-up of Geri Halliwell (Ginger), the motivator behind the Girl Power image, could stop fans from furthering the Girls' cause.

As for the show, well, even the fiercest critics ate their words. Yes, the Girls could sing, and sing well with good mic technique. Their crack six-piece band, led by MD/keyboard player Simon Ellis, was sourced from members of Simply Red, East 17 and M People, and transformed the music into something of real substance. And enhancing the lively choreography was a vibrant set which pulsated with a powerful lighting design by the show's producer Pete Barnes, and marked the debut of a new generation of LED video screen technology which on technical terms at least was superior to that used on U2's PopMart.

Closed production rehearsals commenced in Dublin in late January 1998, by which time the Girls had hired Richard Jones as their tour manager and Julian Lavender as production manager, both of whom had previously worked with Bjork, and whose job it was to solder all the loose ends together. After some warm-ups in Dublin, the tour opened in Zurich on 2 March and steamed through Europe, arriving at Wembley where it pitched camp over a two-week period.

Being the Girls' first tour, and at such a high level, the production team had a number of challenges to rise above, not least how to deal with the Girls' blissful ignorance of how live productions work. Lavender commented: "At the start the Girls had little understanding of what we have to do technically to put the show on every day, and it can be quite frustrating in terms of having things ready for when they suddenly want to go through a dance rehearsal at 3pm."

"The biggest problems at the beginning were about dealing with the enormity of the whole production," said Jones. "We all went through a vast learning curve and the comms system [Metro Audio/ASL] has definitely earned its keep! With six weeks of the tour completed, the Girls have gained a good appreciation of why technical problems might occur and that it takes time to cure them. People have underestimated just how bright and astute they are."

The light, sound and musical direction team of Pete Barnes, Mike Dolling and Simon Ellis had all worked together on the East 17 Insomniax tour, as had monitor engineer Graham Blake and video director Blue Leach, all of whom obviously shared an ingrained feel for what makes a pop production work at its best. By the time Lavender arrived in December, most of the decisions had been made concerning the crewing and suppliers to the tour, as Jones explained: "After Istanbul, we kept PSL for the video, Wigwam for sound, LSD as the main lighting contractor, and Brilliant Stages for the set, and then made some incremental changes elsewhere."

Lavender interjected: "Because it's got the Spice Girls tag everybody adds another 10-15% on top of what you would think is a realistic price. We've really struggled to not let the costs run away."

The main man responsible for the creation and conception of the show's design was Pete Barnes. As Lavender said: "The whole concept is pretty much out of Pete's head, and he spent a huge amount of time thinking about the whole look – not just the lighting but also the stage set and the opening video introduction."

This five-minute intro piece of outer space-obsessed footage was created, with Barnes' input, by Robin Aristorenis at Sensible Music's Motion Graphics Suite and, with no expense spared, featured a voiceover from *Star Trek*'s William Shatner – "Spice, the final frontier"... inevitably.

Barnes explained his intro idea further: "It's a bit of a follow on from the 'Spice Up Your Life' promo. This time, the Girls are on a spaceship and when it lands, your attention becomes focused on the screen which by now appears as the doors of the craft. The letters S-P-I-C-E give way to the doors opening [actually the screen parting in the middle] which then reveals the Girls standing there in silhouette. Deafening screams kick in, and they step forward to perform the opening number – 'If You Can't Dance'."

The thirty-six square metre, 2.7 ton central screen referred to here represented the latest generation of LED technology supplied by XL Video of Belgium, and manufactured by Frederic Opsomer's System Technologies using LEDs and control systems by Montreal company SACO Smartvision, headed by MD Fred Jalbout. These were the two principal men behind the unmistakable U2 PopMart screen.

Barnes was introduced to the screen by XL's Guido Rusysschaert. Ultimately, his favouring of LED over CRT came down to physical practicalities. "The Sony JumboTron would have been much heavier than the LED option were we to get a similar size screen," Barnes explained. "With a JumboTron we'd have also needed a ground support system which would have meant increasing on the stage depth and that would have impacted on the audience capacities."

It was a basic maths exercise for Richard Jones: "XL's was the only screen we could use in the end. The set's big enough as it is. We're taking ten trucks [from Stardes] and with a larger support system we'd be into another truck plus the associated costs."

At one point in the set, the screen split again to act as a "cryogenic chamber" from which the male dancers emerged to be "brought back to life" by the Girls. With a box depth of 152mm, the screen allowed all cabling to be neatly concealed within itself.

Thanks to horrendous ice storms in Canada, the screen arrived late for the Dublin rehearsals, however, when it was eventually rigged, the production team were delighted with its performance. Lavender said: "It's been very reliable; it goes up and comes down really easily, and it's amazingly bright. Consequently, it has to run at a very low operating level."

The high density resolution images were afforded by a much tighter pixel formation than previously used for U2's screen, and unlike the U2 version, the Spice screen really did lend itself to arena applications. Yet there was still a way to go before perfection could be reached, according to Barnes. "You sometimes get a bit of 'noise' when the screen can't decide whether the image should be black or non-black. We can compensate for that by switching the screen to its lowest level of grey, so you don't get total blackness but it gets rid of the noise problem."

Of the creative side of the video presentation, Blue Leach said: "The video is wicked, with two and a half hours of really nice camera work, mixes and cuts. Apart from XL's LED screen, we also have a Barco 9200-projected soft screen high up at each side of the set, both of which carry the same magnified live camera images. They also show deaf and dumb signing in a little circular window, which was an idea of Pete Barnes' who arranged it through Kaleidovision, the people who also put together all the ravey graphics.

"The hard LED screen is used for a mixture of live images and VT material which is triggered by Dataton software from Simon Ellis's keyboard and is frame-locked for accuracy. While the opening 'Space' sequence runs off Beta, the remaining VT material we show on the centre screen is accessed at great speed from three Flamingo Digital Systems hard drives, and was edited from old documentaries and other footage I found along the way. For songs like 'Say You'll Be There' we feature the non-lipsynched passages from promo rushes.

Leach described PSL's Portable Production Unit or PPU (allegedly designed by Richard Burford for Genesis, but unused when the production budget was ruthlessly cut) as a monster. He said: "Digital video effects vary from show to show, and I'm using the Magic DaVE by Snell and Willcox for a mixture of very light strobes, some black and white inserts, and things like the funky picture-bending stuff that appears on 'Stop'. It's really just to jazz up the live pictures rather than just having regular twenty-five frames per second pictures in a box – it makes it a little more pleasant to look at.

"I think the three screens complement each other perfectly, because when there is no VT material I still put live stuff up on the centre screen but we tend to swap all the cameras round. Each screen will carry a different camera but we alternate all the images by cutting on the For-A FDM-V162 sixteen-input digital switcher. It's a high energy show and the camera and the cutting reflect that very well.

"Our cameras are manned Sony 16 x 9 switchable D30 digital cameras and two Toshiba 'lipstick' minicams. I suggested we get a Jimmy Jib camera crane and a Cartoni Dutch Head for two of the pit cameras. The latter is a dolly and track device which enables the camera to be tilted from side to side in a liquid movement. The lipstick cameras are on drums and keys, and cut away to the band when the Girls are offstage and the band's playing on. One of them sits right above the drummer's head so we've got the whole drum kit in there and the wonderful view of him hammering away."

Pete Barnes devised a look for the show which went several steps further than that of Bill Laslett's 'rollercoaster' Istanbul set. "The Girls wanted an hydraulic ramp," said Lavender, "and something more modern. Pete's idea was to tie it all in with a space link, hence the 120' starcloth behind the huge painted scrim."

After drawings were finalised with Hangman via a steady flow of faxes, the set build was handed over to Brilliant Stages who, prior to

Dublin, pieced it together at Three Mills Island Studios in London's Docklands. The result was stunning, comprising elegant staircases, catwalks and podiums, and providing much scope for the diverse scenes throughout the show. Jones commented: "It's a very classy, beautifully-constructed set, and easy to put together for the back-to-backs we've done in Europe."

Barnes acknowledged the twenty-year relationship he maintained with Hangman's Alan Chesters: "I have concepts like the splitting video screen and other cosmetics, and Alan does the artwork and the painting side of it."

These "cosmetics" included the central rampway which turned into a catwalk for 'Move Over'. "The hydraulic section lifts up out of the centre of the ramp and projects forwards. It's picked up by a thrust at the end so the whole centre section forms a catwalk for the Girls to perform on. There's a very large area up in the back centre to accommodate the Girls' eleven costume changes, which is quite important because there's no time to go to dressing rooms."

Highlighting the set was yet another magnificent lighting design by Barnes, whose fascination with owls earned him the nickname of "Swoop"! In addition to 64' of front truss and 120' of back truss, the four concentric circles of truss (15, 11, 7 and 4 metres diameter) suspended above the stage were retained from Istanbul.

Rattling off a mental spec sheet, Barnes' kit was everything one would expect from LSD and Vari*Lite. "LSD supplied forty-three Icons, the ninety-six Par 64s, the Icon desk which runs everything, and the trussing, while Vari*Lite supplied thirty-five VL5Arcs. There are six Xenon troupers at FOH and a lot of non-neon lighting around what we term the 'tiara' which is the video wall surround, and other areas of the set such as the staircases."

The other lighting supplier in Europe was French company Cote Scene which brought in twenty Martin MAC 500s, thirty MAC 600s and two MPBB Black Boxes. How did this arrangement evolve? "While we were rehearsing in Cannes last year, Cote Scene introduced me to the new MACs and Martin flew me out to their Danish factory where I saw them properly for the first time. I particularly like the MAC 600 – it's got some quite nice effects such as on 'Move Over' where its random strobe effect against the catwalk simulates photographers' flashes.

Also, all of the backdrop is lit by them because they give you multiple colour changes, and again there are a few instances in the show where they give a shimmering, lightning sort of effect behind the set."

The moods created by the lighting in this two-part show were extremely varied, as were the songs. 'The Lady Is A Vamp' was mock-cabaret, with architectural lighting giving a Las Vegas feel. On 'Viva Forever', the last single to feature Geri, a four foot mirrorball dropped down to lend a dreamy atmosphere, and at the other extreme was the colourful Seventies disco flavour of 'Who Do You Think You Are'.

Barnes did not forget the power of pyro – Shellshock supplied aerial bursts and 0.5 second gerbs which shot across the front of the stage between the encores. There were also four Cirro Lite cracked oil machines dotted around the stage, plus two Le Maitre G300s in the truss. Where there's smoke, there's fire...and the Girls had plenty of that.

Having worked with East 17, FOH engineer Mike Dolling was no stranger to hysterical audiences. "That kind of mass hysteria can wear the ears," he said. "However, I try to run this show as quietly as possible because I'm conscious of risking the hearing of a predominantly young audience. But most people seem to think we run the show at a good level; it's a big sound but not harsh."

The rig he referred to was d&b audiotechnik's 402 system – the same brand used for East 17. This was configured six cabinets wide and seven deep, with double rows of tops on the main left and right for long throw, with (per side) six 402 subs and six B2 subs with matching amplifiers and built-in processors. For infills in the centre of the front of the stage there were six full range d&b 902s giving good coverage at a sensible volume. At Wembley, there were also a number of Meyer MSL-3s around the sides of the stage as fill-ins for the additional guest seating. The delay system was also d&b 402s, in a four wide/four deep configuration.

Dolling commented: "The formation of the delay cluster helps to provide sufficient bass up in the bleachers, rather than having a bassy sound on the floor and light and toppy up above. The d&b system is very good for that."

In fact, for many years, Dolling maintained a huge belief in d&b, and was no less a fan of Wigwam, the sound rental company for this tour. "My crew chief, Nick Mooney, and I are constantly finding new, improved ways of running the system, just as Britannia Row did with Turbosound Flashlight. I do like small box, tight-Q systems – this is like a giant hi-fi."

Assisting the d&b cause was the new RIB system which ran from a rack-mounted PC and provided remote control of gain, EQ, power and level of all the amplifiers for the entire rig. Dolling: "We run it all up from front-of-house, and we can trim and high frequency compensate the top boxes for extra throw, and we are now getting into its time align functions. I'm actually looking at using it in conjunction with a BSS Omnidrive, which might be the next step in getting even more out of the d&b system."

Quite simply, the show was outstanding, especially from the audio perspective; a major factor in which being Dolling's Amek Recall console. As the tour hit the States, the desk was subjected to a significant upgrade when it was fitted with Amek's Rupert Neve 9098 mic pre-amp and parametric EQ modules, which Dolling had previously used in rack mount format. He commented: "It's a magic box, really. You put the 9098 across a microphone and like any high quality mic amp it fattens and stabilises the sound. Plus, with the quite astounding parametric EQ you are able to gain far more control as far as dialling out any nasty frequencies, and tailoring the mic sound to the Girls' individual voices.

"Having used the rack version before, I knew that having those facilities within the desk itself was going to be vital. When you use the rack mounted ones, you have to insert them so the result is not quite as clean because you're still running through the desk mic amp and then out to the 9098. So having the facilities within the desk itself allows for a clearer signal path."

Dolling was particularly sold on the Recall's automation and insisted he simply could not run this show without it. Two automated auxes handled dedicated delay and echo settings for each girl on each song, while the desk MIDI-controlled a bank of Yamaha SPX-1000s for all the effects, and also triggered compressors and gates whenever required. Each song was set up as a scene, and the Recall communicated via MIDI with two Yamaha 03D mixers, one of which sub-mixed the close-miked percussion, and the other sub-mixed

Simon Ellis's keyboard set-up.

"The Recall generally takes a lot of the hard work out of mixing the band," enthused Dolling, who ran a total of seventy-four inputs, including effects, across the three mixers. "That allows me to concentrate on the vocal cues and harmony balances. With five [or four, after Geri's departure] lead singers, you get very busy on the cues and I don't have the luxury of spending much time on mixing the band. The Recall takes care of that for me and does it brilliantly. Without the automation I would need another pair of hands."

The Spice Girls' sponsorship by Shure is very much in evidence. Apart from a range of SM91s, 87s and 57s spread across Andy Gangadeen's drum kit, ten UHF Beta 58A hand-held radio microphones with super cardioid heads have been chosen for the Girls' – two mics each – and Wigwam built a special rack for the systems, as Dolling explained. "We have a buffered switcher for each of the Girls' A and B mics. If there's the slightest problem with the main mic, we hit a switch, the B mic is handed to the appropriate girl, and it switches the mic over on the desk channels. There's no patching or spare radio channel to EQ – it's all automatic and I don't even know if they've changed mics."

Shure's presence on the tour also extended to stage monitoring in the form of the PSM600 Personal Stereo Monitor in-ear system, employed by the Girls. Monitor engineer Graham Blake discovered this new alternative to Garwood when the band performed at the MTV Awards and, as he says, they haven't looked back since.

"There's a facility on them called 'Mix Mode' which you can run two receivers off the same transmitter and the same frequency," said Blake. "You just pan hard left or hard right, running two inputs into the same frequency, and it's got us out of trouble quite a bit in Spain and Italy where you do get interference. The packs are also sturdier and we've had no trouble with drop-outs at all. We just have the percussion player left on the Garwood system.

"Of all the acts I've worked with who use in-ear monitoring, the Girls have probably been the best; they've taken to it like a duck to water. In-ear monitoring obviously helps in achieving a clean sound, and microphone spill is further minimised by having perspex shields around the drummer and percussion player."

Despite the in-ear systems, the stage is not entirely free of loudspeakers. There is a side fill of four d&b 402 stacks per side which carries a full band mix (and the Girls' vocals if the in-ears should ever fail), both keyboard players have Nexo LS500 subs and PS10s on top, the drummer has two LS1000 subs and a pair of PS15s, the bass player uses a 2 x 15" TAD wedge, and the guitarist uses two single TAD 1 x 15" wedges.

Band mixes are catered for by a Midas XL3, into which a rack-mounted Mackie CR1604-VLZ sixteen-channel mic/line mixer bounces down the all-important video soundtrack feeds. Yamaha ProMix 01s are also resident on the keyboard risers. A Yamaha 02R, meanwhile, is used exclusively to mix the in-ear channels, and with a fair degree of sophistication.

Blake explained his reasoning behind the kit choice: "When we first started rehearsals the Girls were all requesting different mixes for different parts of songs. With the XL3 pretty stuffed with the band's requirements, we had to look at getting a board which could be programmed for all these intricate changes and the 02R, with its automation and built-in effects, was a natural choice. It's the best piece of gear I've bought for a long time

"I'm also the first live sound engineer to use some new software for the 02R from a Canadian company called Zeep. We've set up something like 128 different scenes within the set and I'm controlling the in-ear mixes from an Apple Powerbook G3 which can also change EQs and effects while the show's running without me even touching the 02R."

As their European tour came to a close, the Girls came to terms with Geri Halliwell's absence and settled comfortably into the idea of performing as a foursome on their all-conquering US tour which started on 15 June at Miami's Coral Sky Amphitheatre, and ended in Dallas on 26 August. Later scoring their third consecutive UK Christmas Number One, it would be some time before the screaming subsided.

CHAPTER THIRTY-ONE

Céline Dion

Let's Talk About Love – 1997-2000

There was no better way to complete this picture of state-of-the-art concert production in the Nineties than to take a flight from a rain-sodden runway at London's Heathrow Airport to the sublime stickiness of the Florida sunshine where, on 3 October, 1998 in Fort Lauderdale, *Titanic* theme song star Céline Dion was appearing as part of a two-year world tour which boasted yet another new phase in visual presentation techniques.

Unwittingly I had chanced upon what was arguably one of the tour's highlights – the opening event at the shiny new, but unfortunately named $192 million, 20,000-seat National Car Rental Centre Arena, complete with Dion's special guests Japanese violin virtuoso Taro Hakase, soul star Diana King and in a rare live teaming, direct from nearby Miami for one night only, The Bee Gees with whom Dion had recently recorded the best-selling international hit 'Immortality'.

The tour was named after Dion's album *Let's Talk About Love*, the follow-up to her double Grammy Award-winning, 25 million-selling *Falling Into You* – not a bad achievement for a singer who was once Quebec's best kept secret. Possibly her most valuable asset, aside from her strident vocal style and manager/husband Rene Angelil, is her ability to communicate verbally with her audience.

Maybe it was the overtly MOR, drama queenish nature of Dion's music which had been lost on me before I touched down in Florida, but somehow the lushness of the sound, visuals and Dion's warmth was all-conquering. This was the Diva as a Human Being – a rare mixture, but one which she made work with the technical assistance of her regular production company, Montreal-based Solotech, which was supplying sound, lighting, staging and video equipment and services.

When Dion's previous tour ended in June 1997, few people expected her to go out on the road again so soon, but for lighting and production designer Yves Aucoin it gave him the opportunity to bring forward his idea of putting together an in-the-round production. Promoter John Giddings of Solo, in Fort Lauderdale to launch the 1999 European stadium leg, which was to include Wembley Stadium dates in July, informed that the design was inspired by Phil Collins' recent success with the format, as seen by the Dion entourage in Toronto in 1997.

"I thought Céline would be a perfect artist for that kind of a show, being such a warm entertainer and keen to talk to her audience," said Aucoin. "I told her that from a 360° communication point of view it would be more demanding. With people all around her, she would have to stay incredibly focused on her performance, so I sat down with her and Rene, and explained everything. They weren't sure at first but I put some drawings together of a heart-shaped stage and the video screens, and gave a computer presentation to them, and they loved it!"

Amazingly, and at substantial expense, Céline Dion purchased four 16 x 12' Saco Smartvision LED screens (one for each side of the stage) and, the highlight of it all, a custom-designed video floor inspired by the technical innovations put in place by the same company for U2's PopMart screen. The Saco screens were supplemented all around the perimeter of the stage by a number of large Sony TriniTron colour TV monitors. Aucoin explained: "When you are in-the-round it is impossible to create a traditional set with drapes and soft goods because you will obscure parts of the stage, and this is where the power of video comes in. Céline first asked if we could have a floor which changed colour, and gradually the idea extended to the possibility of using the whole surface of the stage as a video screen."

For most of the performance, the images shown on the four flown screens were close-up camera shots of the star – there were four manned cameras in the rig and five remotely operated cameras around the stage. However, at one point Dion appeared to duet with Barbra Streisand on 'Tell Him' (a shrewd mix of Dion's live image and session footage of Streisand, synched with the band via a click track). Other dates would see Dion duetting with The Bee Gees with the aid of video, but in Fort Lauderdale we were blessed with the Gibb brothers in the flesh! Elsewhere the screens showed a variety of digital hard disk graphics, including stars and clouds, or pulsating colours, which occasionally made their way to the video floor to create an ever-changing, "virtual" set – a breathtaking sight from the upper balcony!

The heart mutated into the bow of a ship for the Titanic theme encore, 'My Heart Will Go On', but exactly how? At the tip of the heart shape, a double steel rail rose from the floor for Dion to lean against. Meanwhile, the stage itself, being effectively a huge video screen showed the image of a ship's deck, surrounded by water. More than just "giving the impression of a ship", as Aucoin modestly put it, the result was one of the most spectacular multi-dimensional visual effects ever seen on a live concert stage.

A 360° in-the-round production presents a big challenge for any lighting designer. Aucoin explained: "The lighting was certainly my first worry. It's damn hard because if you want to go too far with front-of-house or backlight you're going to cut out some seats. The other option is to wash out the crowd, but that is not the right approach for the Céline Dion audience, apart from maybe on a couple of uptempo songs. For the most part, the audience is expecting the 'big ballad' with Céline very well highlighted.

"On this show, because the video aspects are very important in enhancing a nice, feminine image with the close-up visuals of Céline, it would not be cool to project lots of dazzling gobos on to her face. When I started the design I asked for a 12 x 8' platform to be in the audience so I could put some fixtures there to enable me to have some reference of the depth of the lighting at the back. I have four in the arena configuration and eight in the stadium set-up. I have a lot of Vari*Lites, twenty-eight VL5 and sixteen VL5Arc wash luminaires, and twenty-four VL6 and twelve VL7 spots, plus forty-eight Clay Paky Stage Scans, and eight bars of five ETC Source 4 Pars with Compulite 1kW Whisper colour changers."

With all trussing designed and manufactured by Solotech, other rig elements include sixteen MR16 1500 watt blinders, sixteen ETC Source 4 Lekos, twelve Altman 300 watt Fresnels, Robert Juliat Ivanhoe and Aramis 2500 HMI follow spots, MDG fog generators, ETC forty-eight-way dimming and, for that final *pièce de résistance*, a forty-eight-inch mirror ball for the Dion/Bee Gees performance of 'Stayin' Alive'! "It may seem like I have quite a sizeable rig but it's not a great deal for an in-the-round design," insisted Aucoin.

For control, Aucoin and Gatien Ouellet each used a Compulite Sabre lighting console. "I've been using Compulite desks for many years and I absolutely swear by them!" said Aucoin. "On the last tour I had an Artisan for the Vari*Lites, but I decided to switch to having a Sabre for both automated and generic lighting. We programme in parallel so he has the same cue numbers as me, so if something should happen to either of us which meant we couldn't work one night, we could MIDI up the two desks and it would be a fairly simple procedure for a deputy. I am taking care of all the Clay Paky scans, the audience lighting and key lights, as well as calling the spots, while Gatien looks after the Vari*Lites."

Like Solotech, front-of-house sound engineer Denis Savage and monitor man Daniel Baron are hardly newcomers to the Dion camp, having worked for the star since the mid Eighties. However, what was new for this tour was their choice of mixing consoles – for Savage, a Soundcraft Broadway, and for Baron, a special version of Soundcraft's recently-launched Series Five Monitor.

A Soundcraft user for many years, Savage had previously employed two Europa desks, using them alongside two Yamaha ProMix 01s which handled sequenced signals and percussion mixes. This approach, he said, helped to "clean up the mix" by allowing him to mute any microphones which were not in use at any given time instead of leaving them open. It was an approach which he wanted to continue and develop, and he began to investigate how a single automated console might achieve his aims.

Savage narrowed the possibilities down to three choices: a Neve Libra, a Euphonix and the Soundcraft Broadway, which digitally controls analogue audio hardware and completely resets every audio parameter on a snapshot basis. With audio under remote control, the control elements are separated from the audio elements, allowing the control surface to be as small or as large as circumstances require. Savage explained how he arrived at the Broadway solution: "The thing about the Libra and Euphonix was that they have a more in-line design than live mixing design, and I was initially drawn to them because outside of my live engineering I have a recording studio. On the Euphonix I would have been limited by the amount of EQs, and the more I looked, the more I could see that the Broadway kept meeting all my criteria.

"The way Soundcraft has arranged the VCAs is very good, like when you offset something, if you recall the next cue you don't change your level of the whole band, you keep all these offsets. That's so important when you're a live engineer. The way I run the show, I don't automate the EQs, so when I go from one cue to the other I don't change my EQ. I couldn't do that with all the other consoles, at least not the same way. It was always a bit more complicated. But Soundcraft designed the Broadway to be a programmable live console first and foremost, so it made a lot more sense to go with that and I'm very pleased we made that choice."

Being a console which was fundamentally designed for the theatre market, hence the name, it was unusual to see the Broadway on a mainstream pop tour, but Savage believed that engineers would be employing this console more and more on similar tours. He said: "You get a lot of channels within such a small footprint [the two input racks gave Savage eighty channels]. You have a soft patch and for each cue you can re-assign whichever channels and faders you like, and have them in mono or stereo. I'm using only one surface and that gives me twenty faders plus eight VCA groups, and yet I'm running the same show we had before when I was mixing on two Europas. Every manufacturer is working on this and we're seeing Gamble and Yamaha coming out with their own ideas. It makes sense because it's ridiculous to have huge consoles and run around like a madman trying to mix a show when you can have everything you need in a compact form and at your fingertips. It's all in the way that they designed the software. I'd seen people mixing shows on Yamaha 02R digital mixers but noticed that when they recalled cues it was feeding back, purely because I feel that it wasn't designed to be a live console."

How did Savage view the character of the EQ? "It sounds really good, although it doesn't have the same feel as a normal analogue console EQ. It seems that you need to push it more to hear it, but it's very efficient in that you can copy EQ settings over to other channels for a cue. It's so fast and accurate, and especially good for setting up vocal mics – you can have everything soundchecked in no time at all."

To what extent was Savage using automation? "The only thing I'm not automating is the EQ, but that doesn't mean I have tons of EQ work to do between songs because the way I'm set up, each instrument has its own channel. I have three audio racks and two control surfaces and on each component there is a MIDI in/out/thru, so I can cue a programme change from any part of the system directly from the console."

Outboard was a fairly regular affair, although Savage made a special note of his BSS 901 on Dion's vocals. "When we play all these big arenas I find that I actually do less vocal processing because the buildings are so live and you feel that any processing ultimately muddies the sound. It's different when we play outdoors. So I try to keep her vocal as natural as I can. Compression is very important – Céline is such a dynamic singer who delivers a vast range of emotions in her performance, and that means I have to keep the levels under control. As well as the BSS I have a Manley Tube De-Esser that I use to tame the sibilance."

Monitor engineer Daniel Baron picked a remarkably comfortable place to mix from. Twenty feet from the stage, and out of the range of glaring follow spots he was able to see everyone in the band without having to sit behind a giant PA stack. This in-the-round caper does have its bonuses! His customised Series Five Monitor console evolved after he approached a selection of manufacturers with the idea of building a desk that specifically met his needs.

Like Savage, he shopped around. "Ironically, I was going to have a Broadway but it didn't quite fit our brief for monitoring," he said, "so I looked at ATI, Soundcraft and Cadac, and I chose Soundcraft to build the console. We added some ideas to what they were already working on for the Series Five, and we ended up with a special version. A year ago, my desk was the first stereo module prototype and Soundcraft looked at my wish list and came very close to realising everything. There is no automation, but I get by okay!

"I'm running ninety-two channels [twenty monos and thirty-six stereo channels] in one eight foot frame, which is nice and compact. I don't kill seats and I can see everything I need to access very easily – Denis and I both enjoy this aspect of our consoles. The bar graph meter bridge from the standard issue of the Series Five Monitor didn't fit, but I asked Soundcraft to include it on mine as well as some other buttons. If you lose one side of the piano, for instance, during the concert they have a switch left to both channels and another switch right. If you lose the right channel, you press left to both channels and you kill the mute to the channel that doesn't work, so at least everybody has the piano in both ears."

Baron's special needs included finding a way to sensibly distribute compression around the monitor mixes. "I wanted to use compression in a way that would not influence the musicians' personal dynamic performances, so that meant not including compression in their mixes. However, there are other mixes which need to be affected by compression. My mix is post-fader for everybody, but pre-fader for the guy who plays his own instrument – therefore my fader movement doesn't affect any musician's personal mix. Of course, I insert some reverb and other treatments on backing vocals and guitars, for example, but I might not want everybody to hear those effects, so this is an ideal way of working."

In some ways the Series Five Monitor was designed for in-ear monitoring, which was just as well considering that the Dion stage was absolutely devoid of any traditional wedges and fills, with in-ear mixes supplemented by Aura shakers in the risers and under the drum stool [see Rod Stewart chapter]. "We've been using IEM for about eight or nine years," said Baron. "But now that we have gone out with this in the round show we had to change a few things around, simply because the microphones are behind four stacks of speakers instead of two.

"On the Series Five, we have the possibility to have the shakers before or after the EQ. I prefer before the EQ because if I put a bump in the bottom I could possibly add another 100 cycles which is not good for me because I like to get a wider range at the bottom. For Céline we have a Garwood Radio Station system which suffers from floor noise but that isn't usually a problem for singers who are the loudest in the mix. She has become used to the sound and EQ of the Garwood system so we have stayed with it.

"We have a special Radio Station which has been modified for us by Martin Noar – there's more power and the EQ curves are different to increase the dynamic range. We tried the Shure PSM-600 for her but the EQ point on the highs are not at the same place and there's a bump in the bottom that I can get rid of but we just thought we should stay with what we had. Because we boosted the signal on the Garwood the RF has better reception. We're working with seventy-five different frequencies on this show, so we're at the mercy of our radio systems' performance! The rest of the band are all on Shure PSM-600s because their requirements are much different to Céline's. For them it's better to get rid of the floor noise."

It's by now fairly common to see a rack of Aphex Dominator IIs in line with an IEM system, and this tour was no exception. Baron commented: "The Aphex acts as a brick wall limiter for the in-ears. If my power supply goes down or if I make any mistakes, the Aphex makes sure that whatever happens, Céline and the musicians on stage are not harmed by any surge in volume."

As for the practicalities of the mix, Baron said: "Everybody hears a stereo image – there are six musicians, three singers, plus Céline makes ten. Added to that we have my mix, a 'minus vocal' mix, then a guest mix and reverb sends, plus a mix for Meyer UM1 monitors if ever I need to set up wedge monitors, which will be rare. With the singers and the guests, like The Bee Gees, I prepare a mix that is a basic stereo music mix with reverb. The Bee Gees don't want to spend half an hour doing a soundcheck, so I have consulted their regular FOH engineer Howard Page about what they like to hear on stage, and I have some spare Shure in-ear systems that they'll be using, along with their own personal ear moulds."

Where Soundcraft appeared to rule the control roost, the PA was most definitely a Meyer Sound concern with a flown Self-Powered system divided into four corners of the open, in-the-round set. The PA worked like a front and back system, said Savage. "We designed it a bit differently because we don't want to throw as far on the side as much as on the long sides. So we have long throw cabinets on the top of the rig, and then short throws on the sides, just so we can have the right speakers at the right places. All the shows so far have been in-the-round with the exception of one shed. This is the first tour we've done in-the-round, and everything has been choreographed specifically with this configuration in mind, so it's quite a departure for us. The whole idea was to get the audience closer to Céline."

Each of the four corner clusters was visibly split into five sections. From the top, and left to right, the first row had three MSL-6s and two MSL-5Ps; the second row had six DS-2s and two PSW-6s; the third row contained six tilted DS-2s and two MSL-4s; there were three MSL-5Ps and two CQ-2s on the fourth row, and hanging underneath were two CQ-2s. Additionally, there was a total of twelve UPA-1As (to cover the front rows) and twenty-four 650-R2 subs under the stage.

Commented Savage: "The PSW-6 directional subs (2 x 15"/2 x 18") on the sides are new from Meyer. We've tried to create some low end efficiency by putting these subs on the sides of the clusters, and I think we've cracked it. We also have the MSL-5P which doesn't exist anywhere else on the market – we didn't want too many amplifiers up there in the rig, so Meyer built these Self-Powered versions especially for us, and the Meyer Remote Monitoring System (RMS) helps us to detect an amplifier fault or breakdown via a computer screen. The only things in the array which are not self-powered are the DS-2s which have their Crown Macrotech MA-5000VZ amps in racks on top."

The rest of the amplification consisted of thirty-seven Crown MA-1200s for the UPA-1Ms and 650 subs, the optional UM-1 monitors and Aura shakers, plus a Hafler P-1000 amp for the drummer's monitor system.

Despite the power and flexibility of the live audio technology at his fingertips, Denis Savage was ultimately at the mercy of this new $192 million venue's acoustics. "This is typical of the new 20-25,000 seater arenas being built," he said, scratching his brow. "They all have good height so you can hang quite a bit of weight in the roof. The average buildings sound pretty good because the designers are aware that they are going to be used for sports events and concerts, whereas these facilities have traditionally been built for sport with little consideration for acoustics because a live response enhances the sound of a crowd during a game.

"It's still a battle – we're trying to concentrate audio energy everywhere and have control over it, but the hard surfaces make it difficult because of reflections. It's pretty live, but compared to other large sports arenas, this seems to be fairly concert friendly. Low end is quite good here. We've kept the PA volume down to a sensible level so that the sound doesn't hit the walls too hard and cause bad delays."

To aid Savage's audio battle, system engineer Francois Desjardins was in charge of the PA system's alignment, relying on a combination of a Meyer SIM 2201 sound analyser system, BSS Soundweb, Meyer CP-10 EQs on the MSL-6 and MSL-5s, and Klark Teknik DN-410 EQs on the rest of the rig. "We sub-divide the PA system and EQ each subdivision with a dedicated EQ device, and after that we time-align each section so that when it arrives at the crowd it acts like a single point source array," said Desjardins.

"We set up twelve B&K 4007 microphones around the arena and align every section so that it is as flat as possible, and whether you are listening from the balcony or the stalls it sounds close. Because all the speakers do not sound the same, we use the Soundweb to offset the EQ of the whole system. Soundweb also has high-pass filtering and delay so we can align everything. If you turned on only the top speakers it would sound strange, but when everything is working in harmony it sounds just like one big loudspeaker."

The Let's Talk About Love tour was set to travel the world for close to two years. Céline Dion and her crew spent the remainder of 1998 in the USA and Canada, before moving on to Asia in early 1999, returning for more US dates in the spring, and then heading off to Europe for eight weeks of summer stadium shows. One thing was certain – this was one of the few tours which would ever be able to claim a span of two centuries, let alone two millennia!

index